THE BOOK OF DRUIDRY

THE BOOK OF DRUIDRY

Ross Nichols

Edited by John Matthews and Philip Carr-Gomm

Thorsons
An Imprint of HarperCollins*Publishers*

Thorsons
An Imprint of HarperCollins*Publishers*
77–85 Fulham Palace Road,
Hammersmith, London W6 8JB
1160 Battery Street
San Francisco, California 94111–1213

Published by The Aquarian Press 1990
This paperback edition 1992
7 9 10 8 6

A catalogue record for this book
is available from the British Library

ISBN 1 85538 167 2

Typeset by HarperPhototypesetters Limited,
Northampton, England
Printed and bound in Great Britain by
Caledonian International Book Manufacturing Ltd, Glasgow

CONTENTS

Nine Groups of Druidic Concepts

Greater Sites of the Britannic Islands

Druidic Wisdom

The Eight-fold Year-Plan

FOREWORD

by Philip Carr-Gomm

Many people these days are turning to the native traditions of various cultures in an attempt not only to reconnect with their roots and their heritage, but also in an attempt to find a living spirituality that can lead them out of the psychological wasteland that has been created by industrial society.

Great attention has been paid to the native American Indian tradition, and to the shamanistic practices of such diverse cultures as the Siberian, Tibetan and Australian Aborigine. Less attention, however, has been given to a tradition which lies closer to the ancestral roots of most European, and hence many North American, people—the Celtic tradition, whose spirituality is epitomized in the path of the Druid.

The reason for this lack of attention has almost certainly been the belief that the Druid path has been lost. In reality, although the Druid path has often disappeared from the historian's view, it has never been lost as a tradition—only hidden from the public gaze.

But often that which we think of as lost is only in fact hidden from us for a time, in order that we may discover or rediscover it at the right moment.

For nine years after Ross Nichols' death the manuscript of *The Book of Druidry* appeared to be lost, until in 1984 a strange series of events led to its rediscovery and preparation for publication.

During the last two years of his life, Ross Nichols, the Chosen Chief of the Order of Bards, Ovates & Druids, had been working on a book that he hoped would be able to convey most of what he knew of Druidry to those who were not initiated into its inner workings. Having just completed the final pages of the book, he died unexpectedly in 1975.

The Order that he had led with such competence and enthusiasm soon became dormant, and his successor closed the Order in 'the apparent world'. During the confusion that ensued after his death—from the inadequacy of his Will and the fact that his study and flat remained unlocked for a considerable time—the manuscript, the Order teachings and papers passed into a number of different hands rather than to his successor. Nine years later, these scattered documents were assembled again to revive the Order in its modern form and to bring *The Book of Druidry* to publication in the form that you find it today.

It happened in this way.

A key figure in the recent rebirth of the Order, who wishes to remain anonymous, but who has deep links with both Welsh and English Druidry, found himself several days after Ross' death in a public house that by strange coincidence was not far from the old 'Apple Tree Tavern' in Covent Garden which saw an earlier revival of the Order in 1717. There, by chance, he met an associate of the Order. They discussed Ross' chieftainship, and at a certain point, he was moved to warn him that he should try to ensure that the Order papers were preserved.

'I am sure the lawyers will take care of that,' he replied.

'You may well be surprised,' replied our friend, 'all the most precious documents might well be thrown by those same lawyers into rubbish sacks and left in the street to be collected as refuse.'

Although sceptical, the associate remembered his words, and as if these remarks had been prompted by a vision of future events, the black sacks of discarded documents were duly discovered outside the late Chosen Chief's house in Barons' Court one afternoon.

Thanks to this forewarning, the refuse men never collected those bags. Their contents were carefully stored for nine years, as was the manuscript of *The Book of Druidry*, which had taken a different path out of Ross' house.

To show how these papers and this manuscript came to be rediscovered after nearly a decade, I need to recount a personal story.

I first met the Chief of the Order of Bards, Ovates & Druids when I was eleven or twelve. I interviewed him for a magazine I had started. I can remember very little of our meeting except vague images of a figure who was both warm and authoritative. Three years later, when I had my own darkroom, my father introduced me to him again. He invited me to photograph the ceremonies. Over the next few months, as I photographed the elaborate public rituals on Parliament Hill, in which Druids welcomed mayors and mayoresses, Buddhists, white witches or Morris dancers to their rites, I became more and more intrigued by these strange events which often combined deeply mystical moments of union with Nature with the absurd—as when stray dogs or children would be drawn into the magic circle, or when sudden gusts of wind would sweep off head-dresses, or downpours of rain would remove any semblance of reverence from the proceedings.

I began to visit Ross once or twice a week after school—first of all to show him the photos I had taken, but gradually beginning a relationship in which he became the teacher and I the student of Druid lore.

Some time later, I asked to be initiated, and on May Day in 1969 I formally entered the Order on Glastonbury Tor.

For the next six years I visited my teacher frequently, and he taught me in an apparently haphazard way. After making me a cup of tea, or a meal, he would talk about one or other aspect of the Order's teaching. He would draw diagrams of Stonehenge on sheets of paper that I have kept to this day, write notes to clarify points, and hand me typed or duplicated sheets with written expositions and discourses. It was only years later that I found that all these teachings, so apparently disparate as they had seemed at the time, formed a coherent and practical whole which spoke of an ancient heritage that had become fragmented and lost over the last two millennia.

In 1975 Ross died suddenly at the house of a friend, a few days before we were due to travel to Glastonbury for the Bealteinne ceremony.

When he died, I assumed that the manuscript, which he had entitled *The Book of Druidry*, would be carefully preserved, along with the Order papers, and that the book would duly be published, whilst the Order would be carried forward by the older members who had worked with Ross. In reality, something quite different happened.

The Order was closed by his successor, and other concerns meant I thought little about the manuscript, the Order and its teachings for nearly a decade. It seems that most of the people who had gathered around Ross did likewise.

Nine years after his death, in 1984, I was meditating one morning when I suddenly became intensely aware of his presence. 'Have a look at the teachings again,' he said, 'and you will find that they are immensely relevant to the problems of our time.'

After this experience, I knew that I had to gather all the material together, and begin to meet again with others to work with the teachings.

This unexpected encounter led me through a series of extraordinary synchronistic events that resulted—four years later—in the re-founding of the Order of Bards, Ovates & Druids on St Valentine's Day 1988.

The day of the meditation, I made a list of all those documents which I felt should be gathered together. I began with the three books needed to complete my collection of Ross' published work. That afternoon I visited the nearest secondhand bookshop and asked if they had any of the published books, and although these were small editions printed for the most part during the Second World War, the surprised assistant found that he did indeed have one copy—bound up with string in a package containing letters and sketches by the author. Unlikely as this may seem, I walked for several blocks to the next nearest secondhand bookshop, only to find that they had the twin volume edition on magic that Ross had edited in 1952 complete in its slipcase.

I called a friend, Colin Murray, who ran the Golden Section Order which dealt with Druidic and Celtic matters, and asked if I could see him. I told him the story of the day's events, ending by saying, 'I only have one more published book to collect—*Sassenach Stray*'.

'But I have two copies,' said Colin, 'so of course you can have one of them!'

Next I needed to find the lost manuscript. Colin suggested I try Vera Chapman. Vera was one of the Triad of Chiefs of the Order who had founded the Tolkien Society and is the author of many children's and adult books which combine fine story-telling with esoteric lore. I visited her later that week, only to find that she did indeed have the manuscript, although it had been kept for years by one friend of Ross, who had then passed it to another who had kept it under her bed for several years before passing it to Vera. Thank heavens Vera had it, for the first lady had died, and the second might never have been traced. She handed it to me for safe-keeping—asking me to place it in the British Library if I was unsuccessful in finding a publisher.

So within an extraordinarily short space of time I had obtained a complete collection of Ross' books, both published and in manuscript form. The next task was to gather a small group of Order members and sympathetic friends who would be willing to meet together to work with the ceremonies in an experimental way, to see if they were still suitable for the 1980s. I did this by contacting all those whom I was still able to reach after nine years of separation. To my surprise I found that virtually every one of them had carefully preserved some of the Order documents and teachings. Much was duplicated, but each had somehow managed to gather material that was unique. Together with the material I already had from my days of apprenticeship with Ross, it assembled into a complete collection—including the inner rituals, the Order Constitution and related correspondence and documents, Ross' personal correspondence, and even notes of his on scraps of paper relating to every aspect of the Order's work. It was only several years later that I was to learn of that 'chance remark' in a public house in Covent Garden that proved to be the instigator of much, though not all, of the saving of the Order papers.

The experimental group worked for just one year, but it was sufficient for us to know that the ceremonies and group workings of the Order were helpful, relevant and valid in today's world. For the next three years I worked to transfer the mass of material that had been collected into a sequence of teachings and practical work that could be studied and undertaken not only in a group setting, but also individually—wherever the student happened to live. Up until this time, Druidry had been a path which could only be followed by those who could physically visit a teacher, as I had done. But this limited the teaching. The impulse and inspiration which had come from Ross' message in 1984 made it clear that now Druidry should be made available to all those who sought its inspiration and understanding.

Although by 1988 the work of preparing these teachings for individual study through a form of postal course was almost complete, a natural reluctance to actually take the step of re-founding the Order prevented me from taking any further action. Then the anonymous friend who acted as a catalyst for the saving of the documents in 1975 appeared again in the life of the Order—as if out of the blue. I had not spoken to him nor seen him for years, but a week before St Valentine's Day in 1988 he telephoned and asked if he could visit me on that day, together with some friends.

Although he gave no inkling of the purpose of his visit, I knew in my bones that something important would happen.

On that day I was asked, persuaded and finally appointed Chief of the newly-reconstituted Order. We began the work of printing the course, and within months a steady flow of enquirers became a growing body of enthusiastic students. We held our first Summer Solstice celebration at Glastonbury, and as the year moved on we found that Druidry seemed to answer a very real need in people—not only from all over the British Isles, but also in America and Holland, France, Belgium and Australia. That need seemed to be founded in the desire to reconnect to our spiritual roots and heritage in the hope of finding a way out of the psychological wasteland of our present age.

At this disturbing point in our evolution, when more and more species are becoming extinct each year, we find ourselves turning not to the suited businessman or politician, nor to the white-cloaked scientist or doctor, but to the strangely-robed figure of the Druid or shaman for directions. As we move amidst the debris of the petro-chemical age we are seeking once again a connection with nature, with the Source, that is lasting and sure. For this reason many people are turning to the 'Nature-religions' or natural spiritual paths in an attempt to make this connection, which somehow conventional religion has failed to achieve, or has indeed exacerbated.

The reason for our deep need to reconnect to native traditions at this stage in our history is undoubtedly due to the profound sense of alienation that besets those of us who live in the 'civilized' world. Karl Marx saw alienation in many of its guises as the root-problem of the capitalist system, and attempted to construct a world in which man would become dis-alienated. Seventy-two years after the Russian revolution, when the attempt was made to construct such a world, we can—without bias—say that the Communist system has also created a society in which the majority feel profoundly alienated.

Both East and West have become alienated from the natural world—with the disastrous consequences that we face today. And it is in the light of this fact that we can understand the revival of interest in the 'Earth religions' which points to the growing awareness of the necessity to combine our spirituality with a reverence and care for the Earth.

It is undeniable that there is a renaissance of such an interest in these natural religions throughout the world. A part of this renaissance reflects the need in the collective unconscious to redress the balance that has been disturbed by the dominance in our religious consciousness of the patri-archal religions of the Judaeo-Christian and Islamic worlds. This imbal-ance has resulted in a disturbed relationship to the planet herself; and rather than seeing the revival of interest in earth religions as regressive, as harking back to primitive times, the upsurge of interest demonstrates quite the opposite trend—one of progression, in which we meet the old wisdom at a new turn of the spiral and see that we need its sense of the sacredness of all life if we are to survive as a species and planet.

A great deal of interest is currently being shown in native American Indian ways, and many of their teachings and practices are similar to the Western ways of Druidry and Wicca. Druidry and Wicca are distinct and separate manifestations of the Western Path, and the best way to consider them is as brothers and sisters—within the same family, and therefore sharing family characteristics, but also separate, with characteristics peculiar to themselves.

Druidry is biased towards a reverence for the sun, whereas Wicca is biased towards lunar reverence. Wiccan work is often concerned with working with polarity, whereas Druidry does not stress this aspect to such a degree. Both, however, work in a circle, work with the four quarters and four elements, and celebrate the seasonal festivals.

Druidry has links with Christianity, too, in a way that Wicca does not. The early Celtic Church, whose priests had often been Druids, still maintained its connection with Nature—as a study of their prayers and poetry will show—and the Order is involved in working towards the revival of the Celtic Church. In the summer of 1989 the Order participated in the first conference of Christians and Druids at Prinknash in Gloucestershire, at which representatives from most of the Druid Orders met over three days with representatives of the Christian Church in a number of its forms. We found, during that time, that all of us felt intuitively and deeply that a revival of the Celtic Church could be immensely helpful at this time when the Church needs to throw off its accretions of millennia, and return to the practice of a simple and pure spirituality which is in tune with Nature, rather than holding a position of superiority towards it.

Some readers of this foreword might be pleased to learn of such a dialogue between Druidry and Christianity, particularly when it results in specific action being taken to initiate a new impulse within the Christian movement. Others might be disappointed, hoping that Druidry was exclusively 'pagan'. But Druidry is a way of working with the natural world, and is not a dogma or a religion. It can be combined with Buddhism or Christianity, Wiccan practice or Judaism, or it can be practised on its own. Druidry honours, above all, the freedom of the individual to follow his own path through life, offering only guides and suggestions, schemes of understanding, methods of celebration and mythical ideas—which can be used or not as the practitioner feels fit.

This openness of Druidism can sometimes be infuriating, particularly to those with analytical minds, unused to wholistic thinking. The very word 'Druid' poses difficulties. What exactly does it mean? Where does it come from? Who were they? What do they do now? But we should be wary of trying to answer these questions too readily. William Blake, who stands in the Order's records as one of its Chosen Chiefs, said, 'The wisest of the Ancients considered what is not too explicit as the fittest for instruction, because it rouses the faculties to act.' It is in this spirit that much Druid teaching is conveyed.

Why is Druidry particularly relevant today? We have seen how it answers a need for disalienation, for a rediscovery of roots and heritage, but it is also particularly relevant at this time because it creates a forum into which we can bring three different aspects of our lives. Within Druidry we can bring our concern for the environment, which is our love of Nature, into relationship with our spiritual concerns, and into relationship with our artistic concerns. Ritual and poetry, dance and spiritual practice, personal development and ecological concern all find their place within Druid work. Rather than competing for our time and attention, they mutually interact, one with another, enriching our lives and delineating a sacred space which acts as a crucible to our creativity.

To be able to be an artist and the follower of a spiritual discipline; to be environmentally concerned and active; to be able to combine one's Druidry with whatever other spiritual practices and teachings one finds beneficial —these are the goals of those who study Druidry today.

Ross Nichols' life was a good example of how it is possible to encompass such different objectives.

Philip Peter Ross Nichols was born in Norfolk on 28 June 1902. He completed his MA in history at Oxford in the 'twenties, and began a career which allowed him to teach, publish both poetry and prose, paint and travel. He had always been a practising Christian, and worked for the Church in boys' clubs in the East End of London for many years. He was ordained a deacon of the Celtic Church by Bishop Tugdual of St Dolay, and was also an active Martinist, being able to combine these interests with his Druid work.

Having worked as ballet critic for a provincial newspaper, he became principal of Carlisle & Gregson's, also known as 'Jimmy's', a private college which was known as a 'crammer's', and which had tutored, amongst others, Winston Churchill (before he was initiated into the Albion Lodge of the Ancient Order of Druids at Blenheim in 1908).

In 1952 the Forge Press published an impressive twin-volume edition of *The History and Practice of Magic* by Paul Christian. Ross edited and revised this nineteenth-century French work, which had been translated by his friends James Kirkup and Julian Shaw, and coordinated the supplementary articles and notes written by the famous palmist Mir Bashir, and the former Presiders of the Order Lewis Spence and Charles Cammell, amongst others.

His own published work, apart from numerous articles in historical, poetic and esoteric journals, consists of *Sassenach Stray* (1940), *Prose Chants & Proems* (1941), *The Cosmic Shape* (1946) and *Seasons at War* (1947).

A full selection of his poetry, *Prophet, Priest and King*, edited and introduced by Jay Ramsay, which draws strongly on Druidic and related imagery, is being published by Element Books, and is available from the Order.

Ross, or Nuinn, as he was called in the Order, was an accomplished water-colour painter and had exhibited at the Royal Academy. In addition to his passions for history, writing and painting, he loved to travel, and having few family ties and an academic post with long vacations, was able to do so. On each visit he would make extensive historical enquiries, photograph and sketch archaelogical remains and ancient monuments, and often write an account of his journey. We do not know of all his travels, but we do know that he visited Egypt and Morocco, Bulgaria, Malta and Greece. He was a regular visitor to Ireland and was a good friend of his fellow Chief Druid, Paul Bouchet of the Order in France, whom he visited both officially and unofficially on several occasions. He also visited Wales and Scotland, and in particular Iona and the Hebridean islands.

He joined the Ancient Druid Order in 1954 and took the office of Scribe —ideally suited to his inquisitive nature and literary abilities. When his teacher, the Chosen Chief Robert MacGregor Reid, died in 1964, the Order split into two groupings, as had happened several times before in its history. A group of senior Druids disagreed with the election of MacGregor Reid's successor, Dr Thomas Maughan, and decided to form a reconstituted order with Ross as its Chief, and with the three grades of Bard, Ovate and Druid fully taught and recognized in a way that had not previously been done in the Order's modern cycle. From a study of the Order papers and correspondence, and in discussion with those who remember the events of those times, it was a difficult and sometimes bitter period of separation—as most separations are. And yet, looking back 25 years later, it is clear that it was a healthy and positive development in the life of the Order. There is room enough in Druidry for many different expressions of its truth, and within the last few years there has been a proliferation of autonomous groups working within the Druid tradition. Most of these have come together to form a Grand Council, under whose umbrella they can meet and engage in joint initiatives, including the Order of Bards, Ovates and Druids, the Ancient Order of Druids, the Secular Order of Druids and the Glastonbury Order of Druids.

Just as a tree develops many different branches, so Druidry has developed its different branches, and it would be unhealthy if it were not to grow in this way. The Ancient Druid Order, although not yet a member of the Council, continues to hold the two Equinox ceremonies in public at Primrose Hill and Tower Hill each year, and the Summer Solstice at Stonehenge (when allowed by the police). Although no longer the largest Order, they have received the majority of media coverage of Druidry, thus forming an image of Druidism in the public's mind which is representative of only one stream of Druid tradition. The white robes and patriarchal bias of their ceremonies are elements which were introduced into Druidry during the period of the Druid revival in the eighteenth century, and whilst being quite valid ways of working in their own right, must not be thought of as the only authentic way of working within a Druid context.

The Ancient Order of Druids (not to be confused with the Ancient Druid Order) were prime movers in initiating the Grand Council. Having shied away from esoteric Druidry for more than 200 years, and having concentrated primarily on social and charitable activities, they feel now the spirit of the times urging them towards mutual interaction with the other branches of the Druid tradition and are actively seeking dialogue, as are the other members of the Council.

One of the major achievements of Ross Nichols as Chief of the Order of Bards, Ovates and Druids was to reintroduce the celebration of the five ceremonies which had been abandoned from the repertoire of modern Druidry, so that the reconstituted Order celebrated not only the Spring and Autumn equinoxes and the Summer Solstice, but also the Winter Solstice and the four Celtic fire festivals of Imbolc and Beltane, Lughnasadh and Samhain.

Another of his achievements was to reorganize the Order into the three grades of Bard, Ovate and Druid as it had always existed in the past. During the time of his chieftainship he organized ceremonies at Parliament Hill and at Glastonbury—and for 10 years the Order would celebrate the rite printed at the end of this book on the Tor itself. One of Ross' greatest skills lay in his ability to gather people together. For each event he attracted not only those interested in the esoteric, but local council officials, local children who dressed as acolytes and assistants to the May Queen or the Queen of Summer or Autumn, carrying posies and flowers in their hair, visitors from other faiths, and poets and musicians who would perform within the Druid circle.

With such an active schedule of celebrations, combined with leading the Order and acting as principal at 'Jimmy's', Ross was well aware that he needed a place of retreat. He bought a few acres of woodland in Oxfordshire, and there he built two wooden huts and furnished them with camp beds and stoves. Whenever he felt the need, he would retire there, either alone or with fellow Druids, and live a simple life of chopping wood, fetching water, walking in the forest and cooking by an open fire. Being interested in both the naturist and vegetarian movements, he was able to combine his natural instinct for simple living with the contemporary currents of thought that were translating these ideals into practical models of living.

When he wrote *The Book of Druidry*, Ross managed to combine three books in one: a history of Druidry, a guide to certain ancient sites, and an anthology of Druid wisdom. As such, it can perhaps best be appreciated if it is approached in the following way: the history can be read as one book, and will hopefully give the reader an insight into who exactly the Druids were and what they have become today; the guide to the sites, while it can of course be read as a book, is probably most useful when combined with a visit to the actual site and a reading of the associated literature relevant to the site as given in the Bibliography; and, the anthology of Druid wisdom, by which is meant the section of the book entitled 'Nine Groups of Druidic Concepts', and the section 'Some Druidic Wisdom', together with the details of the Eight-fold Year plan and the Bealteinne ceremony, is most fruitfully used as a resource for accessing the inner nature of Druid teaching.

It is important for readers to remember that this book was written over 15 years ago, and to know that since that time a number of writers—such as John and Caitlín Matthews, Bob Stewart, John Michell and Gareth Knight amongst others—have explored the areas of research covered by Ross in great detail from both a scholastic and an esoteric viewpoint, and a study of their work will add a depth and richness to the understanding gained from reading this book.

It might also be helpful for readers to note that Ross enjoyed playing with the spelling of certain mythological figures and place names, and although we have changed some of these to avoid confusion, we have left others to convey his sense of amusement with language.

Ross' style often involves him explaining a question after rather than before he has discussed it—and once one knows this, one can enjoy the experience of light slowly dawning on a scene which has hitherto remained in obscurity for us. In tackling the more veiled passages, we need also to remember again the quotation of William Blake in which he stated, 'The wisest of the Ancients considered what is not too explicit as the fittest for instruction, because it rouses the faculties to act.' Ross clearly came to a decision in writing this book that he wanted to reveal much of the nature of Druidic teaching, and yet he was still bound by his position within the Order to be discreet and cautious. Hopefully the reader will be able to sense, behind and beyond the words, the atmosphere of Druidry which words alone can never convey.

Philip Carr-Gomm.
London, 1989.

Details of the postal course and other activities of the Order of Bards, Ovates & Druids can be obtained by writing to:

The Secretary, O.B.O.D., PO Box 1333, Lewes, E. Sussex, BN7 3ZG.

I. Introductory General Ideas

Druidry is the Western form of an ancient universal philosophy, culture or religion, dating from the days of early man when the three were one. It is of the stone circle culture, the groves of sacred trees, the circular dance. It has been traced by some as far as India in the cult of Siva; its oak tree burials are not infrequent in the West. With the numerology, orientations and magical square calculations recently made, it is seen to link with the near–universal surveying system, with its meaningful number and mystical geometry, that lends colour to the ideas of a race of highly-developed beings originating from an Atlantis somewhere, or coming in flying chariots from another world or dimension. At no time has Druidry agreed with the idea of evolution from the animal as the main human origin, but has always conceived of a supernal, giant or deific basis to its universal shape.

Druidry has never been tied to the cult of any one god-focus; its members, earlier and later, seem always to have been experimenters and explorers in various lines of learning. Pythagoras, sometimes considered as a founder, in such a perspective was a collector and developer of much earlier geometrical ideas. William Blake was an intuitive teacher, often by hyperbole, of the highest truth: 'Ancient man contained in his mighty limbs all things in heaven and earth.' Always profoundly conscious of a great supernal design, such thinkers linked with the mystical sides of many religions, but found Druidry itself something larger than any of them. The Sufi, the Arhat, the higher Christian mystic, even Augustine of Hippo or the German stigmatist, Theresa Neumann, share certain concepts of Druidry. Meanwhile, the Romans attempted to exterminate, the Roman Church excommunicated, and the seventeenth and even the earlier eighteenth-century Christians decided that on the whole Druidry had been, and was, intolerable. Only an antiquarian vicar who was also an alchemist dared, from his own entrenched position, to break the general rule: The Revd William Stukeley was head of the Order in England from 1722 to 1765.

The intolerant intellectual atmosphere meant that Druidry has largely developed underground in recent centuries, and Druids became as cagey as Freemasons in admitting their connection. So successful were they in laying false trails that one recent professor, writing in full ignorance of modern Druidry, dismisses as laughable the idea that the eighteenth-century movement could possibly have begun its assembly of groves from many quarters under the aegis of John Toland, although he had written papers, later edited as a book, on Druid culture and antiquities.[1] Lord Bulwer Lytton's family in times past furiously denied that he was a Druid, whereas we know the grove of which he was Chief. William Blake,

[1] J. Toland, *History of the Druids*, 1719.

although frequently using Druids as horrifying semi-mythological figures in his writings, managed to keep secret his connection with them so deftly that the chief authority on Blake today, Kathleen Raine, did not know of the link. Yet Blake had told no lies about it, and at least once had announced his Druidry, on the one occasion he came publicly into conflict with authority, at Chichester in 1802 (see p. 98). Blake was indeed a Druid; he was Chief for 28 years, and through him, jointly with Stukeley, appear to come the main inner ideas of Druidry today.

At no time, it now appears, have reasonable records of the Order been kept or, if so, they have been destroyed through the various schisms and quarrels over succession that have occurred from time to time. Mainly, however, it has been the early Druidic prohibition of writing and the insistence upon the learning by heart of long wisdom-poems that have handed on the learning, mouth-to-ear, through the centuries. A sense of secretive power and a great poetic metaphorical ability have indeed characterized the Welsh side of Druidry, so that even when written it has been difficult to interpret the meaning and teaching hidden in the *englyns*.

To give any account of the development of Druidry is therefore impossible in the documentary historical sense. Whilst one may be fairly sure of the general outline, the gaps are larger than the areas covered by what is known. It is easier to give a concept of its ideas and whence they derive.

II. The Shape-Shifting of Recent Knowledge

Archaelogists are now moving towards a realization that many of the older ideas are truer than has been thought, and an article in *The Listener* (3 January 1974) by Anne Ross is enlightening. The Celts are now taken as a really very ancient race, the first perhaps of the large-scale migrants. They it was, she considers, who, as the Beaker peoples, spread in two quite separate waves into Europe about 2300 BC, and also later in perhaps 2000 BC. The culture was marked by their pottery, by personal crouch burials with possessions, by a more aristocratic society with richer and poorer people, and by the use of bronze and of bows and arrows. The second phase varied the type of pottery, and used short daggers and axes rather than bows.

The landing and dispersal place from the eastern Mediterranean voyages was Spain, and the cultures seem to have come directly thence to Ireland and western Britain.

Ireland itself has the oldest legends in Europe apart from those of Greece, as well as the oldest legal system. The legends tell of various invasion races in tales going back to movements of peoples towards the end of the third millennium BC and link Spain firmly with Eire. Excavations agree in dates with what these legends seem to say; the spread of language also seems to agree—the 'Q' Celtic or Gaelic language group keeps a hard 'g' or 'k' sound as in *mac*, 'son of', and is the older group found in Eire, Scotland and the Isle of Man—as well as in Iberia (Spain) and the Caucasus. The 'P' Celtic or Cymric group of languages has a 'p' or 'b' sound so that *mac* becomes *map* 'son of' in Welsh, sometimes *mab*, as in *Mabinogion*. Blood-group analysis tells the same tale: the O-gene is the dominant group in Ireland and Scotland, the 'Q' Celtic part, and the A-gene-dominant group corresponds to the 'P' Celts of Wales.

If the Celts therefore go back so far, instead of the 900–800 BC which has been the most that archaeologists have hitherto allowed, they cannot be separated from the megalithic culture—unless that too rapidly increases in longevity. Nor, although the type of Druidry may have changed, can the Celts be dissociated from their traditional priesthood. It becomes therefore highly probable that in fact, as the Order's Chiefs have frequently suggested, Druids did direct the building of Stonehenge.

Such apparently antiquarian studies as we undertake prove to be pointers to our own psychology, and as it were entrances to temples. Meditation at Samhuinn, at Imbolc, or at the dawn of the Summer Solstice gives markedly different results, one supplementing another. To enter into the Druid house, symbolized by the great trilithon and the mound of our banner, should open doors into many unfamiliar hills where we may find caves of light like the legendary mounds of the *sidhe*. 'The Ancients wrote it in the earth' and we should be able not merely to decode, but to develop and elaborate on these experiences.

For nothing here should be taken to mean that we are merely researching the past. To find the sounder wisdom of the past and to train our powers in the present by it safely, then to use them intelligently and with the right motives, that is the object of a modern Bard and Ovate.

Each year the archaeological shape of things is apt to shift somewhat, altered by a fresh dig. The sum of these amounts to a considerable rethink and most of it moves in the direction of the more traditional or 'occult' ideas.

Successive summers in the west of England have shown Arthur located in death at Glastonbury in the Abbey's old graveyard and the finding of Mediterranean-type objects on Glastonbury Tor link it with the Arthurian-period finds excavated at Cadbury Castle (Camelot). The finding, by pendulum divining, of an oval ceremonial shape on the Cadbury summit and of a track running south-east with centres of power along it like shrines have neither been confirmed nor disproved by the digging.

Digging at Silbury has shown something like 12 different types of earth laid in sectionally, brought from as many different and distant areas of Britain. The traditional astrological layout with an axis running from Stonehenge to Avebury has always specified Silbury as 'earth', and it is earth indeed—symbolical tributary earth from half of Britain joins in a union of whatever kind the vast Avebury circle represents. There are rumours of a crown-type circlet and a crystal goblet found in Silbury years ago that have disappeared—these might be symbols of a spiritual authority recognized here in such a tribal union, like the union in Eire which the councils and games at Tara signified, or the Greek Amphictryonic League.

Attention has been focused more and more upon Glastonbury Tor and upon Chalice Well, between the Tor and Chalice Hill. Undoubtedly there is an indefinable power emanating from the whole region which draws sensitives of all types to it. But it has unsolved problems. Do the Tor's ridges form a maze pattern? Why were St Michael's Tower and its predecessors built? Was it to seal an entrance? Why has the cave below been so determinedly sealed up?

The concept of the 12-mile wide zodiac with its giant figures, which seems a fantastic dream to many people, appears at Glastonbury itself to shape with meaning for this age. The bird representing Aquarius—the age which is coming, or may indeed be here already[1]—turns its head here, and its beak is precisely upon the Chalice Well. Now a bowl is the symbol of the Aquarian Age by tradition—a great bowl, balanced on the head of a man. It is often said that the Aquarian will be the age of free intelligence rather than authority—the bowl, the feminine emblem, is filled with air or intelligence, not water or emotion, which dominated the passing Age of the Fishes.

But also it is true that the bowl or chalice is a 'feminine' symbol, and that this is being upheld by man. So that spiritual refreshment in a feminine elemental form is to be the dominant shape—supported by mankind. This would appear to suggest a return of a matriarchy, but in an intelligent and intellectual form. That matriarchy is due for a return after some 4,000 years, and is in fact returning, has long been observed.

Not least in these revolutions of established ideas is that brought about by calibrated radio-carbon tests. Recent Chosen Chiefs of the Order have never accepted that the evolution of megalithic temples and the art of the circle-builder came from the South-east to these islands—an apparently 'proven' thesis hitherto adopted almost universally. Carbon-dating tests now put Stonehenge as 'at least' 500–1,000 years earlier.[2] That is, the first Stonehenge used to be reckoned as about 1900 BC the finished monument at about 1450 BC; now it appears that the beginnings may be 2900 BC–2400 BC. Avebury is still earlier, say 3200 BC. The earlier dates considerably antecede the Great Pyramid, which is given as 2720 BC by Cottrell but may well be later.[3]

It is too soon for archaeologists of any type to revalue in terms of a west to south-east spread of the wisdom-building architecture. But no one can now call the ideas of Stukeley and Blake on early Druidry impossible.

[1] Astronomically the age began in 1881.
[2] See Colin Renfrew, *Before Civilisation*, 1972.
[3] Breasted gives the Great Pyramid's period as about 2900 BC and Glyn Daniel gives it 2500 BC and the *Djoger* Pyramid as 2680 BC.

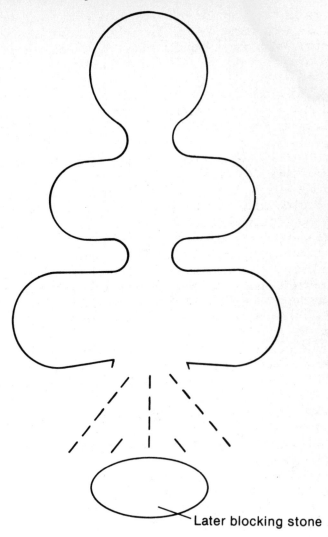

Later blocking stone

Suggestion of significant shape of the interior of West Kennet Long Barrow and its kinship with the Maltese rock-hewn temples of similar shape generally reckoned humanoid. The triple entry here, however, is different.

More generally speaking, their thought now calls for more sympathetic interpretation. 'Ancient Albion contained in his mighty limbs all things in heaven and earth' is only another way of saying 'Man is the measure of all things', a classical dictum. Kathleen Raine has applied the comparative study of symbol and myth to Blake, who emerges as a metaphysical teacher of great scholarship and profound expressiveness. Aubrey's and Stukeley's concepts of Avebury and Silbury begin to look reasonable if supplemented by more recent knowledge. The Windmill Hill people could be the population that created the immense Avebury; the West Kennet Long Barrow, the most complete and impressive barrow in England, is an obvious temple of the old Mother Goddess, and built in her shape, balancing Silbury, the male emblem, one each side of the Avebury-Stonehenge axis.[4]

Many obvious excavations await the diggers, if esoteric ideas are allowed to guide them. After unblocking a limestone cave, known in the eighteenth century, that runs under the Glastonbury Tor, some burrowing under St Michael's Tower could show if it hides a way further down. Although at least one vertical shaft has been found not far away, no one appears to have dug far, if at all, into the actual centre of Stonehenge. There are rumours from years back of some digging-out of steps that was hastily refilled and no report made.

Professor Thom in his book on megalithic monuments has with a wealth of labour worked out angulations that re-form and extend our ideas on orientations. In particular the moon aspects prove to be vital. Early man needed to know when it was full moon so that he could see by night, and its waxing and waning usually made it a feminine symbol, although a masculine moon is known. We already know that in the Aubrey Holes in Stonehenge there is an apparatus to forecast moon eclipses: nights when the moon was eaten up were important to know in advance, probably for both hunting and magic.[5]

Early Druidry or its predecessors in neolithic times must therefore have had a cult of the moon as well as of the sun; a matriarchal and fertility side. The circles are orientated sometimes to stars such as Sirius, characteristic of a season, but mainly to the midsummer sun or to the sun's birth in midwinter. If these were 'life and power' orientations, the 'death' ones were mainly north-west or south-west. An example is the best circle at Carrowmore, Sligo, orientated to a fine cromlech, perhaps the grave of a chieftain, to the North-east, and also to the doubtless 'sinister' power of the old goddess Maeve in the Misgaun to the North-west; so that power was received from the spirit of the old chief, but sacrifices would be on the angle of the old war goddess.

The continual concentration in the past upon directions and their significances, with a good deal of mental effort, seems to be the basis of the awareness men and women can now develop in meditation along parallel lines: the mental paths are already there.

---

[4] See Caroline Malone, *Avebury*, B.T. Batsford, 1989. She pushes back the date of the complex to 3710 BC. For Silbury Hill, see *The Silbury Treasure* by Michael Dames, Thames & Hudson, 1976.
[5] There are reasons to think that early man perceived the fertility and generally 'magical' currents that emanate from the moon, which cycle eclipses break. The elder Druids had a great moon-sense, linked with the 'moony' mistletoe.

III. Cones and Hills: Emergence of a Higher Self

Man's higher intelligence may come in from the stars, winding as a filmy snake inwards, circling through the Milky Way, or Dragon's Path, entering Earth from the direction of the Pole Star, as some of our ancestors imagined.[1] It may come from a series of age-long visits from other and more developed planets, in flaming chariots, wheels, groups of spacemen called angels. It may be called up by the higher or inner sun radiating from a sphere 'behind' the physical. It may be from any of these things, or it may not. What is sheerly incredible is that it should 'evolve' from ape-men with nothing of such a nature to draw it up and forth. Where really is the ape link anyway? The son of Louis Leakey found the oldest dateable remains of man as two and a half million years old, and he is a good deal more modern-looking than the later Australian specimen. (Since then archaeologists in Ethiopia have found remains dating from four million years ago, while elsewhere in Africa the dates are pushed even further back.) From God's breath man became a living soul, in the old story. God's breath might come in many forms, with the Mercury-snake not the least worthy concept.

Whatever the causation—and one notes that modern philosophy shies away from causation and in effect will not cope with the problem—what one can trace is the development, from experience and features of the outer world, of concepts measuring up to these shadowy intimations, whencesoever they came.

One of the earliest joint activities of man was the circular or ring dance. If, as Soviet speculators teach, the rhythm of joint working-parties swinging together began rhythm, song, even speech, as the *Volga Boat Song* expresses the heave-ho of the action, there is quite a good case for suggesting the evolution of such dances. In the furious release of energy, the whirling and mixing of the astral forces involved in the sideways-movements and singing, these forces develop a boiling and rising centre. With custom, practice and some small amount of realization that something beyond the physical was happening, a few natural psychics, then as now, would be able to see this, on another plane, as a rising cone. It would be seen probably as either red (energy, passion) or green-blue (the nature colour); or perhaps a blend of both.

So the concept of this upward vortex became one of the earliest mystical concepts of man. Vortices of this kind are well-known to occult workers now. It was found that force from them could be stored, as the ancient witch communities believed, in certain trees, notably oaks, and in stones. Humans had struck upon one of the basic shapes of life, the rising circle or spiral. T.C. Lethbridge, the Cambridge archaeologist-psychic, in his

[1] Actually, this is not such a merely poetic fancy as it may sound. Our own 'Sb.' classification of galaxy, halfway or so through its life-span, does have spiral arms which are slowly contracting, whilst its planets are expanding from their cores: by Hubble's Constant, the expansion of planets our sort of size is at the rate of 0.6 mm per annum. So, very slowly, the outward arms descend and the worlds themselves swell.

writings on his findings with pendulum workings, made it quite clear that all objects to some extent radiate, and that their spheres of radiation describe elongated spiral cones, both above and below them. Every biologist indeed knows of the curves of growth in nature—this is something of the same kind.

Discovering the life-principle, then, experimentally, early man magicked in game, stupefied the leaders of a rival tribe, and used cone-power for any purpose, good or bad, since it was simply neutral power. They probably also called up the spirits of the dead to prophesy from the fire that might be at the centre of such dancing; fire aptly symbolized the rising power of the cone. This was better than the shaman's possession by the spirits of the dead when near the bodies in the group charnels of the long barrows, those large dark houses of the remains of the revered ancestors. It was gradually realized that men's spirits seemed to be better off when separated from the cult of their decaying flesh, and cremation began—the fire purified the essential life, destroyed the useless husk. Witchcraft's basic ideas come largely from this era and witchcraft knows a good deal about this stage in man's conceptual evolution. Later Druidry included these amongst its ideas, together with orientation and the later knowledge of sun and moon power.

So at this stage there had already been a great mind development, some observation upon what is popularly called the psychic plane—which is at least as common amongst primitive peoples as with ourselves—and an appreciation of collective power. So firm was this knowledge that, finding stones better media on the whole than trees for storage of the forces, men eventually built stone circles for their dancing. The degree of their magical and psychic powers is to be gauged by the extent to which they spread the laborious building of these circles. We move towards an abstract type of mind; not the literal imitations of animals in a magic cave, not the literal contact with the dead to hear their voices, but the rising circle, the cone, voices in the open air, forms that build up as with the Witch of Endor, and so to the representation of these things in the flat, by lines, so that a few scratches really do represent a man or woman, often of late Picasso type, which most folk could understand.

The cone began to be seen as an outline, a pointer. It has an edge one can draw; perhaps things the same shape might have the same effect? So arrowhead shapes, pointed sticks, bones generally were tried out. With due concentration, they seemed to work—and still work. Bone-pointing in Africa is quite effectual as a curse. All these types of magicking techniques work in suitable communities, and not necessarily outside them.

But, equally, now the higher mind of man began to operate. He no longer looked only at his game, his enemies, his physical needs. A cone raised by a large circle must be a pretty large thing, whether psycho-physically perceptible on that scale or not; it was believed to exist and it worked, and eyes began looking upward in areas where there were pointed hills. The cone had drawn awe and respect; the hill, more solid, drew more awe. This is the era of the holy hill upon which so much early ritual took place—the 'high places' detested of the Judean prophets, that high place Lud Hill, or Montmartre. This is moving towards a cult. Whereas a cone of psychic power, personally raised and operated, faded from view after a time, this solid one stayed put, and you could go to it. This represents a basic change. Ideas, appearances, power emanating from a hill have a fixed quality, external to oneself. Man respects power; and power is exactly what such electromagnetic forces as that possessed by Glastonbury Tor convey. From the Middle Ages comes a clerical edict that no one must sleep upon the ground of Glastonbury because it is inhabited by devils—another way of saying the same thing.

Now the neolithic, abstract type of mind developed further. As he looked at the regular pointed hill, the cone of power, man began to conceive the shape of the isosceles or even the equilateral triangle. This is going a long way, and we have perhaps arrived at sky observation, the realization of orientations; the horizontal vision of distance now adding itself to the nearer vision of vertical cone and hill. Bone-pointing had been found to work; what about the 'ghost' or outline of the pointed hill? And so we find cones of power of a different kind—flat ones, isosceles triangles pointing. One very clear one can be seen at Houldstone Down in North Somerset; a more complex scheme is obvious as soon as looked for at Brown Willy. (Both are given in full in issues of the *Ley Hunter* nos. 11 and 18.) They could be noted more generally; so far few have looked for them, and one does not see what is not anticipated. Wherever there is a marked line of orientation it is always worthwhile to look each side for features at symmetrical distances. If present, they are probably bases for a flat cone in a significant direction. Their finding might confirm the intention of an orientation. Ley observers have scarcely, if at all, recognized this phenomenon; they seem to be too busy to use their eyes. A dozen more exactly noted examples would confirm the thesis that these early men were geometers as well as precise observers of direction for luminaries and stars.

We have now arrived at a fresh crucial development. It hardly requires genius to reflect that the concepts of a cone of human psychic power from a ring dance, an arrow-like pointing bone with a trail of objects in a line, and a conical hill, whilst they may suggest each other by shape, are so radically different that they imply differentiated schemes of thought. The pointing bone is on the power-directing line; you set it to aim in the direction you want in order to magic somebody. The hill is a great fixity that towers over you. It may send or receive power, but you cannot sway it. The contrast is total. A hill has a great *mana* of its own from its shape and height, and perhaps a natural magnetic charge as well. To it man begins to attach a devotion that he does not attach to the power-cone that he himself emanates. The height seems to be a kind of unformulated god— the god that man *will* later formulate. (There are virtually no shapes of gods from this neolithic period.) The cone or bone-pointing powers are both in effect using the esoteric magic formula, 'as below, so above'—as we direct, so let wider effects be. But when man begins the observances of a non-human power in a hill, he begins to say to himself, 'This is a holy thing, and if its wishes may be ascertained, *it* should guide *me*; it is (literally) the highest thing I know upon earth.' And he moves towards the contrary adage, 'as above, so below,' which is the basis of religion. 'I perceive the higher and will be guided by it.'

If therefore one accepts that the isosceles triangle of power follows or develops together with a hill–cult, such triangles represent an aspiration to receive, not to force anything, as a man using an actual holy hill aspires to receive. The orientations of these things tell one so. An isosceles triangle projecting to the North-east will be very unlikely to be projecting anything thither; on the contrary, the North-east is the great place for receiving the *mana* from the seasonal high force of the sun, so that the triangle is likely to be a gesture of drawing down blessedness from the sun-god—the magic of induction. It is a new idea, an immense crucial development, the emergence of an attitude that has opened the eyes of humanity to the possibility of a great and perhaps beneficent power beyond itself.

The same triangular technique can, however, be used not to orientate oneself but to project something on a huge scale. Witches consider that they can and have done such things, especially with weather. According to the late Gerald Gardner,[2] England was three times saved from invasion by witches. These patriots in the time of Elizabeth I, probably directed by Dr Dee, caused the winds so to blow as effectively to ruin the Spanish Armada's plans for its landing in England. The next occasion was when in the Napoleonic wars the witches of Sussex (even now a famous witch area) organized a consistently-blowing, south-west wind that prevented Napoleon's pontoons ranged at Boulogne from carrying over the 'Army of England'. The third great coven was one in which Dr Gardner took part, when witches gathered on the Sussex Downs, not to encourage winds but, more psychologically, to project into the minds of Hitler and Goering the idea that invaders could not come over. The projection appeared to work as well as did the others.

The snake from the stars has certainly now wound its way towards man and bitten him into craving for that which is beyond himself. Upon this, later priestcrafts develop.

But confining ourselves to the concepts, not the administrations, of these higher longings, we find them moving ever broader and deeper, until the flight is undertaken to the concept of an 'almighty' something—a word really meaning nothing, for it implies a quality humanity cannot by definition know.

The way thither is a long one, and is traced partly through sexual symbolism. The cobra head, certain fruits and flowers, dead men's fingers

> for our chaste maidens dead men's fingers call them
> but liberal shepherds give a grosser name

[2] Gerald Gardner, *Witchcraft Today*, Rider, 1954.

— these are later fancies for the phallus. For the feminine organ the cowrie shell, the pomegranate and the dolphin—mainly by its name δελφίς, so parallel with δελφος (a womb) have been forms.

Beasts, trees and stones are parents, for the early woman had no idea of the causes of birth; when the quickening of the womb occurred, that was when the living thing entered her. So she looked round and saw a tree, a stone, an animal, even a god, and this was the parent. So we have the Sons of the Bear, the Wolf People, the Stones, and the children of the Seal or the Quicken Tree—for the mountain ash, with its red berries, was reckoned very powerful and quickened the womb often.

Thus the clans and the godlings arrive, and figures in nature take on humanized personality. What about the visibly lustful goat? He seemed to be a cut above the others, and represented nature very capably.

If these rocks, trees or beasts could proliferate in humans, surely that had great *brigh* or *mana*? So personification begins and humanoid myths. There are sons of the goat Pan, satyrs, and sons of horses and other creatures, centaurs. Here early moral teachers found an opening; and from the Greek and Irish myths can be worked out a whole school of philosophical teaching—something not yet properly done, but lying there embedded in the tales, waiting for the collector of gems to string together.

Personification becomes more gross and literal amongst more modern and literal-minded folks. Fecundity in Zeus must be the father of men as well as gods—but if so, then Hera, the wife, who is also the changeable sky, must surely be very jealous? The dead must be in a thirsty dry world, longing for draughts of milk or wine or even beer; they had a tough, dark god of their own. One poured beer into their coffins. And so on. These figures are never truly almighty, not even Zeus—who is merely rather stronger than the other gods, as Homer indicates.

But again the more abstract and reasonable forces in man's mind, or concepts given him from elsewhere, balance up. If the esemplastic minds of the Greeks built these very human fairy stories about the doubtful doings of their gods, and enjoyed their grosser features, the power behind it all began to broaden and deepen, so that we have the wonderful concept of father Zeus at Olympia or the extant and almost magical face of Hera the divine Mother also there, and quite apart from images, which the more thoughtful Greeks tended to despise, we have concepts like Οεμις, 'law', or Σοφια, wisdom, which are philosophic ideas transcending form. On this ground the Greeks match with the anti-graven-image Hebrews, who had the Commandments, the Ark and the holy books of the One God, with plenty of angels, and on these accounts considered themselves a chosen race, chosen by a hill god of the volcano who had impressed them on their migration from Egypt, and whom they had built into a very dogmatic myth.

We have arrived almost at modern times. The purified Greek religion of the great statues and the depth and elevation of the addresses to the Mother Goddess in Apuleius leave no doubt that worthier concepts were there in the minds of the educated—and many of the merely devout too. The One God is visibly on the way; he had arrived centuries earlier in India, infinite, 'almighty', yet in relations with humanity.

The snake from the stars had nestled now into the bosom of man. The Mother Goddess in snake form had united with Ophion, in Greek myth, and produced a red world-egg. The Druids' egg or stone was red. This would be hatched only by Solis, the sun—or the inner sun. This was happening.

STONES, WOOD
AND CULTURE

I. The Great Stone Culture

After surveying this immense prospect of space and time, it does become evident that the Snake's eggs take several well-defined and widespread main forms in which are contained certain teachings. 'The Ancients wrote it in the Earth.'

The evidence is scattered but chronological. Very many dolmens exist. From a good deal of converging evidence it is highly probable that each dolmen was a place of ritual rebirth from the Mother Goddess, the high spot in each man's spiritual life. Then came the long-barrow group temple-graves of ancestors, left for long periods, where the spirits were venerated and consulted; round individual barrows followed, moving towards the burning of the dead rather than inhumation. Later came the menhirs, great stones set up as psychic instruments, either for reverberations to particular ancestral spirits or for power storage generally. These led to a new piece of spiritual mechanism carrying implicity in it a whole system of teaching: the stone (or wood) circle, varied in many ways. Finally a few names appear that contain the concepts of Spirit, Air, and the Supreme God in three forms.

Each of these stages represents a significant station in the evolution of man's higher consciousness.

The power of the Mother Goddess can be horrific and tyrannous; it can also be benevolent and loving. We shall see from the Pacific island of Malekula that her rituals of rebirth were believed to deliver from the clutches of a Guardian Ghost and to activate the winged side of man's spirit, represented by a hawk.

The long barrow represents veneration for ancestors. Maybe offerings were made to them; almost certainly mediums in the shape of shamans purported to give their advice and communicate with the living. How long the sway of the ancestors in themselves held is not clear, but obviously not for very long, because the bones are often unceremoniously cast aside to make room for others, or indeed scarified, that is, the flesh removed.

The round barrow is totally different as a practice. It represents, first, a recognition of the individual as distinct from the family and ancestors.

Much more, it moves towards a new concept, linked with a sun cult, of divine fire. From somewhere, probably Persia, had come the recognition that man's spirit really did survive as a separate thing from his body; his true self in fact survived. Therefore man's mere shell should be burned, to transmute it to essential fire and so to reduce body and spirit to the same otherworld dimension. Man's spirit was akin to the sky-fire above, not to the womb of earth below.

Quite separately from the dolmen, power inherent in upright great stones was recognized. Man had perhaps already found experimentally that in fact stone did store psychic power rather better than trees and that each stone gave an effect of personality. Stones were credited with being the homes of the spirits of ancestors and sometimes their likeness was attempted, as in Corsica, or they were held to be supernal tribal beasts. Stones, like animals or trees, were often parents. If a woman was contemplating an ancestral stone and her womb quickened, that ancestor had entered into her.

As we have seen earlier, by a process of trial and error man had developed the circle-dance and found in it a remarkable technique for raising and directing power and, quite as much, for concentrating it and for self-protection. He now seeks a fixed lodging place for it. In a pastoral setting on uplands suitable for grazing, the wandering nomad is in no position to wait until a circle of trees he has planted grows up, as could happen in a fixed civilization in the plains. If he makes a ring of staves, someone is quite likely to take these useful wooden posts before he is back next season. So he rather laboriously sets up circles of stones large enough not to be easily moved. Sometimes, however, the danger seems less and he feels that smaller ones will do.

Within and around such a *gilgal, cor* or *choir* of giants, great and varied exercises could be carried out, calculations made, sun and moon observed usefully, and communication with the divine established.

Of his home dwellings we have little belonging to early man, and that little is rough, but of these apparatuses for the higher applications of concepts—dolmens, burial-houses, round barrows or burning pyres, impressive stones and larger or smaller circles—we have enough to know that he was an earnest seeker and indeed one who found a great deal.

We know too that his was an experimental mind capable of developing. The dolmen rises by stages from being a spiritual womb to being a great gateway, sometimes still thought of as the great house, more often as the place of coming or departing of supernal powers. Its two great pillars invited concepts of pairs like day and night, summer and winter, man and woman. In Celtdom a pair was often given colours, the northern pillar green, the southern gold.

II. The Dolmen as Rebirth Chamber

The long history of dolmen and megalith clusters, by general archaeological reckoning, begins in Sri Lanka, continues in the plains and mountains of southern India, crosses the Marmataka plains and the Maharesta plateau to Kashmir, so passes across northern Iran, through Syria, then by boat migrates to Cyprus and Malta, goes one way by land along North Africa into Egypt, takes another way to Egypt by the Wadi Hammamat; from Syria it moves by water to southern Italy, to the islands, Spain, the South of France and Brittany. A slower land migration also takes place up the Balkans and across into central Europe. First from Spain, then from Brittany, it crosses to England, coasts up the western shores and what are now the Celtic areas and islands, and seems to find its main end as regular dolmens in Ireland up the Boyne Valley. On the way are notable accumulations of dolmens in Syria and Iran. They are in their hundreds in Ireland.

No archaeologist seems to have suggested any convincing function for these three-stone chambers, as distinct from cists or burial chambers. But comparative ethnology has one from the Pacific—at the very end of the serpent's tail—which links with Ireland, its head.

The Pacific End of the Serpent's Tail

A young Cambridge researcher, J. Layard, went on an assignment to the Pacific, to Malekula Island, following on the work of another, A.B. Deacon.[1] Layard found on the north and west sides of the island some of the last remaining palaeolithic men. Their ceremonial religious life centred round the erection of a coral-slab dolmen. Various preliminary formalities culminated in a man lying in the little sacred chamber where he was initiated or reborn at the age of 25 or 30; at a later ceremony he went up on top and sacrificed. Thus he acquired his higher self, a kind of bird, a huge hawk whose body was always above the club-house. One recalls that in Wales it was a bird, there called a hen, that swallowed little Gwion and from whom he was reborn as Glorious-Brow (Taliesin). Such seem to be the beginnings of the Soul.

A long time ago Dr W.H. Rivers observed, 'In Melanesian dolmens are sacred doors; the initiate crawled through them for the rebirth ceremony.'

Deacon distinguished no fewer than 32 grades of initiation in these societies. All centre round the dolmen, *nevet muogh*, literally the 'stone of life'; and a main rite, the *Nogho Tilabive*, is 'to make men', i.e. a fertility rite.

The earlier series of initiations is called *Low Maki* and involves the ceremonial building of a dolmen over three years.

The first year is spent in the selection of the main coral slab, the second in bringing it to the dance-ground, the third in erecting the dolmen. The fourth year sees the ritual sacrifice of 100 boars and 100 fowls on this dolmen for the group to be initiated; also each candidate chooses a special boar to bear his new name. There is then the 30-day retreat into the

[1] A.B. Deacon, *Malekula: a Vanished People*, 1934 and John Layard, *Stone Men of Malekula*, 1942.

dolmen, which is *na-vot*, the rebirth place. Two more years are needed to complete the feeding back into life from rebirth.

Quite separate are the elaborate sand tracings during initiations which are the complex path of the dead man's soul, guided but also ruled sternly and demandingly by the Guardian Ghost. If the spirit did not know his ritual way, then the Guardian could and did eat him up. *Low Maki* and these sand tracings were probably the original cult, and then *High Maki* was added from elsewhere. The details of this are very similar except that the layout of the ritual is that of a vast outrigger canoe from another island.

Maki Low, then High, take between them therefore a cycle of between 10 and 18 years. The complex of tribes is both matrilinear and patrilinear, and hence they are split into halves, so that when one half's *Maki* has ended, the other's begins, and these figures therefore have to be doubled to give the cycle covering all tribal sections.

Earlier, before a general disapproval of cannibalism had spread, the supreme type of rebirth arose from human sacrifice on the dolmen; the consumption of the corpse of a brave enemy, for instance, gave immense power. Those used to these concepts naturally found extremely easy the acceptance of Christian dogmas about eating and drinking the flesh and blood of Christ, and consequently they made, and make, good converts.

The club-house, *Ghamel*, is erected in each village in a certain way. The front post is the *simbe na-nibul*, the seat of the hawk. Two dolmen-seats are at either end of the hut: the front, called *Wughi*, is the penis and the back, called *Lase*, is the testicles. Up above, finally, is the place of the huge hawk, the sacred image. After death you wanted really to escape the attentions of the Guardian Ghost—although as an insurance you learned all those sand-patterns—and the heavenly hawk was the best bet. 'Each individual performing the rites (of *Maki*) is identified with the mythical hawk who presides,' and the hawk is contrasted with the earthbound Guardian Ghost. Other presences of whom all are aware are the voices of the ancestors, which sound from the uncanny boomings of drums made from hollowed tree trunks.

In Malekula there is little stone; as indicated, the dolmen is made of coral. But the message flashes all the same to the stones at the head of the great snake in Ireland. The dolmens studding the mountains in the Boyne area are known as the Beds of Diamuid and Grainne, that is, the sun-goddess who absconded from her marriage feast with the old Finn Maccumhal and eloped with his protesting follower Diamuid. This is a legend clearly arising from neolithic ideas. From the goddess the soul of each man was born in a mystic marriage—Grainne is in Irish myth the younger form of the sun-goddess. Her function is to lure people away from the stuffy conventional to the song of the spirit. It is the conventional in Diamuid that is constantly protesting, but eventually the immortal chase hunts him into second birth. With just such long preparation for much of his life the Malekulan palaeolithic had also solemnly prepared for this; he constructed this birth-chamber for his own higher self. After the rebirth he had escaped the Ghost and was as a bird, an angel; the bull had wings. It was typical of later denigration that this beautiful concept of early man—another form of which is the little bird rising out of the head, often seen in Amerindian art —should in Ireland be demoted to a story of 365 copulations by an adulterous couple.

III. Long-Barrow Temple Graves

Less detail needs to be given of these, since their function is largely agreed. Usually orientated north-east–south-west, the half-circle of great stones that normally formed their entrances were places of ritual concerned with life and death, forerunner of the gates and tomb-entrances which form the scenes of the great Greek tragedies. Within, the vivid presence of the dead was dramatized by the masked shaman's utterances. It is likely that drama begins here, with dramatization of the dead and the choral mourning over them.

The actual shape of such a long-barrow seems often humanized within in a significant way. Take, for instance, the West Kennet Long Barrow, perhaps the clearest example in England. If the circular chamber at the end is the head, and the four small chambers ranged each side are limbs, then the entrance itself becomes the womb, the way in and out of birth. Death is also the gate of life. We shall find this concept repeated.

Certainly the long-barrow as temple has the cult of a Great Mother deity by orientation. At New Grange, clearly linked with the sun-goddess Grainne by its name, excavations have found that a passage for the conveyance of dawn lights up a specially-built channel precisely from the South-east, place of the rebirth of the winter sun (see p. 239). This is a place and time of motherhood, when the small sun is born from the earth or darkness. Clearly it is a change when the Mother is a darkness which gives birth to the weak new sun. Before this the darkness as ruled by the moon had been the motherhood concept, growth and fertility in the triple moon shapes. The moon is still very important indeed, but the sun, at first feminine, manifestly begins to lead. In the most striking Mother Goddess temple in the West, the *Table des Marchands* in Brittany, the stalks of corn —food and fertility—carved on the central stone are grown under what is clearly a round sun, not a moon. The recognized symbols of the Great Mother are there and elsewhere in Brittany more clearly than in other areas it seems; the plough, the necklet and the snake at least, the others more arguably.

IV. Entries, Initiations, Observations

With all this in the past it is easy to see how the mound chamber stands for the old house of the ancestors and the dolmen sometimes as its entrance.

That entrance itself comes to be a crucial and dramatic symbol. In its earlier birth-chamber form it is the place of spiritual rebirth, as we have seen, and this thought developed into a place of tests and initiations; and so low tunnels of stones develop, mazes for the soul, little buildings to test the young in these grades. Sometimes they are the mazes of the soul's wanderings after death. The thought of birth is still there in the narrow, twisted exits. The innumerable stone avenues, for instance, on Dartmoor, or the miles-long parallel stone lines at Carnac could be variants on this theme.

But in the later, loftier, arched form, with two close-set thick, slightly-tooled stones and a fitted lintel, the portal has much greater *numen*. At such arches were solemn betrothals and curings: lovers' hands and sick children were passed between stones as though they were flames, which were also used in this way—lovers leapt through fires and the sick passed between them. Magicians also dipped or annealed children—Achilles was made invulnerable except for the heel by which he was held when dipped in the river Styx. The child could also be baptized by fire:

> I set the child on the red-hot coal
> to burn the human from his soul.

The link between fire, spirit and stone is quite clear: the stones are as powerful as the flames, both having great divinity.

At another level, great stones and trilithons were witnesses and markers of time and direction, the means of certifying seasons, of risings and settings of the sun, moon and planets. These functions gave them a kind of holy mystery. To this day what do we usually do when wishing to commemorate an event or a person? Is not the answer commonly a great stone? These things go very deep into the subconscious of all. We are all palaeolithics, we are all neolithics.

V. Spiritual Survival and the Round Barrows

Round barrows, as has already been said, embody totally different concepts from those of the long barrows. The individual, with some possessions useful for another world, but usually carefully broken, so as to be of no further use in this world, is placed in the birth position in a small stone coffin or cist. In most cases she or he is facing East, that is, when there is a body at all. More commonly there is only an urn for ashes from the funerary pyre.

The rising sun, the dawn, is the source of new life. Not, as might be thought, the sun-power of the South, but the dawn, whence light rather than heat comes, whence spiritual forces have quite consistently been held to come in most of the cultures we know. The South is quite distinct: 'The fire burns only that which is dross in man'. Always it has been held to be the great transmuter of the carbons of earth, by the oxygen of flame, into the gaseous form that is akin to the etheric. The race that habitually incinerated the dead, then carefully collected the ashes into an urn as good as they could make, and placed goods for them, was clearly expressing a belief in the continuation of life on another plane which, however, still had certain needs rather like this one. This fire-like place was invisible, but flame and the sun were symbols of it.

As one looks at the seven barrows, and in another direction at the six barrows, that are upon the downs above Stonehenge, telling of the wishes of the dead to be laid, or their ashes laid, in the holy area, there is a peace and dignity in which the idea of these barrows being those of seven ancient kings seems highly appropriate.

Round barrows are in clusters from India to Ireland. It is impossible and pointless to list the areas. Everywhere men had made the move from the concepts based on earth, fertility, the power of darkness and the moon to quite other ideas based on an upland culture: the regency of, and teachings behind, the sun, his or her rulership over the world and the idea of holy fire akin to the sun. If not exactly this, then to the recognition of light and spirit from the East, at any rate. This is separately confirmed by the presence in other lines of prehistoric culture of burials with bones painted red facing East. Such are the Red Lady (now thought to be a man) of the Paviland Cave in Wales, and another in the *Font du Gaume* in the Vezère valley of France. In the comparative colour-blindness of early man, red was, it seems, the first colour that became distinct to them; it was life-blood-energy. To paint bones red and then face them East is to express more clearly than in words that life will come again from the place of rising light or intelligence.

VI. Great Trees, Posts, Menhirs

To consider the great isolated stones usually known by the Breton-Welsh term menhir (*maen-hir*, great stone) one is inevitably drawn to the thought of isolated great trees. For trees are in many ways more natural and obvious centres for reverence than stones. Trees live, give fruits or nuts and shade, are useful, hospitable and stately. Indeed for ages trees were a main cult in a forested world. In very many parts of the world even today native populations give as much respect to the living principle in the tree as any up-to-date ecologist would wish, only in a more personal manner. A native will apologize to a tree for cutting it, knowing that it has a living spirit which can be highly benevolent, but has malicious powers if upset.

Each tree and shrub has its own characteristics and tradition according to the old British lore. The Gaelic-Cymric trilithon, and the tree alphabet (see p. 289) contain a remarkable set of observations and poetic identifications between the months of the lunar year, 13 consonants of an alphabet, and particular trees and creatures, with five other trees representing the seasons and vowels. The oak is the king and centre of the lintel of the dolmen, flanked by the beautiful flowering whitethorn and the brilliant-berried holly, both guardians because of their prickles. Prophetic and wise trees look out from the ends of the lintel.

The oak, the yew, and perhaps the ash were the chief sacred trees of earlier peoples in Europe. The oak attracts the heavenly fire, the lightning, and therefore belongs to the force manifested in thunder and fire; it is the tree of Zeus, of Thor, of Yahveh. More than this, its remarkable tensile strength and apparent eternity of age made it divine. Many cults, but especially the Druidic, made the mistletoe that came to be associated with it—although not commonly to be found in oak trees—the plant of a sacred cult. The yew was always guardian of mysteries. Evergreen, seemingly eternal, it brooded over sacred waters, places of sacrifice, academies of metaphysical learning, and poisoned unwary animals. A yew grove of real antiquity always means a holy spot (see p. 152).

In the Gaullish trinity, Hu-Hesus was the force and figure that was at the first fork of the oak tree and represented life. The name seemed a natural link with Christianity when it came.

The ash tree, with its wide-embracing form, especially as 'umbrella' tree, played in the more northern part of Europe something of the same part that the bo-tree played in India: it was the Great Mother, eventually the cosmic World-Ash Ygdrasil, whose triple root goes to air, to water and to *hel*—the fiery land beneath earth. In these two trees, the oak and the ash, the concepts of the All-Father and the all-embracing World Mother found the widest lodging. They are still found by many to be deeply symbolic and meaningful.

VII. Circles of Wood and Stone: Woodhenge

When men began to realize the utility and power latent in the circle, the planted groves of trees seemed a cumbersome natural form of this. True, elaborate circles and avenues of trees are found in patterns which may well stretch back into indefinite antiquity. Great Yews, for example, near Salisbury must form one of the most impressive woods in the world. A great circular space centres radiating avenues of huge old yew trees often of fantastic shapes. Ideas of sacrifices to the gods arise—the yew is always the death-tree *eadha*—and the grim description of the Druidic Groves hung with victims near Marseilles given by Lucan in the *Pharsalia* comes to mind.

Such groves mean waiting a long time, especially with oaks and yews, and compromise was attempted with wooden circles of posts. Elaborate circle patterns were made. For example, at Woodhenge, near Stonehenge, we find an egg-shaped ellipse some 81 ft × 73 ft oriented north-east at the smaller end. Its six-fold rings of posts, around double centre posts, form a suggestive numerological sequence. The third ring is the key. It was of

16 large tree trunks apparently each 2.88 ft across, and the perimeter of its ring is exactly 200 Megalithic yards. Two rings outside it are of 140 MY perimeter with 32 posts and of 160 MY with 60 posts respectively. These numbers of posts are in Mother Goddess figures, multiples of 4. The 16 tree trunks (4 × 4) probably held a biggish roof some 93 ft × 80 ft broad so that the other rings were under cover. The figures of the next two rings inwards are of quite different sorts of numbers, decreasing by ratios of 20: 80 ft with 19 posts and 60 ft also with 19 posts. Finally, when the perimeter at 40 ft is one quarter that of the outermost ring, the number of posts becomes 12 (or 13 with a central post), the zodiac number. The meaning

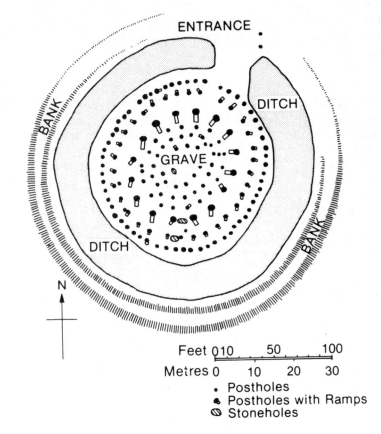

Woodhenge.

therefore seems to be a house of the Great Mother, all multiples of 4, realized towards the centre as also the moon with her sacred number of 19. By the orientation one could read it that the midsummer sun was to enter the secret cells—the inner circles—of the moon. The whole thing looks like a tribal cult-house; yet it was structured as a temple. It may well be compared with the Sanctuary at Avebury.

The build-up of the geometry of this elaborate plan is based on the sixth of the perfect triangles of the Pythagorean system: 12–35–37. With such expertise present one is justified in looking for sophisticated meanings in the numerology also. With wooden post circles we are already in the presence of the mathematical mind. All things may have meaning. One is prepared for the still more remarkable calculations of the great stone circles. It is natural to assume that, wood proving impermanent, there was a general movement towards stone, and indeed this seems to have been so in the upland areas where stone was available; but wood circles may well have continued as the holier form for some time, and then again, near the warm seas the stone had to be coral.

A great deal of careful and systematic work has been carried out over recent years in surveying not only the stone circles generally, but their actual shapes. These are much more complex than expected, and form parts of ley line systems with wide implications of meaning. Professor A. Thom has spent some 30 years on megalithic sites, circles and others, measuring and surveying. His work has resulted in the firm establishment of the megalithic units of length, the Megalithic yard (MY) of 2.72 ft and units very often of 2.5 or 5 of these; also, as seen in the above example, a preference for ratios of 10 or 20 MY. He has worked out a megalithic calendar based on observable stars; it is a year of 16 months, their days varying between 22 and 23 with one month of 24 days. The calendar needs seven observable check marks for seasons on the horizon.

A large number of rings are thus found not to be circles but to be ellipses, 'eggs' and other constructions. These are based, like Woodhenge, upon the double triangle structure of what was later the School of Pythagoras. One of the most complex is Avebury. Based on a Pythagorean triangle 3–4–5 in units of 25 MY, its sides are 75, 100 and 125 MY. The great circle has 4 or perhaps 5 curved 'corners', and arcs that are part of it are drawn based on the apices of the structural triangle (see p. 166).

Alignments have been found for most of the ring structures, circular or not. Professor Thom found, up to the time of his *Megalithic Sites in Britain* (Oxford University Press, 1967), 262 observation lines, of which 117 were sun alignments, to the North-east or South-east generally, the moon had 42, and various stars used for determining seasons had far fewer circles— Capella 13 and Arcturus 8, for example.

Obviously one has to postulate several types of use and several kinds of mentality using these rings and circles. There were marked-out dance-grounds for ecstatic raising of power; this is hardly made by the same type of mind, one would think, as that which revelled in the type of geometry displayed in the making of complex circles, arrangements for notching up yearly seasons and working out units of time to divide the year. Amongst the greater examples, Avebury might well be a setting for vast ring-dances, but Stonehenge hardly had the space; any revels it fostered were surely outside, in the avenue or cursus.

THE CELTO-CYMRIC
TAKEOVER

I. *The Celtic Druids in Britain*

Modern archaeologists and prehistorians have posited a possible great centre in southern Asia around Sumeria whence—3500–2000 BC or earlier—dispersed a certain type of priestly culture, with right-hand dancings, wisdom-poems of length, taboos on certain animals, and perhaps a belief in personal survival in certain forms, later spreading down south-westwards into India. There it developed a concentration of dances round stones, the cults of sun and moon, and beliefs in reincarnation with the dance-god Siva and the use of his triple sign—undoubtedly corresponding to certain teachings. From Mohenjodaro this enriched culture then gradually spread, a main part coming down through Egypt about 3100 BC or earlier, and adding to its ideas there a massive architectural skill with large stones, a visualization of the death-ship and some symbol shapes such as axes. Probably here they realized *hega*, magic, the realization of a mystic North, South, East and West and the fuller possibilities of stone circles, which thenceforth they began to spread along North Africa. Their main culture developed in Syria, but then their land-limited ideas took to water from the Syrian-Palestinian coast in the calm Mediterranean and, seeking relief from the undue heat there, they sought the islands and crossed into Spain and southern France. Why should they go to a chilly climate? The answer is that it was not. The greater temperatures in Britain implied in the finding of remains of Mediterranean plant life, say, 10,000–2000 BC certainly meant quite an excessively warm climate further south. A pastoral race sought pastures in more temperate areas.

Observing favourable currents and winds, they ventured further—unlike the indigenous Mediterranean sailor, who hates to be out of sight of land. In the summer one tried the voyage from northern Spain to Brittany or Ireland and others followed. We are at about 3000–2000 BC or earlier, and these are the Megalithic Berber-like peoples who settle most of Europe and are in Britain.

They came from Asia, perhaps from the same area that had given rise to the earlier movement south, where the continual drying-up of the Central Asia series of seas (originally one great sea)—perhaps already owing to man's cutting down of vegetation—was making life difficult. From this area came a new series of waves of peoples into Europe from a different direction—those later called *Celtae*, who developed a natural ability with metals, invented the long sword in the Swiss area, and with its aid and that of the horse, formed a forceful aristocratic tyranny over much of Europe, and over the more peaceful spread of an earlier settlement of their own Celtic race. Of their ideas, beyond a few god-names, we know little. With their metallic skills they invented enamelling, and with their better horses they developed speedy chariots from the lumbering cart depicted in the earlier Halstatt silver pieces or shown in stone engraving in Bulgaria.

They needed all their quickness to cope with what they found of the older Druids in Britain. For they then crossed over and found there the most polished and philosophic of the areas of megalithic beliefs. They did not, however, quick as they were, penetrate to the higher ranges of those early Druids' numerology of the heavens; they were perhaps not allowed in. The Celtic Druids took over the organization and much of the learning, but not the innermost learning which, with the exception of a few clues generally known, was henceforth lost, unless indeed we can now unlock it. What remained and was cultivated was wisdom, mystic quarterings, and sun and moon observances, often put into poems; but this becomes complicated by Greek culture. The Celtic Druids knew Greek writing from about 600 BC, and the Druid Abaris, mentioned by Diodorus Siculus, is recorded as speaking Greek perfectly. They also acquired some of the classical philosophy. The Greek-Celtic Coligny calendar appeared on the Continent at this time. It is this mixture of Celtic and Greek that survives in *The Black Book of Caermarthen* and elsewhere.

The cults of the oak tree and the yew were probably already in Britain. The oak tree belonged to the high god, probably the Hebrew IAO, who showed himself as Esus, and to Taran, the bull and thunder god. To these votive fires were offered. Human sacrifice—for which there is little or no evidence in Britain—looks different when viewed from the angle of a quite literal belief in a pleasant afterlife together with a preliminary judgement. Some crimes the Celts, like the Hebrews, found too foul to permit their doers to pollute the community, and the cleansing by fire was necessary. In any case, the dead were usually burnt now so as to free their spirits; so that all you were doing was to accelerate the process of inevitable rebirth, however many of the criminals—or prisoners—you burnt up. On the Continent such sacrifices were aimed at influencing the various gods, though there were none, we think, in Britain, although possibly some in Ireland—but there we have to take evidence through the hostile sources of the monkish chroniclers, who were always denigrating the heathen.

The megalithic cult of the oak and yew and the knowledge of the properties of the mistletoe we may confidently ascribe to the earliest Druidry. Everywhere the oak seems to have been sacred—Greece, Rome, the near East (where the kerm-oak was taken as substitute), both Germany and southern Europe—in all places the immense age, the knotty strength, the horizontal lines of the tree, so different from others, gave the impression of its being the king of trees. The oak takes 500 years to mature, is 'ripe' for 500 years and takes 500 years to die, but is often flourishing well after 1,500 years and until 1,800 or 2,000 in some cases. Such ages were beyond man's lifetime, and the toughness of the wood, the deep indentation of the leaves and the suggestiveness of the shape of the acorn combined to make it the tree of the divine and of the initiates, the tree of the most sacred functions of life. Upon its mast fed the most tremendous of beasts—the humanoid wild boar, whose mate was an incarnation of the Mother Goddess.[1]

Then there was the mistle, that mystic plant of the air, whose roots were up there and not in earth, whose sperm was carried from tree to tree by birds. The berry itself seems to contain sperm, and it was considered sperm from heaven—the gift of the Gods—both a poison and a cure to men. The writer had failed to perceive why amongst Druids the mistle was always referred to as the All-Heal, until he contacted the clinic which uses the whole mistle plant, and little else, for the treatment of rheumatic diseases, with singular success. The megalithics were known to be skilful with herbs and cures, as are the witches of today, and this stemmed from their culture. They knew the magical effects of mistle, properly used, upon the ills that commonly afflict folk living in this climate, against which the later Romans proliferated their sweat-baths. That which cures the worst of the diseases can also be used for many others, and All-Heal becomes an appropriate name (see p. 153).

So the oak tree stands for eternity, the quality of the ancient upright stone also; and the mistle becomes life, its magical moment of pleasure, its ability to cure most ills. It comes from the air, symbol of the spirit. When then we learn from Caesar and Pliny that a main action of the Druid magical calendar was the cutting of the mistle from the oak tree, at a season worked from the lunar calendar, this custom's importance is now obvious. Only the symbol of sun-and-moon could be used to cull such a holy thing, and only at a special moon-season—'slivered in the moon's eclipse'. Gold is always a symbol of the sun and the sickle's shape is that of the new moon. A golden sickle sounds a singularly ill-adapted weapon with which to cut, but ritually it is perfectly intelligible. Once a year, then, the Chief Druids sought out an oak tree upon which mistle grew, and they must have sought a long time, for mistletoe is not common upon oaks; the plant favours another sacred tree, the apple, in which grows the spirit of eternity, of the land of the *sidhe*, of the dead. It is gathered principally in the sixth moon; if possible on the sixth day of the moon. They chose this day because the moon, though not yet in the middle of her course, already has considerable strength. They called the mistletoe by a name meaning in their language 'the all-healing': *Vilice*. Having made preparation for sacrifice and a banquet beneath the tree, they brought together two white bulls, whose

[1] See p. 150 for fuller treatment of the oak.

horns were bound then for the first time. Clad in a white robe, the priest ascended the tree and cut the mistletoe with a golden sickle, and it was received by others in a white cloak. Then they killed the victims, praying that God would render this gift of his propitious to those to whom he had granted it. They believed that mistletoe, taken in drink, imparted fecundity to barren animals, and was an antidote for all poisons.[2]

What they culled was seen as the union of the high moment of life—symbolized by sexual ecstasy—with eternity; the eternal life and the moment. There is no suspicion in Caesar that he is being fed a piece of symbolic teaching, that Divitiacus, the Aeduan Druid, was seeing if he would swallow the idea of literally cutting with a golden edge. The literal Roman swallowed it. So, apparently, have the copyist historians ever since. None has even commented upon the lack of cutting power in a golden sickle, which is fairly obvious; none has even looked for a metaphorical meaning, which is, after all, not particularly obscure. This is typical of the sheer stupidity with which things Druidic have been treated.

Even in Caesar's time tribes were still crossing over to Britain. When we have the Pindaric Ode that refers to somewhere in the North-west, the Land of the Hyperboreans, 'people beyond the north-west wind', which seems very likely to be Britain, Ireland or the Outer Hebrides, we cannot be sure whether it is megalithics or Celts who are rejoicing in the 'hecatombs of wild asses'. It sounds, however, rather Celtic. A 'famous round temple' sounds like Stonehenge—but it could be any great stone circle. But let us see the passages, one of which is from Pindar, *Pythian Odes X* (Trans. Sandys):

> Neither by ship nor land canst thou find the road, O reader, to the trysting-place of the Hyperboreans. Yet in the olden days Perseus, leader of the people, shared among them in the banquet on entering their houses and finding them sacrificing famous hecatombs of asses in honour of the God (Apollo). In the banquets and praises of that people Apollo chiefly rejoiceth, and he laugheth as he looketh on the brute beasts in their ramping lewdness. Yet such are their ways that the Music is not banished, but on every side the dances of maidens and the sounds of the lyre (Celtic harp) and the notes of the flute are ever circling; and with their hair crowned with golden bay-leaves they hold glad revelry; and neither sickness nor harmful eld mingleth amongst that chosen people, but, aloof from toil and conflict, they dwell far from the wrath of Nemesis. To that host of happy men went the son of Danae, breathing boldness of spirit, with Athena for his guide. And he slew the Gorgon, and came back with her head . . .

This therefore is a frankly fabulous land, an elysium without fate (Nemesis). Its herds of asses belong to Apollo, the sun-god. It is Wisdom (Athena) who leads men thither and it harbours the Gorgon. Yet it agrees in many ways with Diodorus Siculus' description (Book 2, Ch. 47, of his *Bibliotheca Historica*, mostly lost):

[2] Pliny, *Natural History*, XVI, 249

Opposite to the coast of Gallia Celtica is an island in the ocean—not smaller than Sicily — lying to the north, which is inhabited by the Hyperboreans who are so named because they live beyond the north-west wind (Boreas) . . . In this island there is a magnificent precinct (or grove) sacred to Apollo and a remarkable temple of round form, adorned with many consecrated gifts. There is also a city sacred to the same god, most of the inhabitants of which are harpers who continually play upon their harps in the temple and sing hymns to the God extolling his actions . . . The supreme authority in that city and sacred precinct is vested in those who are called Boreadae, being the descendants of Boreas, and their governments have been uninterruptedly transmitted in this line. This island Hyperborea had remained untainted by foreign power; for neither Bacchus nor Herakles, nor any other hero or potentate had made war upon it.

If the round temple is Stonehenge, the city might be Amesbury—named from Ambrosius, which is a form of Mercury, via the Welsh Emrys.

Links with Greece are very clear, especially from Herodotus (Book 4), who relates that offerings from the Hyperboreans wrapped in wheat-straw were said to be passed on from people to people until they reached Delos, which was Apollo's main shrine, apart from Delphi. Earlier, he says, they had been sent in charge of groups of Hyperborean girls, guarded by five men. Concerning north-west Europe he says that, although he knows little of it, 'It cannot be disputed that tin and amber do come to us from what might be termed the ends of the earth.' He is elsewhere aware of the Tin Islands and of the Baltic (Book 3).

Pliny treated Britain as separate from Hyperborea, however, and Solinus (c. AD 200) follows him. Britain is noted for 'great stones', its people are proud of their deep tatooings (the Picts, the 'painted' or tatooed people), and the Goddess Minerva, presumably Sul, presider over the City of Bath, which keeps alight a perpetual fire, seemingly of coal. Hyperborea for him is beyond the North Pole (Book 25) and its inhabitants practise suicide with general approval by jumping off cliffs.

Toland[3] very definitely makes the Hyperborean Island to be Lewis in the Outer Hebrides, for a number of reasons. Here there is a balmy climate and fertile land, warmer and balmier then indeed; he points out that the land is capable of double cropping in a year and only the slackness and ignorance of the natives prevents its being extremely rich. Apollo he identifies with Beli (Belinus) through a form Arbelio, unknown one thinks to anyone except him; but then Toland really did have sources that we have not. In Lewis the harp is the commonest instrument and always has been so. The place is full of what might well have been round sacred groves. The peculiar dialect spoken thereabouts is a form of Erse (Scots Gaelic). Apollo's temple of wings, where he hid his arrow after slaying the Cyclopes, was, if this involves birds, most likely on Lewis, because a fantastic number of birds of many kinds do crowd this island.

Above all Toland relies upon this word *Boreadae*, said to be the hereditary

[3] John Toland, first of the modern Chosen Chiefs, letters to Lord Molesworth. See p. 99.

ruling family, as being good Erse for the name for the tribal chieftains, collectively known as *Boireadhach*. It certainly looks a close fit. Nevertheless, a 'famous temple of round form' does sound much more like Stonehenge. It is true enough that the Greeks did visit Lewis. It really remains an open question.

Now who was Boreas, and has Apollo any links? In Greece Boreas was a half-serpent, an oracle, who lived with other winds in Mount Haemus in Thrace. He particularly impregnated the sacred mares, who conceive from the wind and have no equine sires. This horse-cult, indeed the mythical hen-horse, existed by the evidence of hillside figures all the way to India, and horses may have therefore been brought by the earlier migrations thence. In Britain the horse was always sacred, and Epona was a venerated mare-mother of the Gauls. In the Pin-hole Cave, Derbyshire, is carved the figure of a man wearing a ritual horse-mask. Apollo was called the Horus of the North; he is so placed on the late Greek Zodiac of Dendera. Moreover, Apollo's mother Leto is also Brizo, who is the same as the Celtic Brighid. Between Hyperborea and Delos frequent visits were exchanged.

The Ceryneian Hind of Wisdom was driven to Hyperborea by Herakles in his third labour, and he followed it to seek wisdom. The hind sheltered under the Apple Tree, the Celtic Tree of Paradise. The apple-trees of the Hesperides in Herakles' eleventh labour were death-apples, and the Hesperides, again, may be a dreamy version of Britain. Perhaps the very earliest vision of this country is as the White Islands of the Odyssey; the White Rocks (the Dover cliffs?) are the last sight of land of the living, beyond the Pillars of Herakles, before the mariners, Odysseus and his aged comrades, row slowly on their last voyage entering the Portals of the Sun; the darkness of the West. Plutarch uses the very adjective of chalky white, *leukos*.

Such are some of the more striking classical records of this land and its culture. Into these legendary pictures comes the first named Briton, Abaris, a Druid, i.e. a Hyperborean Priest of Apollo, and Toland thinks his Apollonian arrow is part of his Druidic equipment.[4] With a bow and quiver he travels Italy and Greece; he is wrapped in what sounds like a plaid, girt with a gilded belt, 'wearing trousers from the soles of his feet to his waist', as barbarians are represented in classical sculpture. He visited Pythagoras[5] at Marseilles; he spoke perfect Greek, as it were from the Academy or the Lyceum. Pythagoras gave him unlimited praise and judged him ready for the reception of wisdom—unlike most of his own Greeks. A cloud of marvels hangs around this visit. With later writers he delivered oracles, he rode through the air on his arrow, he cured diseases. Less marvellous is the account that Pythagoras in return was initiated into the

[4] John Toland, *History of the Druids*, 1719: second letter to Lord Molesworth.
[5] Lobeck, *Aglaophanus*, reckons Abaris as about 570 BC, which makes him Pythagoras' contemporary.

Druid wisdom at Marseilles, for the master was constantly seeking new initiations, and the Greek and the Celtic were manifestly in close touch.

The first of the names for Ireland appears about now from Marseilles sources: Aristotle, de Mundo, cap.3, gives 'Ierne': Diodorus Siculus, lib.5, gives 'Iris'; and Strabo, Book I 'Ierna'. Abaris' legend seems confirmed from Ireland, by the way, where a tale is told of one 'Abhras' who travelled to distant lands and returned via Scotland, bringing with him 'a new religious system'. Was it from Marseilles?[6]

II. The Romans in Britain

We know that Caesar found the Druids of Gaul a main obstacle: they urged on the resistance. Caesar was one-third a general, one-third an intelligent inquirer into alien faiths and beliefs, and one-third literary leader of a Roman circle with dogmatic ideas about literary style, like the earlier T.S. Eliot. Hence the unnatural terseness and congested sentences of his style, then much admired. He was capable of winning over and making friends with the Aeduan Divitiacus the Druid and learning from him all that he would tell him about Druidry. Eventually, however, continental Druidry compromised itself with Rome, and so lost its power, despite preserving its forms and temples.

Not so in Britain. Constant help from Britain to his enemies forced Caesar to make two demonstration raids, temporarily conquering some of south-east England and frightening its kings into allying with him. The real Roman conquest came later, in AD 43 directed by the Emperor Claudius in person—a humane and enlightened affair without battles. Military rule was set up, as was customary at first.

Little humanity characterized the Roman rule when Nero succeeded Claudius. Orders were given for the extortion of all monies possible, and Roman law did not recognize matriarchal rights, which prevailed perhaps generally amongst the tribes settled in Britain, but certainly amongst the Iceni of Suffolk and other wide areas of eastern England. When Boudicca (Boadicea)'s consort died, his whole fortune was seized, not the legal state share. Her daughters, heirs to herself, were unrecognized and outraged. By now Britain had had time to experience what Rome's military rule was like, and most of the East and North at any rate decided on rebellion. In the West rebellion was constantly urged on by the active, politically-minded Druids based upon the sacred island of Mona (Anglesey). East and West seem to have collaborated. The very able Roman governor, Suetonius Paulinus, was goaded into marching north-west to exterminate the Druids, while Boudicca gathered the tribes and swept down through the half-Romanized countryside to sack Verulanium (St Albans), Camulodunum (Colchester) and Llyndunum or Londinium (London). (See pp. 205–7 for a full account of this.)

[6] Godfrey Higgins, *The Celtic Druids*, and Springett's *Secret Sects* may be looked at here.

Rome now realized that the military rule which produced such reactions should be changed, and Britain was organized as a civilian province under a *vicarius*. More equitable law prevailed. Rome optimistically laid out well-planned cities and proceeded to educate the sons of chiefs as good Romans. But they had reckoned without the Celtic nature, chary of being enclosed or dominated. Celts deeply distrusted towns, and although the Romans' places were partly filled and some schools for chieftain's sons worked, evidence for a number of sites shows cities unfilled, villas abandoned and a general exit on the part of a large number of the populace to other areas. For Rome did not occupy the British Isles, far from it; the Pennine area, central Wales, all Scotland (not at all dominated by the Roman Wall), not to speak of the totally untouched Ireland, were refuges and racial rallying grounds. It is true that Julius Agricola planned the conquest of the whole country, but just as he had begun he was recalled (AD 83).

Modern educated man equates civilization with buildings. Because Egypt and the classical countries built houses, baths and temples, people who did not value these things must be barbarians. The Romans led the way in this estimate, understandably; it is less understandable that modern historians have mostly followed suit. Whilst paying lip-service to the demonstrable facts of jewellery, chariots, armour and weaving of high quality, these folk could not, they feel, really have been cultured. But the Celtic culture is a different thing; it is musical and eloquent, values the individual more than the concerted achievement and personal adornment more than built-up walls. It has great abstract designs on its metal work and on some incised stones. Celtic buildings were purely temporary and utilitarian, clay and wattle, with thatched roofs. Of the reasonably recent great hall of Tara only mounds remain. In all the areas of Celtdom not one piece of truly native architecture in the normal sense exists.

Was there further Druidic activity in Britain after Boudicca's revolt? Probably, in an underground way. At Stonehenge there appears to have been a considerable cult, for a large quantity of pottery has been found, enough to argue a considerable use, not the equivalent of modern tourists' litter. How much the Celtic Druids knew of the meanings of the measurements of the monument is anybody's guess—they may only have known the main orientations, a tradition of ceremonial approach, and perhaps circular dancing or movement—they can hardly have known less if they used it at all. Oak tree burials with ceremonial objects like sacrificial knives seem to indicate Druidry. One Latin inscription actually uses the title 'Antiquus' as though it were of an Ancient of the Order of Druids—one of the names now used for a Chief. In 1834 a rather earlier Bronze Age burial was found at Grisethorpe in Yorkshire, an oak coffin covered with oak branches and mistletoe remains; the old man's skeleton within had ceremonial stone and bronze magical instruments by it. Similar finds have been made on the Continent.

What is certain is that in Wales the mountains held a number of highly intelligent, mystic-minded people who were studying the Graeco-Roman philosophies and linking with an older wisdom. In Ireland, after Padraic (St Patrick), a disguised Druidry held some sway; customs evidently held as before, and seemingly unchecked, for Scotland.

III. Irish Druidry Christianized

We have a good deal from the old books and other records of Ireland, collected by the Irish Gaelic and Cymric-speaking Toland, probably from sources now no more. One can do no better than follow him with discrimination.

The outstanding and 'constitutional' recognition of the dominant advisory position of the Druids is most marked, and the Bards and Ovates continued it when 'Druid' became a dirty word under Christianity. King Cormac first instituted a law that the king must have a Druid to be advised by in judging the law, as well as for prayer and sacrifices. He must also have a bard, a chronicler, a physician and a musician, as well as three 'controllers' of his family. The leading nobles had to have the same set-up of seven. When Christianity came, the Druid was simply replaced by a priest; the rest carried on. The priest was not necessarily a non-Druid, often he was a converted one. Druidry as a scheme had features that enabled it to adapt easily to the new faith.

It is quite clear that St Padraic—not by any means the first missionary saint of Eire—went much further than St Augustine was later to do in adapting to heathenism. He himself was born in England and had been taken captive; he sounds typically Celtic, for all his Christian training. He had blue-painted eyelids and hair shaved across his head in the Celtic, not the Roman, tonsure. He travelled like a chief, with a mass of followers, craftsmen, bards and musicians. Not at all the style of an Italian monk.

Finding out (or knowing already) all about the high standard of life and learning set by the Druidic colleges, he proceeded to the rather easy conversion of the Druids to what must have seemed to them only a more dramatic version of their own ideas; after all, both cults taught survival of death, both believed in an in-dwelling supreme spirit, only represented for the vulgar by the stones now called 'idols'; and Druidry had an essential spirit called Hesus or Esus, linked with the oak tree, which seemed a plain anticipation of Jesus upon the tree of the cross. So the Druidic training colleges were taken over and called monasteries or nunneries, with schools keeping intact most of their internal arrangements. Druids became Culdees ('Chaldeans' or magic-workers) or Magi (Seers); the word 'Druid' was strictly forbidden. They did not, however learned, hold top positions—those were given to dependable Christians—but Culdees were lesser clergy, or dwellers in monasteries.

IV. Christian Druid-Bards in Scotland and Ireland

Many went over to Scotland, where, after the mission of St Columcille

(Columba) they were in fact the only missionaries until the eleventh century. In the registry of St Andrews are shown 13 hereditary Culdees holding their own property and with families. A settlement is recorded as dedicated in true Druidic style with nine circumambulations. This was in AD 825 and for 300 more years this Druidic colony of Kilrimon continued.

Some of the hereditary lines were the O'Duvegans, bards to the O'Kellys; the O'Clerys and O'Brodins were antiquarians, the O'Shiels and O'Canvans hereditary doctors.

We have the names indeed of many Druids allied to mythical heroes and related to kings in Eire as well as in Scotland, and these were distinguished in various ways. No one name stands out. Cathbaid was grandfather of Cúchulainn, the legendary Celtic battle hero; Tadhg was grandfather of Finn McCumhal, the other great leader; King Eogain married Moinic, daughter of the Druid Dilliu, and so on. Nobility were Druids as well as nobles, and Ida and Ono were two Druidic lords of Corcachlaun (Roscommon). Ono presented the fortress Imleach-Ono to St Padraic, who changed it into the famous monastery of Elphin (*Aillfinn*, white stone). The Archdruid of King Niall of the Nine Hostages, called Laighichin mac Barrecheadha, induced him to war furiously against King Eocha of Munster for killing his son. Druids might not take actual part in war, but they could and did urge it on and direct it. Dion Chrysostom, in *De Recusatione Magister in Senatus*, says, 'Without the Druids, who understand divination and philosophy, the kings may neither do nor consult anything; so that in reality they are the Druids who reign while the kings . . . are only their ministers.' It is recorded that Bachrach, Chief Druid to King Conchobar Nessan of Ulster, is said to have described most movingly the passion of Christ at the time it occurred.[1]

Another, now the second, grade of the Order Toland distinguishes as the Greek *Ouateis*, Latin *Vates*, which he says is from the old Celtic *Faidh*, a prophet, as used in the Irish Bible—where, incidentally, Druids are substituted for the Three Wise Men from the East. *Vates* or *Faidh* were, it seemed, doctors, diviners and natural philosophers. They and the Druids both went in for predictions which, according to Cicero, were quite fallacious (*De Divinatione*, lib 1, cap 41).

Within Christian times, at a general assembly of 597 held at Druimceat (Londonderry) under the eleventh Christian King Aodhmac Ainmhire, together with Aodheumhac Gauraine, King of Scotland, and St Columcille (Columba), a decree was issued that every king and lord should support a Bard. Schools of bardic learning were set up, and it was enacted that the High King's Bard should superintend all the rest. These schools and some educational Druidesses are recorded as teaching royalty such as the daughter of King Laoghaire.

Bards, as indicated earlier, were considered harmless, not being identi-

---

[1] Myles Dillon, *The Cycles of the Kings*, Oxford University Press, 1946.

fied with Druids, who were remembered more for their alleged sacrifices. To what extent Druidry did in fact continue as Bardism is problematical; obviously it was good coverage to be a Bard.

These were the kind of people therefore that Druids were in Eire—learned, distinguished, sometimes deplorable, but always leading figures. It appears to be true that the organizing missionary to Eire, St Padraic, nevertheless destroyed all he could lay his hands upon of their learning, as a rival to Christian learning. According to a fairly reliable older historian, Dr Kennedy ('Dissertation about the Family of the Stuarts') he 'burnt 300 volumes, stuffed with the fables and superstitions of heathen idolatry; unfit to be transmitted to posterity.' Obviously this was done with the assent of the converted Druids themselves. It is mainly why we have less of the Druidic learning than we might have; a monkish holocaust of books, in its way losing us as much proportionately as the whole of Europe lost by the burning of the great library of Alexandria.

But how much idolatry was there really? And what is an idol? Padraic threw down some 'idols', but left, and seems to have re-used, many more. The most famous of his overthrows was the idol covered with gold and silver called *Cromm Cruach*, the 'bent' or 'bowing one' in the Plain of Slecht, Co. Cavan, with 12 bronze-decorated companion stones standing about him, the place being known as the *Maghsleucht* or 'field of adoration'. Even so, we are not told he was humanoid in form, only decorated. The saint 'dented' Cromm Cruach, and the others were sunk in the earth as far as their heads.[2] There were in fact no 'idols' in the usual sense of the word; the severely abstract neolithic mind rarely ran that way, and their successors did not either. It was Christianity that introduced human figures. The great Cromm Cruach may be compared in name with Cruim and with *Tairneach Taran*, meaning thunder—Taranus the thunder-god being a Jupiter.

Mostly, then, 'idols' were sacred stones. We are said to have one divinity's name at Clogher; he is *Kermand Kelstach*, translated as 'the Mercury of the Celts'. Other consecrated stones' names are the 'High Stone', *Ardcloch* (Arklow), and the 'Yellow Stone', *Buidhe-cloch* (Wicklow). Toland remarks that just as Mercury at Clogher proves to be merely a stone, so in heathen Rome Mercury's original was a square stone; the Irish were neither more nor less idolatrous than the Romans.

Stone in fact was symbol for the stability and power of deity, which is beyond representation and so is not represented. Most of the cairns were set up to Beli/Belinus/Abellio, a form of Apollo, and all forms of the sun. They were also set up in Palestine as a record and a witness to the covenant between Yahweh and his people: 'That day Joshua made a covenant for the people; he laid down a statute and an ordinance for them at Shechem. Joshua wrote these words in the Book of the Law of God. Then he took a great stone and set it up there, under the oak in the sanctuary of Yahweh.

---

[2] Stokes (ed.), *Tripartite Life of St Patrick*, London, 1887.

And Joshua said to all the people, 'See: this stone shall be a witness against us because it has heard all the words that Yahweh has spoken to us; it shall be a witness against you in case you deny your God.' (Joshua 24:27.) Stone therefore possesses the power of recording the imprinted message, a power theosophists attribute to the akashic records.

Witches, and apparently Druids, have always further realized that energy as well as records is stored in stones of particular kinds, and it has been suggested that a particular atomic structure in certain types of stone facilitates this process. In about 20 different kinds of crystal structures lies a capacity for storing a particular type of electrical power known as 'piezo-electricity'; they can 'step up' transformers, producing voltages up to 20,000 volts.[3] This might be why so many ley lines concentrate on the Giants' Dance; it could be why the bluestone circle was brought probably from Ireland and set up so honorifically by numerology. Such properties in stones are the subject only of quite recent research which may go very much further.[4] That our forbears used stones to store a form of psychic power that they could draw upon is evident from witch testimony; whether, when set in ring structures, they formed power stations to boost the motive power in flying saucers is another possibility.

The greatest of stones was of a rare green quartzite and called the *Lia Fail*, the stone of fate, or *cloch na cincamhna*, stone of fortune. Wherever that stone rested, one of Gaelic blood was to rule.

> Mark this O Scots; if fates not fail,
> where this stone shall be set,
> there is your kingdom's seat.

> Cioniodh scuit saor an fine
> Man ba breag an Faisdine
> Mar a bhfuighid an Lia-fail
> Dlighid flaitheas do ghabehail.
> (Carmena Gadelica)

When the Irish colonized Scotland they therefore sent the stone to King Fergus, at Argyll, to confirm his rule, and the Scots kings held it as coronation seat there until Kenneth II took it to his new capital at Scone about 842, whence Edward I seized it in 1300. Mysteriously, however, it is still pointed out at Tara, thus rivalling the bilocation of the tomb of Abraham. It was supposed to have had a 2,000-year-old history and to go back to the daughter of the last reigning princess of Judah, who brought it with her to the West. Was it Jacob's stone pillow at Bethel (Genesis 28)?

There are far vaster altars and stones than these. At Hoy, in the Orkneys, there is an oblong stone ironically called Dwarfy, which is 36 ft × 18 ft

[3] See H.D. McGraw *Piezo-electricity in Crystals* (Methuen) or Alan Crawford's article 'Piezo-electricity' in *Discovery*, November 1964.
[4] In the case of contemporary computer technology it has been found that crystals are more efficient storers of information than magnetic discs, and light (through optical fibres) a more efficient medium for the transmission of electrical impulses than wires.[Ed.]

× 9 ft hollowed out with a stone door cut out with two bed-and-pillow shapes and a fireplace. In Herodotus (Bk 2) is a description of a building 21 cubits long, 14 wide and 8 high, all one piece of stone.

Dolmens, or *kist-vaens* in Welsh, Toland generally thinks of as Druid altars. We gave an alternative suggestion (see p. 33), for no altars as usually conceived are needed in such profusion as that in which dolmens are found in some parts. But certain ones have clearly been used for an altar function.

Stones and fire are basic to the roots of civilized conceptions. Ur of the Chaldees, Abraham's city, could be the city of fire or light (*Ur*, old Gaelic) while the Hebrew name for the mother-city of Egyptian religion, Heliopolis, is On, (Gaelic *Oan*, a stone). Both are dedicated to light or sun —Bel; and Ba-bel sound similar.

In Eire, then, chieftainships lightly combined under the elective high Kings of Tara, a kind of loose confederation linked by Tara gatherings at intervals for games and festival, not unlike the Greek unity based on the Olympic Games. This prevailed before the coming of Christianity, and for a while afterwards. It suffered two sea-changes, the first from the earlier Greek and the second from the Roman missionaries; both compromised with Celtdom and its Druidry to some extent and Druidic priests were energetic missionaries. Columcille of Iona, for example, obviously considered Christianity simply as a more 'revealed' form of the basic truth of Druidry—'Christ is my Druid' he said. Roman Christianity only later developed a detestation of these independent Irish, with their alien customs, when Augustine was sent to shepherd them into the right way.

V. Social Organization—Ireland and Wales

What of Britain, that is, present-day England and Wales? It had gradually become reconciled to a great extent with later, more lenient, Roman rule, which had become partly a native thing—local tribesmen served in the army in Britain, and the Roman Wall became a bond and a harmonizing area for North and South, rather than a defence. Both aspects were upset, however, when the elvish, tricky, quick-witted Picts, the tattooed, disguised fellows, replaced the heavy Caledonii on the Wall's farther side. The Picts played unfair games on the Romans. They disappeared into mists, landed on coasts behind them, popped up out of the heather. It became increasingly difficult to manage the Wall.

Moreover, the provinces developed a remarkable partiality for setting up rebel emperors and backing heresies they fancied. The Celts were still an independent lot. Albinus started it in AD 196. In 287, when the raids began, Carausius and Alexander began a separate empire, and in 296 Constantine the Pale (Chlorus) was sent to reorganize and discipline the province and did so. He organized naval defence under a Dux Brittanorum (leading general of the Britons), and a number of admirals, one the Comes Saxonici Litoris (Count or Duke of the Saxon Shore, that is, the shore the

Saxons raided). The next disturber was the great Constantine, who in 306 was proclaimed Emperor at York (Eboracum), before eventually gaining the whole empire, at first with the help of troops from Britain. Then in 383 Magnus Maximus led an army to back his revolt to gain the empire, but was defeated in 386. Even in the year of withdrawal, 407, Constantine III led off an army to Europe to back him, only to be overwhelmed in 412. Thus Britain was left defenceless without men.

Pelagius the Briton became a dominating influence in the church, and he taught a much more humanist version of Christianity about the time of the Empire's fall (c. 360–420). He held, against St Augustine, that men possessed free-will to deal with temptation. 'If I ought, I can,' he said. Man was immensely helped by divine grace, but was quite free to save himself. Augustine and the church, however, decided that the fall of Adam had impaired man's will, so that the divine will to save—the universal priesthood of Christ—took the initiative in all cases. Pelagius and his follower Coelestius escaped from the fall of Rome to Africa. Later they were both condemned by the Western and Eastern churches.[1]

About now and for the centuries immediately following we can to some extent build up a picture of the social life and of organized Druidry in Wales and Ireland from the old books. The Irish are the older; we have the books of Armagh and Kells, *The Red Book of Hergest*, *The Book of the Dun Cow* and others, and in Wales, *The Black Book of Caermarthen*, and, rather later, *The Book of Taliesin*.

For over a thousand years the High Kings of Tara, the *Ard-ri*, ruled. Loose as the confederation might have been, it fitted the Irish temperament. The age of this throne is impressive; but its kings tended to go for plunder abroad rather than constructive work at home. Niall of the Nine Hostages (397–405) was an arch-marauder in a time of marauders; he did not add to the harmony of Europe but saw his chance in its weakness.

The various tribes, the *Tuatha* or 'baronies', were turbulent. Yet even so peace was to be had in Ireland rather more than elsewhere, and fleeing scholars and civilized Romanized 'barbarians' generally began to settle and build up a great culture. Under the Brehon laws Ireland was settling down by the end of the eighth century.

The power of the Ard-ri was balanced by that of the *Coibhi Drui*, the chief or 'helpful' Druid, right up to the Christian advent.

The Organization of Society and Learning

From Wales we have listed nine classes of society, although some look suspiciously like later borrowings from Britain: *Bremin* was the king; *Twyrog* the duke; *Jarll* the earl (Norse); *Arglwydd* the lord; *Barwn* the baron; *Breir* the squire; *Gwreange* the yeoman; *Alttud* the small owner and *Kaeth* the slave. There is listed a hierarchy of degrees of learning too. If the years each degree takes are added—and reckoning the doctor as also studying for

---

[1] It has been suggested that Pelagius was a Druid.

a few years—we have some 20 years, the same as Caesar's estimate of the Druidic training-time.

We begin with three years of poetry and music—*Disibliysbas*. Six years more of the same give us *Disgiblisg ybliaidd*. Nine years more are the *Digiblpenkerddiaidd*. We come with relief to the learned product, the 'doctor', who is merely *Penkerdd* or *Athro*.

There are three kinds of poets and they all wear long robes; the *Prydudd* sings of the lands and praises the doings of princes and nobles; the humbler *Tevluwr* has a country beat and tells of jests and pastimes; more sinisterly, the *Clerwr* gives out invectives and speaks 'of country matters'. We know that invectives and satires could kill, and amongst some peoples the corresponding act of despisal still does.

But these poets are to be distinguished, it seems, from the Bards. All Bards are Herald Bards, who tell of noble acts, assign arms and make prognostications. These are considerable powers to wield. They are steeply graded, and the highest grade evidently includes great originals. Members are called Princes (*Privardd*), who are inventors of rhythms and forms, and go by the titles of Merlin Sylvester, Merlin Ambrosius and Taliesin. Amongst them shone the chief harpist of the land who lived in the king's palace, the *Bard Telyn* (Harper).

Compared with these glorious ones the next grade seems paltry; the *Poswardd* or *Prydiddion* set forth and teach the music or prognostication that the Privardd began—they are in fact the administrators of the learning.

The third rank is different, they are ensigns or heralds-at-arms, who declare blazons and keep records, a kind of college of arms in fact, called *Arwyddvardd*.

The greatest of all Bards had died, we learn, in the year 2067 BC after the Deluge, the fifty-sixth Overking of Britain, called Blegywryd ap Geisyllt.

It is all a noble and courtly set-up, moving towards the medieval. A great deal of what is typically medieval in England was in fact Welsh, when not French.

VI. The Irish Invasion Races

We have looked mostly to Wales, but the Irish version is as poetic. A long look in the backward and abysm of time produces a story of transformation that not only focuses, but seems to interpret the half-real, half-immaterial history which is as much of the development of the Irish consciousness as of the Irish races.

The setting of the tale, from a book of the eleventh century, is that Tuan mac Carell is a chief from whom the abbot St Finnan (sixth century) seeks shelter not far from his monastery at Moville, Co. Donegal. He is refused but waits, and at last makes friends with Tuan. On his return visit to the monastery Tuan tells the story of his shape-shifting.

Partholan was the first of men to settle Eire. Tuan's father, Sarn, was Partholan's brother. A pestilence came—all were carried off except he, Tuan. He wandered from one uninhabited place to another for 22 years and became aged. But then came the son of another brother of Partholan. Seeing this cousin, Nemed, from the cliffs he avoided him; but in sleep in Ulster he was changed into a stag, the king or son of the deer (mac Carell).

The Nemedians had reached Eire with great difficulty, in 32 ships each holding 30, but all save 9 perished. They then increased to 8,060. Then they all died.

Again Tuan is aged but this time his body changes into a wild boar, king of the boar-herds. Then Semion mac Stariat lands and three tribes arrive, mainly the Firbolg ('bag-men'). In their time he changes into a great eagle of the sea, in anticipation of the coming of the race of the children of Dana. He is still an eagle when the Sons of Miled arrive, who defeat the gods. But after fasting for nine days he changes into a salmon. For many years he is happy, then at last he is caught and taken to the wife of Carell who eats him whole and he passes into her so that he is born again, as son of Carell, which brings him up to date.

Let us examine these races awhile. The Partholonians and their cousins the Nemedians are from the regions of the dead, and they have to fight the Fomorians. They are children of darkness, Domna; one of them is specified as Buirraineach who is under a tumulus and is cow-headed. What is a giant? Further east it had been someone who built with giant stones and came from overseas. So here, for 300 years, these Partholonians from the Summer Country—somewhere warm, maybe even Sumer itself or Somerset—they land on Bealteinne, only 24 of them, but as they increase they enlarge the size of the land—maybe they drained and dyked. Then these Partholonians are destroyed by pestilence. The Nemedians come and also fight Fomorians, whom they defeat in four battles. But again the dark force of pestilence carries them off and the Fomorian regime is unchecked.

Tory Island was the Giants' stronghold, and the noble stag now has to change into a boar as suitable to the times. Their exactions from all Ireland were appalling—two-thirds of the milk and the children went to Fomorians. Three chiefs again lead the Nemedians who land on the island and kill one of the Fomorian kings, but the other king routs them, and the 30 survivors leave in despair.

The Firbolg are said variously to come from Spain and/or the land of the dead, but actually might be of the Belgae. The daughter of the king of the Great Plain, i.e. the land of the dead, called Teltia, marries one of their kings, and they have a palace at the place called Tailtin (Teltown). This is the start of the great games and assemblies there.[1]

The four great kingdoms of Ireland are now created, with a fifth centre: Ulster, Munster, Leinster and Connacht with Uisnecht as the central hill-kingdom.

---

[1] See M. MacNeill, *The Feast of Lughnasa*, (Oxford University Press, 1962).

At last come the Tuatha dé Danann, the folk of the Goddess Dana or Brighedd, daughter of the race's head, the all-father Dagda the Good. Her three sons manage between them only one son—the mystic one to the three, the three becoming the one again—and he is Ecne, 'knowledge' or 'poetry', for knowledge was conveyed in poetry. Only this race does Tuan call gods.

Dana (Ana, De-ana) is the mate of Bile, the god of the dead, and her son was Nuadha of the Silver Hand or Arm—or Ray. But her darker form is Gwrach, the virago, or Morrigan.

The Dagda, also called Fath, or great father, weds Boann the Boinne-spirit and from this union come the main deities—Brighid, the active mother-goddess; Midir the Proud, he of the shadowy other world; Badb or Bov, a more warlike deity; Aenghus mac-in-da-Oc, the love and beauty god, son of the great force Og or Oige, youth, the sun or summer, as well as of Lugh, and Ogmas, the inventor of the Ogham script.

Ler or Lir the sea-god of mystery is usually considered the Dagda's brother. He belongs to all seas and their distances, and his son is the showy Mannanan of Man, guardian of the commercial ships of men in that central Celto-Cymric sea. He is between the worlds and a bridge between the sidhe-people and the humans. He fails, however, to make friends with Columcille.

Whence do they come then, these Children or Tribes of the goddess Dana (Tuatha dé Danaan)? They link most plainly with Greece—indeed this name, Dana, is one of the clearest evidences of ancient identity between the two races, the Danaans of Eire and the Danaoi of Greece, both being the sons of Dana. They are from a kind of paranormal world, in a reality and unity of a different kind. They are Greek, yes, but is it a Greek legendary world? There is music, there are bright forms and fair hair, magic and magical equipment; there are the lands of enchantment, the land beneath the sea, Tir-fa-tonn, and the land in the magical mounds and hills, Tir-na-n'Og, that land of eternal youth and summer. If we are to allot the place of these dream-realities, they live on the plane of the higher astral, they correspond with the magical-divine number 7—the seventh tribe. In their time Tuan is an eagle.

Yet this world of faery does not last, beautiful as it is. At the fading-out time between one age and another, the older world has a sunset perfection. The greatest things remaining from the classical-heathen world were some of the latest—the *Meditations* of Marcus Aurelius and the pious vision of the Great Mother Isis in the *Golden Ass* of Apuleius, both well within the Christian era. So this magic *sidhe* country and its people are driven out by the Milesians, sons of Miled, and the world droops; the swan-children of Lir transform into shrivelled old men and women and accept baptism. Baptism represents the more spiritual form, but it is a drab affair—only the chapel bell rings. The new faith is austere if more exalted; it is the sphere of the Jesus-number 8, of the new double-balance of 4s, universal but of lower pitch than the magical 7.

Yet the Milesians (perhaps from Miletus, a Greek colony) make a reasonable treaty with the *sidhe*, who are to inhabit mounds and hills, not the daytime lands. Their realm is there, but out of normal sight; those who wish may contact them. Some Danaans went to the within-earth area, Tir n'an Oige, and others into the *sidhe* hills themselves. But Aenghus mac Grein, or mac-in-da-Og, returns. His dwelling is upon the Boyne, he is son of its goddess and creates another bridge between the worlds.

Throughout Ireland mounds may be seen lit from within, with mesmeric music coming from them. If you listen you will be drawn within and vanish for seven days, or years, or for always. The entrance to the Other Land is between two stones or trees in a field, where the air is somehow different and dizzy. People disappear at intervals.

Miled, patronymic of Milesians, arrived with Scota as mate, patronymic of the Scots—who were an Irish race. Scot was a daughter of the Pharaoh, so the Scots are Egyptians. Maybe about the same legendary era Amergin and his Chief Druid arrived in Wales.

The earliest races, then, represented the darkness of ignorance; upon them preyed the active evil ones, the giant Fomorians, then the Firbolg, who sound like a rather inferior trading race—perhaps Phoenicians, or even Minoans?

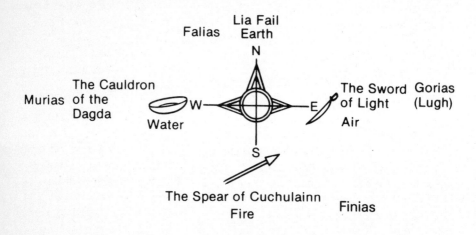

Danaan Four Lands and Symbols.

A general and profound symbolism came with the Tuatha dé Danaan. They came from heaven or from four great cities, whence also their four treasures. From Falias came the *Lia Fail*, the stone of destiny, where the High King stood when he was crowned, and which roared under him as a sign. From Gorias came the invincible sword of Lugh of the Long Arm; from Finias the magic spear, and from Murias the mysterious cauldron of the Dagda which could always feed a host of men.

VII. *The Pattern in Scotland*

And what of Scotland? Thither had returned a large number of the Culdee-Christians, Druids who, however Christian by conviction, preferred the virgin territories of Pictish and now Scottish heathendom, with its varied races, to being subject to church control in Ireland, where as ex-Druids they would never make the grade of Bishop. So the hereditary, married Druids in this form spread over Scotland doing excellent work, their skills in Druid specialities giving them no small advantage, and taking with them the Greek way of keeping Easter. For some 300 years this Druidry sent its roots into the Scots peoples and affected them profoundly. It is a long period in a people's life. Rome regarded the Celtic lands askance but they were strong in their own homeland. Wilfred of York curbed their Easter datings and seemed to roll back the Celtic church flood at the Synod of Whitby in 667, but although some of the spreading missionary work turned back, the settled monks in their houses and Orders remained. The noble families built up their power in the glens, and hereditary bards were kept in many households of the lairds. Druid stones and circles were reverenced and Druid practices went on rather more freely and later than in Ireland. When in the thirteenth century mother church did wield some measure of authority over these distant lands, she seems to have disciplined the flat Ireland more successfully than rugged Scotland. Papal complaints had been loud; Celtic habits ran quite counter to the strenuous reforming ways of Citeaux. Monks and nuns worked together—what scandal!—and abbacies and other offices were hereditary, priests were married against the new reforms, and divine dates were still kept wrongly. All this was Druidic, although the word was not used even objurgatorily.

Up to the thirteenth century at least, then, Scotland was the last remaining area where Druidry dominated, in a light disguise. English ideas made little impact upon Scotland's daily life, but elsewhere things were more conformist. Wales had deepened its bardism, developing that aspect of the cult; Ireland was torn, firstly by civil strife, then by the encroachments of the English; Cornwall went on in its rather secretive way.

By about the eleventh century Eisteddfodau began to form in Wales while hereditary chiefs harboured hereditary Druids or Bards in Scotland. Clan quarrels did not allow much substance to the Scots national kingship on the whole, and it had to be content with an almost nominal suzerainty over the proud chieftains in their inaccessible valleys. It is not really surprising that it was from Scotland that the later Druid revival started which resulted in the launching of the modern Order (see pp. 96–8).

VIII. *The Cymric Culture of Bardism*

We left the Welsh recovering from Roman military domination, yet proud of the half-Roman valour of Arthur; a fiery Cymric people, yet fascinated with the problems of philosophy, especially the setting forth of the due ordering of the heavens, which was partly classical in inspiration.

In the comparative safety of the valleys there was an early flowering of poetry in the fifth to seventh centuries; but there came also the smothering of the inspired independence of the Druidic-bardic culture with its Gorsedd laws. Poetry went on in its peculiar local language forms, but it became, with some exceptions, either the inspired lyric or the eulogies of princes and occasions.

Eventually there followed the bitter wars with the Edwards of England, and with the death of the last reigning Prince of Wales in 1282 the earlier Wales came to an end. Yet the later English power, especially when in the hands of a Welsh family, was not insensitive to Welsh culture and encouraged it, without sharp political limits.

A Gaelic/Cymric Anthology

To look at some of this development in more detail, we need to consider the fifth to seventh century Bards, and typically Llywarch Hen (the Aged). He was by tradition the great poet who in his life bridged the space between Arthur and Cadwallon, so that he was alive in 542—the date given for Arthur's death—and also in 646 when Cadwallon died. Llywarch is said to have been born about the beginning of the sixth century and lived to the middle of the seventh, a span of some 150 years.

About 150 poems thought to be of the fifth, sixth and seventh centuries exist; the north British ones are considered to be those by Aneurin, Myrddin ab Morfryn and Llywarch Hen; the Welsh ones are by Taliesin. William Owen in his collection prints 73 pages of Llywarch Hen, in both languages.[1]

Aneurin is given the late sixth century *Y Gododdin*, heroic poetry written in southern Scotland. To Taliesin are attributed some poems written concerning Urien of Rhegard, in north Britain. They are full of mystic boastfulness and shape-shifting; the main source is *The Book of Taliesin* which is much later but embodies material that is earlier:

> No mother nor father
> made me at all;
> substance and shape
> were the ninefold senses;
> they are springing from fruits,
> from the divine roots,
> from wild flowers—primroses—
> blossoms from the hills, trees and shrubs—
> and I am of earthy clay
> on my birth day
> and of nettle bloom
> and the ninth wave's foam—
>   *Cad Goddeu*

The best known mystical poem is the *Hanes Taliesin* (Life of Taliesin) found

[1] W. Owen, *Bardic Remains*, 1835.

in the *Myvyrian Archaeology*. Nash's translation, here somewhat shortened, follows:

> An impartial Chief Bard
> Am I to Elphin.
> My accustomed country
> Is the land of the Cherubim.
>
> Johannes the Diviner
> I was called by Merddin,
> At length every King
> Will call me Taliesin.
>
> I was nine months almost
> In the belly of the hag Caridwen;
> I was at first little Gwion,
> At length I am Taliesin.
>
> I was with my Lord
> In the highest sphere,
> When Lucifer fell
> Into the depths of Hell.
>
> I carried the banner
> Before Alexander.
> I know the names of the stars
> From the North to the South.
>
> I was in Caer Bedion
> Tetragrammaton;
> I conveyed Heon (the Divine Spirit)
> Down to the vale of Ebron.

★　★　★　★　★　★　★

> I was with my King
> In the manger of the ass;
> I supported Moses
> Through the waters of Jordan.
>
> I was in the Firmament
> With Mary Magdalene;
> I obtained my inspiration
> From the cauldron of Caridwen.
>
> I was Bard of the harp
> To Deon of Llychlyn;
> I have suffered hunger
> With the son of the Virgin.

I was in the White Hill
In the Hall of Cynvelyn,
In stocks and fetters
A year and a half.

I have been in the buttery
In the land of the Trinity;
It is not known what is the nature
Of its meat and its fish.

I have been instructed
In the whole system of the universe;
I shall be till the day of judgement
On the face of the earth.

I have been in an uneasy chair
Above Caer Sidin,
And the whirling round without motion
Between three elements.

Is it not the wonder of the world
That cannot be discovered?

Llywarch Hen's poems are often now attributed to a period as late as the middle ninth century. Laments over age are usually quoted:

Before my back was bent I shone amongst men
first was my spear, I was the head of spears—
now, round-backed, heavy, wretched.
O my wooden crook it is autumn for us—
the ferns are rust-colour, the grasses yellow.
The man I refused is now equal with me.
Wooden crook—it is now winter . . .
my bedside is not jovial.

Wooden crook, it is spring
and the cooks are red with their work,
in the hall are the feast and the lights;
But no more am I the girl's delight.

Myrddin ab Morfryn appears to be sixth century; he is Myrddin Wyllt, the Wild One, both Druid and Bard, and an active fighter as well. Was he the figure known as Merlin of the Arthurian legends?[2] He belonged to north Britain and lived towards the end of the sixth century; the legend is that he went mad in battle and retired to the Scots wood Coad Celyddon. The tale has a common Celtic source. There may be four figures fused into one. The central part of *The Black Book of Caermarthen* is attributed to him. A

[2] See: R.J. Stewart, *The Mystic Life of Merlin*, Arkana, 1987, and N. Tolstoy, *The Quest For Merlin*, Hamish Hamilton, 1987.

little maybe is as early as the sixth century, but most of it is a great deal later in its present form.

Indeed, some Welsh poems written in the margin of a Cambridge psalter may be as early as anything; they were actually written down, however, in the first half of the ninth century.

The mid-ninth century marks a break and a transition, when, under the pressure of Saxon culture, much of the educated population moved from British Celtic areas and the south-west of England to Brittany and on the whole stayed there, until in the twelfth–thirteenth centuries the great Welsh princes had built up realms that created security and invited return. The monasteries were then well-established, and there were some technical advances in the pattern of life. Writing goes on all this time and there are technical poetic advances, especially the complex alliterations called *cynghanedd*. In the tenth century we have the laws of Hywel Dda, who already recognizes several grades of poets.

From this Breton period comes much of the *Four Ancient Books*, compiled by adding on to the earlier material. A lullaby about Dinograde's Petticoat makes an incongruously domestic break in the records of a heroic and grim period. It comes from the Derwent region and one has constantly to remember that 'Wales' or 'Britain' at this time has a great area, and is hardly to be distinguished from the western parts of England. As another break from historical chronicles, here are two verses of nature observation from *The Black Book*. The cuckoo's note, *coo*, or *cw* in Welsh, equates with the Latin *quo* or the French *ou*, both meaning 'whither' or 'where'; so the cuckoo's song is one of desolation for the past:

Cuckoo

The month of May is the finest time
but finest not for me;
the loud birds sing, the leaf is green,
merrily spreads the tree—
furrow from plough and its yoken ox
the lands are quilt-work, green is the sea—
But 'Where, where?' the cuckoos cry
aloft in the high tree,
'Where are my lost ones—all the past?'
The greater their 'cuckoo' on high,
the greater the grief to me.

I cannot bear the smoke of inspiration,
I cannot sleep, for the injuries done to my kin.

Wisdom stanzas in *The Red Book* seem to depend upon rhyme and a certain off-handed *non sequitur* for effect:

Heard you what Rhydderch sang
the third of the generous lovers of love?
Too much love makes too much hate.

> Heard you what the fish sang
> floundering amongst the stalks?
> Nature is stronger than education.

The Black Book has the 73 'Stanzas of the Graves' which are *englynion* about the burial places of heroes, and this is one of the few places in the early period where we hear about Arthur. Most graves were otherwise unrecorded. They mention him, but tell us no more:

> There is a grave named for Mark,
> and for Gwythur a grave is named,
> Gwgawn Redsword is marked by a word:
> but the grave-place of Arthur shall not be proclaimed.

Already there is a small Arthurian *mystique*. The other heroes named are sixth century, so the basis seems to belong to that time.

A happier poem is of the ninth century, praising the qualities of a fine castle and its hospitality, a series of *awdlau*, ending with the praise of loyalty even to death:

> Dishonour was offered, they refused it:
> blood was upon the hair—and from the harp a sigh of sorrow.

Only the later *Book of Taliesin* has a Christianizing blend in the mythology and pagan tales, and there are some truly Christian poems both here and in *The Black Book*. But in such poems as those of the Judgement Day the poet has taken over the Vates-Druid function, obviously:

Doomsday

> . . . When the All-Father descends—
> with his ranged hosts descending for the judgment of the creation—
> at the four corners of the earth the great horn is blown,
> the sea begins burning—
> the ungodly people of all the earth are burning—
> only the embers of them remain:
> let the wilderness of the world be on fire—
> before the great Doom is proclaimed.

This sounds much more like the Norse Ragnarok, the fall of heaven and the old gods.

The 'Praise to God', apparently orthodox, makes a peculiar selection of material creatures who bless the Lord, whilst the placing of the three wells recalls the three roots of a Norse World-Ash, in air, water and hell.

Praise to God

> To the Sun Lord, to you be a hailing.
> The blessing of chancel and church

both of them be upon you
and both plains and hills
give again blessing.

Three wells are above:
two that are of air and fire
are above the wind: one that is of water
is above the earth.

There is daylight, there is shadow—
there are shrubs bedecked with scents,
humans are bedecked with silks—
for these gifts we bless
with blessing of Abraham for his flocks and herds.

And here are birds and bees
the feathered and the insect worlds,
and the luxuriance of growth:
Aaron and Moses for this blessed you.
Even back to the first divisions,
Male and female, you created them:

And the Seven Days
and the Heaven of the stars—
the air and the aither above it:

all that is cited in books and inscriptions.

May fish in the water bless you,
may sand and may soil bless you.
May you be blessed by deeds following thoughts—
so may he who has done good actions praise you:
so may I too bless you, the Sun Lord—
all hail, all hail . . .
Anon—*The Black Book*

Hatred for the Saxon invader links with a Welsh Christianity under the
banner of St David; the re-arisen Cadwaladr and Cynnan will lead in the
following poem:

Cynnan and Cadwaladr

Two pillars of judgment
Two that are terrible as commanders,
Two in the cause of God will conquer Saxons.
They will be generous with the lands of those plunderers.

They are united, ready for battle,
with one faith, united whatever the hap.
These two are the protectors
of our holy and lovely Britain.

> Let them be baited daily by the enemy,
> these Bears will show their strength.
>
> (about AD 930)

Prophetic poems in the Black and Red books foretell the coming of four heroes again, and the broken-down state of society. Myrddin, according to earlier accounts, went mad in Scotland, and eventually he seems to have been in Wales. The Apple-Tree (*Avellaneau*) and Little Pig (*Horianiou*) poems tell something of his loveless life and lonely age.

The apple tree grows in a clearing which Nature protects from Rhydderch's men:

> There's been trampling about her
> but treasure of a lord is she . . .
> No longer Gwenddydd loves and talks to me.
> and Gwasawg hates me now
> since I killed her son and daughter.
> Death takes all, but calls not me.
> Gwenddoleu's dead, no lord respects me
> no girl will visit me, play's delight
> no longer holds me. In the battle
> at Arfderydd my torque was shining
> all of gold—today is nothing,
> I am no treasure of a swan—white girl.
>
> *Avellanau*

Historical facts and comparison of texts lift the obscurity of this. Gwenddydd is Myrddin's sister. Rhydderch, possibly married to Gwenddydd (his 'apple tree'), fought the battle of Arfderydd in 573 in north Britain, and Gwenddoleu, King of the Scots, Myrddin's patron, was killed there (*The Red Book of Hergest*). This therefore is a real light on Myrddin's later unhappy life.

Prophecy mingles with his personal feelings and his dreams:

> Greetings, little pig with sharp hooves . . .
> Rhydderch Hael tonight at feasting
> little knew my wakefulness—
> snow to my knees, I was amongst wild dogs
> deep in the woods, my beard was icy,
> weary weary was my way.
> But Tuesday comes, a day of fury
> between the Powys lord and Gwynedd.
> Hiriell rises from long resting
> to defend against the foe
> Gwynedd's bounds . . .
>
> *Horianiou*

Rhydderch Hael is unknown but obviously Myrddin's patron, and

Tuesday, the day of Mars, is the day to predict a war, which was always an even bet between the aggressive lords of Powys and the rich land of Gwynedd. The north Welsh had a variety of hero saviours who were coming to help them; not merely Arthur but Urien, Owain, Caedwaladr —and Hirioll—all awaiting the call.

It is customary to take as the next natural division of Welsh cultural history the time from 1094—the Welsh rebellion against Norman rule— to the death of the last independent Welsh ruler in 1282. North Wales was now fairly stable under various princes; monasteries had been set up and did remarkable work, notably that of Strata Florida. To such monastic industry may be ascribed the preservation of a very great deal of poetry, especially that of the fourteenth century. It must not, however, be thought that work patronized by the abbeys and monasteries was the mainstream of development, for poetry and its bardism in Wales was a truly national sturdy independent growth, patronized by the princes and much less influenced by dogmatic Christianity than poetry of the period elsewhere.

The main poetic and other culture now tends to return from its industrious exile in Brittany; poetic forms strengthen, the traditions of the past are studied, revived and developed in heroic forms. For this time under the princes is one of a national revived consciousness. This was due largely to Gryffydd ap Cynan who was instrumental in bringing over Irish poets and spreading their influence. It immensely strengthened and inspired the Welsh poetic vein.

Meilyr, for example, is a main poet of the period whose verse even in translation may be seen to be remarkable; in this passage the sheepfold and the parish become synonyms for the graveyard.

Deathbed Poem of Meilyr

May I have the patronage of Peter at the gate
to whom I have been pilgrim.
May I be awaiting the Call
in a sheepfold near to the evermoving sea,
for this is a real honourable hermitage,
the sheepfold, with a briny bosom
lapping about the graves.

O Island of Mary, Ynys Enlli,[3]
island that is pure and the holy type of resurrection
beautiful it is to be there!
Christ of the cosmic cross will keep me
out of the pains of that distant lodging
the dark gates of hell
my great Creator will admit me
to the parish of the people of Enlli.

[3] Bardsey Island, traditional grave of thousands of monk-martyrs, and also the supposed retreat of Merlin.

His son Gwalchmai is another important poet; he was the honoured bard of the prince Owain Gwynedd. Poetry by this time is often a weaving together of jewel-like phrases into recurrent patterns, sometimes with little development. One guesses that the singing of these to the harp afforded endless variations, lost on the written page.

> The sun is rising quickly, the summer's in a hurry,
> the song of birds is splendid, there is fine constant weather.
> Now I am golden grown and fearless in the battle,
> I am a lion that flashes out even against a host.

> All through a night I watched along a frontier—
> there were ford waters murmuring in bad weather—
> again, open grassland was very green, the waters clear together—
> loud was the nightingale, and with glistening feathers
> the gulls on the seabed were seen, being turbulent together.

> —And now my memory returns
> into the early summer
> with my young love from Caerwys.
> —Oh you are far from and unlike
> the lively people of small Mona,
> with its safety and secrecy.
> To your lips I listened on occasion
> to real things, the virgin of the swords,
> to the need of Owain, who links me so closely,
> whose service is an honourable fetter.

> Before my sword
> the English are retreating.

It will be seen that such a poet is also a warrior, which in turn means a radical change of status; the noble warrior is in fact a noble or a prince, and we change over from a folk tradition to an aristocratic outlook, without altogether leaving the large field of sensibility that is in common between them, particularly in the love of nature and the attraction of women. Poets, if not noble themselves, praise nobles, their patrons in fact; a writer like Cynddelw (second half of the twelfth century) praised great leaders like Owain Gwynedd or the Lord Rhys, he himself being a warrior. In some ways he started a new tradition in poetry as well as guarding jealously the old ones, for regard for craftsmanship was always of the essence of how poetry was judged in Wales.

Hywel ap Owain Gwynedd, then, was a noble of the second half of the twelfth century. With him and with Owain Cyfeliog, Prince of Powys, we enter a phase of Welsh poetry when aristocratic themes dominate and poetry itself rises in the social scale—the difference between the freeman chanting in the hall and the noble himself, doubtless with a better education, at any rate with a totally different approach, performing largely to a literate audience. Hywell has brilliant pictures of nature and an easy way with girls. Of the land of the north, and

> the varied growth that borders the river Lliw—
> I love its coast and its mountains,
> its castle near the woods, its fine lands,
> its water meadows and its valleys,
> its white gulls and its lovely women . . .
> I love its fields covered with the little clover
> where I found a place of triumphant joy.
> I love its regions to which valour entitles,
> its wide waste lands and its wealth . . .
> I love the coastland of Meirionwydd
> where a white arm was my pillow.
> I love the nightingale in the wild privet
> where two waters meet in the valley of worship.

Hywel has a genius for discovering girls in all the castles around and glories half-humorously in them:

> I had a girl of one mind with me one day—
> I had two, the greater be their praise;
> I had three and four—and Fortune;
> I had five, splendid in their white flesh—
> I had six, for I will not conceal sin.
> But Gwenglaer, daughter of the White Tower,
> she brought strife; with her I had seven
> and a grievous time there was of it.
> I had eight, paying part of the praise I sang.
> Teeth are good to keep the tongue quiet.

By the twelfth century these educated nobles were consciously reviving the earlier epic style and there is an element of propaganda. Nevertheless, Welsh poetry's style can be shown to be earlier than that of its continental contemporaries the *Chansons de Geste*, which seem to have been the glorification of heroes whose shrines and relics were in various monasteries, which naturally promoted such poetry.

These two princely poets, Hywel and Owain, both carried on the great skills of the poetic past and also widened the scope of poetry considerably. We cannot follow this development here, only mention names: such as Llywarch ap Llewelyn (1173–1220), the Poet of the Pigs, a warrior-poet who delighted in violence and blood but who also wrote notable elegies upon the deaths of the sons of Llewellyn ap Iowerth, the Great, and of Llewelyn himself. One son died when he attempted to escape from the Tower of London, for the background of much of this warlike poetry is the wars with England under Henry III and Edward I.

At this point more general comparison may well begin. The Bards had long passed from power. Even in the post-Roman times of the fifth century, the Italian clergy began to dominate. Until that time the priest-hood had in fact been exercised by the various Druidic grades but all called bardic, not Druidic. Then the Roman clergy debarred them both from patronage and from all but minor religious offices. Druidry now had no official standing, even as bardism; but Bards and their poetry of course continued. The old rules of the Gorsedd tradition could only be carried on in a limited way. The setting up of the legendary code of Prince Beli marks the change.

The Bards, as we have seen, developed as gleemen, as honoured minstrels who had positions in princes' courts; then they changed into patriotic princes themselves in an age of national defence. Hereabouts we have the poetry of Phylip Brydodd who is important less perhaps as a poet than as the organizer of a revived Druidic organization. From many centres he drew Bards to unite in a Gorsedd recognizing the old rules of Hywel Dda; although we have few details, this is recognized as a focal date (1245) in the continuation of Druidry as distinct from bardism. There are half-a-dozen poems to princes attributed to him in the *Myvyrian Archaeology*. An elegy to a prince-leader, Rhys Ievange, by Phylip Brydodd has this vivid imagery:

> Surely it is the trickery of a mirror—
> Did I not today see him commanding, head of his army?
> How is it that I am holding up this body of a lifeless king?
> —Yet all men are but grass.

We are moving towards the end of this period, and with the death of the last effective Prince of Wales, Llewelyn, in 1282, followed the next year by the ruthless execution of his brother Dafydd by King Edward, England definitely ruled or was at any rate exercising suzerainty over Wales; political liberty therefore was no more. This was fully recognized as Wales' major disaster and Welsh poetry rises to a crescendo of horror. Gryffydd ab yr Ynad Goch's magnificent ode is personal and passionate, in its climax, the end of the poet's whole world, a disaster to the universe. This, by any standard, technical or inspirational, stands as one of the great works of Western literature:

> Under the fearful breast cold is the heart,
>   lust is like dry branches shrivelled.
> Do you not see the manner of wind and rain
>   how the oaktrees beat each other—
>   how the sea stings the land?
> Does the sun not drive through the sky
>   and are not the stars fallen?
>
> Madmen do you not believe in a God?
> can you not see the end of an existence?
>   O we sigh to you O God,

let the sea rise over this land:
why are we left, lingering here?

From this prison of fear is no escape,
nowhere to dwell—
nothing is enclosed safe anymore, nor truly open,
the sad counsels of terror hold us . . .

By way of comparison it is illuminating to see how poets and minstrels were faring in England, which by now of course was really and not partially separate from Wales, and the term Britain can be used for both.

Minstrels—*jongleurs*—had a long history. Gawain listens to songs and music in the hall, according to an early text about *Gawayne and the Green Knight*.[4] Minstrels sang of deeds of long ago, of the cycle of Charlemagne, the *Chanson de Roland*, of Arthur and of Brutus of Troy—that Third Troy that was the predecessor of London, with Brutus the founder, it was said, of the British race. The numbers of minstrels grew as halls grew in size and galleries were built. They played the early violin called the *veille* and the little drum, the *tabor*. At the marriage of Margaret, daughter of Edward I, the presence of no fewer than 426 minstrels is recorded. Minstrels and singers, although occasionally retained with regular allowances, were on the whole wanderers; they had no special status or honour such as tradition and custom gave them in Wales, in continuity with the Druidic–bardic customs.

A word is due here to the part played by the Church. The Roman-Christian form in Wales reverted to something much nearer to Culdee-type Christianity as the great invasions cut off Wales from contact with the Continent in the sixth and seventh centuries. Or perhaps one should say that a unification between Church and people occurred, the Church giving a national anti-English lead in the struggle with the eastern neighbour. There was rebellion in 1094 led by the Welsh Church against the new Roman monk-dominated disciplines recently developed at Citeaux that held sway under the Norman aegis. Yet later on we have Cistercian abbeys in Wales playing a great and honoured part in the national life, notably that patriotic rallying-place and centre of the poets, the Strata Florida Abbey. The religion that was to win the people, in fact, had to profess the popular anti-English sentiments. To this extent, the Church succeeded to the political leadership of the Druids.

Strata Florida seems to revert in its structure to much earlier ideas. Its central feature was a great baptizing-place, just as it had been in the fifth or sixth centuries at open-air sanctuaries such as St Cybi in Anglesey. A wave decoration surrounds the abbey's remaining great arch, of a type not seen elsewhere. Something very Welsh and very early in feeling comes through the shattered remains of this national shrine.

---

[4] *Sir Gawayne and the Green Knight*, Early English Text Society, 1864.

He who is perhaps Wales' greatest and most lyrical poet lived in the shadow of Wales' loss of nationhood. The newer trading towns of Edward I's founding, around his castles, were despised by the Welsh aristocracy and those trained in classical lore amongst whom was Dafydd ap Gwilym (c. 1325–1380). The Cymric as well as the Gaelic tradition has always been against towns and traders. Dafydd was always shunning the age's tendencies; he managed in the interest of a quiet life not to protest outwardly, nor to praise the English king for bread-and-butter's sake. Is he therefore trivial? Not really. He makes clear his contempt for the English and retreats to the countryside. Not his part to breathe fire like Iolo Goch. Owain Cyfeliog could revive the nationalist-heroic Gododdin manner, but by Dafydd's time it would have sounded absurd. No, Dafydd accepted the demise of the battle-heroic poetry and looked to the new troubadour movement. He knew French and found suggestions in the *trouvères*. Maybe he went to the shrine at Compostella and actually experienced the land of the *Chansons de Geste* and the troubadours. English influence was felt too, for love lyrics were now being written in south-western England and Dafydd's uncle, with whom he lived for a time, was an English government official in south Wales, and his chief patron, Ifor Hael, was at Masaleg, and neither was immune from the currents of English culture.

We do know enough of Dafydd's poetic contemporaries to realize that he was no isolated figure. Gruffydd ap Vadda, a poet of whose brilliant work only a small amount remains, died from a sword-cut in a friendly fight in 1344. Another figure, Cadog Benfras, has a very small corpus of poetry left—but more important it may be that he married Dafydd to Morfydd in the woods by a 'bardic' ritual, which sounds as though Druidic practices were not dead. This is likely to be linked with Phylip Brydodd's revival of Druidry a century before. Gryffydd Gryg, a contemporary, wrote for Dafydd a memorial *cywydd* (see below) with the fine couplet:

> Yr ywen i or euwas
> Ger mur Ystrad Fflur a'i phlas.

that is:

> The yew tree to a Master
> By Ystrata Florida's wall and manor.

So we have Dafydd representing a fine flower of the age of wandering clerics and poets. Although he uses of himself the phrase *y gler*, which is the usual Welsh term for these folk, it is doubtful whether he was a wandering minstrel. However, there is a mixture of Church phrases and imagery from ceremonial which mingle with his general open-air feeling. Troubadours were always celebrating the past and so is he, with his echoes of twelfth and thirteenth century poets. He is fully trained in the bardic crafts; although he breaks free often, he returns again. Phrases repeat and pick-up and echo, there are medial rhymes and other devices. Few have been more skilled. Mystery surrounds his life; John Rees of Penrhyncoch indicates that he was a small landowner unable to live from his own land. Dafydd adopted as his own, however, the *cywydd* and stamped it upon much future poetry. A *cywydd* is verse of seven-syllable rhymed couplets, with multiple alliteration, usually of 30–100 lines. After hearing Dafydd's work a number of Bards studied and copied the *cywyddau*; they were forerunners of the champions of Cynghanedd, the period 1400–1600, when Welsh poetry reaches its peak in alliterative metres. Leading names are Llewelyn Goch Amheirig Hen, Iolo Goch, Sion Cent, Dafydd Nanmor, Lewis ab Edmwnt—of the 24 metres—Tudor Aled Gruffydd Hiraethog, and Wilhaim Llŷn. Hundreds of minor and also worthy poets were writing also.

For subject matter, there are five Dafydd poems about people, one being on Ifor Hael, and four elegies, a few poems concerning his own life, and the rest all love and nature. Two girls' names repeat but they seem to be typical rather than personal—Morfydd is fair-haired and Dyddgu dark-haired. Girls, wives or nuns, Dafydd wants all to share the woodland reverences and revelations of nature. These connect with frankly physical love, but he does not go into detail.[5]

Translations are always unsatisfactory, but here is a poem on Morfydd, possibly to the Morfydd that Dafydd married:

> God made the colour of your forehead
> daisy-white, and gave you red-gold hair
> like a flaming tongue:
> Your straight neck, your breasts
> full spheres, your cheeks
> of sunny scarlet.
> Brows you have of London black[6]
> eyes are confines of brightness,
> a sweet girl's nose
> over your smile of five delights—
> and your lovely body
> which tempts me from the faith . . .
>
> Come to the hillside my beauty
> and our bed be high on the hill,
> four ages under fresh birch-trees
> on a green leaf mattress still
> edged with the shining ferns
> and against the rains
> the coverlet of branches turns.

A different technique is required for nuns:

[5] See R. Bromwich, *Poems of Davydd ap Gwyllym*.
[6] A black material of the day.

> For the sake of God and Mary
> No more this bread and water—
> these thin water cresses—
> stop your thin prayers.
> For its all the Roman monks.
> It is spring, don't be a nun
> lurking in places darker than groves:
> this faith of yours is firm against love—
>
> Be ordained in a green mantle
> with the warrant of a ring—
> come to this spreading birch—
> the cuckoo's church:
> we win our heaven in a greener grove
> where none forbid or mock:
> remember Ovid's book—
> forget this faith.

To the English, Wales was troublesome in the early fifteenth century. Welsh minstrels were now denounced as causing, by their inspiring power, rebellion against their suzerain lords. This was in marked contrast to the earlier Norman kings, under whom the Lord Rhys—Rhys ap Gryffydd —ruling from Cardigan Castle, caused the celebration of the first Eisteddfod of which there is certain record in 1176. Already the North was more poetic and the South more musical, the musical contest being won by a south Welshman, the bardic competition by one from Gwynedd.

'Rhymers, minstrels and vagabonds' were now forbidden to be maintained in Wales, as they were 'partly causes of the insurrection and rebellion now in Wales.' Authority must have had in mind that, after all, it had been a popular song which had been the notorious text for John Ball's speech at Blackheath in 1381:

> When Adam delved and Eve span
> Where was then the gentleman?

This had sparked off or expressed the Peasants' Revolt. The Robin Hood ballads also were all in the direction of sympathy for the rebels, the men of the greenwood.

The later phases technically were brilliant. Dafydd ab Edmwnt with his 24 metres of the *Awdl* had opened the door to experimental alliterative metres and the *englyn* with its 30 syllables became popular. Alliterative poetry divided into two schools, the Bards of Glamorgan and those of the North.

Dafydd ap Gwilym's fascination and influence went on right until the 1490s. Then things changed, when the *cymghanedd* were made more complex—in subject more modernist, above all more nationalistic. In the nineteenth century the subjects were scenery, seasons, love, character, and a torrent of patriotic songs started; now the tradition continues almost exclusively in patriotic form, thus changing the texture as well as the themes. The standards remain different but very high; better use was and is made of metres, work being far more intricate. There is a general scorn for masters of the recent past such as Edward Thomas or Alun Lewis.

Returning to the Renaissance period for the development of organization, it was a long time before the tide turned and gatherings together of the poems of the past began to be made. Welsh poetry was a very real movement but it had been sporadic, individual, without proper collections. Then Sir Michael Neville came to hold a Gorsedd, and eventually William Herbert, Earl of Pembroke, held a historic gathering in 1570, and for another under Sir Edward Lewis in 1580 definite collections were begun. The Welsh indeed in a sense had now reversed the historic defeat, for Welsh monarchs were upon the English throne.

In 1681 a sort of canon of Welsh poetry was finalized by Edward Davydd of Margam under the authority of Sir Richard Bassett and sanctioned by a Gorsedd at Bawper. In this area of Glamorgan or nearabouts occasional Gorseddau continued to be held but more sparsely.

HOW FAR UNDERGROUND: A STUDY OF AREAS AND FESTIVALS IN FRANCE AND BRITAIN

I. Areas and Festivals from AD 1245 to the Eighteenth-century Renaissance

We have now to account for the centuries between the apparent vanishing of Druidry and the renaissance of the late seventeenth and early eighteenth centuries. How far was that a romanticism taken from classical sources, how far was it a genuine regrowth from existing roots?

Undoubtedly much went underground, including for the most part the word Druid; Bards are increasingly heard of instead. But here and there, now and then, Druidry emerges, and great tracts of what are, with little doubt, Druidic-Celtic rites, customs and cult, implying known deities, suppressed or not, can be easily found—not far underground at all.

Starting from the darker half of the Dark Ages—when presumably knowledge was being groped after with candles—we find at Oxford before the foundation of the university usually attributed to Alfred, from about the year 800 a grove of the Pheryllt called Cor Emrys, which linked Penmaenmawr and Dinas Affareon on the Eryri Gwyn *massif* with the Thames-side city.

The word *Feryllt* comes from *ffer*, Cymric for 'that which is solid' i.e. metals, and it indicated workers with fire and metals. Thus it has been taken to mean early metallurgy; but at this period alchemy is much more likely.

Cor Emrys ('Circle or City of Ambrose') links us with Ambrosius Aurelianus, from the Romano-Celtic borderland between fact and legend. Amesbury near Stonehenge is derived from Ambrose; the earlier form of the name was Ambrosbury. The Penmaenmawr circles are the most carefully designed perhaps of all circles—a large circle with a small one as pointer at some distance to the exact North-east (see p. 220). It is unlikely to have been itself a workshop centre for either metallurgy or alchemy; but it is very likely to have been the temple, the dedicatory place for spiritual direction, of a substantial experimental station a little way distant down the slope.

Dinas Emrys has the legend of the fiery dragons who quaked the foundation of the castle that King Vortigern ordered to be built; Myrddin's test was the discovery of these dragons and dealing with them. It all sounds exactly like later alchemy, where one can see dragons imprisoned in cucurbits.

The centre of the Oxford cult was the Mother Goddess, the mysteries of Ceridwen Cariadwen. Christianity found and suppressed this cult and long before 1056 the Cor Emrys Oxford Grove was suppressed. Not very efficiently; the teaching of Druidry in this alchemic form went on somewhere, or how could Haymo of Faversham have revived it? We constantly hear of these 'revivals': revivals from what source? Obviously something had continued.

Haymo, then, renewed Druidry in some form; and on his death Phylip Brydodd, the Welsh poet of Llanbadarn Fawr (1200–50), is given by Gwywn Jones as the contender with the 'vulgar rhymsters' over the presentation of poems. He was a specialist in metres and stood out as defender of the official and regular style of poem against upstarts 'without grammar or honour', whatever that exactly meant. He reconstituted existing groves in a number of areas, apparently partly in Wales, partly in England. He was one of the most erudite men of literature in its third period i.e. after Eneurian (c. AD 510).[1]

There was already the Bond or circle of Druid fellowship between them, called the Caw, and companions of these several bodies founded the present-day Mount Haemus Grove in 1245.

Now Mount Haemus is a real mountain in the Balkans, and either this or another of the same name was the classical prison of the winds. They were ruled by Aeolus, who let them out as it were on parole for brief periods, otherwise the Earth would be continuously torn with raging tempests. The Aeolian Isles off Sicily are also, however, given for this windy prison. It was, whatever the location, the allegorical name for powerful inspiration which lurked beneath the surface.

From now until the mid seventeenth century at least all record of ritual Druidry appears to be blank, with one startling exception. Can we fill in these four centuries at all, or are we to agree with the many writers who assume that seventeenth and eighteenth-century Druidic reconstruction was simply based upon Roman account plus romantic ideas and a general desire to be sheeted in white—if not in Roman togas, like English statesmen in sepulchral effigies, then in white Druidic robes with Egyptian-style head-dresses? Undoubtedly this element came in; it was the age of romantic revivals already.

In the British Isles, Druidry in these long centuries could not be explicit; although in Wales and Scotland it could be bardic. The Culdees spread a Christianized form of Druidry to Eire and Scotland in the Celtic Church, based upon the Greek forms. The Celtic and Greek, similar at the root, again came together. Customs and ceremonies survived—but they were not to be called Druidic.

In one remarkable instance, however, a god-cult survived in wholly

[1] See 'YBrython' of 1860, p. 222.

Romanized form. It is known that in Londinium a Roman temple of Diana surmounted Lud Hill. A church, then a cathedral, topped the hill, but Diana's cult continued: a ceremonial blessing of her hunt and the acceptance of a sacrifice continued at Old St Paul's until 1557.[2] The canons of the cathedral assembled twice a year wearing garlands of flowers; a buck or doe was received and killed on the steps of the high altar. The offering purported to be a token rental for certain lands belonging to the Chapter. The line of development is clear. The pre-Roman circle had been, as is common with hills, a temple of Lugh or Lugaidh the god of Light. Now Lugh or Lud had far-shooting rays . . .

But let us now look at some evidence outside the British Isles. It is on the other side of the Channel that Druidry solidifies with evidential remains, and it is perhaps to France that one looks for this post-Roman evidence.

The Romans themselves reasonably substituted a suitable surrogate for the deity of the stone circle on the hill. Apart from Diana, another figure often so substituted was Mercury the Messenger—as in Paris.

In France there is clear evidence that Druidry survived the Romans and had a revival. At Poitiers is a baptizing church built on a Celtic temple foundation, but this is over a Roman temple. This triple series shows that the Druidic-Celtic faith was flourishing in the first and third centuries AD. Only afterwards comes Christianity.

This Baptistry of St John of Poitiers is distinctly not Christian, hence it must be a Druidic initiatory baptistry. A number of these initiation places, for instance at Veselet (Yonne) and Nages (Gard), have been discovered. These are both temples over springs, and it is probable that there was a double initiation, one into darkness and air and another into water. Much work on this Celtic-Christian fringe has been done at the University of Rennes, ancient capital of the Breton area. The magazine *Gallia* gives a great deal of information on the excavations and its articles are from cooperative archaeological studies.[3]

Neither burials nor money here found dating from these times show Christian signs. The cross when used is the sun-cross, as thus on money:

Signs used for protection include:

[2] See Camden's *Brittania*.
[3] For much of the following see *Gallia*, Vol 22, 1961, fascicule 1, published by Centre National de la Recherche Scientifique, Paris. Also Paul-Marie Duval, *Paris Antique*, Hermann, Paris, 1972.

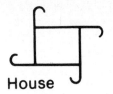
House

Spirit

Guided spirit

Family

Each house seems to have had a sacred hearth. The design for these shows the function clearly. In the tilework at each corner we see the house guarded; between these signs runs each side a pattern similar to the Greek key-pattern—a labyrinth in which the foe loses himself. Within this general protection is another pattern: at each corner are alternately protection for the family and a glyph for the guidance of spirit. Always the whole is surrounded by three enclosing lines.

Upon such a hearth the mystic cauldron boils. The decorations of extant cauldrons say something. Upon one found in the Druidic grotto at Bouchets is a row of knobs under the rim similar to that round the lip of the Glastonbury Bowl. Round the base of another is a series of delicate representations of deer, a very holy creature, the fawn being the symbol of the young learner, candidate for initiation.

It seems the same with the tombs: none bears a Christian symbol, although some may be of Christian date.

In these southern parts of France Islam conquered and tolerated—mingled with—the surviving Celtic Druidic colleges. Charlemagne, again, interfered scarcely at all, Christianity still being very superficial. And so, slowly becoming folklore and customs, the old celebrations went on without any great break.

Here as elsewhere it is difficult to say at what point Druidry ceases to be a philosophic type of religion, when it is a combination with local cult, and when it becomes merely a set of semi-holy old customs. Those carrying them out may or may not reckon themselves Druids in so doing. And so we have to the present day the Festival of St John of Poitiers on St John's Day in June, always linked with rain. There is a robing in the Druidic style and a dramatic performance wherein Caesar is made to take a part—but it starts obviously long before the days of Caesar.

Another festival takes place in north Italy, where in valleys reaching up into the Alps the areas have always been bypassed by invaders. Here we have a regular yearly summer festival, again on St John's Day, in Druid-style robes with circular ritual and words, adapted to the dominant religion by being made into a procession carrying an image of the Blessed Virgin.

Even in the region further west and less protected by special circum-stances, it is clear that the great old gods still continued to be given reverence. Under Notre Dame in Paris was a Druidic circle-temple, not preserved; one is still buried in the foundations of the new London St Paul's (recorded in the memoirs of the son of Sir Christopher Wren). Under the Basilica of the Sacred Heart on Montmartre is quite a collection of

Romano-Druidic exhibits. In Paris were also found statues of Esus emergent from a tree, Teutates the warrior and herald, and Cernunnus, the god of the deer,[4] honoured with torques hung on his horns.

There may also be said to be a Gallic-British spirit-bull trinity (see p. 126). The creative spirit Esus is seen not only as a figure emergent from a tree but as Hu the Origin, and Hu is embodied in the sacred bull forming a triad with Taranus the thunderer (bull-roarer) and Teutates the warrior.

In fact the spirit of life, Hu, linked with the male form Hesus in the form of the oak-tree, with Bel or Beli the sun-disk, and also with the sacred Bull Taruos Trigaranus ('of the Three Cranes') the thunder-god, with his triple stripe, surrounded by three trees and with the cranes of wisdom on his back. They form a unity of idea; the spirit Hu developing into and inspiring the great force of nature, in trees typified by the oak, in man seen emerging from the oak, and in animals shown by the noble bull. The Zeus concept is embodied in the thunder of the bull; the tree-spirit embodies a gentler concept of growth and revelation, Esus is man as adult coming from the tree; but Hu remains as the seed-spirit behind all. One now understands just how easily Druidry fitted into Christianity.

In England one is inclined to think superficially of the Helston Furry Dancers in Cornwall and the Bromley Horned Dancers, and perhaps of Snap the Dragon of Norwich, and to conclude that there remains little else of active myth.

If we direct our attention, however, to the north of England—and English people speaking of England too often mean only the south and the midlands —we find one widespread custom that is highly significant: the New Year first-footing. This extends throughout Scotland as well as northern England. It is the pre-Christian opening of the year; in classical areas Januarius was naturally understood as the gates of the year from *Janua*, a door. The second King of Rome Numa, is said to have instituted the month as the initial one about the year 672 BC. The celebration, really the Solstice, was transferred to the alleged birthday of Jesus, 25 December, then again transferred 11 days by the 1751 calendar revision to 6 January, 'Old Christmas Day'. This battered date was then put back to 1 January and so remains.

The significant thing is that it is a festival of a Dark God. Originally he had a train of riotous followers. He it is who must enter each house, a dark stranger who first sets foot over the threshold in the first hours of the New Year—in some places he must carry a coal to emphasize the blackness. Now the dark or horned figure is always surrogate for a main god of the earlier ideas—Cernunnos, Herne the Hunter, or Old Nick.

If it is still generally observed, how much stronger must the observance have been centuries earlier?

---

[4] Most of the statues, plaques and bas-reliefs mentioned are in the dark-age and middle ages departments of the Musée de Cluny, Paris.

Taruos/Taranos Trigaranus.

A good example of the old New Year spirit, with flames and the first-footing of the stranger, is known from Allendale, just in England but in the border country near Scotland. The fire festival is New Year's Eve. Those who carry out the tar blazing activities are all men. They are in feminine disguises and known locally as 'Guysers'. Beginning with music about 9.30 p.m., towards midnight tar barrels, 'tar borles', are lit, being then called 'tar kits'. They are in fact not barrels but barrels cut down into substantial pans. When loaded with fuel they are very heavy, some 40 lbs. The number varies but lately has increased to 40. With effort they are carried, alight, their dangerous flames licking around, into the village square and to the prepared bonfire which is lit by the flaming and running tar. All are blackened by the smoke.

As soon as midnight comes first-footing begins. The first-footers start now in cars, but their drivers must not be devils—that is, besides not having anything to drink, they must not have meeting eyebrows and not have a squint—sure popular marks of alliance with dark powers. Owing to abuse the custom is not now so general. The idea was that each visitor should be given wine and a light refreshment, but toughs ruined it all. First-footing in this instance seems to have spread from Scotland about the middle of the last century.[5]

For the successor to the Winter Solstice ceremonies rather further southward in England we have to look to Twelfth Night and its Eve, 5–6 January. The Twelve Days of Christmas were from 24 December, the Eve, to 6 January, and the end parts were more distinctly characteristic of the festivals predecessor, the Roman Saturnalia, and of the older wisdom in the Three Wise Men, the Epiphany.

The country areas had something special and seasonal. It was general in Somerset and Devon, and in many other areas, to hold a wassailing for the fruits of the earth, especially for the apple trees and for the oxen. The trees were danced round and libations of drink poured; in Hertfordshire the owner and his party entered the cattle sheds and drank healths to the bulls.

In England a King and Queen of the 'bean' were always elected. Twelfth Night was a popular court and city, as well as a country, festival, at least down to 1689. It was fostered by both Charles I and Charles II. A remnant of the feasting is the Twelfth-Cake.

It was now the Bromley Horned Dance time, when the Horse-Man rode in and made alarming sounds and the dancers wore helmets with huge deer antlers set on them, as they do to the present day; nor is this survivor by any means the only locality in which this was done. So we have the recalling of the Horned God, Cernunnus.

Also the general carnival period began from now until Ash Wednesday —a long time, but in practice it was shorter. In Italy, where they like carnivals, it became the last eight days; in Paris, where life was more serious,

---

[5] Article by Venetia Newall in *Folklore*, Vol 85, Summer 1974.

it was three days. There were races. In Rome horses were raced without riders.

Two other astronomical dates got themselves transferred also. The spring equinox on 21 or 22 March became Lady's Day on 25 March, then, with the calendar alteration, 5 April. Now the equinox had originally been the year's beginning, but the transferred day seems to be without real meaning.

In Scotland, in the wide uplands of the Lowland border country, is found a most living and ceremonious tradition. Peebles, which is in effect capital of the upland centre, is the leader and exemplar of this, together with Melrose. The festival is known rather misleadingly as Beltane, although it takes place at midsummer.

In the week surrounding the Summer Solstice, an inaugural service is held at the old pilgrimage Cross Kirk on the Sunday. On the Solstice itself, at the parish church, the Provost installs the Cornet for the year and his Lass with sashes of office, and the Cornet is given the royal burgh's standard to bear and guard. The Lass 'busses' this. The Cornet is provided with Right and Left-hand men as well. Thus equipped he acts as a kind of mayor for contacts—corresponding to the Druidic office of Maenarch. He pays ceremonial visits to other towns, and his election marks the choice of whoever is deemed to be the worthiest and most presentable citizen. A ceremonial riding follows, a whole troop of riders accompanying the central figures, and there is a proclamation of right-of-way through the main streets. At Neidpath Castle the Warden receives them; they canter up Morning Hill which overlooks all Peebles and beyond, and after surveying the landscape, go down to the Tweed and ford it just above Fotheringham Bridge. The Beltane Bell Races follow on the race track. Afterwards the ride resumes, going back to Peebles, where stirrup cups follow, and the Cornet's Reel is vigorously performed in the streets. By this time it is evening and the day finishes with the presentation of the Beltane Bell, the Callant's Trophy and various cups.

On the following Saturday the week concludes with the coronation of the Beltane Queen by the Crowning Lady, during a well-patronized and historical fancy-dress parade on the steps of the parish church. The Queen and her court are normally Peebles schoolchildren.[6]

Originally—that is, pre-Reformation—the Beltane was on the first Monday or Tuesday of May, the normal time in fact. It was a large pilgrimage which many Scots kings attended, and celebrated the finding of the True Cross by the Empress Helena in Jerusalem. The title of the Cross Kirk might be from this, but in fact a fine cross was discovered locally in 1291 and this was probably linked with the Jerusalem revelation. Another pilgrimage represents the season of Lughnasadh in August and

---

[6] See *Official Guide to Peebles* and *Peebles Beltane Festival Jubilee Book*, Kerr, Peebles, 1949, with lists of holders of offices.

was called Roodmass or the Exaltation of the Cross.

In England the whole celebration of the popular Solstice seems to have passed, as in France, to St John the Baptist's day 24 June, taken as Midsummer Day, the festival of water, of midsummer fire and of flowers. There was a great bonfire on the Eve, then a night of vigil and prophecy. All the watchmen of London, a large assembly, carried flares on poles in the time of Henry VIII. Branches were collected and houses heavily decorated. Also often collected was a strange assembly of special plants; fernseed which gave invisibility and belonged to the fairies; vervain, traditionally the cure and improvement for sight, linked with the Horus-eye of the sun; St John's Wort, a herb of the season which shows red spots on 29 August when St John was executed and keeps off devils and thunderbolts; trefoil, which marks the footsteps of the spring goddess, and rue, herb of exorcizing and disinfecting. At least two of these are used in outer Druidry today. The day itself seems to have had no special celebration beyond being a holiday with branch decoration of houses.

It is impossible not to see in all this celebration, especially in Peebles, the strongest possible indications of the Celto-Druidic ideas and figures. The Triple Goddess is most surely there. In her young sprightly form she is the Lass, mate of the Cornet—and one recalls that although the later Tarot packs of cards show the Chevalier and the Valet, earlier ones had the Chevalier and the Princesse—the older sibylline form of the mother is obviously the Crowning Lady, who stays in the background and weaves spells, and the crowned Queen is the regnant form.

In the minimizing necessary to get by with this in either a Catholic or a Protestant Scotland, the powerful Queen Goddess became a figure in a children's festival—no possible harm in *that*. The young Prince-Ruler, exercising the Queen's powers—the kind of role Arthur had, if legends have some truth—becomes a municipal figure, built up when towns were pushing their powers and leaguing with each other everywhere, usually against the king. One cannot but see a triad in this Cornet and his Right and Left-hands. He ousts the Queen in significance, a patriarchy replacing a matriarchy.

Here then in a kind of living fossil form is the key to a good deal elsewhere fragmentary and enigmatic in the British Isles. Races on tracks belong to the ritual games of Stonehenge and Tara. The riding about probably derives from the beating of the bounds of an area, both to define it and to expel evil. The reel is the active dance of inductive magic bringing power to the crops.

It will be seen that we are dealing with three types of man's economy: the hunting age; the age of tamed animals, flocks and herds; and the age of agriculture. Somewhere in these last two comes the conquest and use of another animal, the horse, with immense consequences to the mobility of the people and to war usages.

Autumn and spring are two further natural astronomical dates, like the longest and shortest days. No one who systematically observes at all can fail to remember these. Yet they make comparatively little ritual impression compared with some other year divisions which are more natural to man's activities, being fixed by the state of the foliage, by his beasts, and by his agriculture. All three have their own rhythms. Moreover, these again vary, adapting to climate under the varying skies of the Mediterranean shore-lands, of the desert areas, and those of central and northern Europe.

The true Bealteinne (pronounced 'beltinner') of May is the maximum time of blossom and its magic, when sheep and cattle naturally drop their young and give milk, and when in mountainous areas it is usually warm enough for them to go up to the lower Alpen pastures. Summer approaches.

Balancing Bealteinne is the approach time of winter, Samhuinn in November, with the sinister threat of the ending of vegetation and the beginning of the long sleep. Man has to use his stores of food.

Between these come two others, also of the very earliest impact. If Samhuinn marks the visible end of the year, Imbolc or Brighid in February was its first stirring of life, when rains washed the land and when man's plough could most usefully till it in many areas. Six months brings the reaping season of August, the time when John Barleycorn meets his death, when man gathered in his crops for all the year, rejoiced, wedded and made sacrifice. All this is in Lughnasadh.

These four dates are the first functional divisions of the year in the times of the Celts and of many other races. The year began in February; probably it had ended much earlier, at Samhuinn in November, the period between the two observances being a no-man's-land of darkness and propitiation to the dark gods. Magical summer began with the blossoms of May and ended with the ritual cuttings, killings and weddings of Lughnasadh.

The Celts may very well have known of the astronomical dates, but they meant little to ordinary life. Considering the amount of hunting and killing that are implied, the hunting ages would appear to be the originating periods, Lughnasadh being the time when most animals were in rut and most dangerous to hunt. It was the age of the grimmer shape of the Mother Goddess.

Taking Bealteinne first, we find it important enough to be anticipated: the Roman Floralia celebration began in April, and in south Lancashire the great day was anticipated by carollers called Mayers. There were two songs, the Old and the New, collected in the eighteenth century and given in Chambers' *Book of Days*, (Chambers, 2 vols, 1881) as follows:

Old May Song

All in this pleasant evening, together-comers we,
For the summer springs so fresh, green, and gay;
We'll tell you of a blossom and buds on every tree,
Drawing near to the merry month of May.

Rise up, the master of this house, put on your chain of gold,
For the Summer springs so fresh, green, and gay;
We hope you're not offended, (with) your house we make so bold,
Drawing near to the merry month of May.

Rise up, the mistress of this house, with gold along your breast.
For the Summer springs so fresh, green, and gay;
And if your body be asleep, we hope your soul's at rest,
Drawing near to the merry month of May.

So now we're going to leave you, in peace and plenty here,
For the Summer springs so fresh, green, and gay;
We shall not sing you May again until another year,
For to draw you these cold winters away.

New May Song

Come listen awhile unto what we shall say
Concerning the season, the month we call May;
For the flowers they are springing and the birds they do sing,
And the baziers are sweet in the morning of May

All creatures are deem'd, in their station below,
Such comforts of love on each other bestow;
Our flocks they're all folded, and young lambs sweetly do play
And the baziers are sweet in the morning of May.

The Old May Song seems to go back to the Gaelic period when gold was plentiful as ornament, and worn as torques which seem indicated. The New seems to give some hint of later date by using a local word *bazier* for the plant auricola which came from Switzerland about 1567. The Latin word means 'little ear'—could not *bazier* be a vernacular for 'base ear', i.e. an ear-shaped flower near the ground?

The word May itself comes, it seems, not from the goddess Maia, but from the Latin *Maiores*, elders or older statesmen in the Roman Senate as distinct from their juniors. It also had the name of *Tri Milchi*, the time of thrice-milking. However, Bealteinne chiefly meant to the neolithics what its name implied, the lighting of fires, mainly upon hilltops as signs of rejoicing. Until very recently, and here and there today also, the festival was so marked generally in Eire, Scotland and the Isle of Man, always upon the Eve, that is the last night of April.

In Britain generally, hawthorn branches and flowers were picked the night before and brought home with the tabor and flute at dawn to decorate all doors and windows. At Hitchin they say a song which was collected in 1823:

Mayer's Verse

Remember us poor Mayers all,
And thus we do begin
To lead our lives in righteousness,
Or else we die in sin

We have been rambling all this night,
And almost all this day,
And now returned back again,
We have brought you a branch of May . . .

In other places, Thaxted for example, the girls waved branches but did not sing a ballad. To quote Chaucer's *The Court of Love*, before dawn 'forth gooth all the Court both grete and lest, to fetch the flowres fresshe.'

Much later Henry VIII with Katherine of Aragon met the holders of the main offices in the city corporations gathering May on Shooter's Hill. Returning, they proceeded to elect the prettiest girl as the May Queen. Let Spenser describe all this:

Siker this morrow, no longer ago,
I saw a shole of shepherds outgo
With singing, and shouting, and jolly cheer;
Before them yode a lusty Tabrere,
That to the many a horn-pipe play'd
Whereto they dancen each one with his maid.
To see these folks make such jouissance,
Made my heart after the pipe to dance.
Then to the greenwood they speeden them all
To fetchen home May with their musical:
And home they bring him in a royal throne
Crowned as king; and his queen attone
Was Lady Flora, on whom did attend
A fair flock of fairies, and a fresh bend
Of lovely nymphs—O that I were there
To helpen the ladies their May-bush to bear!
The Shepherd's Calendar Eclogue 5.

Linked with the central cult of sun and growth is the Maypole. This has a history long indeed, almost as far back, one guesses, as circular dancing itself. In warmer times and areas when a fire was not acceptable as a dance centre, the erection of a pole in lieu of a natural and more awkward tree enabled a special dance to develop at sites considered sacred; for instance above the fertility-inducing Long Man of Cerne—it was his generative organ not his height that was 'long'.

Multiple ropes, later ribbons, were elaborately woven and unwoven by the circular dancers in a continuous hey around the pole, recalling the mazes of earlier man. From other types of Maypole triple circular garlands were hung. Such was the most famous of Maypoles, that re-erected in 1661 after the Restoration by London's citizens who disinterred it from Scotland Yard, whither the Puritans had consigned it; with flags, drums and music it was uplifted by the combined efforts of a posse of sailors sent by the king's brother, the Duke of York, the future James II. It was erected opposite Somerset House at the beginning of Little Drury Lane, and was a cedar tree no less than 134 ft tall.

France celebrated spring with little Olympiads, contests of poets for a golden violet. This, as might be guessed, originated in the south amongst the troubadours of Toulouse, perhaps in 1323 when troubadours were invited to assemble upon May-day. Later 'Les Jeux Floraux' were expressly encouraged by Louis XIV, when in 1664 he appointed 40 members to a 'nouvelle academie' provided to ensure their development. May Queens were now throned in a more stately manner, under Gothic arches, and dressed like little statues.

Part of the celebrations in England related to the chase, and its popular rebel-hero, Robin Hood and his crew, were mimed, together with a dragon and hobby-horse, in a kind of carnival with Morris Men. This account in a novel, *Queen Hoo Hall* by Strutt, gives the general effect well:

Six young men first entered the square, clothed in jerkins of leather, with axes upon their shoulders like woodmen, and their heads bound with large garlands of ivy leaves, intertwined with sprigs of hawthorn. Then followed six young maidens of the village, dressed in blue kirtles, with garlands of primroses on their heads, leading a fine sleek cow decorated with ribbons of various colours interspersed with flowers; and the horns of the animal were tipped with gold. These were succeeded by six foresters equipped in green tunics, with hoods and hosen of the same colour; each of them carried a bugle-horn attached to a baldrick of silk, which he sounded as he passed the barrier. After them came Peter Lanaret, the baron's chief falconer, who personified *Robin Hood*; he was attired in a bright grass-green tunic, fringed with gold; his hood and his hosen were parti-coloured, blue and white; he had a large garland of rosebuds on his head, a bow bent in his hand, a sheaf of arrows at his girdle, and a bugle-horn depending from a baldrick of light blue tarantine, embroidered with silver; he had also a sword and a dagger, the hilts of both being richly embossed with gold. Fabian, a page, as *Little John*, walked at his right hand; and Cecil Cellerman, the butler, as *Will Stukely*, at his left. These, with ten others of the jolly outlaw's attendants who followed, were habited in green garments, bearing their bows bent in their hands, and their arrows in their girdles. Then came two maidens, in orange-coloured kirtles with white courtpies, strewing flowers, followed immediately by the *Maid Marian*, elegantly habited in a watchet-coloured tunic reaching to the ground. She was supported by two bride-maidens, in sky-coloured orchets girt with crimson girdles. After them came four other females in green courtpies, and garlands of violets and cowslips. Then Sampson, the smith, as *Friar Tuck*, carrying a huge quarter-staff on his shoulder; and Morris, the mole-taker, who represented *Much*, the miller's son, having a long pole with an inflated bladder attached to one end. And after them the *May-pole*, drawn by eight fine oxen, decorated with scarfs, ribbons, and flowers of divers colours, and the tips of their horns were embellished with gold. The rear was closed by the hobby-horse and the dragon. When the May-pole was drawn into the square, the foresters sounded their horns, and the populace shouted incessantly. The barriers of the bottom of the enclosure were opened for the villagers to approach and adorn it with ribbons, garlands, and flowers. The *woodmen* and the *milk-maidens* danced around it according to the rustic fashion; the measure was played by Peretto Cheveritte, the baron's chief minstrel, on the *bagpipes* accompanied with the pipe and tabor, performed by one of his associates. When the dance was finished, Gregory the jester, who undertook to play the *hobby-horse*, came forward with his appropriate equipment, and frisking up and down the square without restriction, imitated the galloping, curvetting, ambling, trotting, and other paces of a horse, to the infinite satisfaction of the lower classes of the spectators. He was followed by Peter Parker, the baron's ranger, who personated a *dragon*, hissing, yelling, and shaking his wings with wonderful ingenuity; and to complete the mirth, Morris, in the character of *Much*, having small bells attached to his knees and elbows, capered here and there between the two monsters in the form of a dance; and as often as he came near to the sides of the enclosure, he cast slyly a handful of meal into the faces of the gaping rustics, or rapped them about their heads with the bladder tied at the end of his pole. In the meantime, Sampson, representing Friar Tuck, walked with much gravity around the square, and occasionally let fall his heavy staff upon the toes of such of the crowd as he thought were approaching more forward than they ought to do; and if the sufferers cried out from the sense of pain, he addressed them in a solemn tone of voice, advising them to count their beads, say a paternoster or two, and to beware of purgatory.

Scotland had games in great variety at a number of places, especially Edinburgh:

At the approach of May they [the people] assembled and chose some respectable individuals of their number—very grave and reverend citizens, perhaps—to act the parts of Robin Hood and Little John, of the Lord of Inobedience or the Abbott of Unreason, and 'make sports and jocosities' for them. If the chosen actors felt it inconsistent with their tastes, gravity, or engagements, they could only be excused on paying a fine. On the appointed day, always a Sunday or holiday, the people assembled in their best attire to some neighbouring field, where the fitting preparations had been made. Robin Hood and Little John robbed bishops, fought with pinners, and contended in archery among themselves, as they had done in reality two centuries before. The Abbot of Unreason kicked up his heels and played antics, like a modern pantaloon. Maid Marian also appeared upon the scene, in flower-sprent kirtle, and with bow and arrows in hand, and doubtless slew *hearts* as she had formerly done *harts*. Mingling with the scene were the morris-dancers, with their fantastic dresses and jingling bells. So it was until the Reformation.

Domestic Annals of Scotland, Vol 1, Chap 7.

Samhuinn, as previously remarked, is really the name of a season, not a brief celebration. The dominant power of darkness took over the period when there was no time, when one year or season had finished and the next had not started. In this interim the gates between the worlds were open, the dead and the living could mingle. Feasts for the dead were put out, offerings greater or smaller; the harmful dead were to be bribed off, lest they should injure the living during this their period of rule. The lights, always kept lit, were to keep the darkness at bay.

Samhuinn therefore was the season of the world of the dead. In Scandinavia and in Brittany it links with the death-journey and the ship. The Viking ship burials and burials with treasure, not necessarily Scandinavian, speak of a great stirring of the sea-going imagination. All death was a voyage; all coffins, ships.

In north-western France, Normandy presents it most dramatically in the Pointe du Raz, the grim peninsular with the Baie des Trépasses where the dead are washed in by the currents that race around the rocks towards Sein Island. On certain nights of the year a boatman is mysteriously summoned. At the quay his boat fills with invisible passengers, loading it down to the gunwales, and he is bidden to cast off for the further shore. The boat passes over the drowned city of Ys, whose bells mysteriously ring below. At the landing in England, the invisible but weighty crowd gradually depart, the boat rides high and the boatman returns.

In Britain the spirits then follow their path across the land to the North-west, the direction of death, later known as the Roman Watling Street. Now Wat-Wip was one of the names of the dog of death in Egypt, Anpu or Anubis the embalmer. No one has suggested any other origin for the odd name Watling.[7]

Gradually Samhuinn has shortened from being a whole season to a few weeks, then to a week, now to three days (31 October–2 November), but the influence of the Druid ceremony can still 'take over' a sensitive, so that normality is not wholly returned to the consciousness until the end of the old period.

Hallowe'en is Samhuinn's more usual name in Christian England—the night of all the 'hallows' or saints, when the door to the other world opens. It was often called Nutcrack Night, and in more recent centuries all sorts of light-weight divinations were performed, mostly by girls wanting to see future husbands. Nuts and apples and candles were the main mediators— and one notes that both nuts and apples are of the foods of the other world, those that are kept stored throughout winter and linked with fairies. In Ireland nuts were cast into the fire representing a girl and two lovers. If one jumped he was, or would be, unfaithful; if one blazed he would be enthusiastic; if the girl-nut and the boy-nut burned together, this meant marriage.

---

[7] See Rendel Harris' series of essays *Caravan* and *Sunset*, series 1931, for many fascinating if wrong-headed etymological suggestions.

Apples were bobbed for in tubs, only the mouth being used. A candle and an apple are at the ends of a suspended stick which is then whirled round. Trying to catch the apple in your teeth you are quite likely to have your face spattered with burning wax. Readings of marriage were taken by choosing blindfold one of three bowls; one was of clean and one of dirty water, and one with none. The clean water was a maiden, the soiled water a widow, the empty bowl meant bachelordom. And if you looked into a mirror whilst eating an apple—that magical food—a future husband appeared.

The dead could be more responsibly evoked by various spells. Not all were good, and protection against them for the living was essential; there were garlick and henbane, and the nicer-sounding angelica could be worn, more to attract good protection than to repel evil.

1 November came to be All Hallows or Saints. It emphasizes the complementary pattern of Samhuinn and Bealteinne that in Rome, when the Roman Pantheon became a temple for the Blessed Virgin and all Martyrs, the day chosen for them was at first 1 May, but it was altered to 1 November.

The feast of 2 November is quite different, it is All Souls' Day, for the dead generally, whether particularly holy or not. It was a ninth-century Abbot of Cluny who propaganded for it in France, but the observance did not establish itself until the close of the tenth century. Bells came to be sounded at all street corners to bid the prayers of the faithful. In Italy, with typical literalism, the tombs in Naples were thrown open, the skeleton robed, torches lit and flower decorations set out. Moreover on Hallowe'en in some Italian cities a full feast was laid out in the house for the departed whilst the family went to church. When they returned in the morning all had been consumed. The tale of Bel and the Dragon in the Apocrypha part of the Bible indicates the general nature of the feasting of the dead. In less elaborate form the feeding of the dead was general in northern countries; offerings were set outside the doors or in cup-holes in stones on the moors said to be frequented by folk of the other world. Milk, beer, wine and water were all provided in different places; cakes, bread and salty nuts, apples and other fruit are some of the general eatables supplied.

Thus the original Samhuinn would seem to have been amongst the most primitive ceremonies known, part of the religion of consulting the dead in one way and of aversion in another, to avert malefics.

Soon after the Winter Solstice the nights begin to be perceptibly shorter. By the beginning of February life is a little easier; it is very wet, and seeds will, if planted now, ingeminate quickly. So it was generally taken that Imbolc (2 February) was the time for ploughing; it is the First Furrow in Eire. Similarly it is the time of the Great Mother of fertility, Ceridwen Cariadwen in Wales, the Nurse of Seeds. As an old crone she had guarded them; now they are in the ground she begins to transform into the young form in which she will appear in May. Indeed the very first flowers, the snowdrops, have appeared already, as the edelweiss appear at the edge of the snow in the Alps.

An act of inductive magic was made at this time when many lights were lit to induce the flame of life. Candlemas is the form as taken over and emphasized by Christianity. As we have it now, Imbolc is a day of the Mother, the Purification of the Blessed Virgin, the festive day of Brighid, with water and many lights. Earth is then washed by rains and indeed by February floods; seeds are sown, perhaps mass matings were arranged, as six months later at the complementary season, that of Lughnasadh.

Lughnasadh or Lammas (1 August), the Gwyl (festival) in Wales, or Hlaf Mass, has claims to be the most widespread and popular of all the early festivals. It is largely Scots and Irish in provenance now. This time when the god of light (Lugh, Lugaidh, Lud or Lot) wedded Eire, the fair Earth, summed up the thankfulness and festivity for the grain crop just gathered or about to be gathered, with a fire festival on every hill. The Lughnasadh races and contests were held at Tara and elsewhere; there was a general wedding of lovers; a sacrificing and feasting that went on for days. A most learned book has been devoted to this one festival by a considerable Gaelic scholar: *The Festival of Lugnasa* by S. Maire MacNeill, 1962.

The grain-sowing of February has now had this end product; it is the high tide of vegetation. Fraser brings examples of its being the main sacrifice season, when the old Mother Goddess changed her mate who was honorifically slain, and the new mate taken. Certainly there is evidence of this having happened, but still more of its being evaded and surviving mainly as a horrific tradition. We are excused from believing in it for Britain by the Arthur legend, which runs totally the other way. But in the woods near the gloomy Lake of Nemi outside Rome a priest, perpetually armed, prowled constantly about looking for an attacker who could, on killing him, succeed him in the words of Macaulay's *Lays*:

> the priest who slew the slayer
> and must himself be slain.

This strange local phenomenon was the origin of the vast Fraser work *The Golden Bough*, which is the mistletoe.

The Hlaf Mass name seems to survive from the mass at which a loaf by tradition was offered, symbol of the plenty that was ground from the threshed wheat; and 'Hlafmas' became Lammas. Little remains in Britain of accompanying festivals, but originally there were ritual contests. One such survives in Lothian, where cattle-tending boys, with little else to do, build by groups their 'towers' of sods, and attack each other's fortifications in gangs.

II. The Eight-fold Year

It may be reckoned that these multiple old customs are merely interesting, without definite link with the religious-philosophic ideas of our ancestors.

Yet a little reflection will show them to be very directly related indeed to the actual figures of the French-Gallic, the Irish-Scots Gaelic and the Cymric-Welsh mythologies, as well as to some more distinctly English myths. We have already seen some of them in ancient France. Let us see how those, and others, relate to the seasonal observances, and in fact still constitute a kind of natural and unrealized Druidry that continues.

Winter Solstice (Alban Arthuan)
21 December
Essentially a death-birth—the death of the old sun and temporary victory of the dark, the birth of the child-sun from darkness on the horns of the moon, the seed-period of the life-spirit. Hu as the tiny light-seed or the first ray of Lugh the Light is represented as coming from the horns of Night as mother. We have numerous names for seasonal mother figures—probably Ana is as good as any, without actual hints here from prehistory. All Christmas and New Year celebrations are from these ideas.

Imbolc
2 February
This is the earth, its washing, clearing from debris and soaking with rain, personified as Mata—the first plough is usually a synonym for first intercourse. Dana is the Mother of Men, Brighid is the most practical and one of the most widespread of earth-mother forms.

Spring Equinox (Alban Eiler)
21 March
Astronomical observance—days begins to dominate nights. The growing youth, therefore, of foliage and love is Aenghus mac-in-da-Oc, young love-and-life god of the Boyne, son of the sun's summer disk-god Og. His temple on the Boyne is oriented both to the Winter Solstice and to spring.

Bealteinne
1 May
The magic and blossom of the young May-queen is certainly that of the maiden tricksy form of the mother-goddess, who is Grainne in Ireland (she who tricks Diarmid into taking her off). There are Niwalen and Helen in England, and Olwen in Wales. The Horned God, Cernunnus, is fairly certainly also here, considering that the horn dances are held on this date. He links with Robyn Hode, whose name is phallic—the Robyn was a synonym for the male organ.

Summer Solstice (Alban Heruin)
21 June
The male, or bisexual, powerful mature sun. The sun's orb is Beli, the season and its god are Og; with classical influence he adds the shape of a

Herakles, with 12 labours and a club. Later Og suggests George. Herakles is probably the fertility-giant of Cerne. To this season has also very probably been attributed Teutates the war-and-energy god, the proclaimer and vizier. He can well link with Tehuti or Thoth of Egypt, as the ruler under the sun-god Ra. All this links with Maypole dances everywhere.

Lughnasadh
1 August
The basis is the marriage of Lugh, or Lud, the Light, with Eire, Earth; but also the goddess at maximum, the ripenings and some harvest. Lugh or Lughaidh therefore, and the powerful Brighid form of the Mother Goddess probably are here. If she was to do the masterful mate-sacrifice, it was about now that these weddings attributed to her by Fraser would take place. One suggests it may have been a birth-time as well as a death-time; John Barleycorn may have been partly cut down, but also it is about nine months from the *magnus intercursus* of Samhuinn, when it was not only the dead that had intimate communion with the living. There is some evidence of bull-sacrifice now, and the bull-god, who is Taranus, is likely to belong here. In every field the Corn-Dolly represented the Mother Goddess.

Autumnal Equinox (Alban Elued)
21 September
Now is the main season of gathering the crops, for the general ingatherings of many fruits and for reflections upon life; for the storage of grain and apples and for a plentiful thanksgiving—but also for a realization of dark days ahead. Here is likely to be the Dagda, the wise old man, with the gift of endless food, and undoubtedly the time of the elder sibyl-form of the Mother Goddess, Ceridwen as Nurse of Seeds. The symbolic pair of August are older in September–October.

Samhuinn
31 October–2 November
At first the general date for both consulting and propitiating the dead, then of the opening of the gate of the other world for a long, then a shorter period, and also of the opening of the gates of time. Considering the prophesyings and foretellings involved, one cannot avoid linking this with Ceridwen as Sibyl. But if classical interpretations mean anything, this should be the season of Mercury, the Guide of the Dead, whom the Romans equated with Lugh. And amongst a people whose cult firmly believed in metempsychosis, what else can Lugh be but the vital guide between lives, who not only guided you in the paths and tests following death, but led you back to the land of the living—one hoped into a noble family?

It rather sounds as though early man now semi-hibernated, taking no account of time, sleeping a great part of the days and eating dried foods until the sun reappeared, say in February.

God-Names Grouped

By this analysis, the sun or male god-saviour appears in his usual phases as in other mythologies: the infant Hu as a seed, a little Horus or Christ-infant; the boy-youth Aenghus as Horus on the Mount of the Noon, or Christ in the Temple; the mature young man of power Og, as Herakles, corresponding to Horus revenging Osiris and becoming the first Pharoah, as the classic Herakles fulfilling his labours, Christ fulfilling his teaching and miracle mission; and when rather elder, the wise elder who teaches, the *Dagda Mor* or elder sun-god with the magical harp.

The Mother Goddess is in many shapes: Ana or Dana the earth (Gaelic); Ceridwen Cariadwen ('the dear one'), a general name for the Cymric Great Mother; the tricksy Grainne; Niwelen or Olwen of spring; the strong mother Brighid (Eire) of summer, also the moon-mother; the crone Sibyl and prophetess Ceridwen, the Nurse of Seeds, or autumn-winter; and likewise the Sow, the Old Hen and the Hind, not to mention the Wolf-mother.

These forms in fact comprise some main figures of the Gallic-British and Gaelic pantheons. It is a less definite and more shape-shifting pantheon than the classical and there are literally hundreds of lesser names, mostly synonymous with one another, or shapes of local river-spirits and mountain-godlings. The functions are apt to be mixed, as we saw in looking at some of the French set. Taranus or Taruos, the great bull and bull-god, seems like Jupiter, but has little in common with the classical Father of the Gods except his thunder-bolt and his attribute the oak tree; whilst Lugh is a strange Mercury indeed. Goddesses are an equally mixed set, Brighid especially. She was war goddess of the British north in the days of the Brigantes tribes, patroness of war crafts, yet the typical nurse, e.g. of the infant Jesus, the goddess of the *teinne* (sacred fire), which probably was the little fire of the moon, and finally the spiritual sister of Padraic.

Everything speaks of vividly imaginative but very localized people, who wove deity into their surroundings. Yet certain figures they had in common, and certain ones were understood in a higher sense by their Druid-educated nobles. Lugh, Taranus, Teutates with Dana, Brighid, the Morrigan, these were for the common crowd, but Lugh, likewise, would have been an 'inner god', tor the Druid-Celts were not great cultivators of child-gods—that comes with a later stage of civilization usually—but one, the little Hu the Mighty, carried a name in common with that of spirit in many different lands and ages. He was not always the adult male as shown in Gaul—more often he was the child at the forked branch. He was particularly a Druidic deity, understood by the few, a name to the many. Between and behind the violent shapes of some of the main deities is always the still small voice, the little one who is the greatest, whilst both as Lugh, Light and as Mercury, the guide, he had meanings one feels that varied with education.[1] Dana too seems to reflect a more aristocratic feeling than say Brighid or the Morrigan.

We have, therefore, festivals now being carried on that observe the old Gaelic-Cymric tradition—and one cannot separate the Gaelic-Cymric from the popular, or completely even from the more secret Druidic tradition. Peebles gave us two shapes of the Mother Goddess and one of her regnant son as a triad. First-footing appears to mean Cernunnus the Horned God, the spring's trefoil is the goddess's footsteps, the vervain may be of Horus, hawthorn is a Welsh giant Uspiddaden Penkawr. 'Robyn' Hood is a vivid form of the general Green Man or Horned God. Maypoles are linked with Teutates-Herakles; they stand for fertility, but also they are the apogee of circle dancing; and the very literal communing with the dead in Italy makes Mercury-Lugaidh a living figure. Above all, the canons of old St Paul's gives us Diana-Dana of the chase (for Dana as great mother is always linked with beasts such as deer and hounds), and a prehistory of Lugh who is Lud, with perhaps Grainne also on Ludgate Hill.

The British bull, a *Punch* evocation called John Bull and also the real Dr John Bull who wrote our national anthem, are peculiar links with the bull-deity, that noble beast from Paris. England was earlier known as the Enclosure of the White Bull, and there is one traditional white herd still in Scotland, the Chillingham Herd, with its pedigree reckoned to be of 2,500 years at least.

The hillside horses tell of Epona, the horse goddess or the centaur of the Roman period, in much earlier form. We are in fact surrounded and entangled with Celtic-period and earlier concepts, an unconscious Druidry, perhaps of the more physical cults, less philosophic than today's Druids would easily admit. Of a suppressed cult, the more popular and less enlightened part would go on outwardly; the philosophic—the truly Druidic element—would become a mouth-to-ear tradition here and there.

III. The Druidic Renaissance

Intermittent recognition of Druidry as a possible philosophic system or a local cult seems to have occurred from time to time since AD 1245 and obviously the tradition went on in hereditary groups who kept it to themselves. One of the best traditional evidences, if substantiated, would be that of Kernow, the family we mentioned under Cornwall, which states that it belonged generation after generation, from the year 925, to some group that represented bardic Druidry. The tradition was also confident of itself in Scotland, where some Chiefs kept hereditary Bards; the same had been true in earlier Ireland. Elsewhere, a foretelling, a rune, a scrap of wisdom, would be known in the countryside here and there; there were stones with suggestive names. There was a musical side, and a quality of

[1] See also the youthful god Mabon, Son of Madron in *Mabon and the Mysteries of Britain* by Caitlín Matthews, Arkana, 1987 [Ed.]

prophecy—a mediumship-plus, one might say, that went on in Wales. Old customs such as we have shown in Peebles provided such interest as there was in a Protestantized land.

With the new values of the Renaissance culture—some two centuries late in reaching England at all fully, as these things normally are—the exclusiveness of Christianity began to break down. The wisdom of the past generally, not merely that of the Greeks and Romans, began to be more acceptable. John Dee, a Welshman of some psychic power, but very much lined up with the English establishment under Elizabeth I, must have known something of Druidry; his silence in itself is a kind of evidence of an activity in Wales that was unpopular with London. He knew something of a 'water of life', presumably the Chalice Well, at Glastonbury, otherwise he does not cross our path.

There is a statement (unconfirmed) in one of the chronicles of the time that on a royal progress in Wiltshire contact was made with the 'last Druid of Stonehenge'. If substantiated, this would be of great importance, and show the continuance of some sort of local tradition. It was the kind of thing that would excite the seventeenth century, for it was above all 'curious'; the weird and the odd mixed with real learning in the minds of those not absorbed in the strife of religion that characterized the period.

Amongst the most curious-minded was John Aubrey (1629–97) who did a great deal to stimulate a taste for the past. He went to, and did some work on, the two greatest Druidic monuments; by 1692 he had compiled *Monumentae Germanica*, which included his observations on Stonehenge and Avebury. He knew all about the Mount Haemus Grove of 1245 and the reports of an earlier grove at Oxford, where he lived. He determined to revive Mount Haemus, and a group began to wear the robes and to carry out some of the ceremonies. This would have been in 1694 or soon after. We do not know which ceremonies—probably the equinoxes.

Now the rumbustious young John Toland was in Oxford from about 1694 and was closely in touch with Aubrey. Born in Ireland, he had been educated in Scotland and taken degrees. He detested the dogmatic Christianity of both camps and had made Scotland too hot to hold him. He absorbed Aubrey's Mount Haemus ideas whole-heartedly, especially as he belonged to the Celtic area, knew their languages, and was acquainted with their antiquities. Indeed, it may have been that it was Toland's ideas that stirred Aubrey, already an elderly man, to action—it all happened when Toland was 24 and Aubrey 65, and thus either Aubrey or Toland could have been responsible for this first small revival.

It is the Order's tradition that John Toland was the founder, not so much of this earlier renaissance as of the unity of many groves, which unity is given as having begun in 1717. From this time it is more convenient to tell the story of modern Druidry in terms of events in the lives of the Chosen Chiefs. But first some general remarks seem necessary.

The conditions of secrecy in which most of them wrapped themselves leads to misunderstandings. Sometimes indeed they seem to have deliberately provoked such misunderstandings. The offhand and cross-grained character of John Toland leads a recent writer to scoff at the very idea of his being the Druid founder in modern times, presumably because his writings on Druidry seemed hostile. But this comes from ignorance of the nature of cover-up and camouflage. It is quite easy to imply a total condemnation by criticism or tone, when actually one is writing no such thing. To be the Chief of a secret or almost secret Order, and at the same time to write critically and tersely about it, was just the kind of joke to appeal to Toland's satirical mind. Blake, again a singularly truthful man, saw his created shapes under two guises—each had its Spectre and its Emanation, its dire form and its blessed one. This to him was so elementary a truth that any who did not understand these two aspects of the same figure were not worth explaining things to—in fact, he just would not explain; people had to understand. Acquaintances protested that he had said Druids were bloody sacrificers in one passage, in another that they were the wise philosophers, and that the early patriarchs were all Druids. He replied, in effect, 'Yes, yes—ha-ha, ha-ha.' It never occurred to them it seems that he could be a Druid himself. Yet he had never denied this—because no one had asked him.

In 1803 there occurred an incident when Blake fell foul of a soldier, Trooper Schofield, who plainly did not understand his hyperbolical expressions and apparent approval of the French Revolution, and he was charged with attempting to seduce a member of His Majesty's forces from his duty. Blake took this to heart; it was in fact the only brush with officialdom recorded throughout his life. The trial occurred in January 1804 at Chichester Assizes, and Blake was found not guilty. Called upon to testify, he refused to take the oath, because he was a Druid. Indeed he mentioned that he was a Druid in the preface to one of his books, but it was taken as one of his hyperbolic utterances. None of this proves conclusively that he was Chief, but these facts, combined with his inclusion on the traditional list of Chiefs which gives the dates of their chieftainship, and which has been handed down, argues strongly in favour of the idea that Blake led the Order from 1799 to 1827.

There have been 13 Chosen Chiefs to date.[1] They are chosen for life, with an interesting check system however. On election by the senior grade of the Order, a Chief is known merely as Chief Elect. Within 21 days he must name his Pendragon, and usually also his Scribe; and only upon the appearance of this Triad does he become Chosen Chief. If one of these chooses to voice a public disagreement with him, the Chosen Chief ceases to function and a new election is held. Thus it is a system of despotism tempered by the possibility of group denunciation. It might be recommended to political constitution-makers. So long as the Chief has two substantial fellow-members acting in total accord with him, all is well, but no longer.

[1] 1975 [Ed.]

IV. Three Centuries of Chosen Chiefs

We give here a list of the past Chosen Chiefs of this particular line of succession [Ed]:

John Toland	1717–1722
William Stukeley	1722–1765
Edward Finch Hatton	1765–1771
David Samwell	1771–1799
William Blake	1799–1827
Godfrey Higgins	1827–1833
William Carpenter	1833–1874
Edward Vaughan Keneally	1874–1880
Gerald Massey	1880–1906
John Barry O'Callaghan	1906–1909
George Watson MacGregor-Reid	1909–1946
Robert A.F. MacGregor-Reid	1946–1964
Philip Peter Ross Nichols	1964–1975
John Brant (in custodial capacity)	1975–1988

We begin then with the contentious figure of **John Toland** born 1670 and Chosen Chief 1717–22, or Janus Junius Eoganesius, a Latinization of the peninsular Enis Eogain, where he was born; he was also Britto-Batavus and Patricola, commonly considered the philosopher of materialism. More correctly perhaps he philosophized what would later have been called positivism. He was also reckoned a panthiest, by which was indicated that he saw God in many forms. He was born in Londonderry, educated there, then in Glasgow (1687) and after three years was in Edinburgh (1690–9) obtaining a diploma in the liberal arts. He was in Glasgow in 1688–9 during the violent persecution of the Scottish church. He then had a wandering career, first in England, then in Leyden for two years, then back to Oxford. From London in 1696 he produced *Christianity not Mysterious*. He had been in turn Catholic, Protestant, a Latitudinarian in Holland, a Socinian, and a Deist; then, influenced by Bruno, he settled into what was called Materialism. He expounded the philosophy as 'all is matter' (*materia*) or dynamism, and 'all is motion', each being based on Nature, which had both. Reason he considered to be the true First Law; unlike Locke, he admits no flaw in it, human reason is absolute. (Locke had carefully postulated 'sound' reasoning.) Reason was the ray of divinity in man and also a revolutionary thing. Yet he did believe in two levels of teaching, one for the multitude and a secret one for 'the recesses of the private chamber, to men of consummate probity and prudence', and on this necessity for a double standard he quoted Parmeneides. Freedom was the following of reason, alias the law of nature. The Universe was essentially intellect and motion, intellect being basically material. Matter, however, meant with him also organic matter, and in this he differs from other philosophers;

'seeds' of things are the essentials, whether of ideas or in biology; everything is organic. This is a concept which became basic to the Druid teaching, wherein the seeds of knowledge, essential living concepts that take root in the heart of man, play an important part.

Christianity Not Mysterious brought upon his head the thunders of the orthodox in all quarters. He moved to Ireland in 1697, the year when his book was ordered to be burnt by the common hangman, and he was there coupled in reputation with Locke, both denounced as Socinians. Toland was thoroughly indiscreet, and when religious troubles added themselves he retired abroad. Scotland and Ireland had made themselves impossible, being now filled with Jacobites, and dodging them he came down to London in 1711 and busied himself in getting together groups that could fulfil his ideals. In public he appeared as a scrivener for the Whig interest, which could and did pay him; he published *The State Anatomy of Great Britain* in the same year, 1717, in which he published the prophesies of St Malachy of Armagh about future popes, which have proved so accurate, and which tell also of the end of the papacy. Also, after reconstituting Aubrey's Oxford Grove of Mount Haemus, he quietly founded the modern Druid Order combining groves from some ten centres, some from overseas Celtic lands, into a Mother Grove, *Antich Geata Gairdearchas*.

Soon afterwards he was living at Putney, where he seems to have remained. Three years later he issued the *Pantheisticon*, taken to be raillery, but quite possibly it was a rather fantasticated description of what he knew and had founded already; it is in the form of lessons, responses, a canon of philosophy, and a litany. He describes a 'Natural Religion' in a Socratic society. Select bodies now have the deposit of truth. 'There are,' he says, 'in several places . . . not a few pantheists, who . . . have their private assemblies where they feast together and . . . where they philosophize over it.' They were similar to, but not identical with, the Lodge of Freemasons, also founded about 1717. Toland, as distinct from Voltaire, started a sort of philosophic sect, made a ritual based on metaphysics, and closed it to the greater part of people; in fact he created a mystery.

Such were the beginnings of modern Druidry. Many sects and philosophies also started and were confused with each other about now, and they had members in common. Thus it is impossible to say who was in which, or to reckon it a proof that a man was not in one because he was in another. Toland wrote profusely; in all, he produced over a hundred works. The year 1718 saw *Nazarenus*, and 1720 *Tetradymus*. Other books are *Clydophorus*, *Hypatia* and *Mangoneutes*. Toland emerges as a primitive Christian, disliking all that the churches had added to the teachings of Christ and the Apostles. 'I solemnly profess to your Lordships,' he wrote to the Bishop of London and through him to the rest of the bench of Anglican bishops 'that the religion taught by Jesus Christ and his Apostles, exclusive of either oral tradition or the determinations of synods . . . was no less plain and pure, than useful and instructive; and . . . equally understood by everybody.'

There does not seem to be much left of the philosopher of materialism. In his self-composed epitaph he speaks of his spirit being united to the Heavenly Father, and of his body's rising to Eternal Life—'but will never be the same Toland.'

When exactly his three letters to Lord Molesworth which, together with *Questions and Answers*, constitute his *History of the Druids* were written is unclear; they were first printed in 1726, four years after Toland's death.

In this work Toland gives a very fair survey of the classical accounts of the Druids and Hyperboreans, whose island he takes to be Lewis, in the Hebrides, of which he gives a lyrical account, including a description of Callanish. He gives fully the link with Pythagoras and rightly gives the accounts of the earlier Greeks, especially Pytheas of Marseilles, more credence than the Romans where they contradict. The famous Temple of Wings of Eratosthenes he gives to the island of Skye, whose name means the winged island, *skianach*.

Toland, coming from Londonderry, had a fairly accurate knowledge of things Gaelic and he added to it a knowledge of Welsh; he was very proficient in languages. He describes a large number of Great Britain's monuments. In reading Toland one is struck by the modern and undogmatic approach; his account of the megalithic sites such as Callanish is excellent. When he is not arguing religion, he appears as a genuinely detached observer, not letting his ideas cloud his facts at all. His concept of ancient Druidry agrees with what one may say now—except of course that he had not the archaeology to take it far back.

The Rev. William Stukeley, born 1687, and Chief 1722–65, was a typical eighteenth-century *flaneur* of antiquities, yet much harder-working and more sincere than most. Born in Lincolnshire country (Holbeach), he early drank in a love of the country atmosphere and its ancient monuments. He went to Corpus College, Cambridge, in 1703, and in 1708 took a degree in medical studies. He became one of the erudite anatomist Dr Mead's circle in London. From 1710–17 he lived in the country, partly in Boston, and began his series of rather arduous archaeological journeys summer after summer until about 1725, usually with Thomas and Roger Gale.

In 1717 he became a Fellow of the Royal Society; in the following year he himself founded the present Society of Antiquaries and became its secretary. In 1719 he completed his professional qualifications with a medical degree at Cambridge. Next year he became a Freemason and in 1722 joined the Society of Roman Knights—Lord Winchelsea was Cingetorix and Stukeley Chyndonax, names one recognizes in Druid lists of members.

He was by now a valued member of the erudite upper-class group of his day, which really esteemed learning, even if its standards were erratic; he was, for instance, a friend of the Deist, Isaac Newton. Apparently he quietly took over the probably small Druid organization on Toland's death, in the offhand and secretive way which often characterized the Order. Three years later in 1725 he went on a revealing expedition along the Roman Wall.

A satisfactory income, however, seems to have been lacking, and it was suggested to Stukeley that entry into the Anglican church would provide him with one. He had already left London for Grantham, and married in 1726. He adjusted himself to the idea, and after ordination disappeared in 1730 to the congenial country around All Saints Church, Stamford, as its vicar. Here he did much good parish work and continued his writings and studies. He began identifying the sacred classical figures, such as Bacchus, with Jehovah, *Stonehenge Restored to the British Druids* appeared in 1740, and *Abury* (Avebury) in 1743. But, all in all, he must have missed the intelligent contacts of London, and when eventually he heard that the incumbency of St George's, Queen Square, in Holborn, with a nice vicarage, was vacant, he applied and obtained it through patronage. Here then he lived from 1747, adding a cottage in Kentish Town, some way off, from 1759.

It was probably to this period that his studies in alchemy belong, linked perhaps with the Royal Society. The writer has a copy of a unique alchemic working which by internal evidence seems likely to have been Stukeley's version of alchemy. It is far clearer in language than are most such books, and it is related to ritual as few, if any, other workings are. Whether at this time Druidry had a ritual, or was a learned discussion group with a few customs only, cannot really be known. But there is a basic use of alchemic concepts in the rituals that might well come from this time.

Stukeley was much uplifted when, in 1753, he was summoned to Kew Palace to give his opinion on an antiquarian matter to the Dowager Princess Augusta, mother of George III. Soon she was sharing his enthusiasm for things Druidic and he enrolled her as a patron of his Order; maybe she was even a member. There were a number of visits.

Stukeley died peacefully in 1765. He had twice been happily married, and his life generally one may reckon as having been serene and fruitful. He had demonstrated, in spite of Toland's reputation, that Druidry was quite compatible with Christianity, at least in its more Latitudinarian aspect. His later utterances on archaeological matters had become erratic; his suggestions that Stonehenge might have been built by intelligent elephants was rather typical of other remarks which were will-o'-the-wisps rather than illuminations. He had done fine observational work at Avebury and Stonehenge, and devised a speculative Avebury scheme that makes sense, though doubtful in its development.

He handed on the chieftainship of Druidry, it seems, to the family of his patron, the Earl of Winchelsea, whose brother, the Hon **Edward Finch Hatton,** now headed the Order from 1765 to 1771. Hatton was one of His Majesty's surveyors, which probably meant antiquarian interests. Virtually nothing however seems to be known about him or his influence upon the Order.

We enter public Druidry with the coming of **David Samwell** (1751–99), Chosen Chief 1771–1799. Samwell was a qualified medical naval officer and an explorer; he travelled with Captain Cook on *Resolution* and *Discovery*, and it is he who gives us the narrative of Cook's death at the hands of natives in Hawaii. He was son of a Welsh vicar and was in fact Welsh–English. Himself a minor poet in Welsh, he was a main promoter both of the Welsh Gorsedd in London and of various Eisteddfodau in Wales. He was secretary of the Gwyneddigion Society from 1788 and president in 1797. He spent a good deal of his career in ships, but meetings were held in London at intervals. He did useful editorial work on Huw Morys and Dafydd ap Gwilym.

It was a period of the building up of nationalities, of romantic legends and poetry; of MacPherson's romanticized *Ossian* and of Iolo Morganwg's earlier years. Iolo had begun enthusing Wales with his ideas; modern stone circles should be put up, he said, according to ancient custom, whenever and wherever Eisteddfodau were held. Samwell joined with Iolo in a ceremony upon Primrose Hill, Regent's Park, for the autumnal equinox in 1791, when stones were placed on the hilltop where an offensive sundial now sits. A joint declaration was made on behalf of English and Welsh Druids, that the English language was to be considered of equal authenticity with the ancient Cymric for all bardic and Druidic purposes. This implied brotherliness and the equality of the two Orders. But Iolo apparently could not permanently carry his fellow countrymen with him; old distrusts of the English extended even to its Druids. Violent recriminations followed in a few years' time and the English were humiliated by an unbrotherly denunciation of them by the Welsh on language grounds. The English group was sadly disorganized.

It was during this chieftainship that one Henry Hurle, an artisan of some intelligence, founded the body called the Ancient Order of Druids. Blake seems to have linked with it. [2]

We now come to the great enigmatic figure of **William Blake,** born 1757, recorded as Chosen Chief from 1799 until his death in 1837. He took over the disorganized and discomfited English Druids after the recriminations from Wales thrown at his predecessor, and seems also to have worked with Hurle's Ancient Order. It is obvious that he took certain decisions. Public

[2] Organized in lodges, with an Arch Druid chairing each lodge, the Order was originally formed for the purposes of social improvement. Today their members in Britain total over 3,000 and they engage in numerous fund-raising activities for charities, particularly for the handicapped and for children. Affiliated Orders exist throughout the world. In 1833 a number of lodges broke away from this main body, and remodelled their rules to include in them the payment of sums of money to members who by sickness or accident were unable to work. This movement named itself the United Ancient Order of Druids. In 1878 the group was registered as a Friendly Society, and now has lodges in Europe, Australasia, America and Guyana. While using some ceremonial in its meetings, the United Ancient Order of Druids Friendly Society mainly acts as an insurance concern with an unusual history. [Ed.]

Druidry only led to compromise and confusion; the Welsh were more language nationalists, and not of the philosophy to which Blake enlarged the old Druidry. Therefore Druidry would return to the inner illumination; he would organize it with universal rituals, no longer in those public music contests, the Eisteddfodau.

It is notable that Blake's clearest setting forth of shapes and meanings was engraved in 1796, three years before his assumption of the Chief's office, in the 'Four Zoas', which hold the heart of his mysticism. Until recently it has not been known, except in the Order, that he was its Chief. Even the expert on Blake, Kathleen Raine, did not know. And yet the proof was not far away. It was the year after he took over, in 1800, that Blake at Hayley's instigation went to live at Felpham in Sussex.

With his very positive character one could hardly imagine Blake taking the definite teachings in Druidry for long from anyone else. Moreover, a great deal of his basic quarterings in the 'Four Zoas' are found embedded as basic ideas of the Druidic rituals. Some years ago, before the present writer had gone deeply into this subject, a lady librarian from the Aylesford Brothers community (Carmelites) was asked to give a public talk to the Order on the formidable poem *Jerusalem*, which she had been studying for ten years. From this the shapes emerged as almost precisely those of the concepts used in the Order today. This outside and unbiased evidence added to a strong presumption for Druids that Blake was indeed their Chosen Chief for 28 years, and the probability of this is strengthened by the fact that his house, when he returned to London, was very near the Apple Tree Tavern in Charles Street, Covent Garden, which is where the Order's gatherings had been started by Toland, curiously enough on Blake's birthday, 28 November. It is probable that in Blake's day the Order continued to meet there.

Once the hint is given, it is easy to see Druidic indications throughout Blake's work. From his predecessor, Stukeley, Blake drew his serpent-temple of Avebury in an illustration to *Jerusalem*. The Flea's Ghost told Blake about the transmigration of souls; how blood-thirsty men become 'fleas' like himself. William Owen, the early Socialist, identified Blake with the Bardic system, both being patriarchal.

From this time onward Druidry, so far as England was concerned, whilst duly claiming and fostering the Cymric-Celtic wisdom, had something more; it was a scheme for the world, for mankind. Jerusalem was for all men; archetypal England was universal. It is only Blake's ambivalent treatment of Druidry that has caused scepticism, and with the clearer realization of this as his characteristic mode of writing, we can with a certain amount of confidence put him in his proper place, as a probably very punctilious and careful director of inner ceremonies, parallel with what we know other people were also fashioning about them.

No one, obviously, could truly succeed Blake; nevertheless the next Chosen Chief, **Godfrey Higgins** (Cingetorix) was a learned and original writer, with his own contributory ideas. Born 1773, he was Chief 1827–33. He was a Freemason and a Fellow of the Society of Antiquaries, and specialized in the history of religions. He went deeply into Egyptology as then known. He designed a massive work in three parts, the first being his *Celtic Druids* (1829), followed by the two volumes of his *Anacalypsis* (1836), still very well worth reading. It is 'an attempt to draw aside the veils of the saitic Isis; or an Inquiry into the Origins of Language, Nations and Religions.' He was largely influenced by ideas of phallic worship. A final part of his work was to have dealt with Christianity, but he died before achieving this. He regarded Christ as a Nazarite, belonging to the Pythagorean Essenes; he was a Samaritan and a hermit. The *Anacalypsis* is something of a landmark in the collation of religions, anticipating much future work, although written in a strange style.

William Carpenter, a miscellaneous self-educated writer and journalist, succeeded Higgins; born in 1797, he was Chief 1833–74, over 40 years. He was an ardent crusader for political reform, besides being a writer on esoteric themes. It was he who introduced the Lost Tribes concept: he wrote *The Israelites Found in the Anglo-Saxons* (1872). He went interestingly into numerology and produced *A Critical Study of Ezekiel's Temple.* By this time it appears that public Druid ceremonies were again being held, but we have few details.

During his chieftainship the Order was joined by Edward Bulwer-Lytton (1803–73). Lord Lytton was the popular sensationalist-mystery-monger of the day; perhaps without any profound grasp of occultism, he did however know a great deal in queer directions. *Zanoni* intrigued the Victorians, and dark hints of mysteries were worked into his other books. He was a sound historical novelist as he showed in *The Last Days of Pompeii* and *The Last of the Barons.* Possibly he did know more than appears in his books; at any rate the famous French occultist Eliphas Levi thought it worthwhile to pay Lytton a considerable visit.

Relatives have the peculiar habit of often furiously denying that an eminent man has had any links with organizations they think unrespectable, and so it has been with Bulwer Lytton. We know, however, the title of the grove of which Lytton was chief in this Order; it seems quite clear that he was a Druid, as well as quite certainly a Rosicrucian, but improbably a Freemason.

It was in 1865 that Dr Robert Wentworth Little founded the Societas Rosicruciana, during this chieftainship. Later, in the time of Keneally, he founded in 1874 a Druidic Lodge within the Masonic movement, called the Ancient and Archaeological Order of Druids. To what extent its membership was in common with that of the Societas Rosicruciana is not known. It was members of the latter who later on created the Golden Dawn.

It is true that from a Nuremburg source came or seemed to come initiatory rituals of great power. But it is even more worth noting that they were only the lower grades, and that Nuremburg absolutely refused to hand over those of the Adeptus Grades. It was MacGregor Mathers and Crowley who between them faked up the higher grades. Mathers announced that the Secret Chiefs had given him the Second Order rituals. We only have his word for it—as also for Crowley's later self-promotions. Mathers' experiences of fierce, hot and great power are similar to the descriptions given by Hitler of his awesome adventures. To that extent one bears out the other.

The higher grades of the Golden Dawn are beautifully composed. How 'high' they really are and what relationship that which is printed—without the Order's consent, by one man not in the higher grades himself—bears to the truth as experienced, cannot be known save by the Order's higher personnel.

The Druid Order now fell under the doubtful leadership of an ebullient barrister, **Edward Vaughan Keneally,** who was born in 1819, and was Chief 1874–80. He took silk as QC in 1868, and was on the Oxford circuit. He became leading counsel for the claimant Orton, in the Tichborne baby case, a *cause célèbre* in its day. He conducted this in a violent manner that twice earned the rebuke of the judge. Defeated in court, he by no means gave up the struggle, but was disbarred for his manners in 1874. Still on the Tichborne platform, he had himself elected an MP in 1875, aiming constantly at an inquiry into the case, but never succeeded.

Besides these rather flagrant activities, Keneally was a genuine occultist; he wrote *An Introduction to the Apocalypse* and *The Third Messenger of God*, both still quite readable and suggestive.

Gerald Massey (Chief 1880–1906) was a successor as it were, to the Godfrey Higgins tradition, continuing with most scholarly transcendental studies. A poet and mystic, his books include *The Book of the Beginnings* (1881), *The Seven Souls of Man* and *Man in Search of his Soul* (both 1887), *The Coming Religion* (1889) and perhaps his best-known *Ancient Egypt: the Light of the World* (1907).

In these manifold works, Gerald Massey, who had come up the hard way but had made himself a real scholar of Hebrew, Sanskrit, Greek and things Egyptian, delivered a basic attack on historic Christianity, not as a disbeliever so much as the exponent of the eternal verities of the Mysteries which Christianity caricatured. Above all he held that spiritualism was the root and ground of what we know of another state of being. He traces in detail what can be inferred from comparative studies about the split in the early church between those based, like St Paul, upon direct revelation, and those who faked an unhistoric personality out of Jewish traditions incorporating a distorted past, and then put into the mouth of the Jesus so created the real wisdom of the mystery tradition, mostly from Horus of Egypt. The fanatics who came to believe in a historic Jesus grouped round the Peter tradition in Rome; the Gnostic mystics who knew the truth became heretics. Paul in truth never believed in a historic Christ, only in the mystic Christ revealed to him; his epistles were doctored to conceal this. John stands half way—the mystic who accepts but for whom the vision is basic.

Most of this was compressed into ten lectures given by Massey in 1887, issued in ten pamphlets, now rare. Curiously little is now heard of this most original researcher, perhaps because he was no atheist, rationalist, orthodox Christian, or even a spiritualist of the accepted type. The time must come when the Ninth Chosen Chief's massive scholarship—his very name hardly seems accidental—must be either recognized as valid, or detailedly refuted. Mme Blavatsky treated Massey and Higgins as authoritative scholars in her *Studies in Occultism* (Esoteric Character of the Gospels) and was quite right to do so.

Massey therefore led the Order into the new century with a greatly improved reputation for producing scholarly but unorthodox studies.

Of **John Barry O'Callaghan** (Chief 1906–9) little trace seems to remain. It was an intermediate sort of leadership for only three years. He was in effect deposed and replaced by a more forceful figure.

This was a well-known manufacturer and 'naturopath', **George Watson MacGregor-Reid,** called Ayu Subhadra Savvanus as a Druid, and he was Chief for a long period, 1909–46. Fairly early in life his interest in natural foods led to his manufacture of the powder called Sanatogen, which developed a great sale—one of the few health foods to do so—and it must have made him a considerable little fortune. At any rate it set him free to pursue his mystical and curative interests. From 1907 onward he had edited the *Nature Cure Annual, a Health & Pleasure Guide,* which had articles on treatment and diets and advertised curative establishments, resorts and hotels. A number of his books had a wide vogue in their day: *The Natural Basis of Civilisation, Rational Dietetics, Women's Place & Importance, The Feeding of the Invalid,* and *Educational Aids to the Young.*

At some period in his life, MacGregor-Reid visited Afghanistan and India, evidently for some time, for he received a mystic initiation into Buddhism in the famous Kapila monastery in Northern India—as one might presume from the Druidic name he adopted. It seems that he did not so much become a Buddhist as receive Buddhism into the conflation of faiths characteristic of the Druidic philosophy. Blake had already displayed Hindu and Buddhist concepts. MacGregor-Reid was capable of working all this into a wholly Western form, so that only if one looks for it does one perceive the Buddhism—as well as a generalized Christianity and Islam — in the public rituals of Druidry.

The regular visitations to Stonehenge now began, sometimes with tempestuous incidents; on one occasion, considering that circumstances and behaviour in the *Cor Gaur* were unfitting for a mystical ceremony, MacGregor-Reid led the Order out and held the whole impressive ceremonial in an adjacent field.

He defended Druidry and fought authority in a heroic manner, and brought in substantial allies: Sir Oliver Lodge and Lord and Lady Glenconnar appeared as his supporters, Sir Oliver in fact entering the Order. Reid was a tallish man who could dominate crowds and he used repeatedly to speak on Clapham Common.

A little way from Stonehenge itself, at Normanton Gorse, he found a natural amphitheatre to which he drew the local population of Amesbury, together with his own followers, with the help of a local band and hymn-singing. This became a considerable annual feature of local life. He was apt to be ahead of the crowd, although he was a fine orator. Yet his personality and ideas never seem to have left those who heard him. One of his repeated sayings was 'God is too big and too great for any church.'

MacGregor-Reid's chieftainship was marked by the presence at Stonehenge of a remarkable man. Of the known Druids of locality undoubtedly the greatest was John Soul of Amesbury (1866–1942), the Shepherd of Stonehenge. He lived in Ambrose's town where he had a business and an antique collection. He seemed to know the whole history of the neighbourhood and its land properties in considerable detail. He linked with MacGregor-Reid and was initiated into the Order at Normanton Gorse, together with Walter Rodway, in 1918. He was constantly at Stonehenge, and was a familiar figure in his white shepherd's smock and crook, always ready to expound as much of the truth as he judged his hearers equal to understanding. He was naturally regarded as the monument's guardian; he understood its structures and interpreted its shape with intuitive correctness long before any recent studies. June after June the Druids would meet at his house and thence go out to the Giants' Dance under MacGregor-Reid as Chief, before or after the Dawn Ceremony.

To John Soul as to many others of the deeper philosophic trend, Druidry was as much a private as a public mysticism. Placing a few stones in a formal way, or merely taking the circle shape, they would contemplate regularly. As any trained mystic knows, illumination results when this is correctly practised; and many valid Druidic truths were developed. John Soul wrote an account of Amesbury of the period, and gives valuable information both about the town and the monument. Some of the Order's inner knowledge is derived from him.

At this time there were still only two annual outward events, the autumnal equinox at Primrose Hill, and the Stonehenge summer vigil and sunrise. As though it were something that called to a basic instinct, people increasingly came to Stonehenge; the monument took on life, it began to convey again a deep, if hardly understood, message.

The Second World War was interruptive to these activities. The 1939 observance, led by John Soul, was the last formal one until 1946, although groups always gathered. In 1946 the Druids assembled in robes on the Solstice at noon coming from South Harrow, and performed rites that included a form of communion; they wore oakleaf wreaths, and especially memorized John Soul. The performing body was described in the local newspaper as the Ancient Order of Druid Hermetists from London.

In his later life MacGregor-Reid's universalism took an unfortunate form; he tried to make Druidry into a religion, which in modern times it has never been, and he discovered and adopted a certain Universalist Church, announcing that it and Druidry were in effect united—they were aspects of the same thing. He must have lost some support over this amongst normally religious people who took their Druidry as a quite innocuous philosophic addition to it. The bitterly anti-Church Toland might have been heard turning explosively in his grave—except that he hadn't one, having handed over his body by his will for experiment. The early altar of the Order's inner working was therefore given over to this Universalist body, and it seems that it is now somewhere in America. The writer has seen a photograph of it—it appears to be an early eighteenth century stone piece, with the carved signs of symbols astrological and religious upon it. It might well have been the altar of Stukeley as alchemist, for instance.

Moving firmly still in this peculiar religious direction George Watson MacGregor-Reid died, having indicated his successor as one known as Smith of Clapham. Thereupon the Order split. Those who wanted philosophic Druidry, as it had earlier been, would not follow a leader who identified it with any religion, however universal. After a few months, encouraged by several friends who urged him to help them salvage Druidry from a wrong turning, Macgregor-Reid's son, Robert, allowed himself to be put forward, and a valid separate working was declared; any substantial body of senior Druids has by custom such a right. A large number of his father's followers came with him and helped.

Robert MacGregor-Reid or Ariovistus, Chief 1946–64, had hardly been a favourite of his father, who considered him to lack both philosophic depth and leadership. But what he did have was a considerable spiritual depth and an immense range of contacts. Although less interested earlier, he had developed great insight and had an almost unrivalled knowledge of the ancient high sites and the moorland areas of Britain, knowing Marlborough Downs in particular. He was deeply convinced of the megalithic mystique, and could genuinely convey this.

Earlier in his life Robert had been in touch with the main figures in the esoteric movements which had their beginnings in the 1890s, and he knew several of them well, including McGregor Mathers. He was in the Golden Dawn circle at some time during the 1920s, and knew figures such as Aleister Crowley and Dion Fortune fairly well, but he always kept his own judgment and was never carried away by the movement. At some stage he had received ordination from a Nonconformist source, and although he never took up a cure of souls locally, he did consider that he had a mission to the young, and to all enquirers. Towards the end of his life he would talk for evening after evening to groups of young people in Soho restaurants on metaphysical subjects, and sometimes he drew them into Druidry. For the sake of stability he obtained a Civil Service post between the wars and stayed in it; this interfered little with his chosen Druidic work. He had small organizational capacity; twice at least those working with him in the Order left, exasperated by his lack of system, and new groups formed. Two or three main figures again drew groups round him, however, and the Order did enlarge considerably, though not always in ways he liked.

Robert MacGregor-Reid was a sturdy Scot by build, and in earlier years would tramp immense distances and acquired thus his personal knowledge of a large variety of important prehistoric sites. The last occasion for an extensive expedition in his more frail years was that to the Breton Annual Gorsedd of 1963, when he was taken to visit many of the Breton menhirs and dolmens, the Mother Goddess temple known as the Table des Marchands, and the greatest fallen menhir Er Mane Hroeck or Ergrah. Within a few months he was dead, from a sudden but not unexpected heart attack, leaving a widow and one son.

The range of knowledge of Robert MacGregor-Reid was immense. A special grove had been formed to record the teachings that he gave and the facts he knew, often quite extraordinary; and these records were in fact carefully kept, covering the last three years of his life. In spite of his lack of system, the public ceremonies were, in his time, carried out in better style and with larger numbers.

Indeed considerable developments marked his chieftainship. A part of the organization for some time had been the Presidency, to which distinguished writers sympathetic to the Druid cause were invited. Lewis Spence, the authority on fairy lore and Druidic matters generally in a number of books, became linked to the Order in this way, and Robert's personal contacts led the Order, after Spence's death, to invite the elderly Charles Cammell, an authority on art who had earlier been associated with the Golden Dawn and whose book on Crowley is much better balanced than most others, to associate himself with the Order in this office. Cammell was editor of the *Connoisseur*, being a friend of and personally linked with artists of many types, especially with Salvador Dali and Pietro Annigoni.

Rex Atherton, the reviver of the modern Essene movement, also linked with Druidry to the satisfaction of Robert MacGregor-Reid.

In the 1940s Robert's father had busied himself with international Celto-Druidic links, and this led eventually to the assembling at Stonehenge of a large Druidic congress with representatives from the many countries that had Druidic customs, Celtic-type dances or other qualifications—the concept of 'Druid' being fairly loosely applied. Finland, Italy, Russia and Hungary, for instance, have pockets of Celtic settlements and were drawn in, as well naturally as the Bretons, Cornish and Welsh. It was a much more varied gathering of the Celtic clans on a broad basis than the Celtic congresses held in recent years; some 40 nationalities were present. The after-effect of this was the realizing anew of the Universal Bond concept started so much earlier, represented now by a useful card-index of names from all over Europe.

It was in the 1950s that a remarkable and energetic man associated himself with the English Order, Dr Leigh Vaughan Henry. He had been received into the Welsh organization, since he had Welsh blood, and he was indeed on its directing council. He was also a member of the Cornish Bards, and of the Breton triple Order. Thus it was Pierre Loisel, the Breton chief, already friendly with the English Order, who introduced him. It was suitable to revive for him the office of Maenarch, or 'keystone', a word indicating the Druid who acts as a real link in the 'arch' of the several orders and areas of Druidry. This function he performed until his death in 1963, as far as circumstances allowed. Ceremonial visits to the Breton Gorseddau began, which proved enlightening and fruitful. These take place in August at one or other of the many traditional sites of Brittany, and usually form part of a 'festival folklorique', a gathering of teams of regional dancers and musicians in varied local traditional dress.

The Order owes Dr Leigh Vaughan Henry a considerable debt on this wider 'international' front, not a least part of which was his use of a mysterious fund he administered for cultural purposes to hold a ceremony in Scotland in 1953. He argued that whatever was done in London people took little notice, but go to a distant area where nothing much was happening, and an immense effect is produced. At considerable expense members of the Order were taken up to Oban, thence by ferry to Mull, and conveyed about this quite large island by several motor coaches. In the town hall of Tobermory, Breton musicians played the binou and bagou, and a festal night of Scots-Breton music and dances was held in the presence of the Duke of Argyll. The next day, at a fine stone circle at the southern tip of the island, known as the Ross of Mull, a notable assembly gathered, drawn from a large part of western Scotland. Newspaper reports and photographs were manifold, and it appeared that Druidry, absent since 1717, had made a considerable impact, whilst no theological objections were raised.

About this time another picturesque figure appeared. There are still in Britain a number of independent Druids of locality not necessarily belonging to, or created by, any formal Order. James Duncan was one of these, and used to say that of his personal knowledge he knew of the existence of several hundred more of such 'hereditary' Druids. He fraternized with the Order at Stonehenge, white-bearded and in white robes, carrying always a large crook—a kind of successor to John Soul. It was noteworthy that no official ever dared to demand entrance money from him when the monument came to be girded with wire, which he reckoned —on good grounds—to be of doubtful legality. He had many schemes, one of which was for putting a sensitive electric cell on the Gnomon which would sound off some dulcet note when the sun's rays actually came to it at the solstice sunrise, thus dramatizing it for wireless transmission. He eventually came to attend other ceremonies of the English Order.

It had been evident for some time that the year-scheme of ceremonies was unbalanced. Why had the eighteenth century started up the autumnal equinox and not the vernal one? There seemed to have been no reason. A traditional site of one of the places of free speech in Britain was Tower Hill, or the *Bryn Gwyn*. It seemed suitable, and the Rev. 'Tubby' Clayton, the famous war-time padre and founder of Toc H with its lamps of remembrance, afforded hospitality for changing-room space. Unfortunately the guardians would not let Tower Green itself be used, but a paved site near the Toc H church of All Hallows-by-the-Tower was available, and the observance was revived in 1956. It at once became apparent that the choice was a good one. Crowds were used to gathering to hear speeches a few yards away on the Thames embankment, and they flocked readily to a new diversion which they soon learned to take seriously. On these occasions, as Chosen Chief, Robert MacGregor-Reid had something of his father's oratorical power, with an evident earnestness and a plainness of speech that impressed the crowds.

It is obviously difficult for the writer to assess the features of his own period of office, but it cannot well be omitted. This will be made as factual and objective as possible.

From the first there were difficulties about the choice of successor to Robert MacGregor-Reid. A paper-thin majority decided on a second ballot in favour of the then Pendragon.[3] After a few months a number of senior members of the Order decided against his leadership. Now there was a repetition of the events in 1946; these seniors declared a separate working, held a solemn investiture conducted by the Scribe, and declared the reconstituted Order in public in the autumn of 1964. Whilst in full continuity with the past, the opportunity was taken to shape the Order into three grades. The eighteenth century had a passion for white—it was the era of powdered wigs and ever-so-white classical statues—so that Druids, undifferentiated in spite of the old documents specifying a hierarchy, in white robes based upon the Autun bas-reliefs, seemed a natural conception. By the twentieth century it was realized that Druids, properly speaking, were the third product of separate trainings represented by the bodies of Bards and Ovates. Wales, influenced by the doubtful scholarship of Iolo Morganwg, made the first grade that of the Ovates on the false etymology of *ovum* = egg, whereas the word is from *vates* = a prophet. The English Order started correctly with the Bards, making the Ovates those who had begun the inner studies.

The Order of Bards, Ovates and Druids announced the holding of observances to complete both the astronomical and the Celtic year-cycles. It was obviously unbalanced to hold a Summer and not a Winter Solstice; for the death-and-birth of the year is quite as important as its highest point. Holding that England had quite as good a title to be called a Celtic country as, say, the majority of France, and that Celtic culture was basic, the four

[3] Dr Thomas Maughan, a homoeopath who was responsible, together with a colleague, for initiating the training of lay homoeopaths in England. [Ed.]

Celtic fire ceremonies were reinstituted: Imbolc, Bealteinne, Lughnasadh and Samhuinn. Thus the OBOD now conducts more celebrations than any other part of the Druidic complex. Avoiding deliberate clashes with the rump of the old Order, which continued to meet at Stonehenge, Tower Hill and Primrose Hill, the OBOD sought new sites for celebration.

The former Chosen Chief had been keen on a ceremony at Glastonbury, and after an experimental visit which won local support, the Bealteinne observance was located there upon the Tor;[4] that is upon the eve of May Day with its blossoms and May Queen, or as near to that date as was practical. Lughnasadh, the wheel-ceremony of harvest and the year's decline, was held in a private wood in the Chilterns. The Summer Solstice, which had become increasingly rowdy at Stonehenge, where the Office of Works had begun to keep out the public from the monument which was its proper temple on the Solstice morn, was first held near Northampton, in a magnificent wooded site overlooking the Northampton plain called Hunsbury. This and the two equinoxes, however, were subsequently moved to Parliament Hill, Highgate, where great cooperation was found and where the people of England's capital could easily reach what may well have been their old centre—the proper name of the eminence is the Llandin, which is very near to *Caer Llundain*, the Welsh for London; the very name Parliament Hill means a great assembly-place for discussion, and the area is still one of the unfencible places, like Hyde Park Corner, a place of free speech. The Wessex area was the busy hub of the Bronze and Iron Age rulers; in later centuries the trading port of the Pool of London had the dominance. The Winter Solstice has to be held indoors and a suitable small hall was found in south-west London. The other two more Celtic feasts, those of Imbolc and Samhuinn, which also needed indoor shelter, have been held in a large basement room.[5]

Regular public meetings have been held on matters of general esoteric, occult or archaeological significance, with papers given by many distinguished speakers. Separate groves of instruction and practice for the three grades of the Order are held within it. The custom has been observed, in accordance with the old Welsh direction, that first admissions to the Order should be by way of a public ceremony, as part of one of the eight observances.

The time is probably soon coming for an extension of the ambit of the Order from the intensive basis of research and ideas laid in the last few years to the holding of groves covering a much wider area.[6]

---

[4] Under the Chieftainship of Ross Nichols [Ed.]
[5] This refers to the Barons' Court home of Ross Nichols [Ed.]
[6] For the subsequent history of the Order see Foreword by the present Chosen Chief, Philip Carr-Gomm.

V. Other Groupings

For the last 2,500 years at least, Druidry never seems to have had an authoritative governing body, being typically Celtic in this. And although there are, no doubt, many minority groups of Druids and Bards in various countries, to which we could attend, it is more important now to trace the development of the main movements in Celtic and semi-Celtic countries.

The Bards of Cornwall (Cernow)

Although the Cornish bards purport to have been instituted in 1928, there is evidence suggesting that the Druidry there was very early indeed. If a tradition in the Kernow family is to be trusted, a migration came over from Wales in the tenth century, including the Sept[1] of Kernow, being already expert miners, to settle and to act as a nucleus of loyalty to King Aethelstan, Alfred's grandson, who was engaged in expanding and firming up his boundaries especially in the West, where he fixed the river Tamar as the boundary of the south-west Welsh after defeating Hwl, King of the West Welsh, and his ally Owen of Gwent. It was an era of movements and changing loyalties. Aethelstan considered he had achieved being the Basileus or Emperor (Gk.) of the west, had the imperial peacock fan carried before him and was for a time guardian of the 'Spear of Destiny', said to have been that spear of Longinus, the centurion who pierced the side of Christ on the cross. The spear was later a treasured possession of Charlemagne, and has had an extraordinary history ever since. Large grants of land were made to the Kernow which finally became known as the land of Cernow, Cornwall.

From the ninth century until now it is stated that the family has never lacked a Bard in the Gorsedd. Therefore there must somewhere have been a Gorsedd to link with. However all this must rank as unproved assertions until further research is made. One recalls that from family histories many valuable new aspects of history have in recent years been recovered.

In the nineteenth century a feeling of nationalism or Cornishness began to be cultivated together with societies to foster the ancient language, likely to die out. William Borlase in the eighteenth century had already made the Cornish conscious of their great archaeological heritage but rather in the spirit of his contemporary William Stukeley, that is that almost any ancient remains not obviously Christian were Druidic. A number of English people helped with this, such as the famous vicar of Morwenstow, R.S. Hawker, who wrote the patriotic *And shall Trelawny Die?* But the language did die, and the bardic Cornish had to be revived when in 1928 the Gorsedd Byrth Kernow was inaugurated by Archdruid Pedrog of the Welsh Order with Henry Jenner as Grand Bard, at the Boscawen Un. The most distinguished of the scholars whose efforts had resulted in this revival was Dr Morton Nance. One grade only—that of Bard—was instituted,

---

[1] A division of a tribe. [Ed.]

wearing deep blue robes designed by Sir Hubert Herkomer the academician. Members may be language Bards or non-language, in which case they must have shown appreciation of or done something for the culture of Cornwall. Ritual is based upon the Welsh model. The ceremony is commonly moved annually between east and west, and is normally held in August. The Order is numerous and membership is by initiation based usually on cultural services over many years.

The Welsh Gorseddau of Bards

Many people would think of modern Druids as Welsh, and certainly the movement is strong in Wales, if nationalistic rather than mystical. On the cultural side, Welsh musical contests go back to an unknown date, before that of King Hwl the Good (about AD 950), whose Pencerdd or Chief Poet already had a special chair in the court. Some sort of meeting like an Eisteddfod was held in 1176 in Cardigan Castle, patronized by Lord Rhys, but nothing is later recorded until 1450 at Carmarthen. The next held was in the North, at Caerwys in 1523, and another in 1568, where a committee appointed by Queen Elizabeth examined Bards and granted licenses to wander and earn money by performances. The earlier tradition against written records has prevented our knowing much more until the eighteenth-century almanacs begin to advertise meetings.

With Thomas Jones of Corwen, however, we come to the beginning of the modern Eisteddfodau when he organized a large meeting at Corwen in 1789. A proliferation of Welsh cultural societies followed, and in 1792 Iolo Morganwg (Edward Williams) started the modern Gorsedd, or ceremonial circle ritual. In 1821 the Caernarvon Eisteddfod was a huge affair, much patronized by the nobility and gentry.

Not until 1860 was it decided to hold a national Eisteddfod annually, alternately in north and south Wales. This was rather a different thing, purporting to be Druidic in form and to be national not regional. It was a development from the ideas of Iolo Morganwg on a large scale. Nowadays the National Eisteddfod Court organizes the occasion, while the Gorsedd must be proclaimed, according to the old rule, a year and a day beforehand. It is all very distinctly Welsh and concerned with poetry, prose and musical competition and performance. The robes, a few formalities and prayers are all that really links this organization to anything more than bardism. Inner teachings of any mystic or esoteric type are totally lacking, but this is not to say that they lack elsewhere in Wales. Such an organization is properly bardic but hardly Druidic. However, it is very assured of itself.

Brittany and Cornwall are regarded as having merely 'branch-Gorseddau' not as existing in their own right, through their own traditions and languages, while the French and English Druidic movements are not recognized at all. And yet, when the Gorsedd movement was started under the aegis of Iolo Morganwg, it was proclaimed on Primrose Hill in London, jointly with leading Druids of the day, that English was to be considered a bardic language to rank with the 'Ancient British' for all bardic purposes. By contrast with this, a few years ago an Archdruid was reported as saying that only Welshmen could be Druids, following which a fraternal delegate from Brittany was refused admittance to the National Eisteddfod.

The Welsh mystical-symbolic side is in fact seen only in the ritual. Admission to the three Orders of Ovates, Bards and Druids is by way of examinations or honorary invitations, the Welsh language being compulsory. The Archdruid is elected for three years and has a committee of officers, without whose agreement no decision he makes is confirmed.

The Triple Order of Brittany

Another country where the Druid idea flourishes and where it fosters nationalism is Brittany. It is not always recognized that this area, almost one sixth of France only became part of the French area of direct government with the marriage of Louis XIII to Anne of Brittany its heiress, the great Louis XIV therefore being half-Breton and conceived after a long period of barren marriage following a pilgrimage to St Anne of Auray, Brittany's patron saint.

For centuries Brittany was under independent rulers, for other centuries it was a fief of the British crown, governed by various seigneurs, often royal.

Brittany, old-fashioned and very Catholic, reacted with hostility to the French Revolution and a great slaughter of the Chonans was carried out. At each stage indeed of French history Brittany has been dissident to some extent, including the Second World War, when a considerable element was prepared to deal with Germany, in consideration of Breton independence. The de Gaulle regime was therefore bitterly hostile to the area, which found itself markedly downgraded in administrative ways and, when at the same time one of Brittany's main cities was annexed by decree to France and the vigorous Breton language was forbidden to be taught in schools, unrest broke into defiance for a time.

Brittany has memories of much Druidry and Arthurian legend. The centuries that saw the temporary settlement from Cornwall and Wales left behind some Druidic and bardic practices and a peculiar version of the Merlin tradition. Brittany also had the memories of the famous Druidesses of Seine Island mentioned by classical writers. Myrddin (Merlin) in their version was over-attracted by the sinister arts of Vivienne the witch daughter of a local seigneur. He told her his secrets and falling under his own spell, was imprisoned by her under the Fontaine de Barentin in the enchanted forest of Broceliande for some years . . . One can visit this beautiful old area, a forest still, although diminished, and find the traditional fountain; the route is by way of the Valley of No Return which was where Arthur's sister Morgan le Fay imprisoned unfaithful lovers, and a farm-hamlet called Merlin's Folly.

It was in this area that the Breton Order for some years held its annual Gorsedd, at the village and beside the *étang* of Paimpont, the ceremonial following the Welsh–English pattern.

The Bretons, then, have a strong Druidic and Arthurian tradition from classical and medieval times; but it was only at the beginning of the twentieth century that Druidry became an organized force in Brittany. The Druidic revival in recent times was due mainly to one remarkable man, Taldir Jeffranou, a poet in Breton and a great story-teller.

The Gorsedd Breizh was begun in 1899 and then authorized on behalf of Wales by the Archdruid Hwfo Mon in September 1900. After certain differences, the relationship was confirmed with different wording in September 1971. It was stressed that Wales did not actively govern or administer other Gorseddau, but had a seniority and leadership.

The English Order's links with Brittany began when Dr Leigh Vaughan Henry was Maenarch—a kind of minister of foreign affairs—and member of several Gorseddau including the governing council of Wales. The writer as his successor in that office developed the links further. Several times therefore the Order made robed appearances at Brittany's summer Gorsedd and the English Chief was placed in an honorific position; the Breton chief also paid a few ceremonial visits to Stonehenge. This inter-course has been checked by Wales, which refused further links with Brittany so long as the Gorsedd was on any kind of friendly terms with the English Druids. Such is nationalism in contrast with universalism as a principle.

Gorsedd Breizh has a large membership and stands for a reasonable form of independence movement. Several years ago its council decided to press for a separate governorship for Brittany, rather on the lines of France's colonies in Africa, linked with an elective council. There should be double nationality, Breton and French. These are far more workable ideas than anything the intractable Welsh have ever suggested as an arrangement with England.

The *Drois Meur* is now [1975—Ed.] Pierre Loisel (Eostig Sarzhaw) and the *Drouis an Tribann* is Aldrig Russon.

The Druidry of France

The Order of Bards, Ovates & Druids is glad to have established cordial relations with another non–nationalist Druidic Order of integrity and learning, the French *Collège des Gaules*.

Druidry in France, as we have seen had in earlier centuries, especially in the post–Roman ones, a stronger hold as evidence by the remains than anywhere else. Later France had always been a seed-bed for the growth of mystical movements, orthodox or otherwise, and Druids never seem to have been widely condemned there by Christianity, nor laughed at particularly by later archaeological know-alls.

After the decay of later medieval mysticism a strong occult movement grew in the eighteenth century with Freemasonry, the Martinist cult and other movements—there were some 700 Masonic Lodges, with royal patronage, before 1789. Other developments are linked with the names of

Martinez de Pasquales, Jean-Baptiste Willermoz, and the most spiritual of them, Louis-Claude de St Martin. Two very great and soundly-based occultists dominated the middle nineteenth and early twentieth centuries: Eliphas Levi (Dr Alphonse Louis Constant), 1810–75, whose scientific background gave a modern and convincing turn to his systematic and comprehensive writings on mystical matters in many directions for many years, and Papus (Dr Encausse), 1865–1916, who had immense practice in the world of prognostication, and who fostered and spread Martinism from being a small, very worthy group as left by Louis-Claude de St Martin, into the large movement it is today. It was he, too, who called up the shade of his father to Czar Nicholas II, whence came an exact prophesy of the date of the 1916 revolution and its outcome.

Thus there were strong countervailing influences in Paris to the spate of scepticism that flowed in France as in England at this time, and the re-founding of modern Druidry took place amongst the educated in a far more sympathetic atmosphere than it did in England.

Phileas Lebesque (1869–1958) and Gutuater were the two names most prominent. Very learned in general occultism, Lebesque belonged to the Beauvais–Oise region and, with that feeling for locality so characteristic of the best French minds, continued very largely to work thereabouts. He was a story-teller, a romantic but equally a philosopher and humanist, a master of several languages and a poet. He saw that France, after the abrupt transition of revolution, should link with her earlier traditions and so recondition her awareness to something deeper. With him worked a great orator, poet and musician, Gutuater, an inspired exponent of a faith other than Druidry, and therefore standing for an independent natural religion.

Lebesque felt that the Druidry of old Gaul, when Paris was Lutetia, from which a wealth of remains had been lately found, had much to say to the spiritual basis of modern France. He made contact with Wales. A bronze bust of him, the work of a fellow-Druid Cestalder, is in a public park at Beauvais.

The Druid movement in France is now several hundreds strong, and has its headquarters a little way outside Paris. It has four grades of *Bardes, Ouates, Eubages* and *Druides*. It is under the direction of a distinguished author, Paul Bouchet (Bod Koad), whose *Le Mystère de Perrière-les-Chênes* was widely acclaimed. He is also an inspired astrologer. His Pendragon is Count Paul de Fournier de Brescia (Ker Peoc'h) [1975].

NINE GROUPS OF DRUIDIC CONCEPTS

I. Principles, Circles and Deities analysed

Distinguishing between the Celtic-racial and the bardic-Druidic, the teachings are known most clearly from Wales and France. The air was spirit universal—the medium, with light, of universal creation. The first and basic principle of the substantial creation was water, with its complete purity. When earth was created this caused the water principle to be adulterated. Even so, all issues of water were holy—springs in particular —and so were trees, which were the channels of water and expressed its nature variously. Earth had its own sanctity in life as qualified by water.

That which was of non-living earth substance naturally formed, as in large stones, was a channel for spirit and allied with air, but when tooled or formed into bricks by man it was inferior. Thus God must never be worshipped under roofs, only the sky-vault, and preferably amongst trees. The temples are groves. The air as spirit naturally held men's souls between incarnations.

The two principles of sun and moon operated throughout this framework. The sun was active life and creation; the moon, the instinctive reflection, was therefore the lesser and more feminine thing which partook of the mixed nature of man. Naturally then it was the moon which was the location of ordinary souls between lives; they rested in a state of impercipience. They were first in the earthly clouds of water vapour.

When progressed beyond incarnation, souls then went to the sun, 'an ocean of bliss'. Three times they were there cleansed absolutely before passing on to spheres outside this solar system. Some thought that the meteor was carrying the high soul to a paradise.

The One God was mediated in forms at various levels, mainly triple. The principle which is expressed by Teut or Teutates becomes with the Druids a father universal whence emanates the things of wisdom such as speech, specific wisdom or writing methods—Ogham writing symbols cut upon corners or the Boibel-Lot tree-writing by symbolic leaves. Teut may very well be the Egyptian Tehuti, westernized as Thoth, the Vizier of Ra and Osiris.

Hu the Mighty is in effect difficult to distinguish from Teut and seems to be a different side of the same universalism. He is Esus (an early god in Gaul is Aes), which obviously relates to the Scandinavian Aesir; he is growth, the seed Hé or Hu developing into the great Hu Gadarn, a Herakles who leads the Cymric race; also the tree-spirit in growth. He is very much linked with another Zeus-like figure, the great roarer Taranus the Bull-force. He is likewise the child Gwion developing into the Glorious Brow Taliesin.[1] Hu-Hesus is considered the specifically Druidic form of the deity.

The sun specifically was distinctly Beli, Bel or Belinus, and forms a pair with the Great Mother expressed in the horned moon, for the *Cer* root means horn and her main name is Ceridwen. Beli is naturally the orange disk or ball. There is also the feminine and probably earlier form, Sul or Sult. These popular cults had inner meanings with Druids. Ceridwen is the darkly-smiling mother of the mysteries. Beli has the green form of his complementary colour, which becomes spiritual growth, Sul is a water mother as at Bath.

Teut, Hu and Bel may be reckoned a trinity of shapes of the One; but there is always the fourth, the feminine balance, the all-mother Ana. In the circle she becomes the Unapparent not descended into matter, the dark mystery, in fact the North—or, contrariwise, the unraised *matter* of the alchemists.

But it is a different triad we see as the Druidic glyph fastened and carved upon the tree in Paris. Centrally it has Taranus the Thunder-Bull, the divine strength and the voice of God. Level with the main trunk are the heroic pair either side, Beli or Sul and Aesus—Sun and Life. Over all is the holy sign 'T'. So Teutates is therefore not found in these names—but he may be signified only by the initial 'T'—he whose name may not be uttered, more holy than the others.

Last there is a common pair of lesser deities of Nature who animate the spirits of hills and valleys: Penninus, he of the hills—consider the recurring Pennine and Apennine names of mountainous hills—and Cisa, he or she of the valleys.

Circles

In the open air there is formed the circle. Its ritual officers and position likewise formed anciently a trio and a pair, plus one.

The presider over the ceremonies in the East was Cader Iriatte, the Most Elevated Chair and the Eastern Principle. Opposite was the office of the moon Goronwy, the place of entry. In the South was the flaming energy of the sun Fleidr Flam, the sun at meridian. But the North was the place of the Unmanifest, the mother principle of darkness, the Becoming.

There were two others. The first is the Guardian of the Mysteries called *Swyedydd*, by which title only we know the Chief Druid of Boadicea; he who would give out the records when asked and who might correspond

[1] See pp. 60–2 especially the third stanza.

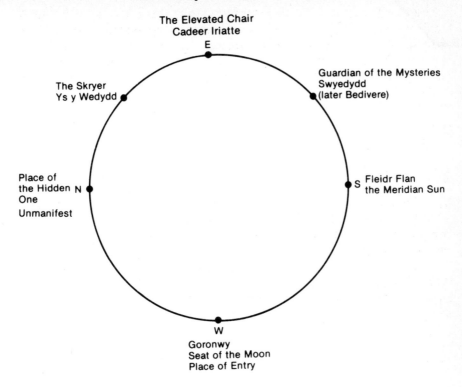

The Elevated Chair
Cadeer Iriatte
E

Guardian of the Mysteries
Swyedydd
(later Bedivere)

The Skryer
Ys y Wedydd

Place of
the Hidden N
One
Unmanifest

S Fleidr Flan
the Meridian Sun

W
Goronwy
Seat of the Moon
Place of Entry

The Ancient Ceremonial Circle.

to the later function of *Bedhwyvar*, who in the Arthurian mystique represents record and witness. The second is the inspired one, the Skryer or
wielder of the Third Eye, called *Ys y wedydd*, the Revealer of Secrets. His
were the inner meanings of what was in nature around them and its
portents.

The dominant pillars of South and North, sun and moon, we can take
back as far as we wish, even to Atlantis as reputed. There the Ruta Temple
was that of the main god who comes to us as Poseidon, life through water
and sun; and opposite to it was Orichalcun, the great white death-shape
or moon. And out there in the mysterious western ocean still rises the shape
of this paradisal land which the Irish call Tir-na-n'Og, the land of eternal
youth, and later times called Hy Brasil. It was seen repeatedly and placed
on maps, expeditions were sent to discover it, but no one ever landed.

Nowadays the circle is rather more detailedly officered. The Chief or
Ancient One is at the East in the *Aberth* or high chair of light; it is the West
not the North that is reserved for guests or special figures like the Mabinog,
and the western officer is merely guarding the stone if used. Each side of
the Ancient are the reflections of the Two Pillars, that is the Pendragon on
his right hand, who wields the disciplinary powers of which the sword is
the symbol; and on his left the Scribe or recorder of doctrines and events.

These two have on the opposite side of the circle their reflections, the Pendragon's in the Swordbearer, who leads processions, guards the circle and admits to it, wielding, that is, the Pendragon's mystic sword; and the Herald who is the announcing voice, the more active form of the Scribe. The axes Pendragon–Swordbearer and Scribe–Herald form the lower or administrative and teaching pillars in the outward showing. At the West is an outer officer, a guest.

Beside the Swordbearer is the Bard, in whose care is the music and who sounds the harp or sings if so requested. This corresponds to the Arts or Venus principle. Here stand any outside musicians or performers invited to come.

At North and South are twin officers bearing emblems of water and fire —moon and sun—respectively, with symbols or actual elements according to the ritual. There are nine officers in the public ritual.

To the further left of the Ancient or Chosen Chief is the representative

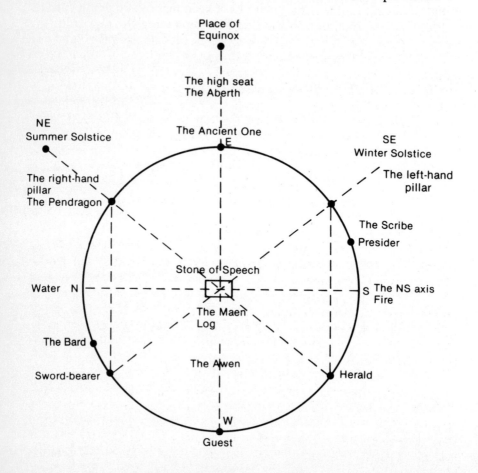

The Modern Ceremonial Circle.

of a function that has been hived off as it were, originally to a local friendly noble: the Presider, who utters the high principles and motives that must guide all. He must not be an actual Druid. He represents the spirit of Locality and the Arts and is usually a distinguished friend of the Order.

At the centre is the place of utterance or inspiration called the Stone of Speech, called in Brittany the *Maen Log*. The Welsh and Bretons make this a stone platform, usually of three slabs. The British Order of Bards, Ovates & Druids has it simply as a moveable stand. Generally, the use of stones, although impressive, limits the mobility of Gorseddau or circle meetings; the modern stones idea was started by Iolo Morganwg and, whilst good to emphasize continuity between past and present and the true nature of that for which stone circles were made, it may now be rather backward-looking when we realize a circle as a structure mentally realized for the operation of psychic faculties.

Playing through the three chiefs on the eastern side are the triple forces of light, which in some stone circles have been marked by pointer stones outside. The centre stone to the due East represents the rays from the equinoxes, the times of balance; the stone to the North-east is the high force of light at the midsummer solstice, that to the South-east is the place of rebirth of the sun in midwinter. The triple rays from these stones play upon the circle's centre. Then they pass over the centre and form the descending form of light, the *Awen*, the Three Rays of Light or Three Pillars of Wisdom, also called in Brittany the *Tribann*, in India the *Tri-Sul*. This is the giving-out form, and their giving-out constitutes evocation, they have been evoked. As the three rays come in on the east side they form the reverse pattern of power descending in concentration; which is invocation, a calling down.

The symbol in the evoking form is the normal Druid sign, although in India and on the scratch drawings of the Wadi Hammamat it is clearly the reverse form; they are merely two aspects.

Placed within a circle the sign shows three aspects of deity—Truth, Beauty and Love—operating within the circle of creation or the world. They are called sometimes the sign of the sacred dove; as the Prince of Wales' Feathers they have been given a false etymology of their motto as *Ich Dien*, I serve, which should of course be the Cymric *Eich Dyn*, man's power, that is the power of God acting in man—a comprehensive term for what the Three Rays of Light should achieve.

The Two Pillars of Pendragon–Swordbearer, representing the basic principle of order and strength, and of the Scribe–Herald, being the opening out of teaching and wisdom, involve naturally the Third Pillar, to Qabalists the Middle Pillar. It will be perceived that it emphasizes the ancient link between western stone—either a ceremonial hand-laying stone or a pillar—and air, the East, the place of the power of the higher mind that echoes constantly through the high tension of most stone. It is dramatized in the centre by the place where inspiration is given out, at the Stone of Speech. This place can in some forms be an actual fire or place of transmutation; it is the centre of the forces working within the circle for its objectives.

The Centre Pillar in fact is the very life and inspiration of the whole.

II. The Celtic and Druidic Principal Deities

The main gods of the Celtic tribes can be taken as a selection from numerous more local ones, of which hundreds of names remain. Moreover they change names and blend with one another in a bewildering way. When identified by the Roman writers as similar to one of the classical pantheon, one is certain that this is only a rough similarity and that other characteristics have been omitted. Moreover there is a different stress upon the varying figures in Gaul from that in England and again from that in Eire.

Let us begin with the pleasantest one: Hu or 'Heu'c', who is also Hu Gadarn and Hesus or Esus. The Heu'c sound seems to identify with the name or sound for spirit, identified with breath, very general and coming from very far in time and space. Hû is the seed, the child, the little one that grows into a giant—and Hu Gadarn is he who leads the Cymric tribes into western Europe in the Iron Age migration. Hesus is the spirit of growth in the tree, he is seen at the first fork between a tree's boughs. Silvanus comes in here as a less definite kind of forest god.

Lugh ('loo') or Lugaidh ('louis'), or Lud of Ludgate, is undoubtedly Light, and the light that guides and shows a way. He probably belonged to hilltops, those guide-places. But there seems to be evidence that he was much more than this. The Roman identification of him with Mercury indicates that he was the god and guide of the dead; and amongst peoples that believed so firmly in metempsychosis, he must also be the guide back into life. One might suggest that the not infrequent three-faced Lugh-Mercury is facing the different worlds. The later Celts anyway had a threefold other-world scheme. From these realms comes his importance and the enormous prevalence of his name everywhere, for he was both a way-shower on this plane and also, more importantly, on the next several planes.

The Horned God is a god of Nature, natural forces, fertility. He shows both as the half-human deity with horns, Cernunnos, between supporting animals, and more powerfully as Taranus the thunder-god, identified with the roaring bull and the power of the heavens. By now we are very near to a classical Zeus-Jupiter figure, for lightning and thunder were the sky-forces of the father of the Gods. Moreover this bull comes to be a beneficent creature of great dignity. A magnificent bas-relief in Paris shows him as though his four legs are stable pillars of the world, with a back as broad as the bull in the Irish epic whose back was the playground for 50 young children. Three cranes of wisdom and record stand on his back and head; three noble trees surround him. Three stripes are down his chest. (See p. 81.)

Teutates is a hero-god with a voice, a warrior. Visions have been seen of him of vast size. But he is not only that; his name may go back to that of Thoth in Egypt and he may well be the executant or vizier of Taranus, if this figure is considered as a Zeus, as was the ibis-headed Thoth for Ra. Hence the cranes—wisdom and writing-birds—around Taranus: 'Ra hath decreed; Thoth has spoken' in the Egyptian phrase.

The specific natural forces have their own representative figures. The Great Og in Ireland is one form, but in that contradictory land the sun also has a mother shape Grainne ('Graun-yer'), feminine of a masculine form Grian that seems of little importance. Possibly Og is the sun-disk—it is also the word for youth and for the summer season, whilst Grian and Grainne were originally the animating pair of principles behind. The figure of Herakles appears to come in fairly often, perhaps a borrowing that had a rather similar hero-god to identify with. The Cerne giant has Herakles' club, but is mainly a fertility figure of a very different kind.

Og has the main love-god for his son, Aenghus mac-in-da-Oc of the Boyne palace 'New Grange' or Cashel Aengus; he is a youth.

An older pre-Celtic sun-god who is also the earth appears to be the Dagda, with one eye, a huge cauldron which can feed armies and a vast spoon in which can lie a man and a woman, presumably to generate. He is the great one, Dagda Mor, and father of the chief goddess Dana. He also has far higher functions as harmony, with the lyre of the seasons.

The main race and country deity in Eire is without doubt the goddess Dana, always supreme. Significantly she is both in Ireland and in Greece. She is easily recognizable as ancestress of both the race of the Greek Danaans and of the Tuatha dé Danann. She seems to remain as the most highly evocative race-figure; but the usual attributes of the Mother Goddess separate into three which for the British Isles are:

Grainne, Olwen, Ellen, Niwalen, etc Forms of the tricksy spirit of the young spring goddess; Eire, Wales and England.

Brighid. Central form of nature and strong woman; deity of crafts, war, nursing and motherhood; the summer of life but also the moon of mystic fertility; Eire and England. (The male forms in Ireland on the crafts side were Diancecht the healer with herbs and Goban or Goibniu the Smith who forged the heroes' armour.)

Ceridwen. The main form in Wales; the autumn crone and sybil, prophetess and 'nurse of seeds'. There are two younger forms of Ceridwen, but they are minor.

On the Continent Epona is a main goddess form—sometimes a centaur, sometimes sitting sideways across a horse rather inelegantly. The horse, when it appeared, must have had an enormous mythical effect as well as a physical one—a means of swifter travel, an agent of conquest, a fulfiller, as it were, of dreams. The flying horse is familiar both in myth and dream-analysis. People took a long time to grow used to the possibilities of horses; as late as the time of Arthur cavalry troops were his surprise weapon against Saxons.

Of these deities, in Gaul Taranus in bull form; Teutates, a kind of Mars, but also a teacher; Cernunnos the tree and animal Nature-god and Lugh in Mercury and other forms, together with Epona, are the chief. And of course Ana or Dana.

One cannot really make a classical-type pattern out of this group, only find misleading parallels here and there. The Celtic deities exist in their own right, as our own consciousness and imagination react to them.

Hu-Hesus or Esus is the distinctly Druid concept amongst them—the little seed that becomes a giant, that is the tiny Maban and also the mighty white bull.

Lughaidh as god of metempsychosis would have a Druidic aspect. The deity of Stonehenge is, probably at least, in general the popular Lugaidh or Light, but in particular Beli or Belin, the actual sun-disk. *Heol* is Breton for sun, and is the obvious correct name in place of the ridiculous 'heel'-stone.

III. The Druidic-Celtic Shape

In the East the Lord Visnu descended into Mauraya as a vision of the holy White Elephant and Gautama Siddharta, called the Enlightened One, was born. In the West wisdom descended much earlier into the lands of the Hyperboreans where the Sun Lord was celebrated constantly with song and dance. At the rebirth of Light two white bulls were sacrificed and a white herd of cattle is here still. One of Britain's earlier names is the Land of the White Bull.

A mysterious age passed. Then was seen in the sacred groves of the Celtic time, upon the tri-formed oak on the middle tree, the name of Taranus, the Bull, who is divine strength in manifestation.[1] On the branch to his right was Beli the sun, external form of Og or the heat of summer, when the sun is highest. On the branch to his left was Esus, the being who inhabits the tree itself. He is to be seen in stone form emerging from a tree and may stand for completed man on the material level.

Above on the middle tree and over the divine Bull the letter 'T' indicated that which was not to be written, the name of the manifestation Teut—Tehuti or Thoth—the cental syllable being *hu* or *hé*, given in classical times as Teutates. He stands with upraised arm conveying the lightning flash of power and life from heaven to earth.

Below at root one can assume was a bowl personified as the All-Mother Ana, feminine form of An, who fosters all that is manifest and whose proper elements are both fire and water—which in later form comprised both water and land in *terra* and perhaps did so earlier.

Unbounded light and air are the two divine elements in which live the spirit of man and the creative forces generally. Light is the more divine and

[1] Bas-relief found near Notre Dame, now in the Cluny Museum, Paris.

the least material, only to be perceived. In more intense form it is the fire that transmutes. Air is an element that can be felt and is a feeder of this visionary life.

Water in pure spring form conveys refreshment and strength that are also divine in a more material way. Trees are the embodiment of these. But water that is imprisoned turns evil, for it has a seed of darkness within it. Thus Ana is both a purity and a darkness.

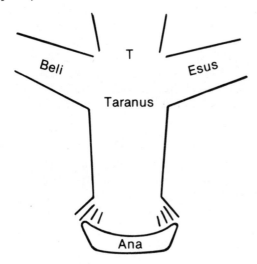

The Holy Druidic Tree.

Earth at its densest in rigid stone carries the tensions of the divine lightning of Teut and his immortal word, and so is akin to and represents air into which the tall stone rises. But earth, either as stone or brick, if handled by man loses divinity and becomes a prison, and common earth is merely dense matter. The slighter the prison between men and the divine light and air the better: for the divine may not be truly reverenced under any cover, only beneath sky near the aspiring trees or tense stones.

Fire, the more vigorous form of light, is sent to purify and change darker earth. It is the great transformer and links with woman who has the pot of fire.

From the trees Teut draws out many beautiful spirits with healing, cathartic and defensive powers, whose chief is Esus. Into the stones Teut writes the records and infuses the messages of the higher worlds.

Air and stone are the first tutelaries of the human spirit which is seeking Spirit. In the shadow between the stones is the first initiation, the baptism of air and darkness. Stone in its hollow bears water, and water at the dawn of new light is lifted in crystal to the ray. In the light-changed water is then the second initiation of baptism.

Thus the principle of fire as light is the completed gift through life-bearing water, for which the preparation was in the darkness given by spirit in stone and air, for instance between the tall stones of the northern cove at Avebury. So out of darkness, summer light comes over the stone of the Heol at dawn, as Beli, and so the midwinter ray reaches the elevated water in the temple of Cashel Aenghus (New Grange), or as in the upheld bowl of African tribes when they have not been unduly 'civilized'. All bowls, circles, horseshoe shapes and water are considered feminine, but a male element may be in them; all fire and light may commonly be male or sometimes female; menhirs are male.

In the sacred stone circle three positions were filled, not four: offices represented the stone of light in the East, the water of growth in the West, the fire of divine life in the South—but the North was the place of the Great Unmanifest, the seed, the hidden growth. So in the mystic Hebrew letters there are *Aleph* the air father, *Mem* the water and *Shin* the fire, only.

One of the five named aspects or figures came to have more prominence than the others. We know that Hu or Hé was the seed and essence, the form of deity that like little Gwion is transformed from least to greatest: Hu, the 'u' pronounced either with a light *i*-sound as *hé*, or *heuc'h*, is the creative word, the seed of fire, the first sound. At first sight he does not appear upon this glyph, until we investigate the mysterious 'T' above and realize that in the older Egyptian form Teutates is Tehuti—more or less, for we do not know the Egyptian vowels—but at any rate there are two 't's and between is an 'h'. Now the syllable *hé*, the sound of breath, Greek **E** is not only that of the later Welsh *Hu* or *Heuc'h* but is known to have the same essential meaning of creative breath or life in many tongues. **E** was over the tall gateway entrance to Apollo's temple at Delphi, signifying divine breath or prophecy. So it is a fair inference that here the *hu* sound from between the two 'T's or trees descends from the high level of the first manifester and unites with Aesus as Hu-Hesus or simply Hesus, in the same manner that the letter *Shin* descending between the four letters of the mystic Tetragrammaton changes YHVH into YEHESHUA (adding the vowels). We have this combination of the seed or word in all things; Hu is with the grown tree-spirit, which also represents man, as seen emerging from the tree. Three such tree-spirits stand around Taruos Trigaranus in Paris.[2]

These were the earlier ideas of the Culdees, seekers whose dwelling was still the Druidic college, re-named as monastery or convent. Twenty-two Druidic centres of learning are recorded as having been in the British Isles, and there would have been at least one college at each, giving sections of the 20 years of complete Druidic studies and also giving teaching generally to the sons of chiefs.

The deity under five or six aspects is shown as originating light, spirit and design at the top of the scheme—that is to the East, if it is conceived on compass lines—while the centre pillar or tree continues down as heavenly strength and energy in matter, shown in oak trunk and bull. Tara,

[2] Stones from the 'sailors' column; Musée de Cluny, Paris.

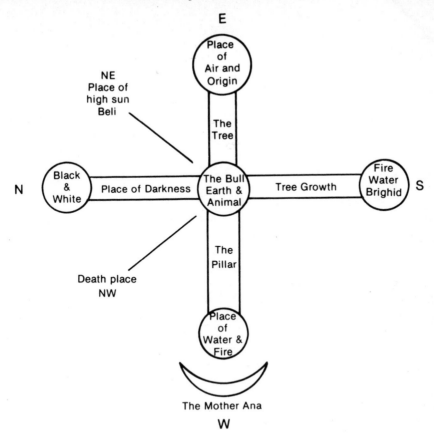

An Oriented Scheme.

Eire's early holy place, is obviously likely to have been dedicated to this bull Taran. The root and base is in Ana, combining the fire of growth and the sustaining life of water. On the left or North-east is Beli the summer sun —in some versions it is Sul, the feminine sun of Bath—but also at the North proper, the lofty root of darkness. On the right or South is vigorous growth or Aesus cherishing Hu the essence. There may also be a feminine firebowl there humanized as Brighid.

There are assumed to be two feminine bowls: one of the moon-water-earth in the West and one a fire cauldron in the South. We know they both exist mythologically; their placing here completes the scheme.

Without any derogation from the One (triune) God Teut and the Creative Seed or Word Hu or Hé, we have therefore a number of change-able forms, recognized as images, which helped the Celts to separate the One Spirit's functions.

These could also be expressed in the pentagram, probably already worked out in a philosophic way in the Near East:

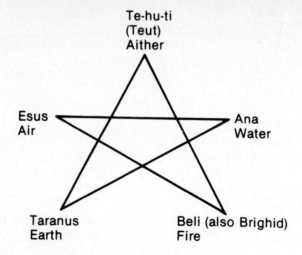

The Druidic System on the Pentagram.

Here the seed Hu is the principle of design in the whole, within *aither* taken as light; the bull is the solid and fruitful earth, the mother is the water bowl. Hu is descending the other way to the sun disk to the fostering fire principle, and goes up to the tree aspiring into space which is air or growth fulfilling the seed Hu. The inspiration of all is still the father-origin Teut, *aither* as light. The seed has come down from between his two trees to Esus —shall we say the paradise Trees of Wisdom and of the Knowledge of Good and Evil? A summary of the names of spirit in two main schemes may help to make things clearer.

The Names of Spirit

1. *Transformation and Continuity of An̥*

Sumer

The trinity of An̥, Enlil, Lord of the wind, and Ana.
An̥ has vanished, leaving this duad as regents.
Enlil develops a power Enem, the 'word' that supports the burden of the world (Tamil *enam* = thought that creates).
Enlil develops seven forms—or eight, with Enlil himself.
An̥ divides into the eight of the Sumerian zodiac, all aspects of himself.
An̥ is seen with three rays of light in the Wadi Hammamat.

Mohenjodaro

An̥ the first of a triad, as Lord, with Anal and Ama the mother. Modern Tamil has Andavar.
Enal and An̥ both have eight forms; there is an eight-fold zodiac, perhaps of 4980 BC.

India
A̦n: god with the 4–3 headpiece-trident.
Hé is Isvara (the Lord).
Siva, the historic counterpart, is an alternative name, and *Vak* = a translation of A̦n and means sky.

Egypt
(1) Ra is Dravidian for 'light'.
Ra's city = Anu; Anur = city of A̦n; Bible translation is On; Green Heliopolis, 'city of the sun'.
Ra's symbol is the obelisk and A̦n had a fluted column.
Ra also has eight forms as a family. He is born from the abyss of Nu (probably 'An' reversed).
(2) Osiris (Greek)—better version 'Ausar'. Egypt invaded by Set who defeats Ausar, and his and Set's followers appear to mingle forming the Egyptian people. The word Ra now appears as general deity. Set rules awhile.
But Ausar's true successor is Heru (Horus) who replaces Set, and the A̦n ideas return.

Hebrew
An appears in some inscriptions as 'El', a basic name of God: both mean simply 'lord'.

Persian
A̦n = basis of name 'Iran'.

Breton and Cymric
Three pillars of light sign = Tri*bann* (Breton) and *awen* (Cymric).
Ana the Great Mother: feminine form of A̦n.

2. The Hé Development

The aspirated *E* sound, shown also as 'u' 'which in North Welsh is sounded as a short *i*: generally connotes fire, light or air as spirit.

Egypt
Hu = the Sphinx' name, as Lord of Two Horizons, i.e. moonrise and sunrise (and settings).
Hru = Heru = Horus, the Hawk of Light.
S-hu = wind and spirit.

Greece
E is the inscription over the gateway at Delphi meaning divine breath or prophecy.

Gaul
Hesus = Esus plus Hé: figure upon the fork of the oak-tree.

Teutates the leader-god is Thoth or Tehuti: the central divine principle is Hu.

In Cymric Hu (pronounced 'heu'c') Gadarn, tiny seed or divine atom, growing into a great one: name of half-divine leader.

In Hebrew: *yod-he-vau-hé* is the Tetragrammaton, the fourfold divine Name.

In Mexico: Oldest divine image in Mexico is *Huehuetcotl*, ancient god of fire, with firebowl on head marked by equal-armed cross.

IV. Nine Arthurs

The Historic Arthur

It was late in the third century AD that western Europe generally became afflicted by the eruption of boatloads of plundering pirates from the Germanic areas. They were known as Saxons, and were led, like the later Danes, mainly by young adventurous princes. They were of a backward civilization, and, although their war-bands did successfully settle eventually, they were in comparatively small numbers. Their crude gods gave us some of the days of our week and eventually contributed somewhat to our language. But at this stage they were merely marauders to be checked. Rome had to set up a special naval chief, the Count of the Saxon Shore, with a navy based in a number of ports, to guard the whole eastern and south-eastern coasts, not always successfully.

After its rather superficial introduction to Christianity, Rome left in AD 407, its legions summoned hurriedly to defend the Rome which, however, fell in 410. They were invited back later by a large section of the new well-Romanized Britons, and there was apparently some help sent; but on the whole the British, both the Romanized and those non-Romanized, were left to face the Saxons alone.

Britain, at any rate the South-west and perhaps the centre, was by now classical to some extent, used to Roman ways and values, partly literate and inclined to be proud of being Roman, for Roman had come to mean British-Roman, the civilized as against the barbarous peoples around. This is where the historic Arthur comes in, with whom the name of the last of the great Romans and imperial relatives here, Ambrosius Aurelianus, is always linked.

In the lands Rome left there was always a yearning back to that firm, rather decorative and cultured rule. Its figures are romanticized. Thus the romanized Artorius (probably the Cymric *Arth* or *Aradr*, 'a bear', or 'strength', Latinized) became symbol for a great legendary realm of peace and spiritual strength, later mingled with the chivalry of subsequent centuries.

Arthur was in effect rehabilitated as history by a remarkable piece of research called *The Battle for Britain in the Fifth Century* by T.D. Reed (1944). He emerges as an energetic general who has the answer to these marauding Saxons. He had not the fleet to fight at sea, no, but he did have a Romanized expertise with cavalry. Moving from area to area faster than foot-soldiers could march, he defeated the Saxons again and again; finally he beat a large combination of them at the battle of *Mons Badonicus*—Mount Badon, possibly Bath—and the land had peace. Whereas the rest of Europe was largely broken up, Britain then had a respite for some 30 years.

To this historic Arthur we owe it that Britain is still largely a Celtic area. It had time to consolidate itself. When, later on, Danish invaders came, they met resistance, they only penetrated a certain way, and the Celtic and the Cymric peoples later mingled with them. The Celtic reconquest was a very real thing, and eventually Alfred stemmed the invasions and Wessex emerged—almost the same western area as the old bronze age Megalithic culture of the early Druids. It is as true that areas shape peoples as that peoples colonize areas.

The Rescuer from Hell

At the centre of the British occult tradition is the figure of Arthur and the hallow called the Graal. They are linked by the Graal ritual; but they are two quite separate concepts and are each on a number of separate planes —as anything at depth is bound to be. The historic Arthur has already been dealt with; but also one can distinguish between eight separate meanings in Arthur and at least five meanings in the Graal.

The earliest and maybe the most basic Arthur is that of a saviour who goes down to harrow hell, to free the prisoners of Annwn. The ninth century poem *Spoils of Annwn (Preiddeu Annwn)*, which follows, is allegedly by Taliesin, but little Gwion interjects bits. Aradr is of course Arthur, Pwyl and Pryderi are lords of the dead in Pembrokeshire.

Prydwen is the glass ship representing trance or vision, in which the seer moves. Gwair is Arthur's page who had rescued him before and whom he must in return rescue. Llaminaweg is the faithful Bedivere (Bedhwyvar). Of the castle (*caer*) names, only the first is an identification—if indeed even that is, for *Caer Wydr*, 'the glass castle', appears to be a pun on Glastonbury, whose blue chain (line 9) is water; the rest are synonymous, some pene-trable—*Caer Sidi* (tower of the *sidhe*, or spirits) is the dark tower of the dead, and the other names characterize it as *Rigor* = royal, *Colur* = gloomy, *Pedryvan* = four-times-revolving, *Vidiwed* = of the perfected ones, *Vandwy* = on high and *Ochren* = of the shelving sides. So that the Dark Tower of the Dead is a royal place, gloomy, containing four-cornered cists, which truly belongs to the perfected ones, for it is on high, and has the shelving sides (of a high place).

And who were the seven who returned from the Castle of Death? There were quite a few in classical legend who ventured down to Hades— Theseus, Herakles and Orpheus come to mind—and of the Celtic-Cymric heroes, Cuchulainn, Amaethon and Gwydion visited the mystic Annwn. Aradr (Arthur) is following precedents.

It has been hazarded that Aradr is only a synonym for Jesus; but it seems more likely that he is a peculiarly illustrious folkhero-ruler. His god may well be a version of Anubis, the god of death.

There is nobility and grandeur in this hero vision of Aradr in his work of rescue.

Preiddeu Annwn
(The spoils or prisoners of Annwn)

Praise to the Supreme Ruler, the Lord
who touches the shores of this world:
To him be the praise.

In Caer Sidi completely confined
lay Gwair ap Geirion, and no other
could enter, for its rulers
were Pwyll and Pryder —
[Pwyll Prince of Dyved, Pryderi his son].[1]
A heavy blue sea-chain
bound the page of Aradr
and he sings eternally
over the spoils of Annwn
a mournful song.

And we entered the glass boat, being three times
the complement Pridwen could carry,
Pridwen the good ship of Aradr.
Save for seven, none returned from Caer Sidi
[the castle of the spirits].

Should not I be heard, I a singer for fame,
four times revolving in Caer Pedryvan
that four-centred castle?
When my song is heard, that is my first word from the Cauldron—

The Cauldron of Annwn
is warmed gently by the breaths of nine damsels;
for is it not the Cauldron of the Chief of Annwn?
On the rim it is fashioned with a ridge that is pearls.
It boils not the food of the coward
nor of those who swear hastily.
A bright flashing sword shall be placed
in the hand of Llemynawg,
[in the hand of Bedhwyvar].
Before the portals of the cold place [the pit]
the horned lamps shall be burning.
And we went with Aradr in his journey,
in his splendid labours:
save for seven, none returned from Caer Vediwid
[which is the Stronghold of the Perfected].

[1] Lines in brackets do not appear in the original mss. [Ed.]

Yet shall I not be heard, I, a singer for fame
in the square-angled enclosure,
in the island of the strong door,
where the twilight is and also the jetblack night
and they move together?
Indeed the armed ones drink wine that was bright:
we were three times the complement for Pridwen.
We went by sea; yet but seven
returned from Caer Rigor
[the stronghold of royal ones].

To those reputed great in literature
I shall not permit praise
for they saw no prowess in Aradr
after he entered Caer Wydr [strong Island of Avalon].
Three times twenty hundred
stood there upon the wall, and hard it was
talking with their sentinel.
Three times the number for Pridwen
we ventured with Aradr.
Save for seven, none returned from Caer Colur
[that gloom-filled enclosure].

I will not allow praise
to the trailers of shields,
for they do not know the day or the hour of birth
of Cwy the splendid one, or who has prevented him
that he went not to the Devwy's meanders.
They do not know that brindled ox
who carries the heavy headband,
who has seven score knobs in the collar of him.
When we went with Aradr of mournful remembrance
save for seven, none returned from Caer Vandwy,
[the castle of high rising].

Men whose courage droops I cannot give praise.
They do not know the day when their chief rose up,
what hour of day the owner was born,
what animal it is they have with a silver head.
When we went with Aradr in his mournful fight
save seven, none returned from Caer Ochren,
[castle of the shelving approach].

The grave of the sanctified one is vanishing
from the foot of the altar
I will pray to the Supreme.

We are here in a world of earth-magic, kindred to the matriarchal fertility
world, belonging, one would guess, to the lower megalithic cultures (not
to its higher mathematical one). To the same world might belong the great

cauldron which is also a pit of the benevolent Dagda, which can feed whole armies—a vision of a benificent earth producing endless food. And this is maybe the first Graal—very earthy indeed.

The Ceremonial Magical

We pass to the ritual form of vision. To this Arthur Myrddin (Merlin) is clearly a great Druid who is instructing a king in the mysteries and involving him in them—the position that the authorities all describe any great Druid as holding. In this legendary form it is brought to life; we seem to experience close-up how the magic worked. Myrddin as hierophant called up the more-than-living world of the brilliant *sidhe*; warriors (later knights), ladies, swords, magic boats, a whole world of convincing phenomena. And we are in a ritual, directed by Myrddin but commanded, on the lower material plane, by Arthur. It is he who announces the quest, organizes the participants; Myrddin is the inspirer behind it, who knows the moves beforehand. In the quadrature of the Danaans the knights work; Peredur (Percival), to the South, has the exuberance and the blunt violent weapon—the spear—of youth. He makes many ventures, he has fiery enthusiasm, he absorbs what lessons are proper to him. He never sees the Graal.

At the West is the aspirant who has mastered all natural magic; he is the Green Man, Tristram or Gawain, who knows all simples and healing perhaps, and is on terms with the world of spirits beneficent or tricksy. He travels in the marshlands, for his is the place of water; he wanders in forests. He goes further than Peredur; but his is the old magic, belonging maybe to the megalithic past—he does not achieve.

The next aspirant is very different. He is the disguised God of Light, Lugh—disguised indeed in the dark north, alien to him but personified in the gallant and glorious person of Launcelot, the peerless knight. By this figure is intended one who is trained in the white magic of a higher tradition, who is in effect a kingly soul. Yet the higher one reaches, the more overwhelming is the temptation. At this level it is hard not to covet the beautiful things and people of this world, beauties that are good in themselves but evils to one bound on a quest or bound by knightly oaths, and Guinevere represents not so much beauty as possession. That we have been in a matriarchal world is clear by Arthur's possession of a kingdom by right of marriage to her—which is the motif in the tales of adventurous fairy princes—the kingdom goes with Guinevere. So high and spotless as Lancelot seems to be, the very perfect knight, he still has this desire for the material that prevents his finding the Graal—he has only one glimpse of it. He is turned aside from the visionary good by average possessiveness.

Then who can make the grade, if the enthusiasm of youth, the persuasions of natural magic or the dazzling equipment of chivalry and its greatest exponent are not fit for it?

The answer is the purity of youth, Lancelot's son, the next generation, one who achieves upon the basis that the last one has built up. Galahad and

Gawain are both Lancelot's sons in this sense. To Galahad the Graal appears almost without seeking. It is something to do also with his being Gwalchaved, the hawk of summer (the Solstice, the vision, the ripened year), rather than his brother Gawain's Gwalchmai, the hawk of May (magical apogee). The great truths of life come so easily:

> He came al so stille
> as his mother was,
> as dew in Aprille
> that falleth on the grass . . .
> Stephen Hawker, *Quest of the Sangraal*, 1864.

The sword given to him supernally—he did not at first have to draw it out of any stone. And there *was* the Graal, a brilliant vision.

The Arthur of this working is a good earthly king, not a supreme mystic, with Bedivere (Bedhwyvar, also Llaminaweg) his trusty recorder and inspired witness. At the circle's centre is the hierophant, Myrddin, his kingly creation, Arthur, with the King of Mortal Castle, Bedhwyvar, the mystic recorder in time.

At the quadratures Peredur is South, Gwalchmai or Gawain West, Lugh

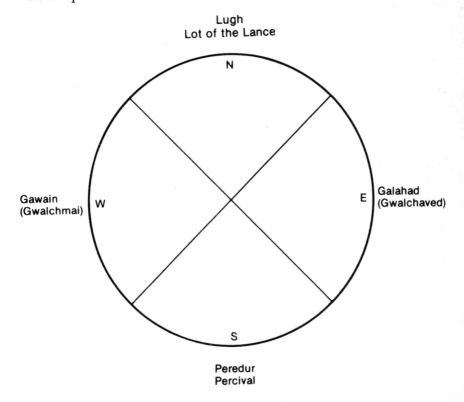

Arthurian Scheme.

or Lot of the Lance, with the representative of *materia*, to the earthy North. But Gwalchaved is at the place of the sun's rising, the golden East.

The Aboriginal Fighter

The vision fades: the vision comes again. On the horizon are the embattled hosts of the heavens, in their four regalia colours; the horses and chariots move over the blue floor of the sky. The battle ranges from peak to peak . . . So it was in Wales, in the mountain range of the Cymru, Eryri Gwyn; and so the poet of Cornwall, Stephen Hawker, has it in his one great poem, which Tennyson acknowledged to be greater than his own Idylls.

> Sirs! we are soldiers of the rock and ring:
> Our Table Round is earth's most honoured stone;
> Thereon two worlds of life and glory blend,
> The boss upon the shield of many a land,
> The midway link with light beyond the stars!
> This is our fount of fame! Let us arise,
> And cleave the earth like rivers; like the streams
> That win from Paradise their immortal name:
> To the four winds of God, casting the lot.
> So shall we share the regions, and unfold
> The shrouded mystery of those fields of air.
>
> Eastward! the source and spring of life and light!
> Thence came, and thither went, the rush of worlds,
> When the great cone of space was sown with stars.
> There rolled the gateway of the double dawn,
> When the mere God shone down, a breathing man.
> There, up from Bethany, the Syrian Twelve
> Watched their dear Master darken into day.
> Thence, too, will gleam the Cross, the arisen wood:
> Ah, shuddering sign, one day, of terrible doom!
> Therefore the Orient is the home of God.
>
> The West! a Galilee: the shore of men;
> The symbol and the scene of populous life:
> Full Japhet journeyed thither, Noe's son,
> The prophecy of increase in his loins.
> Westward Lord Jesus looked His latest love,
> His yearning Cross along the peopled sea,
> The unnumerable nations in His soul.
> Thus came that type and token of our kind,
> The realm and region of the set of sun,
> The wide, wide West; the imaged zone of man.
>
> The North! the lair of demons, where they coil,
> And bound, and glide, and travel to and fro:
> Their gulph, the underworld, this hollow orb,
> Where vaulted columns curve beneath the hills,

And shoulder us on their arches: there they throng;
  The portal of their pit, the polar gate,
Their fiery dungeon mocked with northern snow:
  There, doom and demon haunt a native land,
  Where dreamy thunder mutters in the cloud,
Storm broods, and battle breathes, and baleful fires
Shed a fierce horror o'er the shuddering North.

But thou! O South Wind, breathe thy fragrant sigh!
  We follow on thy perfume, breath of heaven!
  Myriads, in girded albs, for every young,
  Their stately semblance of embodied air,
Troop round the footstool of the Southern Cross,
  That pentacle of stars: the very sign
That led the Wise Men towards the Awful Child,
  Then came and stood to rule the peaceful sea.
  So, too, Lord Jesus from His mighty tomb
  Cast the dear shadow of his red right hand,
To soothe the happy South—the angels' home.

A touch aroused the monarch: and there stood
  He, of the billowy beard and awful eye,
  The ashes of whole ages on his brow—
  Merlin the bard, son of a demon-sire!
High, like Ben Amram at the thirsty rock,
  He raised his prophet staff: that runic rod,
  The stem of Igdrasil—the crutch of Raun—
And wrote strange words along the conscious air.

Forth gleamed the East, and yet it was not day!
  A white and glowing horse outride the dawn;
  A youthful rider ruled the bounding rein,
  And he, in semblance of Sir Galahad shone:
  A vase he hold on high; one molten gem,
  Like massive ruby or the chrysolite:
Thence gushed the light in flakes; and flowing, fell
  As though the pavement of the sky brake up,
  And stars were shed to sojourn on the hills,
From grey Morwenna's stone to Michael's tor,
  Until the rocky land was like a heaven.

  'Ah! haughty England! lady of the wave!
Thus said pale Merlin to the listening King,
  'What is thy glory in the world of stars?
To scorch and slay: to win demoniac fame,
In arts and arms; and then to flash and die!
Thou art the diamond of the demon-crown,
  Smitten by Michael upon Abarim,
  That fell; and glared, an island of the sea.
Ah! native England! wake thine ancient cry;

Ho! for the Sangraal, vanishe'd Vase of Heaven,
That held, like Christ's own heart, an hin of blood!'

He ceased; and all around was dreamy night:
There stood Dundagel, throned: and the great sea
Lay, a strong vassal at his master's gate,
And, like a drunken giant, sobb'd in sleep!

We have touched already on the third Arthurian shape, which is the aboriginal fighter in the mountains, with his ritual brother or twin, a kind of Gog and Magog.

Eryri Gwyn is the whole complex of Snowdonia, the Shining Nest of the Eagles, or simply the High Land. Centrally stands the Great Tomb, *Yr Wyddfa Mawr*: it looks like an uplifted *stupa* in natural form. It is the tomb of Aradr's enemy or tanist brother, the giant Rhita Gawr, slain in the epic fight.

Nearby is the *Carnedd* or grave of Aradr on the dramatic ridge *Bwlch y Saethrow*, Pass of the Arrows, running between Yr Wyddfa and the 'solidified wave' of rock called the *Lliwydd*, also interpreted as the 'wind summit of the breaking wave' by one poet. Also it is the Stained One, for it is rust-red. At this was the last battle, where Aradr was killed. There is, certainly, an old cairn there.

The 'knights' had been driven up Lliwydd; a great cave near the top opened to them. It closed over and there they lie, 'the lads of Snowdon' (*Langcian Eryri*) asleep on their shields awaiting the Call. (They sleep elsewhere as well, in Craig y Ddinas, Glamorgan, and in Caerleon-upon-Usk.)

The mountain lifts up to the heavens the opposed hereditary forces represented by Aradr and Rhita Gawr. Sun and moon, day and night certify and cleanse their forms in the abode of the sun-birds the eagles, who are images of the Second Sight. The fight of the Twelve had ranged all the way up from the Castle of Myrddin, where the seer had invoked this magical strife, up to the Red-stained One. For strength and rulership, Arth the Bear, must die even if well used; but the Twelve Principles are ever ready to come again. Therefore they sleep intact.

The vast view of Wales, with the tiny Glaslyn the blue-green lakelet immediately below, is the backcloth to the cosmic drama of the heights. Glaslyn, looking harmless, was in fact bottomless, and that was the final fate of the monstrous, desolating Avanc, the Giant Beaver, to be tipped into this lake and sink through the world . . . The Avanc seems to represent the power of flood. But still more may it represent a personification of waves of hysteria. (See also page 223.)

Such is the myth-power of Wales that the images take hold on all who come within range. No wonder a chief place of the fairies, here called the *Tylwyth Teg*, is at the foot of an Eryri precipice—although their real headquarters was with the undines in a great pool at Creuwyrion. Great dances were held there, to induce human youth to carry off Tylwyth girls, dowered with magic cattle. But you had to be terribly careful, for if a Tylwyth wife was ever struck with metal she would vanish and might take you with her to a stronghold underground, and then where would you be? It all sounds like a small race carrying on in the midst of a larger, slower-witted people.

Above it all rises the yellowish-white Eryri Gwyn, a huge pyramid to the God of Light. At one side is the cave of the last effective hero of Wales against the English, Owen Glyndwr, the Ogof (cave) in Rhyd Ddu, at the end of the path starting at the Tarn y Dywarchan where, says Gerald of Wales, the land floats: an island nine yards long is unanchored to the bottom, for it has a *Puca Trywn* or fairy on board.

In the crater of Eryri Gwyn under certain conditions can be seen, it is reliably reported, a clear and complete ring of tall stones. It appears to be unnoticed upon maps. Perhaps someone will properly survey this.

From that untraceable cave in the Lliwydd Arthur shall come again: he never dies. Charlemagne and his twelve knights shall rise again and so will he, when this world is worthy of him. 'Is it yet time?' ask the knights as they are seen by local dwellers. And sadly we answer with them, 'No, it is not yet time.'

General Fertility

Arthur, again, is the grain god who dies at harvest; when he is absent the land is barren. He comes over the water, as the grain is floated in Egypt's Nile or Glastonbury's inland sea; he is enthroned by Merlin. His glory passes, he has the grievous wound, but unlike John Barleycorn he is not exactly cut down, only wounded—not slaughtered like Osiris by a tanist brother who is the desert storm, but carried away by four dark queens led by Morgan le Fée over the water, to the far western land whence again he may be ferried.

In detail, Arthur parallels Osiris to such an extent that he comes to seem a version of the Egyptian basic myth, and it is necessary to recall that the outer mysteries of Osiris, Isis and Horus were in fact open to all visitors —there was much travelling in Egypt—during the hundreds, even thousands, of years they were available at Abydos. This cult is only exceeded in age by the cult of Ra at the other end of Egypt.

Arthur's birth is organized by Myrddin when Uter Pendragon cuckolds Gorlios of Cornwall with his wife Igerne.

Geb similarly cuckolds Ra with Nut and thereby produces Osiris whose Egyptian and more correct name is more like Ausor. Osiris, after death at the hand of his brother Set, is ferried across the Nile on the usual funerary barge with his weeping sisters Isis and Naphthys to Aalu in the West, a place of plenty where he awaits glorious resurrection.

Arthur, wounded by his nephew Mordred, is carried off by his sisters headed by Morgan le Fée on a barque to the apple-island of Avallach, in the inland western sea. He awaits the day he is needed.

Osiris penetrates the lower world Amenti in his barque and battles with water demons, while Arthur descends to Annwn in his crystal ship to despoil the magic cauldron.

If we parallel Arthur with Horus, we see that both attract a band of warriors devoted to destroying monsters. Extending our view to the Graal or cauldron as a vessel of plenty, and especially to the Blood Chalice of Glastonbury, in Egypt Osiris as corn-deity is refreshed by the red water of the Nile, Egypt's very life. The mythical Nile arose from two breasts in a cavern; Hapi the Nile god is a male with breasts. The Graal specifically supplied food and prosperity; the Fisher King or Rich Fisher is the name of Arthur in his death-in-life state in Avallon or Avallach.

The sources of many rivers are known as cauldrons. In Caer Pedryvan Arthur discovers a Graal form—according to Sir John Rhys, the original one.[2]

So some main features of the near-universal Osirian mystery came to England, either earlier, from 3000–2500 BC or so in the race's migration, or later by the neo-Platonic philosophic fusions. Considering the total differences in style and feeling, in spite of the resemblances, the earlier time may be far more likely.

The *Sidhe* Vision

In the other dimension Arthur appears with the greater *sidhe* in their mansions in the hills. There he and Guinevere lie, robed and beautiful, still as statues, until those worthy to raise them up shall come. They are the archetypes of Celtdom.

These concepts are much more important in the national psyche than the historic general of the name in the fifth century although as hinted he is indeed important, giving Britain the chance to be a truly half-Celtic kingdom, and not Saxon. But there are yet two other aspects.

The Burying of Arthur

Wales had been conquered to an uncertain degree; Henry II had a vast realm to look after—he and Eleanor of Aquitaine, who presided over the great area of knightly chivalry and romance in the South, between them had a vaster empire than anyone since the Roman Empire. But unity rather lacked. All these troubadours, could not they do something? What about a national epic? That was how the sage Augustus had cemented his empire, by patronizing Virgil into writing an epic all about a very shadowy national founder the Pius Aeneas. The Aeneid had been taught in every Roman school and did the trick . . . What about Arthur? So Chrétien de Troyes (such a suitable sort of name) was found and wrote a good deal of the history of the Holy Grail before he died. But kings cannot command Virgils to appear, and whereas Augustus had one of the world's supreme poets to hand, Chrétien was no great flier. He was an efficient romantic

[2] Rhys, John, *Studies in the Arthurian Legend*, Oxford University Press, 1891.

medieval performer and no more. In due course Henry's empire wilted, largely owing to his obstreperous sons; yet whether any poem, however great, could have held together Angevins with English for long is more than doubtful.

Meanwhile on a more material level a strange thing had occurred. The bodies of Arthur and Guinevere were found, not in wild Wales, but in sober Glastonbury. Henry had been wanting to locate Arthur, to prove that he was really dead and not in cold storage ready to come again, as his Welsh enemies kept saying. It would be a good thing for English morale. And just this happened. A mysterious monk from Wales came and told Henry just where to look; and he found a coffin, and their names, this king's and queen's, were written on a leaden cross a foot long above it, so obligingly. It all sounds too suspicious, although Giraldus Cambrensis saw and believed. Yet it was true, and we can tell this better than the finders. We know that burial in a hollowed-out oak-tree only belongs to the fifth century, or even earlier—already in the Bronze Age in Schleswig-Holstein, says Christopher Hawkes (*Foundations of Europe*). We know that the particular Latin forms in the inscriptions are in keeping also. And a few years ago we had ocular proof to some extent.

Edward I had had the bodies translated to a magnificent shrine before the high altar of Glastonbury Abbey. Came the Reformation, and the peculiar thoroughness of Henry VIII's hostility to the great rebellious abbey led to the scattering of the remains of the legendary pair as much as to the hanging of the last abbott, probably not on the Tor but on Chalice Hill. But we still have William of Malmesbury's account of the finding of Arthur in the time of Henry II; he was buried, he said, 'between two pyramids'. A medieval pyramid was a little buttress with a ridge top. It was so many yards from the first window of St Joseph's Chapel. The famous Spiritualist who had from the dictations of deceased monks foretold exactly where an eastward chapel would be found, Bligh Bond, dug at the spot and found nothing. The Somerset Archaeological Society's excavator Dr Raleigh Radford later had another think; he recalled that chapels often had antechapels which occupied the first window. So he measured out from the second window, dug and found the two 'pyramids', stone sarcophagi with penthouse roofs in medieval terminology, and the writer had the privilege of hearing him expound this on site. We have therefore concrete evidence of the place where Arthur and his queen were laid—the only physical link of any repute with Arthur at all. And it is in Celtic England, not Wales.

Something further might of course be found at Cadbury, which sounds very like Arthur's stronghold. Several seasons of excavation have established probabilities that it was a great chief's fastness of the right period. [3]

---

[3] See Geoffrey Ashe's *Quest for Arthur's Britain*, Paladin, 1971, for a full account of this and many other Arthurian matters.

The Romance Arthur

By this time the wonder-loving medieval world had done its best to restate Arthur in chivalrous terms. A motley assembly of 'knights' was collected round him, some quite authentic-sounding ones with local legends like King Mark of Cornwall or Tristan; the number was uncertain and although the astrological pattern demanded a twelve, it is a most variable roll-call. Tales multiplied. Did the whole thing originate in Brittany, which has the Forest of Broceliande and the fountain of Barentin where Vivienne, the 'lady of the lake', kept Merlin under spells? Yet a good deal seems to be Welsh-English. It was all probably exported to Brittany and elsewhere, enriched and returned again. A round table developed and even material-ized—it can be seen at Gloucester cathedral. The whole affair had been Christianized. Arthur, whom there is good reason to believe was on hostile terms with the Church of his day, became a Victorian idyll of the perfect gentleman or a sort of Catholic defender to some later writers. He was in all probability a tough general and cavalry leader using any means to his defensive ends and treating abbeys and monks with scant respect.

Even less are we now in touch with Arthur the saviour of the glass boat, who still gives a real sense of power.

But let us lift our eyes away from graves and fabulous tables, up to the starry heavens. There are the great symbols which are quite probably the origin of the whole Arthurian idea. And the heavens do not invent spurious legends or change much.

Arthur as Astronomical Principle

The fourth of the traditional astronomical seasons is Alban Arthuan, the light that is in darkness, for Arthur is in the place where the sun never comes, around the pole star. There is the mystic sky area of Arthur, the circle *gorolad*; Arthur means the bear, and he is both the Great and the Little Bears. His kingdom is the sky area of the circum-polar stars; his soul or high self points to the pole star, the axis of man's universe. Fixed as the standard of an unchanging truth, stella polaris' ray is received into the forehead of every man whose concern is with truth. Of this the Great Bear is the appointed guardian and the Little Bear the demonstrator. Changing the figure, Arthur is Aradr, the ploughman of the heavens, when the Bear is called the Plough. He sows the seeds of truth perpetually into dark soil.

A whole northern cosmology is based on these ideas, and this northern Arthur is now reckoned the overriding one. It is certainly the steadiest. Aloft Arthur rides, guiding us, guarding us, perhaps saving us, with the regularity of the ever-turning apogee, the heavens at their highest point for the northern hemisphere.

Yet another, more purely Celtic and imaginative shape also has Arthur. He is Airem, a young sun-god who is also Aran of the Aran Isles, and on 20 December the long night waits for Aran the new young sun. Artor also means the workman, and he may link with Aries the Ram—and thence with the Golden Fleece of the ram-sun. One can also accept that if he is the sun-form then he is the Son of the Dragon, Uther, and of the queen representing Beauty. And when we learn that he has three wives and that Hades takes one, it seems we are back with a yearly vegetation cycle as well as phases of the moon—the vegetation of Persephone, her abduction and her return from the realm of Pluto.

As well as the male and intellectual triad of Aradr, Myrddin and Bedhwyvar there may also be a triad with Morgan la Fée, Aradr's sister, that is, Arthur, Merlin and Morgan.

V. Five Graals

The Graal—Welsh *pair*, Sanskrit *pithara*—as symbol and concept has evolved. No longer the chieftain's large cooking-pot or even the feeding-bowl cauldron of the Dagda, it has become the cauldron of the initiatory Mother Ceridwen, warmed by the breaths of nine maidens:

> The first Word from the Cauldron, when was it spoken?
> By the breath of nine maidens is it gently warmed.
> Is it not the cauldron of the chief of Annwn
> fashioned with a rim of pearls at its lip?
> It will not boil the food of a coward or of one foresworn.[1]
> > *Prieduu Annwn*

The nine maidens at once recall the nine muses — and the nine priestess-Druidesses on Seine Island. So this cauldron makes moral choices and chooses whom it will feed. Note that it poisons all for whom it is not intended, such as certain magnificent horses. It belongs to the lord of the other world. The 'Word from the Cauldron' will be the same as the three drops that fly out from it: the essential names of God. Pearls would not seem a practical adornment for the lip of a food vessel; but the little bronze bowl of about 900 BC, about the time when the great bronze cauldrons were first being made, which was found at Glastonbury, has a pattern of little knobs just under the rim, which might well have had an original in a pearl-studded clay goblet.[2]

Regarding the cauldron as a magical brew-maker it seems likely that what goes into the British cauldron is parallel with what went into the waters of initiation in the mysteries of Ceres, that is, water with a decoction of herbs. Taliesin makes a decoction from laurel (that very ancient magical leaf, chewed for inspiration), ocean foam, cresses, wort and vervain from which moon influence has been kept. Another recipe, from the ancient Welsh poem *The Chair of Taliesin*, seems to be for an initiate's bath. There are normal ingredients such as wheat and honey; mystical ones such as incense, aloes and myrrh; and special but natural plants—'precious silver'

---

[1] See the Thirteen Precious Things, p. 288, two of which refuse their magic to cowards.
[2] See p. 79, where the magical cauldron in Gaul has just such a row of knobs.

is a name for fluxwort and 'ruddy gem' for the hedge-berry called *Borues y Gwion*, while 'Taliesin's Cresses' is *fabaria*. Vervain (verbena) is a specially Druidic plant gathered always at the rising of the Dog-star Sirius.

The cauldron is always that bath in which the neophyte is immersed for which purpose the plant *selago* was infused. In Greece the mixture used was of laurel, salt, barley, sea-water and flower crowns.[3] Once initiated, a more interesting-looking holy drink is quaffed by those qualified: in Britain's Ceridwen mysteries it was of wine, honey, malt and water; in those of Ceres wine, barley, malt and water. They sound like a kind of mead.

The cauldron of wisdom belonged to Ceridwen and in it she brewed life and secret knowledge. She is a hideous hag and dragoons Little Gwion into guarding it for her. It overboils and three drops fall out upon his thumb. Sucking it he learns things; one is that her vengeance will follow and that he had better escape. So begin the transformations of Gwion. (See page 159.)

We are in a strange place with the Graal's next avatar, when it appears briefly at Camelot. Two suns shine through the windows of the hall. A damsel carries in the head of Arthur's son Lohot, killed by Kay, Arthur's seneschal, after Lohot had killed the giant Logrin. Later the Graal became symbol of the mysterious heretical Mass of the Albigenses.

It was Chrétien de Troyes who started seriously on the Graal mythos, this Brythonic Cauldron of Plenty, which is both visionary and elusive, with its quests and strange happenings. It became Christianized apparently in a heretical form favoured by noble patrons and perhaps royalty, for the age was one of popular and sensational unorthodoxies—the heretical Albigensian troubadour culture was in full flower and there were secret practices amongst the Templars; the Provençal Courts of Love were fostered by Queen Eleanor; the picturesque prophecies of Merlin from Geoffrey of Monmouth circulated freely. What seems to be implied is a mysterious Mass other than the normal, the Mass of the Mother of God. The Christianized Graal was a cult of the Chosen Vessel, i.e. the sanctified womb of the Blessed Virgin being symbolized by and almost identified with a sanctified cauldron.

Did this link at all with the earlier highly ritual cauldron of Druidry in France? (See page 79.)

The twelfth century poets played endlessly upon a fortunate philological pun, in that the Welsh *pair*, cauldron, can change by the rules of Welsh pronunciation into *mair*, Mary.

---

[3] As well as the *Chair of Taliesin* in the *Myvyrian Archaeology* see Davies' *Mythology of the British Druids*, J. Booth, 1809.
Ceridwen's cauldron is evidenced in local names in many areas of Scotland e.g. *Maidsemnaighe* = 'knoll of the very large cauldron' (*aghann* = cauldron, fem. *aighe*), in Slains; Kettle Hill (*cadhal* = cauldron), Aberdeen; Maiden Stone (*mha-adhann-lia* = 'very great cauldron stone'), upon which is incised a figure, possibly of a cauldron, with the traditional 'Z' symbol for lightning; most significantly, Maiden Casay (*mha-adhann-casach* = 'great cauldron of ascent'), a plain indicated of a Ceridwen initiation. Both these last are from Bennachie. See J. Rust, *Druidism Exhumed*, 1871.

But was the Graal something else as well, a kind of psychic centre, a scrying instrument? One recalls Lady Flavia Anderson's crystal globe ideas,[4] one recalls the Druids' Egg. Certainly visions came as one looked at it. The *Perlesvaus* or High History has it thus:

Thereupon Messire Gawain was led into the hall and findeth twelve ancient knights. They have set Messire Gawain to eat at a right rich table . . . thereon, lo you, two damsels that issue forth of a chapel, whereof the one holdeth in her hands the most Holy Graal, and the other the Lance whereof the point bleedeth thereinto . . . Messire Gawain looketh at the Graal, and it seemed him that the Chalice was therein, albeit none there was as at this time, and he seeth the point of the lance whence the red blood ran thereinto, and it seemeth him he seeth two angels that bear two candlesticks of gold filled with candles . . . The damsels that issue forth of the chamber come again before Messire Gawain, and him seemeth that he seeth three there where before he had seen but two, and seemeth him that in the midst of the Graal he seeth the figure of a child . . . Messire Gawain looketh before him and seeth three drops of blood fall upon the table . . . Messire Gawain may not withdraw his eyes from the three drops of blood, and when he would fain kiss them they vanish away . . . He looketh up and it seemeth him to be the Graal all in flesh, and he seeth above as him thinketh a King crowned, nailed upon a rood, and the spear was still fast in his side . . . Messire Gawain is silent as he that heareth not the Knight speak . . . the knights leave Messire Gawain all alone . . .[5]

The indications of trance conditions are strong, the 'Graal in flesh' is most significant and no one can fail to parallel the three drops of blood with the three drops from the cauldron of Ceridwen that initiate Gwion in wisdom.

Another initiatory vessel is the coracle, when the novice is sent in it for a test. In another poem, under the name Gwydne (the 'husband' of Ceridwen) a herald summoned novices for initiation to embark upon the sea. They are told that 'the ascending stones of the Bards will prove the harbour of life' and 'the conduct of the water will declare thy merit'. The candidate appears to have been battened down in a coracle—'skin bag'—which was sent off in a current that swirls in Cardigan Bay. Another poem alludes to three mystery figures—the guardian, Ciradr and Kai (Kay)—and then to three ministers who may play the parts of deities. All this seems very similar to the classical mysteries. There in the Lesser Mysteries of Eleusis the novices had to be sea-initiated. The sacred play is evidently part of the Arthurian mystique. Gwydno is father of Eidiol, a form of Ambrosius again.

Legends continued to grow; in some ways Glastonbury/Avalon has come to mean more in its desolation than in its physical pride. The Thorn developed an origin in Joseph's budded staff only in the eighteenth century. The intensive sanctity of the place even in total ruin makes it the only

[4] *The Ancient Secret*, Rilko/Thorsons, 1988.
[5] *The High Book of the Grail* trans. N. Bryant, Boydell & Brewer, Cambridge, 1978.

possible centre for an English national mystique. This was instinctively grasped by Blake when he based his national anthem *Jerusalem* on an even more extreme legend of Jesus' coming to Glastonbury and founding the ancient house:

> And did those feet in ancient time
> Walk upon England's mountains green?
> And was the holy lamb of God
> On England's pleasant pastures seen?

Here John Cowper Powys found in the older cauldron the inspiration for his great novel *Glastonbury Romance*.[6] An accumulation of psychic happenings, fancies and wild imaginings have kept Glastonbury to the fore, not perhaps altogether reputably, with the Rev. Bligh Bond and Mrs K. Maltwood adding their own personal visions. For a time too it seemed to be transforming into an English Beyreuth under the spell of the composer, Rutland Boughton.

The main authorities for this saga and legend, and their dates so far as available, are these: Gildas, c.AD 540 *The Anglo-Saxon Chronicle*; Nennius, *Historia Brittonum*, about AD 800; *Annales Cambriae* tenth century; William of Malmesbury, *Acts of the Kings of England* and *Concerning the Antiquity of the Church of Glastonbury*, c.1125; Geoffrey of Monmouth, *British History*, c.1135–40; Robert Wace's *Chronicle* c.1150; *The Grand Saint Graal* (based on Robert de Borron), c.1200; *The Quests of the Holy Graal* (Mallory's source) 1200–10; Wolfram von Eschenbach, *Parzival*, c.1210; *Perlesvaus* (the High History of the Holy Graal), 1225; and John of Glastonbury, c.1390.

So far as the Christian Graal can be identified with any one physical vessel, Valencia cathedral allegedly possesses the object—a red oriental cornelian cup, of Roman date, with additions of the ninth century. It was used by early Popes, until Sixtus II sent it via his deacon St Lawrence to Huesca during the Valerian persecution of AD 258. In 713 it had been hidden in the mountains at San Juan de la Pena, where it remained in legendary seclusion during the main myth-making period until 1399. It eventually arrived in Valencia 1424.

The cauldron is a symbol of the crescent moon, which cannot be separated from the cult of the Great Goddess and birth. The cauldron was to be filled for birth to arise from it.

To call down the moon out of her sphere is to invoke the Great Mother to incarnate in the priestess or maiden. At the North in the deity position, the priestess stands facing South, and the priest gives her the fivefold kiss —in the modern version,

> by seed and root, by bud and stem,
> by leaf and flower and fruit.

---

[6] See also his *Pair Dardeni*, on the cauldron itself, in *Obstinate Cymric*, Village Press, 1968.

The priestess then stands with legs apart, her arms opened wide, forming a pentagram, and utters the Charge, the invocation to the Goddess to descend into her.

It would be surprising if some such 'witchy' rite were not used at Stonehenge in the Great Horsehoe, and if the Great Trilithon were not an entry into new life, as well as into death. The priestess, however, would face the north-east dawn rather than the midday South.

Only very slowly has this great emblem taken on any semblance of Christianity. It is the great bowl of night, the cauldron of the stars—and one remembers that the inside of a Chinese bowl is the dome of sky, whose dragon pattern is the clouds. It is the goblet of strange potions that transform you. What has not gone into the cauldron from time to time? All the enchantments of Circe or the witch of Wookey Hole maybe, all the spells and dreams of men.

At Glastonbury it is not only the customary chalice of the Last Supper, brought over by Joseph of Arimathaea; it gets itself buried in Chalice Hill and from it flows the red water that distinguishes that remarkable spring. An apparently first-century dipper, the kind with which one dips into the *krater* at the Greek friendly feast, has indeed been found in a mysterious way near Glastonbury in recent years and now is kept at Chalice House. Is it part of the hidden intention in things that this dipper, that could well have been used at the Last Supper (if a disciple were rich enough to own it), should come to this holy place?

As the Graal comes reluctantly into the light of Christendom another curious thing occurs; not only does it become a chaste communion goblet but its form changes. In at least one of the Graal stories the hallow becomes a holy stone.[7] What does this mean?

It seems to mean that another glint of wisdom has come from the stars, that a matching symbol has come down to marry with the old dark cup, and that fire redeems water. For a long time the holy fire for the various *teine* ceremonies had to be produced by friction, like the twirling-sticks of the Indians. It was the old tradition. Then came fire from the flint-strike, the Celtic tradition. But the crystal was found and from it came the burning ray. Truly this was the fire from heaven, and that thing through which the fire came was a hallow. Flavia Anderson's Grail book is most suggestive on this.

We have the Arthurian riddle: which is the more important, the sword or the pommel? The answer is the pommel, for from the crystal in the handle the sword of light and fire is directed.

The three drops from the cauldron become three rays of light from the crystal: the circle is complete.

VI. The Druid Egg and Serpent

It is said that an oval ball—apparently of crystal but sometimes called

[7] *Parzival* by Wolfram von Eschenbach.

simply 'red'—hung as a symbol of office from the true Druid's neck. Snakes twined in a mass throw off balls of spittle that combine into a globe, and their hissing casts this into the air. Once a year only do they do this, at one particular moon according to Owen Pughe. The ball must then be caught in a cloth and made off with on horseback at once, for the serpents will pursue until running water is passed over. Thus it is given to us by Pliny the Elder, and his account is reinforced by words in Gaelic and local names: *Glain-non-Druidhe* in Gaelic means 'glass of the Druids', and this as an amulet counteracted any hostile incantations.

The serpent is one of the several symbolic names for the Druid; it symbolized metamorphosis in the casting of its skin and its renewal of life. Rather vaguely Welsh bards call Druids adders, *nadredd*, and they probably meant snakes.

Now Druids did meet at fixed moon-periods during the summer. They may then have indulged in glass blowing, perhaps with a ritual. The very Druidic Bardsey Island, according to the old Welsh poet Meilyr, is called the Holy Isle of the Glain or Druid Egg.

Green or blue glass amulets are called snakes' stones or Druid glass in Cornwall, Wales and Scotland, according to Kendrick.[1] Many of them are very old, estimated at several centuries BC.

The crystal ball therefore resolves itself into coloured glass—green, blue or even red—possibly ceremonially blown by Druids at a gathering during a summer moon. The Druid's Egg was mounted in gold and suspended from girdle or neck. If of clear glass, such a hollow ball may well have been used for scrying—whether a coloured one was equally useful is doubtful. All such objects can be helpful to concentration in a particular way—as can other things.

VII. Mystic and Healing Trees and Plants

Duir the Oak

The dazzling three-pronged thunderbolt of Zeus came down through his sacred tree, whose tensile rigidity impressed as greatly as its age. The tree was the tree of that ancient Gaelic divinity the Dagda of the 12 sun-labours. To the Hebrew god it belonged in so far as he was El.

At midsummer the oak-king was sacrificed or burnt alive, according to Frazer, at the sacred grove of Nemi, and he went up to the Corona Borealis. At all the holy seasons of the Celts oak was burnt for the need-fires, of which midsummer was one. The word for such a fire is *bel-teine*; hence the Beltane name is not only a season's but can be used for any such *teine*: in southern Scotland Beltane is midsummer in the widespread celebrations. In the holiest temple of Rome, that of Vesta, an oak-fire was constantly burning; it was one of the vestal virgins' tasks to feed this.

[1] Kendrick, T.D., *History of the Druids*, Cass, 1927.

In the Mediterranean area generally the oak was the evergreen holm-oak of eternity, as well as a sort of Ancient of Days. The life cycle of oaks is usually considered to be 500 years in ripening, 500 years of maturity, 500 of slow decline—at the end of which, however, the oak is often very much alive.

The boar and sow, feeding upon the holy mast of the oak, were disguised deities of wisdom; one of the Great Mother Ceridwen Cariadwen's chief forms is the sow and her piglets are the disciples of the cult. Such wise swine led the way to the healing waters of Bath.

By the old tree-alphabet calendar the oak (*duir* Gaelic, *drus* Latin) is centre and king of trees, top centre of the trilithon arch; the oak is the tree of Hu-Hesus' mystical manifestation, the tree upon which grew the sacred moon-mistle, cut by the sun-and-moon instrument. The oak also has the gall and the *kermis* insect in its leaves, emblems of red Mercury.

Under the oaks at Mamre sat Abraham and under a 'terebinth' (holm-oak) the angel appeared to Gideon. It was the oak that pronounced judgement on Absalom by catching his head between its branches. Prophets commonly sit under oak-trees (I Kings 13–14). The oak is mentioned some 50 times in the Old Testament.

At Dodona, Zeus made known his sacred oracle by the whispering of the leaves, interpreted by seers. The Gaelic *duir* links with 'door' in many languages, and the centre point of the year over which Duir presided in June was held to be its hinge—as January was its opening latch (Janus). Thus Janus and Cardea his mate of the hinge form the axle of the millstone of the solar system or 'universe' which is at the back of the North Wind. The millstone grinds round fatefully, turned by the strength of the Two Bears in the heavens.

Returning to Britain, perhaps its most famous oak-tree is that in Windsor Forest, belonging to Herne the Hunter of the sky-chase. Gospel Oak in Highgate is that under which Edward the Confessor swore to keep and to defend the ancient laws and rights of England. There are innumerable other distinguished oaks, for they are generally considered by the popular mind as the greatest of trees. Oak is immensely valuable and longlasting for carriages as well as for timber. The desolation of England's main oak forests lies in patriotic defence, for they were cut for some of the main timbers for her fleet, culminating in the considerable fleets of Nelson's time that defended against invasion. After this, Britain's timber has largely been purchased abroad.

Certain esteemed ancients, who were perhaps Chief Druids, or kings, were buried in hollowed-out oak trunks, conceived as boats launching into the sea of the unknown.

Oak avenues, like yew groves, often signify that Druids have been there; such an avenue as late as the eighteenth century led up to the top of Glastonbury Tor. 'The Grove' at Highgate, Coleridge's home, was very probably a name marking the local oak or yew plantation of a Druidic college in this locality around the pool or spring of the Goddess. At

Glastonbury Tor's base is a pair of remarkable old oaks, Gog and Magog. Seemingly well over the 1,500-year lifespan, they still emanate something of the healing power generally attributed to the tree.

On the side of utility, the oak is used to supply tannin for processing leather, whilst the oaks of the south still provide cork commercially.

But for all Druids the holy oak is not only the tree in whose form is the child, the Maban, who is Hu-Hesus the eternally-coming one, not only the tree on whose branches was found the potent mistletoe—the tree itself is a living parable, something that gives deep meaning to its growth. The cornerstone of occult ideas is the ancient Emerald Tablet of Hermes Trismegistos. Just as the great branches of the oak spread above, so wide go the strong intricate roots below. 'As above, so below' is the key.

Iodha the Yew-tree

The deep evergreen eternity of Iodha the yew has a life-cycle of several thousand years—the exact period is unknown. It is never tall but thickens in convolutions. The wood itself is of maximum density. In its groves can be clearly observed the curves of growth belonging to this hemisphere. It stands for the death period of the year, winter, as the last letter 'i' in the vowel order AOUEI in the Sweet Cauldron of the Five Trees.

Taxus (Latin: op. Greek *toxon*, a bow) was the typical tree of the Greek underworld, sacred to Hecate. Also Mercury, messenger to the dead, was linked to the yew, which in the cheiromantic system was given the little finger. The yew groves near Marseilles were where the horror-loving Lucan locates the appalling sights surrounding Druidic human sacrifices for divining. Yew branches were generally carried in the classical world as signs of mourning.

Without doubt the yew stood for sacred mystery in the Druid tradition; yews were planted systematically about the places, often wells, that held sacred truths, perhaps to awe votaries as much as because the trees themselves held sacred properties. Their leaves are fatal to animals; Potter treats the yew as simply poisonous and any medicinal use of the white or red berries as 'uncertain', but Evelyn disagrees about its poisonousness. Certainly the Irish compounded yewberry, hellebore and Devil's Bit to poison their weapons. In tiny quantities it is a proven heart stimulant as valuable as foxglove (digitalis).

Yew is one of the Seven Chieftain Trees, penalties against the axing of which are provided in the Brehon Laws: it is death for cutting down a chieftain tree. Its timber is 'used for household vessels and breastplates', for which something pretty tough was needed.

The most impressive yew plantation in England, almost certainly Druidic, is Great Yews near Salisbury. Long avenues converge upon a round open space that could have been a wonderful setting for a human circle or for any solemnity.

Shakespeare knows 'the double-fatal yew' and 'slips of yew slivered in the Moon's eclipse' (Macbeth). It is always sinister.

Fossilized yew roots have been found in the garden and neighbourhood of Chalice Well at Glastonbury, forming an avenue pattern around the pool of chalybeate reddish water. This water had its twin in the stream from the stalactite-stalagmite tunnel which flowed a few yards away. One came from Wales, the Black Mountains, under the Bristol Channel; the other from the cavern under the Tor. Any yew arrangement here clearly marked a potent and significant spot.

In Ireland one of the Four Great Trees, the Great Tree of Ross, was a yew. It was called the Renown of Banbha—the death side of the Triple Goddess. Youghal's name is really *Eocail*, 'place of yews', and there are other names derived from the tree, always places that might well have been ancient cult centres.

The popular theory is that the Tudor order to plant yews in churchyards to improve the supply of longbows for battle started their churchyard career. There is every reason to doubt this and to realize that the yew was always the solemn plant of death, the branches carried at funerals, sprigs thrown on maiden hearses and the trees grown at burial places.

To Druids, however, it stands for eternity rather than death, with its dark evergreen leaves and seemingly never-dying span of existence. In Druid tree language it stood for the Ovate grade, one who specialized in learning concerning the mysteries.

The All-Heal or Mistle-plant

Caesar's Druid friend Divitiacus the Aeduan told him all about the sacredness of the mistle to the Druids. It had to be cut in the winter, at a certain time of the moon, when found on an oak-tree by the Druid priestly party looking for it, which was armed with a strange weapon, a golden sickle. There were hymns and prayers and the sacrifice of two white bulls, i.e. moon creatures.

This was all clearly symbolical and marries up with other folklore. The mistleberry was generally thought of as being like sperm, therefore a fertility and magical plant; magical, also, in never touching the ground— a 'heavenly' plant whose seed was wind or bird-carried. Not only the Druid tradition has reverenced it.

But the mistle tradition amongst Druids has a further tradition: it is the All-Heal. The medical pharmacopoeia confirms little of this; *Potter's Cyclopaedia* gives its use only as a nervine, narcotic, antispasmodic and tonic, in common with a number of other plants. Powdered leaves only are mentioned. Yet since traditional reputations have so often proved to have solid foundations, the Steiner followers at a Swiss centre have observed and experimented on mistletoe for 14 years with remarkable results, published in the *British Homoeopathic Journal* in 1969.

Viscum album is one of the strangest of plants. It forms its flowers in winter. The flowers appear not only at the tip of the year's growth but also at the joints with that of the previous year. As soon as the flowering of one year is over, buds form for the next. Berries with the seed kernels are not fully ripe before December. Thus flowers and ripe berries, as well as new unripe ones, are all together on the plant in winter. In contrast, its leaves follow the usual evergreen cycle, although they are hardly normal leaves; they drop off after about four years. It is the birds, chiefly the thrush, who by eating the ripe berries in the hungry season, plant the seeds in the first three months of the year.

Steiner had indicated that the two Solstices were the times of maximum efficacy and the research confirmed this. In December the stems carry flower buds on many nodes. Berries take on a golden tint and moon forces are strong in the closed flowers. At the Summer Solstice period the power of the sap is at maximum, showing in test pictures as rose-pink, a sun-filled quality.

Manufacturing preparations from mistle garnered at these two seasons and following Steiner's advice, remedies have been found for many forms of rheumatic troubles and for cancer. All four parts of the plant are used, roots, stems, flowers and berry. But further, it has been found that the plant, after being rotated in a particular way, acts upon imbalances of all kinds in the body. It needs however very great care in administration, this being a highly individual matter. If this quality of healing all imbalances were known to the ancients, then the name All-Heal would be an exact description, not hyperbole.

The moon nature of the plant was clearly recognized by those who gathered it at the Winter Solstice. The white-gold colour of the berries were then at maximum. White cattle were the stars ruled by the moon. The golden sickle symbolized the moon's shape and the sun's substance, combining the two luminaries reverenced by the Druid tradition and indicating the two Solstices.

The Winter Solstice is the beginning of the ancient New Year and the plant was then solemnly distributed to the people as a cure-all. The modern Order does the same—without specific healing implication. Another time for New Year was the beginning of February, and by one working of the calendar the mistle was gathered then.

Beith the Birch-tree

Like the yew, the birch-tree is very generally associated with the Druids; indeed the silver birch signified the young Druid, or the Bard in training. Beth or Beith (birch) had the significance of the beginnings of things, it beat the bounds, it expelled evil, it drove out the spirit of the old year. Roman lectors carried birch rods. The birch is the first tree in the Beith-Luis-Nuinn alphabet.

Now the silver birch in particular was taken as the beginning of the Druid career—the young one under instruction. The word for it seems doubtful; Graves makes it *Eodha*, but he is not supported by Gaelic authorities. The Order as a whole was signified by the oak or Druid, the yew or Ovate and the silver birch or young Bard—a trinity of trees corresponding to the Three Pillars of Wisdom.

The silver birch, together with the rowan, is the most beautiful tree that Nature provides in the more sparsely-treed areas commonly linked with Celts. Its graceful and sensitive outline, fine-hair twigs and shining silver trunk make visiting a birch wood an almost sacred experience. It punctuates the outline of many a glen, standing out against dark firs and distant mountains.

Other Plants of Ceremony

We have dealt with mistletoe (Winter Solstice) and yew (All Hallows); a word is due about snowdrops (Imbolc) clover or trefoil (Spring equinox), may and whitethorn (Beltane), vervain (Summer Solstice) and apples (Autumnal equinox).

The Snowdrop of the February celebration has always signified purity. Alleged to grow amongst snows like the eidelweiss, it is used as symbol of the time of the cleansing of earth's face after winter, in the earliest spring of February.

The Trefoil or Clover is one of the symbolic spring plants that appear in the footsteps of the goddesses Ceridwen and Olwen in their youthful shapes. Primroses, violets and buttercups are others in various forms of the myth. The three of the trefoil leaf has always been significant.

Verbena (vervain) is a modest plant with a very distinctive aroma. How its reputation in classical times arose is difficult to say, but an infusion of this plant in water was held to be of great value in restoring or improving eyesight. The eyes were bathed in vervain water. This cure is unconfirmed by modern records. With this reputation the attachment of the plant to the high point of summer is easily explained. The hawk with his keen eyes has symbolized the far-seeing rays of the high sun for thousands of years; in Egypt the sun-gods Re and Horus were both falcon-headed, whilst by Welsh myth the knight who is clear-sighted enough to win the Graal is Gwalcheved or Galahad, the hawk of summer. If keen sight at lofty heights is attributed to summer figures then the plant that belongs to good sight will be attached there also. Sight is attributed to the element fire and the verbena flower is normally a fierce red.

The *Apple* is the fruit of autumn that kept best through winter in northern parts. Earlier generations were nearly bereft of fruit in winter and the apple shared with the southerly pomegranate a holy and mystical reputation as food of the dead time of the year—and therefore of the dead. Moreover it was mythical: in translating the Old Testament it never occurred, it seems, to anyone to translate the Hebrew general word for the fruit that tempted Eve otherwise than as an apple. Together with the flesh of the holy swine the food promised to humans who joined the *sidhe*-folk in Eire was apples and nectar. Possibly the heavenly digestions of the *sidhe* could cope with this peculiar diet, but one is sorry for the humans.

Trees and plants with various degrees of sacredness and symbolism about them are indeed many—there is no such thing as a complete list. The tree alphabet, consonants and vowels, constitutes a fairly representative selection. The rowan was the brightest thing—except gorse—seen on autumn moorland and was used for dyeing wool red in Scotland. The ash-tree, particularly the weeping ash or umbrella-tree has always been the mothering tree, indeed the tree of rebirth, culminating in the World Ash Ygdrasil of Scandinavia. It was protective against witches; it is actually held to be sacred in Wales, according to the diarist Evelyn. Druidical ash-wands for magic have been found. Yet the ashtree has an evil wife indwelling it, and it is sometimes favoured contrarily as an abode for witches. The alder is another red-bearing tree but from its bark this time—warriors dyed their faces and bodies with it to look fearsome, and so it is the tree of Bran, the raven of the battlefield, a very ancient deity much later reflected in St Brandon. The tree also produced a green colour from its flowers. The willow seems to repeat the theme of motherhood, this time as the water-mother. Tiny complete willows can be grown naturally only 3 inches tall. Willow-bark is a fever cure. The hawthorn and Maytree are holy because of their blaze of white at a magical time of year. Spirits of various kinds constantly inhabit them, but no evil one dares approach. Holly is another impressive red—winter's blood. Defended by sharp prickles, it seems to have symbolized the fighting man. The hazel's edible nuts belonged to another world as much as to this one, for they fed the Salmon of Wisdom. The hazel is essentially also a divining tree, from which the divining rods of dowsers are commonly made. The vine represented inspiration, the ivy made into a drink spelt madness or ecstasy. The reed or rod meant scholarship as well as rules, and the elder was a witch tree, particularly with its white flowers and its black berries. Moreover the elder-mother knew all curative plants. Elders killed serpents, and a crook made from elder was a kind of sceptre.

The gorse or furze was the plant that spread something heavenly yellow, linked with the sun. Another moorland colour was the purple of the heather that mantled the country in September–October. Scotland made the direction and office of the East into the brilliant purple (*airt*), which probably means 'bright'.

The aspen shakes with constant apprehension of the nearness of the world of spirits. The poplars weep amber tears because they are the sisters of Phaeton who misguided the horses of the sun and were burnt up. The elm, originating in Italy, has a doubtful reputation; it is used mainly for the keels of boats and for making coffins, whilst its habit of dropping its heavy arms without warning at quiet times results in a few deaths each year. Its bark, however, makes a good writing material. Pleasanter is the plant dedicated to Apollo, the evergreen laurel sacred to poets, from which the victors' crowns were made in musical contests.

VIII. *The Bringing of the Bluestones by Magic*

The tale of the 'bluestones' of Stonehenge, the rather greyer-looking and smaller stones in the monument's inner part, usually hardly noticed by visitors, illustrates the value of the outside investigator and how dubious it is to leave the running in an only semi-scientific craft like archaeology to the official experts.

It was the Welsh-based archaeologists who pointed out that the top quarries at Mynydd Preseli, north of Milford Haven in Pembrokeshire, South Wales, were the nearest source for spotted diorites of the type of the bluestones. They worked out a hazardous method of transport by rafts and a still more hazardous voyage full of currents and leeshore danger, across the Bristol Channel to the mouth of the Bristol Avon, whose stream did not run very near Stonehenge. None of them happened to be practical seamen.

The late T.C. Lethbridge, an independent-minded but just as well-qualified archaeologist, and by his service in the navy generally and experience of small boats up in western Scotland in particular, far better qualified than anyone else writing on these matters to pronounce on them, was highly dissatisfied. To him the voyage was unlikely and the transport impossible. He looked at a wild story in Geoffrey of Monmouth, added an independent observation and produced a solution much more likely than that still publicized in the official guide to Stonehenge. Here is the relevant passage from Geoffrey, somewhat shortened:

He [King Ambrosius Aurelianus] went unto the monastery nigh Kaercaradoc, that is now called Salisbury, where the earls and princes lay buried whom the accursed Hengist had betrayed . . . He was moved to pity and tears began to flow. At last he fell to pondering within himself in what wise he might best make the place memorable ... Whereupon Tremounos, Archbishop of Caerleon, came unto the King and saith he:

'If man there be anywhere strong enow to carry out this ordinance into effect, let Merlin, Vortigern's prophet, set hand thereunto . . . Bid him come hither and set his wits to work, and I warrant he shall build thee a memorial to last!'

They found him in the country of the Gewissi, at the fountain of Galabes that he wont to haunt, and, telling him what it was they wanted, brought him unto the King . . . Unto whom Merlin:

'If thou be fain to grace the burial-place of these men with a work that shall endure for ever, send for the Dance of the Giants that is in Killaraus, a mountain in Ireland. For a structure of stones is there that none of this age could raise save his wit were strong enough to carry his art. For the stones be big, nor is there stone anywhere of more virtue, and, so they be set up round this plot in a circle, even as they be now there set up, here shall they stand for ever . . .

'Laugh not so lightly, King, for not lightly are these words spoken. Now in these stones is a mystery, and a healing virtue against many ailments. Giants of old did carry them from the furthest ends of Africa and did set them up in Ireland what time they did inhabit therein. And unto this end they did it, that they might make them baths whensoever they ailed of any malady, for they did wash the stones and pour forth the water into the baths, whereby they that were sick were made whole. Moreover, they did mix confections of herbs with the water, whereby they that were wounded had healing, for not a stone is there that lacketh in virtue of leechcraft.'

At that time was Gilloman King in Ireland . . .

The Britons prevailed, and, his Irishmen all cut up and slain, forced Gilloman to flee for his life. When they had won the day they pressed forward to Mount Killaraus, and when they reached the structure of stones rejoiced and marvelled greatly . . . Thereupon at Merlin's bidding they all with one accord set to work with all manner of devices, and did their utmost to fetch down the Dance . . . And when they were all weary and spent, Merlin burst out laughing and put together his own engines. At last, when he had set in place everything whatsoever that was needed, he laid the stones down so lightly as none would believe, and when he had laid them down, bade them carry them to the ships and place them inboard, and on this wise did they again set sail and returned unto Britain with joy, presently with a fair wind making land, and fetching the stones to the burial place ready to set up . . .

Aurelius bade Merlin set up the stones that he had brought from Ireland around the burial-place. Merlin accordingly obeyed his ordinance, and set them up about the compass of the burial-ground in such wise as they had stood upon Mount Killaraus in Ireland, and proved yet once again how skill surpasseth strength.

Book VIII, ch. 9–12

Essential points from this mythic tale are

1. a link with the 'farthest coast of Africa'
2. the name 'Dance of the Giants'
3. the magic stones had come from Eire
4. these stones healed with water and herbs
5. the original set-up was on a mountain called Killaraus

Spotted diorites, although not common, are found in Ireland as well as Wales. There are sources there both north of Dublin and west of Tipperary. 'Killaraus' would be a Latinized form of Killaradh. Giraldus Cambrensis does not help by distorting it into Kildare. Killaradh or Killary means the church on the river Ary, which names Tipperary, and near it is a source quarry. One recalls also the wild medieval legend about the devil having brought the stones over from Ireland.

Giants have always been connected with the enormous stones of early Greek Mycenaean architecture. Classical tradition called them the Cyclopes. A Mycenaean-type dagger is outlined on one of the Sarsen stones of Stonehenge. Mycenae is not Africa exactly but in the eastern Mediterranean, not far off. The corresponding figures to Cyclopes in Ireland are the Fomorians, one of the early invasion races. In the Bronze Age, as we now know, there were strong links with the Mediterranean.

Water poured over certain stones is considered to have healing properties in the highlands of Scotland, e.g. the *clach dearg* granite charm stones. Lethbridge tried dowsing, using chips from the bluestones, and obtained startling results. The pendulum oscillated strongly over Stonehenge and near Tipperary, but not at all at Mynydd Preselli. Tried for dating, the pendulum gave 2650 BC for the original set-up.

The journey by the little Ary river would not have been too difficult. It flows into the large river Suir which enters the sea at Waterford. Hence is a direct south-southeast passage to Land's End. The square sail used at that period could adapt to westerly wind at an angle. Then it was a simple run before the wind along the south coast, and at Christchurch the Wiltshire Avon gives a waterway to West Amesbury—not a long drag to the present site, since the river formerly flowed higher in the valley.

The craft used would have been something like the Eskimo *umiak*, a wood frame covered with skins, light and buoyant, and with blown-up bladders under the gunwales, almost unsinkable. Lashing two of them across with boards, the stones would be slung in the water between them underneath.

All this is given fully in Lethbridge's last book, *The Legend of the Sons of God*,[1] whence the account here is drawn.

Thus it was probably Myrddin with the technical know-how who conveyed the bluestones for the sceptical Ambrosius Aurelianus or Emrys. Nowadays Ambrosius is given a real existence and a ruling period following AD 470, and so he is a contemporary of Hengist and possibly of Arthur — 'Myrddin' standing here for the magic of superior skill, whatever his real dates may have been.

The tale turns out then to be one of Arthurian times, although the event of the moving of the bluestones has been altered 1,500 years or so and thoroughly confused with the larger, more obvious Sarsen stones. It speaks of the reputation of Myrddin, a figure by myth inseparable from Arthur. Ambrosius Aurelianus was, like Artorius (Arthur), one of those Romano-British names.

Recovering from the Saxon ravages, the remnants of the old Roman organizing power stirred again and a strong enough kingdom or 'empire' was formed to achieve a civilized peace over a considerable area for some time. The Ambrosian kingdom is likely in fact to have been continuous with Arthur's.

Geoffrey, on examination, is not such a liar after all. He is weaving a fashionable historical romance, but he builds with some garbled facts which are invaluable to us.

IX. *The Gwion-Taliesin Myth*

The Celtic lands have many myths which have been adequately treated in many books although interpretation sometimes lacks. One however is vital as giving in allegorical form some hint of the nature of the Cymric initiations. It concerns the genesis of Taliesin the Master-Bard, from a seventeenth century manuscript but containing an ancient wisdom tradition.

[1] Routledge & Kegan Paul, 1969.

Avagddu was the ugly son of the Old Mother Ceridwen and her husband the lake spirit, Tegid Voel of Pennllyn. Ceridwen boiled up a Cauldron of Wisdom for him guided by the book of Feryllt (Virgil, also the fairies), putting into it the necessary herbs from time to time, to compensate her child for his ill looks. It had to boil for a year and a day and in three drops of it only the magical essence was conveyed.

Little Gwion (Gwion Bach) and the blind Morda were set to watch the fire and this cauldron. As the period drew to an end three drops of the magical brew flew out and settled upon Gwion Bach's finger. When he put his finger to his mouth, at once he was dowered with the cauldron's insight. He saw that having received what was meant for Avagddu, he would be hated and destroyed by Ceridwen. He fled to his country of Llanfair and the cauldron which had delivered its sacred essence now had nothing but poison, which burst it and, running into a stream, poisoned the horses of Gwyddno Garanhir.

Ceridwen smote Morda and pursued Gwion, who now having the knowledge, changed himself into a hare, whereupon she became a greyhound bitch. He then became a fish and she an otter. He became a bird and she a hawk. Finally he became a grain of wheat and she as a black hen swallowed him. After nine months he was born from her but although she intended to kill him, she could not do so because of his beauty. Instead she dropped him in a leather bag at a sea-weir.

The unfortunate Gwyddno of the poisoned horses also had a luckless son Elphin, which means 'man' or 'mankind', and a rather profitless salmon weir between Dyvi and Aberystwyth. Elphin one day fished out the bag and found the infant. Gwyddno said, 'Look at this radiant brow!' and Elphin said, 'Let his name therefore be Taliesin.' They reared him in their house carefully and he became the prime Cymric Bard, his first poem being one of praise and promise for his foster parents, who then became rich.

Elphin began to boast that he had a more virtuous wife and a finer Bard than any in the court of Arthur. He was imprisoned for this and a test made of his wife's virtue. This being unshaken, Taliesin then had to prove his bardic superiority. He first showed himself a master of magic by rendering the other Bards dumb, then he sang out as the incarnation of the eternal spirit of poetry.[1] A great wind arose shaking the castle, and at his music Elphin's chains fell off him. Then Taliesin was recognized as the great and supernatural Bard singing the many poems attributed to him.

This is the story and in it is embedded much ancient knowledge. The pursuit of Gwion by Ceridwen has the motifs of the four elements and the Hound of Heaven, a training through tests. Like Grainne in Eire she commits the dire action that lifts to a higher plane; she is in fact testing out Gwion. The hare is a most inspired creature to the Celts: it crouched as for sacrifice, it leapt and danced, it embodied the external soul. The greyhound is the sacred dog that appears beside Néhellania, another form of

---

[1] See pp. 60–2.

Ross Nichols.

William Stukeley, reputedly Chosen Chief of the Order 1722–1765.
National Portrait Gallery, London

Augusta, Princess of Wales, patroness of the Order and called by Stukeley 'Veleda, Archdruidess of Kew'.
National Portrait Gallery, London

William Blake, reputedly Chosen Chief of the Order 1799–1827.
National Portrait Gallery, London

Edward Vaughan Keneally, barrister and author of occult books, Chosen Chief 1874–1880.
National Portrait Gallery, London

The present Chosen Chief, Philip Carr-Gomm, being initiated into the Order by Ross Nichols at the Beltane ceremony on Glastonbury Tor 1969. *Brian Peacock*

'Whilst this sword is unsheathed, promise you all that the Earth our home and mother shall be protected and illuminated by the swords of our spirits and wills.' — The Triad of Chosen Chief, Pendragon and Scribe lay their hands on the sword during the Spring Equinox ceremony of 1967 at Parliament Hill, Highgate. *Philip Carr-Gomm*

The Lady Ceridwen Cariadwen prepares to join the procession to the Stone of Free Speech at Parliament Hill for the Spring Equinox ceremony 1972, so that she can hand seeds and wine to the Chief, saying 'At the time of the equal day and night, I bring the seeds and the wine of earth, seeds which have grown and wine that is ripe from the nether years. They are gifts for you, the elders and guardians who have kept and give the seeds of knowledge, the wine of the wise.'   *Stuart Photographic*

An informal Druid ritual in a forest near Utrecht, Holland 1989.   *Theo Steur*

Above Alain Stivell, a Druid Bard from Brittany, plays at the Order's Winter Solstice celebration in London 1967.

Philip Carr-Gomm

Right Representatives of different faiths are often invited to participate in the Order's celebrations. Here Buddhist monks participate in the Autumnal Equinox on Parliament Hill in 1973.

Philip Carr-Gomm

Silbury Hill.   *Janet & Colin Bord*

Stonehenge.   *Janet & Colin Bord*

The stone circles of Callanish in the Outer Hebrides offer the clearest examples of the surveying skills of our ancestors. *Janet & Colin Bord*

Cashel Aenghus, the House of the Love-God, New Grange, Ireland. The magical dawn ray was guided for about 28 ft through the chamber above the central doorway. *Janet & Colin Bord*

The Rollright Stones.

Janet & Colin Bord

The Merry Maidens are a complete circle of 19 granite blocks, overlooking the sea near Land's End, Cornwall, with at least 8 star-alignments, including those to Capella, Antares and Arcturus.

Janet & Colin Bord

Ceridwen, on many plaques. The quick fish is always the silver water representative of the Hermes spirit, probably the trout. The otter is regarded with wonder as an architect amongst creatures. The bird—probably a wren—is the spiritual principle in the realm of intelligence (air) and the hawk has the far-seeing guardian eye of Horus.

Each one of the three successive pairs is a deific principle. With the final transformation we have more—the descent of this wisdom to earth. The grain of wheat is synonym for the seed of wisdom; the supernal bird, possibly really the vulture-mother of Egypt, patiently trains—hatches out —the young initiates. 'Nine months was I in the womb of the hag Ceridwen,' sings Taliesin; nine months may well have been the training in the caves or cells of an early Order.[2] At the end of this the postulant was dropped in a skin bag in the sea; and the test was that postulants battened down in coracles were sent off into the whirling waters of Cardigan Bay —which, however, always returned them to the same spot, so that the process, although frightening, was not a danger.

One remains sorry however for Avagddu, however ugly, and Morda, however (morally) blind.

Those who recognize and foster supernatural qualities will become rich, and the folly of men in boasting may also serve to bring out supernal power. Each time an apparent injury is done, good results. To be thoroughly unfortunate like Gwyddo in worldly affairs may be a sign of pre-election to a semi-divine destiny. Such are some of the lessons of this tale.[3]

---

[2] Nine month cycles are also significant in the training of the modern Order. [Ed.]
[3] See p. 61 for Taliesin's song.

GREATER SITES OF THE BRITANNIC ISLANDS

Preliminary Note:
Selecting perhaps arbitrarily ten centres and their complexes to represent the Megalithic-Druidic culture, it is obvious that much wider linkages with meaning can be made between sites, although space lacks here to deal with them. There is a certain polarization of mystic centres. If one had to name some powerful centres for the British Isles, names springing to mind might well be Glastonbury, Walsingham, Iona, Anglesey, Penmaenmawr (the Meini Hirion) and the Black Mountains. The following therefore cannot take account of many of these wider links, although most suggestive and plausible.

All the following main monuments and their areas are linked in one or another way with Druidic, or at any rate Celtic-religious practices. About all these sites hang more or less clear implications of observances of the heavens or invocations of earth, with seasonal rituals carried out by priests operating a science and resembling prophets more than shamans. The interests indicated would mostly seem to be along the lines thought of as Druidic, with two exceptions: the Rollright Stones are clearly of a different culture, and the Merry Maidens of Lamorna, Cornwall, an apparently complete group, have no cult indication.

Between these sites can be noted certain relationships, and more work on them could well be done. Sometimes it starts with a mystic indication which works out factually and can be demonstrated.

I. The Avebury Complex

Silbury: The Long Barrow Temple: Sanctuary Hill Temple: The Avenue: Great and Little Circles.

Cabiri = North African name of the Dioscuri or heavenly twins.
Abri = a shelter, perhaps the Cove.
Aburi = place of the twin powers, sun and moon.
Silbury: place or burial ground of the goddess Sil or Sul: cp. Silchester and Sul of Bath.

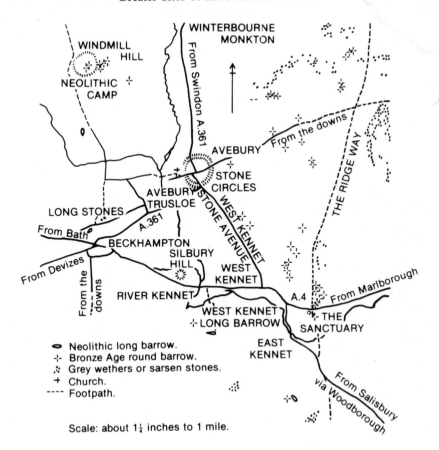

The Avebury area showing the relationship between Avebury, Windmill Hill, Silbury Hill and West Kennet Long Barrow.

When from northern France or Brittany the neolithic far-travellers from Syria came over to Britain they had already created much—or alternatively, they were running parallel with what was being created, according to your dating. The miles-long avenues of Carnac and the vast menhir of Men Er' Broec'h or Er Grnh and maybe the mother-goddess temple now masquerading as the Table des Marchands are of about the same age as Avebury and its first earthwork-ring and the Aubrey Holes and Heol-stone at Stonehenge. Perhaps the cousins in Britain were not quite so artistic— they seemed to leave fewer symbolic shapes. But the main point is that they were all used to planning big forms and had the knowledge of how to handle stones.

The pioneer farmers and pastoralists of Windmill Hill were there some time before they began, probably impelled by settlers—or by a few mystics—from a new migration, to think about putting into stone form some ideas they already had. Their triple-stone-ringed camp up there was an autumnal gathering-place. Quite probably it came to be a place of meeting for tribes over a very wide area—later Avebury certainly was. Besides cattle and sheep they had begun to grow flax for clothing, emmer wheat and Egyptian-type barley; we have their querns. They cleared some forest. They hunted, perhaps for skins; we have their beautifully-made arrow-heads as well as their highly-polished axeheads. They made crude pottery, carved ritual phalli, cups and balls, and there was possibly human sacrifice.

Probably they started with the long barrow in which to consult their ancestors; they made an elongated building some 5–6 ft high within, a central passage with 5 chambers, 40 ft long, laid out humanoid-fashion, head and limbs, head to the west by north, womb-entrance east by south. The shape is that of the rock-cut temples in Malta; the entry is an impressive forecourt. All is in unworked local sarsen stone. Each chamber except the 'head' is built of 5 stones. Over it all they put great slabs, then piled up earth into a barrow 330 ft × 80 ft on a commanding ridge. From the Windmill Hill camp centre, Silbury Hill and this West Kennet Long Barrow, the largest and best constructed in Britain, left open it is reckoned for about 1,000 years, lie near enough in a straight line. This is roughly in the south-easterly direction—the birth place of the new sun of midwinter —but not quite on it, say between south-east by south and south-southeast. The barrow used to be reckoned as built about 2500 BC. Some 46 bodies were found in it when finally excavated by Piggott and Atkinson in 1955–6.

Since Silbury is on this ley line, it is quite likely that it was begun at about the same time. At first, that is, they would see these two low eminences— the little knoll now under the artificial hill and the low ridge rising to a summit—in line; on the further one was built the temple of the dead, to the Mother Goddess of death and birth, on the nearer was to be the symbol of male and tribal unity, the cone-hill.

The writer has testimony to two significant objects having been found in Silbury during the twentieth century which might say something definite as to its character as a 'bury': these were a crystal goblet and a kind of crown, excavated by a then well-known local headmaster. But all traces of these seem to be lost, and the Somerset Archaeological Society, of which the excavator was a member, denies knowledge. Thus the idea of its being some funerary monument to a chief, like the central lith at Callernish, remains unproven.

Another guess has been the angulation of the hill's sides to log calendars. Shadows from logs at certain angles have been used by prehistoric folk in this way in northern Europe. But to go to the enormous labour of con- structing the largest artificial hill in Europe, when not far away slopes could be found equally useful, would seem a work of supererogation.

By far the most probable causation for this vast mound is found in the extraordinary fact, so far known only from a newspaper account, about the excavations semi-officially carried out a few years ago and still not issued

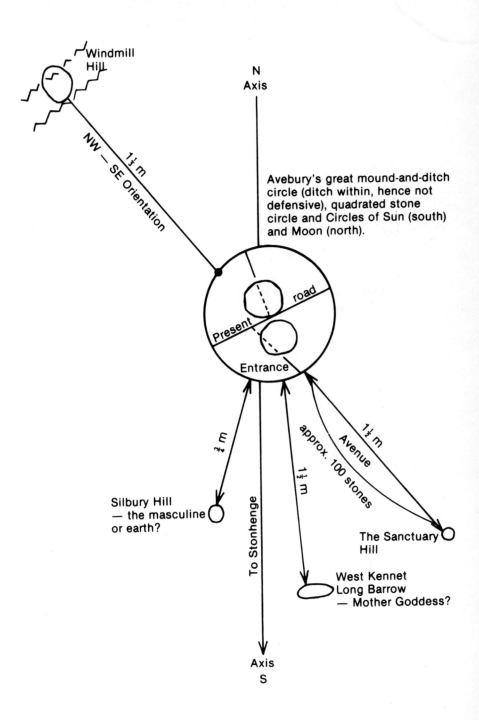

Windmill Hill

N Axis

NW — SE Orientation

1¼ m

Avebury's great mound-and-ditch circle (ditch within, hence not defensive), quadrated stone circle and Circles of Sun (south) and Moon (north).

Present

road

Entrance

¾ m

1½ m

approx. 100 stones

1¼ m Avenue

Silbury Hill — the masculine or earth?

To Stonhenge

The Sanctuary Hill

West Kennet Long Barrow — Mother Goddess?

Axis S

Avebury: General Scheme.

in a proper report. According to *The Times*, it was found that at successive circular layers of the man-made part of the hill were sections of various kinds of earths from many parts of the country. This is the kind of identification which nowadays field-workers can make with some confidence. Here therefore is plain indication of tributary earths being brought in from tribes in many directions to unite in a symbolic way in their hill-mound. It was eventually to reach perhaps 130 ft (present height 125 ft), base diameter 550 ft, summit about 100 ft diameter. It was built doubtless in slow century-by-century growth, one radial earth pattern over another, and the top is approximately the same area as that of New Grange in Eire.

We suggest then that this was the first scheme of this ancestor-reverencing Long Barrow people: the alignment of Windmill Hill's centre with the barrow temple and with the beginnings of the earth-association fellowship of tribes in Silbury.

United in their autumnal assembly on Windmill Hill's cattle-rings, they then conceived the idea of a great open-air temple below for themselves and for their children's children, something really large. The largest thing they knew so far had been 12-rows-wide successive orientations, or the after-life meanderings, shown at Carnac. But their concepts and mathematics were well up to the task. They would illustrate the descent of spirit or life from a higher dimension to this plane by showing a mother-goddess temple on a hill and a life-curve joining it to a great circle typifying this world's horizon.

Instead of using the simple circle—tying a rope to a post and walking it round as an earth scratcher—the first Pythagorean triangle (out of the 8) already held their sacred allegiance. According to Professor Thom's account,[1] they worked the sides 3, 4, 5 in block-units of 25 megalithic yards (MY). The triangle sides are AC = 75, AB = 100 and BC = 125. Striking arcs of 260 MY from the 3 points, a bulgy sort of circle has several angles and at least one flattish side to the south-west. The true radius from a central point 'I' is approximately 200 MY. A point on the circumference at which the distance from B is 200 MY was particularly marked (shown by Thom as point 'S'). It falls in fact within the largest of all the huge stones, that to the left as one leaves the circle by the north entrance.

On a carefully-constructed design on such geometric bases the main stone placings prove to coincide with significant points. In all the 6 arcs verifiable—and over half the circle is destroyed—their lengths in MY are either in units of 5 or 2.5 and for the greater lengths often it is 25. With the perimeters of neolithic circles generally this is the rule. The inner diameter is 1,100 ft or exactly 400 MY.

On this huge scale then, the neolithic tribesmen dug under strict directions with scapulas and antlers, raising a circular bank with the entrances to the north-east, south-southeast, east-northeast and west-southwest whose diameter with ditch was 1,300 ft. From top of bank

[1] Thom, A., *Megalithic Sites in Britain*, Oxford University Press, 1967.

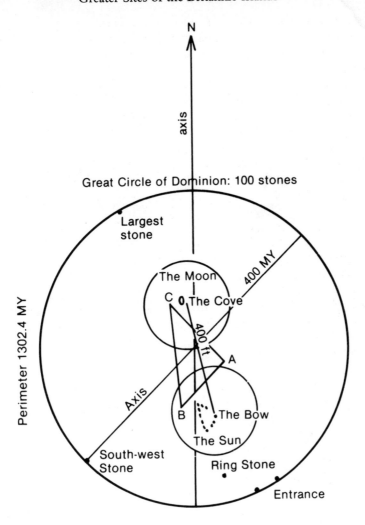

Moon Circle   Total perimeter 1302.4 MY
Diameter 400 MY or 1066.5 ft
Between centres of circles = 400 ft
The Triangle   A C = 100 MY
B C = 125 MY
A B = 75 MY

Diameters of inner circles = 125 MY
Arcs based on A B' and C used to construct sections
of a bulgy circle, others based on southern and western entry stones.
A south-west stone marks an axis. The largest stone marks
an entrance flanked by several more stones and is a geometric key.

The Avebury Circles.

to ditch bottom was some 55 ft, the width of ditch 15 ft. At the circle so geometrically arranged were set about 100 very large local sarsen stones.

There are two inner circles with distinctive features, commonly called, following Stukeley, the Circle of the Moon, to the north, and the Circle of the Sun, to the south. Each is now calculated at exactly 125 MY or 340 ft diameter, circumference 392.5 MY. Note the 25 or 2.5 units in numbers, and similarly in the line joining the circles' centres: 145 MY.

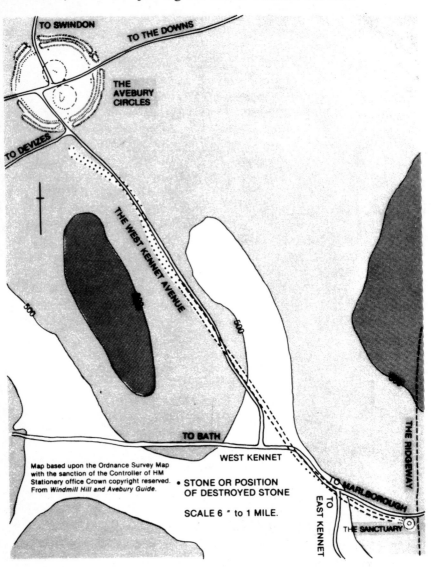

Avebury and the Sanctuary.

The Moon Circle had roughly at centre a pair of very tall stones standing close and possibly a third, now vanished—perhaps a rough trilithon such as may be found in Brittany or maybe just a pair. Stukeley suitably called this 'the Cove'. It is very impressive.

The Sun Circle originally had an obelisk 21 ft tall at centre. To the west is a design like a large 'D' turned eastward, set out in smaller and greater stones.

The mother-goddess temple, now known as 'the Sanctuary', which was from the first reckoned to be the source of the life of the great circle, is on a hill part of another chalk ridge called the Ridgeway, marked by a series of round barrows, by the point where it is cut by the modern road from Marlborough. From Avebury's centre the site is at an angle about east-southeast. Concrete markers are now set in its post or stone holes. Perhaps it had a central post, but its first little circle was of 6 massive posts; 2 rings of stones follow, of 8 and 12 stones; then comes a very close setting, perhaps of stone and wood alternating, with 30 units—a fencing off probably, or even a wall. A little further out are 36 little sockets as for smaller stones, but with 2 larger entrance ones at the north-west. What may be thought of as an enclosure is some way off, a circle of 44 outer stones, diameter 130 ft, with 3 lines of a few stones each radiating to the north-west; a double entry rather like that to the Long Barrow. One notes the posts at the more sacred inner part; wood was earlier and more holy than stone.

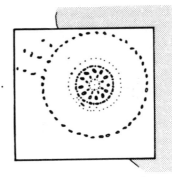

DETAIL THE SANCTUARY
SCALE: APPROX. 1 ″ to 120 ′.

The Sanctuary.

We are justified in looking closely into the numerology of this most sacred temple, since numbers prove so significant in Avebury itself. First note that these are all feminine or even numbers, and the first 3 sets are in the progression 6, 8, 12, up to which it may all well have been roofed in. Only then, when we are at the outer parts, does infusion of odd or masculine numbers come—30 is 5×6, $36 = 9 \times 4$ and $44 = 11 \times 4$. The centre is the number of balance, 6. In the surrounding fence or wall, 30, is the Avebury number 5, probably representing energy on the definite material plane, multiplied by balance, 6. Outside this is a number of external completion, 9, multiplied by the feminine, 4. The outer enclosure's 44 again shows the feminine, but what 11 stood for is vague and perhaps does not much matter. Maybe already they used magical addition; if so it meant the basic feminine, 2.

Between the temple and the Great Circle of Dominion they built the avenue, the curved way down from the abode of the Goddess, whence came birth into this world. Again we have the unit of 100—evidently the dominant number and very significant. The road down from the above was exactly reflected in the world below. Dare we already link with it the Emerald Tablet of Hermes Trismegistus: As above, so below? These stones are fairly clearly male and female alternately in shape—we are intending therefore human generation. The pairs are 50 ft distant from each other and the pairs are 80 ft apart. The concept is confirmed when the avenue curves and narrows abruptly to come into the main circle. This is one of the clear neolithic symbols worked out so ably years ago by Rachel Levy in *The Gate of Horn*: it means birth. Whatever principle descended from the temple is now created and intended to be after the same pattern—100.

If this is general creation, the birth of the solar system or of heavenly bodies, then the attribution of the inner circles to sun and moon is justifiable, for the luminaries came first, according to general later ideas. Around them was created the Circle of Dominion. The Earth would follow —they already had their symbol for that, over there in Silbury—it did not quite fit into the new symbols, but it did well enough. Just as the ancestral Long Barrow would have been better if related to the Sanctuary. Never mind though—this was a bigger and better scheme.

So what was the moon and for what did she or he stand, with that Cove? Not far away they had already quite possibly created Stonehenge's Aubrey Holes, so they had a calculator for the moon that they did not need to repeat. But they lingered in the ideas of the Old Mother of the Long Barrow still, since it was only a half-calculator age. The moon was very magical and had to do with both generation and the entry into life and death. Sometimes you were magicked out of life and came back again, and this always happened at entrances or between two trees or bushes— and above all, stones. If you stood between great stones a haze would come, and suddenly you were not there any more. Such age-old beliefs are to be found still alive in Eire today. It is between these two shadowy monsters, then, that there may be a way to the land of the *sidhe*. The moon seen between them is greatly significant . . .

And what now is the sun, what is he or she? For suns can also be female. At the centre of this southern circle stood a great stone reported by Stukeley and named by him 'the Obelisk', 21 ft tall, say 25 ft long and with 5 ft in ground, since vanished. In this circle is the above-mentioned D-shape. The larger stones form the curve, the very small ones the straight line. In the centre of the curve stood the Obelisk.

No one has suggested any meaning for what is a simple pattern. Yet the pattern appears to be obvious. Is it altogether too obvious to suggest that it may be what in fact it looks like—a bow and arrow? We know this people of Windmill Hill had arrows, and very fine-headed ones. To represent the string or hide thong of the bow you would naturally use the smaller stones. To represent an arrow, why not an obelisk? Both arrow and obelisk are clear sun-symbols in Egypt and indeed generally.

If it is a bow, its shooting directly would appear to be a trifle north of east, say east-northeast. It aims therefore towards some rising sun of early summer. Man's aim is towards the power of the sun—or perhaps he aims to bring down its power as birds are brought down. One recalls that Akhnaton's sun rays had hands at the ends, that is, they were giving; here we aim the other way, at the gift.

Whether this is agreed or not, there does appear to have been a real viewing stone for the sun, called by Stukeley 'the Ring Stone', which has vanished but not quite so completely as the Obelisk—we have its stump. It is on a significant line which, if connected to north-northwest with the centre of the Great Circle, forms a line that runs parallel with the line joining the centres of the Sun and Moon Circles; and it is just south of the Sun Circle. Through it was a viewing hole, says Stukeley, and one guesses it as orientated to the south-east. At what kind of tilt however was the viewing, with that huge mound around? The winter's sun reborn from the old Mother of Night is a regular orientation in periods earlier than orientation to the north-east, which shows the cult of the adoration of the maximum power of the sun, probably masculine. One only guesses, since Stukeley could not leave such precise information and the stone's upper part has gone. All one can say is that this would seem to have been the feature corresponding to Stonehenge's Heol-stone, but aimed at the Winter Solstice.

Let us recapitulate and expand this interpretation. Creation descends from a Goddess level, down the right-handed curve of growth. The male and female stone avenue delivers into a supernal birth—maybe typifying human birth but certainly the creation of sun and moon. This great circle having within it two or more circles will later correspond as at Stonehenge probably with the *primum mobile* and the fixed stars circles; but thought here has not yet become so defined. Have we any planets? There might be some anticipation in certain numbers: 5 is the active material principle and is the number of Mars, and 6 is the number of the sun as balance.

Between the Circles of Sun and Moon would be the place of intense power, especially for healings. To pass between the two fires or Bel or Beli —one of the sun names—was a great healing; on Dartmoor at the two circles of the Grey Wethers one can see the intense blackening. Here, if a ritual were ever to return to this site, is where much of it should take place, at the seat of balance. Take the Druidic catechism in *Barddas*:

Whence come you? What is your beginning?
—I come from the Great World. I had my beginning in Annwn.
Where then are you now, and how come you to be where you are?
—I am in the Little World; I came here after traversing the circles of Abred.
Now I am a Man near the end of that journey.
What then were you in the circle of Abred before you became a man?
—I was in Annwn (the mineral world) the least possible that was capable of
life and the nearest possible to Death.
I came in every form capable of Body and Life to the stage of Man,
along the whole circle . . .

To whatever extent this is ancient and to whatever extent it is due to the poetic invention of Iolo Morganwg (and at the least it does represent earlier Druid ideas) one can hardly deny the elevation and appropriateness of such words to this place of descending creation, between the circles of the aimed-at sun and the mysterious Cove-set moon, within the vaster earth ramparts some 4,000 years old.

The Dragon and the Stonehenge-Avebury Axis

Does creation continue on from the circle, having descended into it? This is where Stukeley's dragon comes in. The dragon or serpent is a very ancient symbol of creative power and wisdom, and the second Chief Druid knew this well. The Sanctuary was obviously the dragon's head, the avenue his neck, the circle his body, and his tail went out correspondingly northwards. No one however seems to have satisfactorily pointed out any stone feature corresponding to the end of the tail, and this so-tidy scheme therefore seems to fall to the ground. Dragon symbols are around certainly; one need look no further than to the remarkable dragon font in Avebury's own church, just outside the great circle. [2]

A new interpretation of the dragon as a near-universal symbol for early man by F.W. Holiday is worth mentioning here. [3] After a good deal of practical investigation Holiday, Lionel Leslie and others concluded that the water dragons, both of Loch Ness and of Irish lakes, were as real and as unreal as flying saucers; both had left immense traces on beliefs and were basic in religions. The sea-serpent's series of coils in the water became the series of knobs on so many prehistoric drawings, and the beaded band, so often seen surrounding circles, especially quartered ones, in his body or tail. Again, the zigzag or chevron on early art would be this. Holiday further goes into the identification of disk-barrows and eye-shapes, usually considered as suns, with representations of flying saucers, which are in fact all-seeing things. *The Dragon and the Disc* is an important contribution to possible interpretations of these shapes and also of pillars of fire.

Inigo Jones had already made a fascinating study linking Stonehenge and Avebury in the seventeenth century. By tradition Stonehenge is a temple of Saturn and Time; and the newer numerology emphasizes the rightness

[2] Traces of a second avenue have recently been discovered at Avebury. [Ed.]
[3] Holiday, F.W., *The Dragon and the Disc*, Sidgwick & Jackson, 1973.

of this. The 2 structures are almost north and south of each other, some 17 miles apart. Was there not a track, an avenue, linking them? Indeed there is. About 7 miles north of the Giants' Dance (Stonehenge) is Casterley Camp, made very squarely indeed. This could be Jupiter's square. Overlooking the Vale of Pewsey and 3 miles on is Marden—this could be Mars. Another 4 miles and we are at the remarkable Knop or Milk Hill, and Cneph is an Egyptian name for the deity linked with Mercury. However we are now having our planetary order from Ptolemy upset: next should be sun-Earth not Mercury. We do, certainly, come upon Earth next, just off the line at Silbury. But Venus, according to Inigo Jones, is way up at Winterton Bassett, thus lengthening the axis by 7.5 miles to 24.5 miles. There are or were certain stone circles near the station. To increase credibility, he placed Silbury as Earth in the centre, and striking circles around, could show Venus' orbit as between Mars and Mercury. Next he showed the moon's circle and then the sun's next to the Earth.

Granted that certain astrologers did so vary the order of the planets, placing the luminaries next to the Earth and the five planets in succession, it still seems forced, especially as we now know of the Windmill Hill site, the West Kennet Long Barrow and the Overton Hill Sanctuary, none of which was within Inigo Jones' ken. A Venus site would be now taken as either the Sanctuary or the Long Barrow; and whether Cneph-Knop or Marden really pass muster is doubtful, however possible Casterley seems. Where the great architect was marvellously right was in placing Silbury at the centre as Earth—earth indeed and how!

Incidentally, on Palm Sundays it appears that the local population was in the habit of ascending the hill to drink hydromel or 'honey-water', which may be interpreted as mead.

That there is a link between Avebury and Stonehenge seems certain and there is an ancient way between. Treated as a ley line it seems full of power. Fresh work now needs to be done on the axis idea.

One estimate has been that Avebury is 800–1,000 years older than Stonehenge, which is now considered over 2,000 BC. It certainly seems all of that in the development of ideas. The short distance between the monuments makes it improbable that wholly different races produced them. This is of course guesswork; but the development of ideas between them is not.

About all this early dating it needs to be said clearly, without derogation to the careful efforts of archaeologists, that we may be startlingly wrong. Radio-carbon dating has placed Stonehenge between 500 and 1,000 years earlier than Atkinson did. So it may be elsewhere, hence Avebury may well be 1,000–1,500 years before this, perhaps 3,400 BC. We simply do not yet know. But dates tend to go further and further back.

Avebury is twice or thrice clearly orientated to the reborn sun of midwinter, implying the Mother Goddess, deity of the hill, from whom life descends hundredfold into creation, which is reflecting its number in 100 liths.

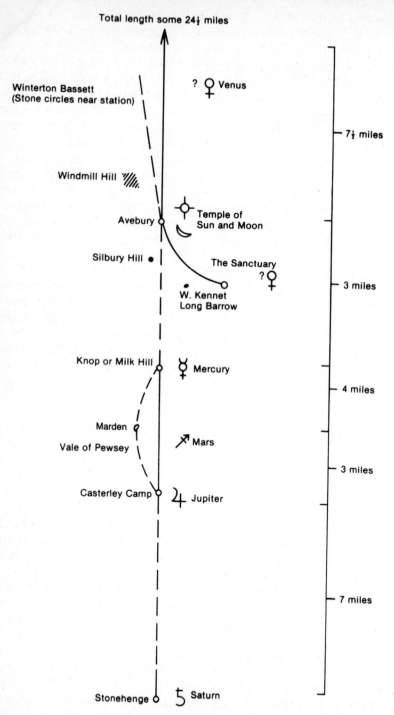

The Stonehenge-Avebury Axis.

At Stonehenge instead of a hill we have the mental structure of a pyramid erected on the diameters of the Aubrey Hole circle and conceived to the proportional height of the Great Pyramid. From this the powers of the planets worked. Stonehenge's triangles develop the Pythagorean basis as of Avebury itself and in many other circles as demonstrated by Thom.

Stonehenge has numbers in circles clearly indicating moon calculations —56 and 19. Avebury has one separate Moon Circle with the mystic Cove only. Some will feel that the depth in its mystery is worth all the calculator-boys' work at Stonehenge.

The sun at Stonehenge is an enclosing circle—370 is the total of perimeter numbers of the square of the sun. It is also the observed rising that passes through several entries to illuminate the central sun-stone or altar at the Solstice. In Avebury there seem to be two symbols: in the Sun Circle may be a bow-and-arrow—man's determination to fetch down sun-power—and there was the holed stone probably set on a line to observe somewhere near the Winter Solstice rising.

Numerology indicates several times that the great sarsen circle of 30 arches at Stonehenge is identified with the Earth, by actual circumference measurements. Avebury by its earlier scheme has the most solid possible earth, built of contributory earths and signifying surely the union of men dwelling on earth, tribe upon tribe.

The size of Avebury suggests huge gatherings with circular dancing and games. Mystically, the vast size spelt failure; it is simply not true that power generated by a small circular group is increased if the dancing circle is larger beyond a very reasonable number of people, say 50 at the outside. The mind boggles at the size of the human circle dancing in Avebury. It was all very jolly no doubt for the tribes, but those in charge of the mystic-psychic side must have realized the lack of true power. Perhaps indeed the Sun and Moon Circles worked better. No psychic known to the writer has picked up any influence that is at all definite from an Avebury monster stone, unless a little lingers in the Great Cove of the Moon.

Hence, recognizing the failure of this popular approach, the observer-scientist-priests made Stonehenge plainly a specialist structure, a physics laboratory. Possibly festivities at some season occurred say around the Aubrey Holes; but it seems a fairly certain guess that minds of the calibre of the calculator Druids, constantly engaged in abstruse work, would never allow a mob of tribesmen to invade their inner sanctuary. They provided, however, a good ceremonial avenue and some way away was a nice big cursus where everybody could race and have fun to their hearts' content.

Most of the ideas found at Avebury therefore are found developed by vastly superior minds at Stonehenge. It is the difference between the intelligent-barbaric, directed in some structures by a mathematical mind, and a sort of wonderland for calculators, an obvious élite with ideas far beyond those of any possible generality of tribesmen, however intelligent.

Stonehenge and Avebury

Since Avebury is the only circular monument in England at all like Stonehenge in complexity and size, a comparison on certain lines seems inevitable. Accepting that the outer ditch-and-mounds of Stonehenge correspond to a creative cosmic force, at Avebury we have a 100-stone circle always known as 'dominion'—perhaps the dome of the heavens shown by numbers of extreme extension and return, 10 × 10. But this has its earlier or higher cause, for the supreme power represented by the Sanctuary temple sends down its power by the snake-like avenue curved and narrowed into the birth-entrance. It would seem like a Great Mother in heaven, sending a long way down into matter and there creating in mystic birth. The numerations of the temple are dominantly feminine.

It is within this general area that the sun, moon and Earth occur, and nearly balancing Earth (Silbury) is the finest mother shrine in England, West Kennet Long Barrow. Was this a fourth feature of the same order? I think it might represent man with its humanoid five-fold shape—its 'laura' of four chapels (four limbs, four elements, etc), and its larger head to the south-east; in cave form it corresponds to the five trilithons of Stonehenge. Mankind is embodied in the Great Mother; and at the other side, Silbury balances it as the cone of many earths raised into the symbol of mankind as the phallus of power. These on the inner (higher) level would correspond to the sun and moon. This would be indeed different from Stonehenge, but a kind of ancestral shape with similar basic thought.

Qualifying all this is the general revolution of ideas between the ages of the two structures. The one is dominantly of the long barrow civilization, the other of the round barrow. One cannot make a complete distinction indeed, for a long barrow presides over the Stonehenge cursus and there are round barrows on Windmill Hill; but the difference between the two types of thought is quite clear.

In the long barrow the dead are laid communally, the revered elders the more carefully. These pastoralists returned at intervals and consulted them, leaving the chamber only temporarily blocked. There were scrying and voices. Emphasis was upon earth, darkness, mystery. Only after hundreds of years was the barrow piled up inside tightly and firmly sealed—both the Bryn Celli Ddu and the West Kennet were so found—packed to the roof. West Kennet indeed is reckoned now to have been open for about 1,000 years.

Ideas about the dead were chained somewhat to their bodies and to the *Kas* which seemed to inhabit them, contacted by shamans. It all forms a frequent kind of primitive cult. But as the circle developed, with its psychic powers, sooner or later someone was bound to think of experimenting in concentrating upon the spirit of one passed on, and this worked. So was it not necessary to have all the darkness and bones? The spirit seemed to live in another world, lightly attached if at all, to the material one. Such ideas have been commonplaces of modern séances; our ancestors were no less experimental and curious. Indeed it has often been noted that psychic powers are primitive rather than a mark of high culture. It now seemed rather old-fashioned to build a massive house for the dead. Surely they were better freed from this decaying flesh?

From the very beginning of civilization fire has had a mystic significance. It is the great transformer, the sign of the god. Fire is bidden from heaven to consume the sacrifice. In a way fire is the abode of spirit, together with air. Fire and air, these are the mutables.

Nowadays we think less of the idea of a new wave of the race, coming from Switzerland and ultimately from the eastern Mediterranean, which, whilst the seafarers had boated it to the islands, had been passing more slowly up the Balkans and into central Europe. These whole peoples from 3,000 BC or so are now generally thought Celtic. But the new ideas came over about fire and round barrows. The later peoples did have aristocracy and chieftainships; they were very class-conscious. These folk are largely identified with cremation, and round barrows usually for the ashes are, one feels, made for the leaders, not for the majority of tribesmen. Whether a race migrated or whether a few people came with a teaching that spread does not matter much.

With these qualifications and in this way therefore fire began to replace earth as the true abode of the dead. Of the four elements by means of which dead bodies can be disposed,[4] this one marks a great advance in thought, surely. Fire links with light, with the sun; the sun, with these new arrivals, begins to take the leading role in religion. Its winter rebirth re-emphasized the Dark Mother—linked with the past in the great barrow—who produced the bright infant; the Summer Solstice is new, it finds magic and power in the maximum elevation of the sun alone, probably by now considered male. Some arrive at a natural monotheism, allied with patriarchy, a monotheism which the mother-goddess cult never included—she was always associated with lovers or sons.

This changeover has been spoken of as a religious crusade, the neolithic religion. The change was doubtless electrifying; one wishes more were known of the contemporary attitude. As it is, archaeology has to serve as the handmaid to reasonable speculation.

Historical Note

Enthusiasm for agrarian progress sometimes took bizarre forms. To give them more cleared land and building materials farmers and owners combined to destroy most of Avebury. Stukeley in his yearly visits from 1694 to 1724 reports bitterly on the destruction. We have a vivid sketch by him of the flames and pits used. Only some time after 1724 did the vandalism cease. Profit-making was reinforced by the idea that the stones were somehow evil in themselves, an idea that still locally persists.

---

[4] The four element burials are Air, when giant kites pick the bones of the bodies exposed in the Towers of Silence; Water, when bodies are launched into sacred rivers; Earth, normal burial; and Fire, cremation on the pyre.

The monument owes its rescue in modern times from almost complete destruction to the selfless interest of Alexander Keiller who became owner and for years had excavations, markings and intelligent restoration done until the western area of the circle stood in pretty good form. In 1942 the National Trust became landlords with the Ministry of Works as guardians. Again intelligent work has been done. The Avebury museum's collection still largely consists of Keiller's own finds.[5]

II. The Dance of the Giants: Stonehenge

Cor Gaur (great circle, Ancient Cymric).
Cathoir Ghall (choir of giants, Gaelic).
Chorea Gigantum (Latin translation).
Claudair Cyfrangon (Old Welsh Triads).
Stonehenge (debased Saxon, 'suspension of stones').

The *site* of Stonehenge is astronomically calculated. Only at very nearly its longitude and latitude could the angulations of the seasons have worked into the symmetrical pattern that they make. It speaks of a long knowledge gained from posts or stones that such a calendar-temple could have been designed without apparently any trial and error; for it was enlarged and developed, but did not need to be changed. Woodhenge, rather earlier, is nearby.

This holy area was and is alive with burial places, obviously for those who wished, or whose tribe wished, for them to be buried or their ashes inhumed within the holy place. Wiltshire has 2,000 round barrows, and 300 of them are near Stonehenge. These are mostly subsequent to Stonehenge's building. Of the 86 long barrows in Wiltshire, there are but two nearby. Beautifully-made flint arrowheads are plentiful in them. One long barrow is very important: it presides over the chariot-racing circus beyond Stonehenge, as the grave of Hector presided over the funerary games in the Odyssey and as the grave of Tailte, Lugh's fostermother, presides over the games at Tailtin (Teltown) in Eire.

The bell-barrows are characteristic of Wiltshire; each has a conical mound 5–15 ft high, a turfed circle and a circular ditch of 100 ft or more in diameter. The disc barrows are more common round Stonehenge than anywhere else. In all these, four out of five hold interred ashes, not the crouched burials in cists found in the barrows of previous generations.

From Stonehenge itself a noble group of seven round barrows, six of them bells, can be seen under a half-mile distant, against the skyline to the north. To the south, about a mile away, is a great number on Normanton

---

[5] However, in more recent times (1989) plans have been put forward for a 'Tudor' Theme Park at Avebury, a dreadful clash of periods which would scarcely help the sacred atmosphere of the place. [Ed.]

Down, some 28, and another long barrow.

The archaeological history of Stonehenge, as we have seen, is of two or three cults and cultures of peoples. Its making and re-making went on for over 500 years, perhaps for 1,000. The residents of Britain, who had in say 2300 BC been here 1,000 years or so, were already agricultural. This was towards the end of the megalithic period and there began to be a little bronze used. They had evolved the long barrow cult of ancestors, had developed big stone entrances, then these round barrows, for individuals or small groups, then the mystique of the great stone, sometimes alone, usually in circles or dolmens. The numbers of things had come to have immense significance. Their experts worked quite complex calculations.

The only monument at all resembling Stonehenge was the great circular stone temple in Odilienburg in Alsace, which was destroyed and of which we only possess partial records. It showed some of the building skill that suggests knowledge of Mediterranean structures, having mortices and tenons like Stonehenge, and it is in the middle of a large area of La Tène culture remains. T.D. Kendrick[1] indeed linked both monuments with classical culture, and reckoned that Stonehenge was a Druid building, a British answer to Druidry's virtual destruction in Gaul by Rome, which shows how clueless quite distinguished scholars could be over dates. Further work on the Odilienburg relics is really overdue.

Modern Druids have always known Stonehenge mainly as a sun temple. Less obviously, it has been clearly linked for them with the moon, by the two horseshoe shapes at the centre: the trilithons and the bluestone horseshoe. It is the temple of Saturn by several schemes, one linking it with Avebury, and by a classical myth and Greek accounts it is the temple of Apollo as the sun-deity. Further, the way in which the central trilithons and the bluestone circle, so far as it remains, increase in height to the enormous trilith at the north-west (of which the single lith remains) shows a cult of midwinter death. A former guardian of the monument pointed this out, in an out-of-print official guide. There are spring and autumn sunrise and sunset orientations also, and similarly with the moon (not needing Professor Watkins to point them out, for they have always been known).

To a large number of people Druidry immediately connects with Stonehenge on the one hand, with the Welsh on the other. In each idea the public is both right and wrong. To link Stonehenge with Druids in origin is to wave a red rag that will draw the charge of all dogmatically-minded archaeologists (and most are very dogmatic), while to suggest to the Welsh that such things as English Druids have a right to exist is to draw an even more formidable stream of oratorical and poetic fury. 'No one except a Welshman has any right to be called a Druid,' was a recent Archdruidic pronouncement.

Yet to deny that Stonehenge expresses that cult of reverence for the

[1] Kendrick, T.D., *The Druids: a study in Keltic Prehistory*, Cass, 1927.

natural powers represented by sun and moon and commonly called Druidic is not possible; indeed if the numerological suggestions we are setting out here mean anything, they mean a link with and a reverence for several other heavenly bodies too, and all in specific detail. And if at such periods the Cymric and Gaelic peoples, or previous races, were using either Avebury or Stonehenge as centres, then Welsh, Irish or English peoples are indistinguishable at such dates, and the whole later nationalism is absurd applied to such early matters. Whatever the Welsh claim, they cannot transfer Stonehenge to Wales, although the early Welsh may very well have been in Wiltshire. This was in fact what Iolo Morganwg and David Samwell evidently knew in their day—more wisely than their successors.

Stonehenge rightly remains a main symbol for Druidry; and the varied and important studies recently made of it are urgently to be acknowledged by present-day Druids and their conclusions applied. All these studies in fact work towards confirming the traditional Druid view of its enshrining Druidic learning and a true mystery teaching.

Preliminary Studies

To appreciate the relevance of the more accurate measurements recently worked out for Stonehenge certain preliminary knowledge however is needed.

It appears that the Ptolemaic-Copernican numbers and ideas commonly known amongst mystics, together with the Pythagorean and Qabalistic schemes, have an immensely older ancestry in human thought than had been reckoned possible. With the extension further and further back of the dating of civilization and with the two revolutionary reconceptions of neolithic abilities by Professor Hawkins and Professor Thom, the existence of what had been usually thought of as classical and medieval ideas some 2–3,000 years earlier can hardly be ruled out as impossible. The Pythagorean system is recognized as a masterly redevelopment of much earlier ideas, and one recalls that Pythagoras is reputed to have been received into the Druid Order at Marseilles, that Abaris from the land of the Hyperboreans (Britain?) visited him there, Abaris being reported as well versed in Greek and 'fit for the reception of wisdom' (Herodotus).

For the general reader, therefore, it seems necessary to set out the general and associated numbers and nature of the planetary bodies and luminaries, and further to make with the writer the assumption that under whatever name, the properties now linked with these numerations were already known in 3,000–2,000 BC. The following therefore are the common attributions of Qabalistic and Ptolemaic numbers, together with some of the links with the Stonehenge features:

One — The one origin, the supreme power, initial force, the male. Certainly applies to the central stone and to the Heol-stone; perhaps also to the outermost earthwork—the circle of origin.

Two — Basic division, pillars of entry, male and female; also it is the feminine generally, in contrast to the 1 male.

Three — The product of 1 and 2 by addition. Hence 3 stands for general creative energy, the triangle or 3 rays. The beginning of the Apparent, identified with the first shapes of matter and its disciplines: hence it is the mother, Binah, in the Qabala, and Saturn in astrology. It can be reckoned the number of the outer earthwork, whose inner perimeter is 333, and this number 333 repeats in 2 other circles.

Four — The number of balance, the distinctly feminine, 2 × 2 or 2 + 2. The four qualities or elements, hence stability, the square. Often the number of Earth, and by Qabalastic-astrological reckoning, it is the number of the creative father-mother Jupiter. The sarsen circle with its squared earth identification is Jupiter.

Five — If 4 is the completed body, 5 has the addition of intelligence; 5 is thus essentially man, his senses, his 5 fingers and toes. Likewise it is the number of intelligent energy, Mars, the energy of 3 but fully directed. Sometimes this is combat, but not essentially; Mars can be idealistic or knightly energy as well. Five links (*vide* Pythagoras) with the Great Pyramid, indeed he makes it the pyramid-triangle shape itself.

Six — This obviously is a double triangle or 2 3s some way arranged. The usual symbol is the interlaced triangle or Shield of Daoud (David): ✡ It stands for balance and the union of male with female. In the Qabalistic Sephiroth it is the sun or heart. Stonehenge being a sun-reckoner, it is not surprising to find the holiest circle, that nearest to the great trilithons, measuring the square of the sun, 666. By one reckoning Stonehenge has 6 circles and there are 6 entrances by way of which light reaches the centre stone.

Seven — This is 4 + 3, basis and creation added. The divine shape, the pyramid, was in later times always given this number, that of its base and its side elevation added. There is reason to link the Great Pyramid with the station stones rectangle of Stonehenge plus its side elevation as triangle (3). By later astrology, 7 is the number of Venus, which is inconsistent with the rest of the elementary numerical scheme. So taken, 7 stands for the Mother Goddess in various forms. Perhaps the pyramid is feminine therefore; matter (materia) is usually so reckoned, and the pyramid may be considered perfected matter. Multiplying the factors 4 and 3 we have 12, representing established forms on the material plane.

Eight — The double 4 by addition or the 4 × 2. In the astrological
Qabalastic scheme it stands for intelligence, Mercury, the
swift-traveller; sometimes called the Christ-number. But if 7 is
divine, then 8 is the divine with a high form of the feminine.
It could be reckoned, if we want a name, as Pallas Athene, the
masculinoid intelligence of Athens' patron goddess. It is also
given as the number of return, or soul and body, by later
medieval reckoning, reincarnation by others. The sarsen circle's
area is 888 sq yds.

Nine — The 3 × 3, energy by energy multiplied, hence power, often
reckoned magical, identified with witchcraft, and above all
with the moon. The whole area of Stonehenge has the number
of the moon in 999, also the moon is figured by the exact
astronomical numbers of 19 (the number of years taken for
moon to return to its place in the sky) and 56 (both the cycle
of the moon's eclipses and 4 times the moon's 14 nights from
new to full). Nine more generally, however, means the completion of creation, the last number in fact, for 10 is the end and
beginning in the primary scheme of 10.

Ten — Here by the elementary numerology we stop, for 10 = 1 + 0,
and we begin another cycle. It is also however the higher
echelon of 1, and hence often taken externally for the sun, most
powerful form of 1.

To unravel further this ancient mystique of numbers it is necessary to know
that each of these number-planets had a magical square. These are usually
started with the Saturn square, 3 figures one way and 3 another. The
definition of a magical square is that each line adds up to the same figure,
in all directions, vertical, horizontal or diagonal. In one square only the
total of all figures adds to a triple figure of the number of the body
concerned, so that the magic square of the sun, whose number is 6, totals
666. The addition of the numbers around the perimeter of the square was
also sometimes significant in linking circles with squares.

Taking the magic square of the sun or 6 for example:

6	32	3	34	35	1
7	11	27	28	8	30
19	14	16	15	23	24
18	20	22	21	17	13
25	29	10	9	26	12
36	5	33	4	2	31

Here it will be seen that the total
of numbers is 666 and that the
perimeter numbers total 370; each
column totals 111.

Since there was held to be a mystic identity between circles and squares, if a circle in circumference, area or diameter is identified by numbers with a magic square, the two were held to be identical in substance; especially if a perimeter number of a square coincided in number with that of a circle's circumference.

The magic squares run from 3 to 9, i.e. Saturn 3, Jupiter 4, Mars 5, the sun 6, Venus 7, Mercury 8 and the moon 9. The first three are those whose orbits are outside the earth's orbit; then, after the sun, come the two which orbit between earth and the sun and are therefore higher; then the moon is highest, next to the high form of the sun in the heavens; for the sun in the midst is that which is in immediate relationship with the Earth, figuring the heart in the body; the moon figured the spirit, as the highest number of completion, 9. A tabulation of the squares' qualities may help:

Analysis of Magic Squares 3–9

Heavenly body	Ptolemaic number	Total of each column	Total of numbers in square	Number of units in square	Total of perimeter numbers
Saturn	3	15	45	9	40
Jupiter	4	34	136	16	102
Mars	5	65	325	25	208
The sun	6	111	666	36	370
Venus	7	165	1155	49	580
Mercury	8	270	2080	64	934
The moon	9	369	8321	81	1333

Square-numbers could, less practicably, be the square of 2 or 1; indeed the figures 111 and 222 in some of these workings may bear some such meaning, as might be supposed.

One more consideration must be given: that of various scales of measurement. The foot and the yard are of respectable antiquity, but the foot is sometimes varying in different areas. The cubit, very ancient, also has several versions. The megalithic yard is an elucidation in which a pioneer was J. Eyre of Cambridge. It is 2.72 feet.

It would seem that the constructors of ancient edifices had all these geometrical and arithmetical schemes and several scales in mind, so that identifications can be made between structures measured by different scales with the same numbers. Thus the inner side of the outer mound–and–ditch circle of Stonehenge measures 333 yards; the medial line through the Aubrey Holes measures 333 MY in circumference; and the outer circumference of the sarsen stone circle measures 333 feet. This is hardly accidental, indeed those who see in this and other numbers more than chance can hardly be denied, especially when it is remembered that by tradition the number 333 is in fact that of Saturn and that the temple of Saturn has been the main traditional attribution of Stonehenge.

The Structure and its Interpretations

Now let us look as visitors at Stonehenge. It lies on an upland plain, not very high or strikingly situated, within a short distance of Amesbury, which we learn was originally 'the town of Ambrose', and as modern Ambrose is the old Welsh Emrys, this is Mercury, the intuitive spirit, by common interpretation.

Up from the Amesbury direction, whence we approach the monument, are supposed to have been floated the circle bluestones and perhaps also the greater sarsen stones, probably upon wide, shallow, skin-covered craft such as Brogger and Haenken have found were common about 2000 BC or earlier travelling up the western coasts of Europe. There is no need to suppose, with Welsh professors, that Welsh coracles were used, nor that the bluestones came from Wales—they could as likely have come from Ireland, and the trade route ran more naturally there. (See pp. 156–8.)

Professor Atkins, who detailed some years ago 16 sun and moon orientations across the great stones, reckoning the heavens as at about 1500 BC (*Stonehenge Decoded*, Souvenir Press, 1966), remarks that only at about this longitude could these orientations have been combined into one workable system. It speaks therefore of long experiments in surveying the heavenly bodies, perhaps with wooden posts, and many postholes have in fact been found in Stonehenge, especially in the oldest parts near the Heol-stone.

Professor Atkins, an American, and Fred Hoyle, the Cambridge physicist and mathematician, together worked upon establishing the Aubrey Holes circle as a computer for eclipses of the moon, which have a cycle of 56. Many were inclined to doubt the startling implications of Professor Atkins, with its revelation of the great calculating ability of people whom Professor Atkinson had led many to believe were of lowly intelligence; until, that is, Atkins' work was conjoined with that of the well-known and unimpeachable Hoyle, famous for his BBC talks and trenchant views.

Professor Thom came later, showing Stonehenge as one in a great system of orientated ovals and ovoid shapes, of which he had by then investigated a considerable number in Scotland and elsewhere.

Thus a series of scientific writers have followed the careful archaeologist Professor Atkinson, whose detailed account, dates, etc. remains basic and cautious. The more precisely these stones were studied and measured, the more remarkable were the results. It was then time for wider comparative studies, and the work meanwhile done on the cubit, the megalithic yard and other measures made possible comparisons of Avebury and Glastonbury Abbey with supernal schemes such as Ezekiel's Holy Oblation and St John's New Jerusalem, and the ideas apparently expressed in the Great Pyramid. Some worthy attempts had earlier been made, but nothing like the daring comparisons and apparent identifications set up by John Michell whose work has caused furious thought, not always friendly but always respectful.[2]

---

[2] Michell, J., *New View over Atlantis*, (Revised Edition), Thomas & Hudson, 1987.

However wonderful the structure and the observations that once came from it, evidently much was lost or went into a world of secret instructions, which is always possible; the later Druids had a tradition of secret instruction specifically about numbers and the secrets of the universe and 'the nature of things', says Caesar. The Celtic elders seem to have been the successors to a system of ancient learning here that had many of the features of that which was later known as Druidry. Leaving this for a later treatment, however, the main history of Stonehenge is one of blank ignorance and even ridicule. Someone cheerfully compared the place—presumably having in mind the five trilithons in their unfallen state—to a set of giantess' false teeth. Its reappraisal was also set about with fantasy. The peculiar antiquarianism of the seventeenth and eighteenth centuries led to a learned tome—one of the first to draw serious attention to the monument—by the great architect Inigo Jones entitled *Stonehenge Restored to the Danes*. This would be in line with a child's history-book once conned by the writer in youth which spoke of it as post-Roman. The second Chosen Chief of the modern Druids, the 'ingenious' Dr William Stukeley, thought that it was quite probably built by intelligent elephants. Wild as this seems, at any rate he was one of the first who realized its great age; his guess was 10,000 years old. Indeed, since Professor Atkinson appeared to have established its period as 1800–1500 BC which he later modified to 1750–1450 BC, radio-carbon dating has estimated it as anything from 600–1,000 years earlier than such figures, and this might make it nearly 5,000 years old—a good deal nearer to Stukeley than to *Little Arthur's History*. It could well be found to be yet older.

With all these clouds of ignorance about it, however, something remained—people seem always to have come here at the Summer Solstice and observed the dawn, with or without ritual. There is some evidence of the cult as far back as Roman times and perhaps rather later.

It is well to look at a good aerial photograph before visiting Stonehenge. This enables one to note the double mounds and the ditch that surround it and form in fact the first circle: the hollow in which lies the Recumbent ('Slaughter') Stone, and the little circle that surrounds the Heol-stone. A wider view shows the great avenue bearing down to the now shrunken stream of the Avon, and a scheme of burial mounds around on the hills, which is very suggestive.

It is easy on the ground hardly to notice the outer earthwork circles; archaeologists agree here that at both Avebury and at Parliament Hill the circles are cult ones, to keep something in rather than to keep enemies out, and are not offensive-defensive. We come across an alien gravel with which a troubled Office of Works has sought to deal with the footwork of thousands of visitors, and the barbed wire that keeps out intruders— possibly necessary, but of doubtful legality, considering the people's common law right of access to national shrines and places of beauty, especially so at a National Observance such as the Solstice dawn.[3]

[3] Written before the stupidly unnecessary actions of recent years. [Ed.]

Stonehenge is a Saxon-based name; this race found nothing better to say about these stones than that they were hung up, a 'hanging' of stones like the 'hanging' gardens of Babylon. It is the *Cor Gaur*, the great circle; the *Chorea Gigantum* or Choir of the Giants; the Dance of the Giants; the Temple of Apollo, it seems, to the Greeks, the Temple of Saturn by another account. The Great Ear and the Stones of Time are other titles. Around all circles hangs the suggestion of dancing or singing; these stones have or had an echoing quality—that is, if one spoke quite low into a cavity in a particular stone one could be heard right across the other side of the circle. The Ministry of Works in its wisdom has now filled in this cavity, and this particular Whispering Giant is silent.

The central altar-stone is of a different quality from any other; it is of a rare pale green Micaceous sandstone and its parallel is with the Coronation Stone, the Irish Lia Fail or Stone of Scone. It was never lying down but upstanding; an earlier generation reported the probable hole, and anyway the altar of the period was normally upright. Pictures of romantic sacrifices, always one notes of beautiful maidens by wicked Druids on a prone stone, are particularly absurd. Oil, wine or incense would have been more likely offerings.

One sees four trilithons, not five; the fifth is only represented by one magnificent lith. The Ministry could quite well erect this feature, as it did another trilithon a few years ago; but there is a dogma that appears to prevent the re-erection of a stone that fell before a certain date. It is time that dogma ceased to work. Then the fallen central stone would be released, and this 'altar' stone could then well be put up again. The public could see much more nearly what this great temple was, and how the rays work in winter as well as in summer.

Some distance away the Heol-stone bows towards the centre. Any observer without preconceptions is likely to be struck by the fish-face that is evident both sides of the untooled stone. It is the oldest and presumably the holiest stone of all; of a peculiar quality and chosen, it seems, for its shape. The usual idea is that it has fallen somewhat to this angle; but also it could very well have been set like that in order to respect the central 'altar' stone. The earth circle around makes it an obvious lingam-and-yoni emblem as in India. If light is marked as coming over or 'off' the head of this upright phallus, then light is conceived as a sexual essence fertilizing something.[4]

On the way back we may note a great flat stone some 21-ft long at one side of a hollow, known as the Recumbent or 'Slaughter' Stone, the latter name being one of those names the eighteenth and nineteenth centuries liked to use to bolster the myth of human sacrifice. We know that in the eighteenth century this was upright, and it seems to have been one of a pair

---

[4] That it is not an exact 'fit' to the Solstice dawn angulation and probably never was is one of those inexplicable facts that bedevil the literal minded but do not alter the central pattern. See Atkinson's *Stonehenge* (Hamish Hamilton, 1956) for details.

of which the other has vanished—together with something like two-thirds of the total stone content of the monument.

Between earthwork circle and the great stones a series of white discs are painted on the ground. These mark the Aubrey Holes, named after the antiquarian Druidic founder John Aubrey. There are 56 of them and form a circle of themselves. The first version was that they were holes designed for stones never set up; it is now reckoned that they were certainly for moveable stones or logs used in moon calculation.

What we do not see are the covered-up excavations of the Y and Z sockets, places of the earlier settings of the bluestones, before the sarsen circle-builders took them down—to replace them later, when tooled, in their present bluestone circle and horseshoe positions. The outer ring had 60 sockets.

A huge number of finds, bronze daggers, worked flints and pottery, have come from the Stonehenge area. Amber necklaces, gold coins and square plates tell of a relatively wealthy community of traders and visitors from great distances.

One can approach Stonehenge up the old avenue, and this is perhaps the best way. It runs from the north-east for some 500 yds and divides. One way runs towards the avenue along which came the great stones, borne first by shallow boats, then slid upon chalk grooves, the other way runs north to the cursus, the barely discernible area some distance away with a rather ruined Great Barrow beside it.

If coming south-west from this direction, the arch by which we re-enter the sarsen stone circle from the north-east is, it will be noted, wider than the rest—evidently made for the honorific reception of sun-rays or of some cult priest representing them. And immediately inside the sarsen arches are a few smaller, rather more slate-coloured stones; these, normally little noticed, are regularly set and semi-tooled, and are the older blue-stones. This is their re-setting by the sarsen-stone builders, who did the tooling, and though few now, their circle can be exactly estimated and numbered. There were two of these bluestones to every sarsen upright, that is, there were 30 sarsens, plus of course 30 lintels, and 60 bluestones, without lintels.

The whole place is encumbered with many fallen stones at awkward angles which, now that all have been duly and carefully surveyed, could mostly be put back and built up again with advantage.

It is soon realized that the trilithon stones rise to a climax in the one lith of the fifth trilithon to the south-west. If we did not know that the summer sunrise was at the north-east and had not been told that this was the point, we should assume that the cult was the other way on. We should quite probably be right, as may later be shown.

We might already have noted, rather further away, two small mounds and two rather inconspicuous natural stones. Only by using compass and calculation would one realize that these are the eastern and western stones, and the northern and southern mounds. Not that they are exactly in these places, but they are calculating stations and markers of a certain oblong, not a square, with mysterious properties.

A Philosophical Numerology

After this conducted tour, it is time for an exposition of the workings of these circles and other features, which should now be more familiar and intelligible.

Two mound-circles and a ditch between form the earthwork. It can therefore be taken as a single structure, and either a medial line be measured, or they can be taken as two features. Taking it as two, the outer circumference measures 1006 ft or 370 MY, the inner 333 yards. The inner indicates Saturn and the outer the sun. The whole area within is 999 sq yds, the number of the moon.

The circle of 56 Aubrey Holes represents the 56-year cycle of the eclipses of the moon and a scheme for 'working' them, a sort of *aide-mémoire*. Their medial circumference is 333 MY—Saturn again.

Upon this holes-circle is based the quadrangle of the four 'compass point' stations, mounds or stones. We would naturally go across from stone to stone or mound to mound, and find that each diagonal—which is also of course the diameter of the circle—is 227.5 ft. Adding these diagonals we have 555 ft, the square of Mars. But 227.5 MY itself is the exact length of one side (base) of the Great Pyramid. Can this be accident? Perhaps, but there is another such accident also. The height of the Pyramid, 480 ft or 176.5 MY, is exactly the proportionate distance, in feet 176.5, from the Stonehenge centre to a point a little beyond the most external reckoning of the great earth circles, where are postholes, probably of a wooden temple. Thus there appears the triangle which is the exact profile of the great Pyramid.

So far we have three outer earth circles: one of holes (the moon) and two of mounds (one the containing sun, the other the inward-working energy).[5] Now we come to the greatest and most wonderfully structured of the extant stone circles: that of the tall stones of the great sarsen ring with their fitted lintels.

The outer side's circumference is 333 ft, a third Saturn feature. The area's square measurement is also remarkable: it is 1,080 sq MY, often taken as the number of the square of Mercury, although that is 2,080; or in square yards it is 888, again the Mercury square. This number has links with the moon, water and the spiritual-feminine principle. These are very remarkable figures indeed.

Doing a simple structure of circles, Mr Michell finds that the diameter 106 ft is just one-third of the total diameter of Stonehenge to the outer earthwork.[6] By circle construction a *vesica* appears neatly enclosing the

[5] Two other circles, of Y and Z holes, may in effect be ignored. They have been excavated and refilled.
[6] *New View Over Atlantis*, ibid.

sarsen circle by the cutting of two circles each of 666 ft circumference. Here is the sun again, the number of the sun's square.

A further working within the sarsen circle results in an inner vesica similarly formed 61.2 ft high by 35.3 ft wide. The circle fitting within this inner vesica is 111 ft in circumference and fits neatly within the bluestone horseshoe. Now 111 suggests a sort of square of ones, and this is the inmost thinkable circle calculation around the one central upright stone. The diamond of the vesica is 1,080 sq ft, the Mercury or Hermes number.

The strangest feature of the numerology here has still to be mentioned: numbers in the sarsen circle make it a model of the Earth itself. The sarsen inner circumference is 316.8 ft. The square containing the earth's circumference is 31,680 miles round. Thus the circle represents the squared or more spiritual or planned aspect of the globe in the proportion of one-tenth foot or 1 ft to the mile.

The square is more 'spiritual', because any square or 4 is both a double feminine principle of 2 × 2 and also a basic principle or divison into 4, the basis and the 4 elements—the Four Causes to the medieval schoolmen—the Jupiter principle of balance, where harmony begins. The square is therefore normally reckoned as foundation or Earth or balance; as the circle is the sign of perfected nature, so the square is of balanced mind.

Thus the general fact of the square—or still more the cube—means a planned balance, in heaven or earth, and the numbers here mean identification with this particular earth, Terra.

The area number links with the 'soul' number of Mercury, Hermes, the guide of spirits and of all spirit, linked again with the water-and-moon syndrome.

The next circle, the bluestone 60, gives us the logical complement of Hermes and the feminine principle: it is the 12, number of external realization and of day and night, multiplied by the intense activity of 5. There is a circumference of 144 cubits, that is, it is identified with the square of the Heavenly Jerusalem, which is 12 × 12 cubits in area, filled with the divine presence represented by the sun. In case the point is missed it is given again; the area in MY is that of the sun's square, 666. So the bluestone circle of the older stones from the previous culture has been set into the most honorific circle nearest the trilithons, and represents the sun as cubic temple, an Apollo temple indeed, in highest form.

Thus all circles have squared-up or three-dimensional forms. Recapitulating, the inner earthwork has the squared form of the basic creative Saturn principle 333, which continues with the next two circles. The Aubrey Holes clearly indicate a squared set-up by the station stones and mounds, which prove to link with the Great Pyramid. The holes themselves are the external moon calculators. The sarsen circle identifies with the temple of earth; the bluestones, holiest of all, give us the sun's own squared temple.

So far it may have been noticed that the number 5 has only appeared once and that is as the doubled diameter of the Aubrey Holes, as 555 ft, sug-

gesting an emphasis on developed energies which the Aubrey Hole circle
and pyramid might well represent. But now we come to the central feature
but one: here are 5 trilithons, the gateways of man's senses, or the 4 bases
of elements plus man's intelligence, symbol of the ancient pentagram, the
5 senses or man ensouled on a first level. The great trilithon can be that of
the spirit, to the south-west. And by this placing is formed a shape ancient
indeed, the horseshoe of the Old Mother.

Centring the sun-temple of bluestones is clearly this symbol. Is she the
moon again? From the general symbolism of the horseshoe one would
think so; and we are, again, not really left in doubt, for within the horseshoe
are yet more bluestones in a formation of the moon's number, 19, likely to
be representing the more sacred cycle and basic idea of moon, since the
Aubrey Holes gave the outer shape in the utilitarian sense. It repeats the
moon-theme with a different accent, not of eclipses but of positive returns
to the same heavenly station, a heavenly cycle of absolute certainty, the
more 'spiritual' side, surely. For each 19 years the moon returns to the same
place in the sky; as everyone then knew and most of us do not. Putting it
another way, the bluestone house of the sun is inhabited rather by the
general Mother Goddess as ruler of humanity and its energies, than by her
as moon in particular; she is a higher thing, the Eternal Return.

Note that the woman, beauty, or moon, as it were Venus, although never
with her number 7, is balanced in the traditional way by the Mars-quality
of the number 5, the complementaries always of warrior and goddess,
bravery and beauty, sun and moon, as throughout most mythologies; the
same balance as is represented in Druidry by the symbol of the golden
sickle reported by Caesar for the cutting of the mistle-plant. The shape is
the moon's, the metal the sun's.

The upright obelisk stone of the centre, the One Alone, origin and force
identified with sun—which is also the sun-child, the Maban, growing into
the Ōg or summer sun—can be taken as just that, or it can be reckoned
as the completing sixth of the central features.[7] If so, the Giant's Dance
concludes centrally, as it began outwardly, with the number of balance, so
much associated with the temple, the double triangle, the male-female
balance, the shield of Daoud. Alternatively it concludes with eight, a still
more holy number perhaps.

No one ever saw a dawn sun ray strike upon anything; at dawn the sun
is a vague general light which catches only with a glow the upper parts of
objects. So here the light caught the probably gold-and-silver coated
central stone which glowed. As the sun became more distinct after rising,
this glow spread down the obelisk, until by noon the light would be
descending almost parallel with the angle of the column; the obelisk in fact
became the ray penetrating earth. So, in a more elaborate shape, in every
Egyptian temple the obelisk personified the sun's ray, at varying angles.

The fructifying ray from the fish-phallus had passed the rings of

[7] Or eighth, remembering the Y and Z holes.

creation, entered between the two flat stones probably meaning the entry into the mother, come into the wide entry of the sarsen symbol of earth and then the two wide horseshoes of the feminine moon. Then it had mounted its obelisk-stone, to descend into earth. So the centre obelisk represents the seed that became a giant, the Maban growing into the Ŏg. Did anyone ever sacrifice upon the awkward tip of a monolith? Perhaps oil and wine, as in the almost contemporary records of the Old Testament patriarchs, but a stand would have been needed to reach it.

The Invisible Pyramid

If we are dealing with people whose constructions and comparative knowledge were as great as they seem to be, the finding in Stonehenge of the proportionate lengths of two sides of the Great Pyramid plus its height would surely mean something more than just that. We have in fact the elevation for the erection here of a pyramid. Place therefore a square of 227.5 ft sides over the Stonehenge plan, centre to centre. We now have a base reaching rather outside the outer earth circles. Elevate the centre 176.5 ft and the pyramid is conceived as towering up, one corner pointing to the Heol-stone and others corresponding, its sides therefore facing to the points of the compass, as does the Great Pyramid in Egypt. It would be containing in its height the squares and circles of the huge plan that lies within the earthworks. Indeed the squares might become a series of in-fitting cubes, like some Chinese box-puzzle.

If we accept this concept, the eye of philosophic faith would see the two mounds with ditch between as first representing the great circular or swirling movement, the first motion in which all things begin, and then as the raying in of actual energy, perhaps from the starry bodies beyond our system. This basic Saturnian energy at the moon's circle immediately erects the perfect cubic form of the pyramid, which further fosters and perhaps causes the particular planetary number-shapes we have traced; at their heart are the sun and moon forms, conceived as further inward than the earth surface itself, in fact in symbol the heavenly bodies within man himself, his heart the sun, his spirit the moon. The whole concept then shows a construction of which Avebury was a much earlier sketch with its great circle of dominion, its sun and moon circles, its cone of earth and mother-temple nearby.

If our speculation as regards the circles is at all valid, at the pyramid we should have something representing the wandering stars or planets. They cannot be reckoned as in one sphere; manifestly there are several spheres. What we do know is that in early reckonings there were 5 of them. The pyramid form has 5 points. True, it has traditionally been reckoned mystically as representing 7, the square base plus the triangle sides, but this may well be a later thing, for 4 or 5 points are the numbers that leap to the eye with the pyramid shape: 4 the base, 1 the tip. There is no evidence that Pythagoras reckoned it as 7; he linked the triangular pyramid shape with 5 and 55. So can we, but perhaps also add in 4; we have had the number

3 with Saturn, and this complex structure may well cover the next 2 numbers. The pyramid is probably here to be the representation of the Great Five planets, Mercury, Venus, Mars, Jupiter and Saturn—sun, moon and Earth are by numerological showing separately reckoned. Mercury (Hermes) is probably the tip, the 4 others at the quarters.

The Earth itself is reckoned from its temple form, since as previously mentioned the great sarsen stone circle of 30 stones and arches has a 316.8 ft circumference which is model of the 31,680-mile-perimeter of the square containing the circle of earth.

The Pyramid as Planets

Accepting the top, then, as the Messenger of the Gods, having the number 8, Saturn, as material basis to the north and Mars as energy to the south; Jupiter would be to the east and Venus to the west or vice versa. This all seems repellently modern, and equivalent shapes can easily be found from ancient Gaul or Eire which would seem less incongruous in the 4–5,000 year old setting than later Roman astrological names.

The tip of the pyramid might be Lugh or Lugaidh, who is light and wisdom, the deity leading the living from birth to birth through the gates of death, corresponding to Hermes the guide. Venus could well be the gracious and dignified Dana, racial spirit-mother of Ireland's fourth race the Danaans, with her long fair hair, accompanied by elkhounds and tall deer. Her earlier form is even more basic, Ana. Saturn as the material can be the former earthy food and one-eyed sun-god, the Dagda, the racial father. Jupiter would no longer be an equivocal sultan of the heavens but An or Aesus, pure Being, radiating from the East, linked with the Ahura-Mazda of the Persians. He might here have already the later Celtic-Druid name of Hu (Hé). Mars would be Teutates, the father of men, who may also be Thoth, the vizier of Rā from Egypt; the great voice and proclaimer of the divine decrees. The sun would be Ōg, (pron. 'aug'), the sun power, or perhaps Beli the sun orb in this scheme, and the moon Ceridwen; basic Earth would be below, say as the fourfold Ainé of Munster.

Summing up, therefore, the successive circles and features from the outward inwards, we have *primary creativity*, Saturn, thrice marked; the *moon* as seen in the sky; possibly the *planetary orbits* as pyramid; *Earth* and the *moisture-Mercury* principle and the *Jupiter* temple; next inwards the *Apollo-sun*, the male force, and his *temple* in the heavens; then *Mars* and the *Mother-Venus* balanced in the trilithons; within this, the specific inner *moon-magic* horseshoe; then the *One* that unites in itself the two, or the One with the Great Five, giving the *supreme balance*. We have therefore the whole pantheon of twelve principles.

Put into listed form, and adding in some previous conclusions, we have from the outermost:

The primum mobile, the activating force of creation, represented by the sun-square.

The *firmament* of the stars, represented by the total area being moon.
The *threefold Saturn* as solid form—perhaps in three stages of solidifying.
The *moon*, in its mysterious physical changing and vanishing forms.
Perhaps the *pyramid*, the five-pointed shape that held the Great Five planets.
The fourfold *Jupiter* temple.
The *model of Earth* within it.
The *Mercury* moisture and *spirit principle* indwelling earth.
The *divine temple*, later to be St John's Jerusalem.
The main deity perhaps, the *sun*, later identified with the classical Apollo.
The masculine and feminine forces, shown in the *Great Mother* or *Venus* shape, and qualifying this, the male energy of *Mars*.[8]
The *Moon* again, now as *magical mother*.[9]
The obelisk as *central sun*, balancing the surrounding circle of creation and the horseshoe moon, probably shown as male-female in its metallic gold-silver mantle.
The central balance of the *six* (or *eight*).
Twelve schematic symbols therefore surround the central sun; these are what were illumined in the days of the Solstice, the realization of spirit upon Earth in highest form. They are not quite as a modern mystic might have placed them, but we can well recognize the logic of their forms.

There is too much numerology and it is much too exact for it to be dismissed as coincidence or wishful thinking. And if it is accepted, it raises strange questions as to a near-universal culture, for the numerology seems to link between most of the places where neolithic or later great temples exist. Was there after all a super-race or a school of divine philosophers? The inner Druid Order has always stated this.

Stonehenge Schemes

Dimensions and Some Meanings

Keys to Diagram
A **Outer mound and ditch:** sun, Saturn, moon.
   Outer circumference: 1,666 ft or 370 MY, i.e. sum of perimeter numbers of the sun's square. This should mean the external temple form of the sun.
   Inner circumference: 333 yards or 999 ft. An emphasis upon the basic number of Saturn, material foundation and energy, facing inwards or the moon, 9.
   Area of circle: 999^2 ft. Emphasis upon the moon, magical mistress of life, and etheric substance.

[8] It is notable that the numbers added in the square of Mars total 65 in each column, and in Venus' square total 165, whilst the perimeter numbers are 208 and 580 respectively. Such numbers would have meant a definite relationship to our forbears.
[9] Again, the columnar number of the moon's square is divisible by 9—an extra significance of some kind.

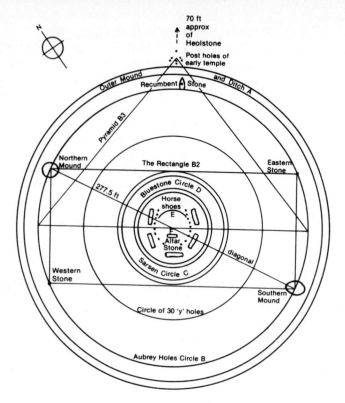

Scheme of the Stonehenge Complex.

B **Aubrey Holes circle:** (1) Station stones rectangle; (2) Outline of the
   pyramid; (3) The moon (its working), Saturn and Mars.
   (1) *Number of holes:* 56 (14 × 4). The cycle of the moon's eclipses.
       Medial circumference: 333 MY. The emphasis upon the basic number
       of Saturn.
   (2) *Rectangle:* 264 × 100.9 ft.
       Diagonals, stone to stone or mound to mound: Each 277.5 ft. This is the
       number in MY of one side of the Great Pyramid. The two diagonals
       added = 555 ft, number of Mars (energy).
   (3) *Pyramid:* If 227.5 ft is the number of one side of the Great Pyramid
       in MY then in proportion the pyramid's height is 176.5 ft, the
       distance from Stonehenge's epicentre to the postholes just beyond
       the entrance, showing a very early wooden temple. The Y and Z
       circles of holes now filled in, each of 30 sockets, occur just here and
       emphasize the 30 motif.

C **Sarsen circle with lintels:** Saturn, model Earth, moon, Mercury.
   Number of arches: 30. A sacred number in Egypt and the number of
   divisions in Egyptian year.

Number of stones: 60.
Outer circumference of circle: 333 ft. Emphasis on Saturn.
Inner circumference: 316.8 ft = 116.4 MY. A square whose perimeter is 31,680 miles exactly contains the circumference of the Earth in miles.
Diameter: 106 ft or 39 MY. A hint of moon, for the regular moon working is a cycle of 39.8 lunar months. As regards 106, centre to centre the lintels prove to be 10.56 ft apart.
Area: 1080 MY^2 or 888 sq. yards. Both numbers indicate Mercury.

D **Bluestone circle (no lintels):** Egypt, the New Jerusalem, the sun.
Number of stones: 60, an Egyptian number for time division.
Medial perimeter: 248 ft = 144 cubits, number of the Heavenly Jerusalem.
Area: 666^2 MY the square of the sun.

E **The Horseshoes, Outer and Inner:**
Sarsens: Moon cauldron, Mars, the senses, quadratures, balances.
Stones, 5 arches: cove or pentagram, the senses and human being, application of Mars forces.
Number: 15 in all, by magical addition 6, symbol of balance. Also this can be reckoned as the sixth concentric feature.
Sightings: The Eight-fold Year is here determined in its quadratures by sightings.
Main Symbol: Clearly the moon horseshoe or cauldron to receive the solstitial sun.
Bluestones: Moon, Saturn, Mars.
Number of stones: 19. A permanent symbol for the otherwise changing moon, the number of years it takes for her to return to the same position in the heavens.
Circle diameter: If the horseshoe is completed to a circle, the diameter = 39.6 ft, i.e. 13.2 × 3, which is more precisely the number of the moon months × the 3 aspects of the moon, or by general creation, 3.
Area measurement: 166.5^2 MY, being 5 times the creation symbol of Saturn, 33.3. Energetic Mars creation therefore.
The Central and Pointer Liths:
Central 'altar' stone: some 16 ft long: when in ground perhaps 12 or 13 ft high.
Recumbent Stone: 21 ft long × 7 ft × 3 ft: almost certainly one of a pair that formed a gateway (Atkinson), say 17–18 ft high with 3 or 4 ft buried.
The Heol or gnomon stone: 20 ft as seen but probably 24 ft in height with 4 ft buried. From Stonehenge centre to the Heol is 256 ft to 264 ft according to how it is measured. It could be significant that 256 = 4^4 —very much the mother-creation number. Taking 264, it is a mixture of 3 and 11 and 8—also suitable by numerology.

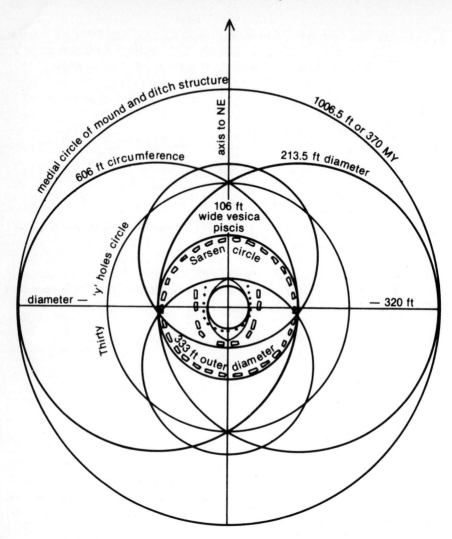

There are three vesicas within stonehenge: the first encloses the sarsen circle, the third the circle fitting within the bluestone horseshoe. This third vesica = 61.2 ft × 35.24 ft and the diamond = 1,080 ft sq. area, the number of Hermes. The circumference of 2 large circles is that of the square of the sun. The middle circle coincides with the circle of 30 'y' holes now invisible. At Midsummer's Solstice the sun penetrates the first and third vesicas — the sacred number 666 penetrating the earth-spirit mercury's number 1,080. Added, they make the number of perfections 1,746, by gematria the Pearl of Wisdom or Grain of Mustard Seed.

Circles, Vesicas and Meanings.

Vesica and Diamond

The intersection of two circles each of 666 ft circumference, on the diameter of the earthwork circle, 320 ft, form a *vesica piscis* 106 ft wide, exactly containing the sarsen circle. The inner bluestone horseshoe circle is similarly contained in a corresponding inner working, the *vesica* being 61.2 ft × 35.6 ft. The diamond shape within this vesica has an area of 1,080 sq ft—again the Mercury-Hermes-wisdom or wayshowing number. Reference should be made to John Michell's books for the full numerological working, in which the sun and Mercury numbers are even more evident. Generally speaking, the measurements seem to say that it is the male and creatively balanced sun force 666 that enters the womb-shaped centre of the Mercury feminine principle represented by 1,080 (or 2,080). This clearly and entirely supports the aboriginal Druidic teaching about the Solstice dawn light entering the central cauldron of earth and Mercury of the 8, being basically feminine.

This leads obviously to another look at the Qabalah in which Mercury (Hod) is taken as masculine. Can the balancing number of 7 reckoned as Netsach or Venus be male? One recalls that the beauty figure of Greece was quite as much Apollo as Aphrodite (Venus).

The Stonehenge Time-Schemes

Stonehenge is above all a time-measurer, hence its identification with Saturn. What were the measures?

Nineteen, the number of the Moon's return to the same place in the sky, has always been a sacred number. (The sacred inner oval here has 19 bluestones.) Also considered sacred has been 56, the Aubrey Holes number, 14 × 4 the moon's cycle.

Several times, it seems, 4 is indicated as the number of the 'holy' lost days at the sun's apogee around the Summer Solstice, especially at the New Grange temple in Eire, where 4 suns (i.e. days) are carved at the north-eastern outer side of the barrow upon the containing stones. Now if it were a year divided by 19s, $19^2 = 361$, leaving 4 'lost' days, if the moon is so taken, at midsummer.

Another, more usual, moon reckoning is 28 × 13, leaving one 'lost' day. (A year and a day is one of the old legal reckonings, e.g. for the hiring of labour.)

Looking at Stonehenge as it stood, there were 5 trilithons with 3 bluestones standing before each, and 4 stones spaced between the trilithon; also there is the space for 3 at the north-east towards the sun's apogee. Is this arrangement indicative of 3 or 4 midsummer days? The space is of course at the right angle for it, north-east, the same as at New Grange. If so, the year would seem to be of 5 seasons like the Egyptian. Each would be of 72.2 days, thereby leaving the 4 sacred days. Three stones before each trilithon ought to mean that each of the five seasons was divided into 3 24.67-day months, 15 months in all.

Such numbers would be agreeable with what we know of old numer-

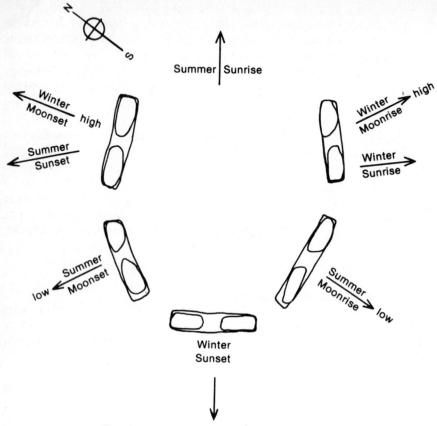

The sarsen stone horseshoes or pentagram.
Through the five trilithons the above are
indicated sighted upon various other stones.

The Stonehenge Scheme of Sightings.

ology, for 72 was sacred as 9 × 8, and 24 was sacred as 8 × 3, whilst 5
is the basic 5 seasons and the number of humanity (5 fingers and toes, 5
senses), so is 4 as foundation, and 3 as a creation number. Above all, 19 is
a 'secret' high number.

The Egyptians had a year of 30 decans of 12 days each leaving 5 sacred
days. Here there are two circles of 30 arches and 60 stones respectively,
with 5 trilithons, or 4 day-arches and one great arch of departure. Also
there are 60 Y-holes.

The Sixteen-fold Year

Professor Thom, working on the sun's declinations and finding orientations to one or another heavenly body marked in many circles, and above
all at Stonehenge, has concluded with considerable mathematical probability that the year was divided into 61 equal parts and has worked out

how many days these months should have—4 with 22 days, 11 with 23 and one of 24, the whole cycle starting with the vernal equinox. Each mark on the horizon served twice, for the spring and for the autumn halves of the year. The sun's appearance can be calculated in various ways, but it seems that the first appearance of the top edge of the sun was usual for the rising, and the last edge disappearing for the setting; but a few observations do show the calculation as being for when the orb completely left the horizon in morning or first touched it at evening. Further work, it appears, may well show the year divided into 32 divisions of 11 or 12 days each.

Summarizing, we have a possible scheme of 24.2-day months, grouped triply into 5 seasons, plus 4 sacred days over. This would be similar to the numerical scheme of the apparent period and chime in with Egypt to some extent. It looks like an intelligent and more accurate adaptation of the Egyptian idea—5 sacred days there, 4 or 3 here, 12-day periods there, periods of 24.067 days here. This too on further scrutiny may well tie up with Professor Thom's ideas.

The Rising of the Sixfold Sun

So far we have built up a series of concentric temples, circular and square, with numbers of profound significance. These by themselves should be convincing enough of the serious and detailed intention of the builders. But to leave it at that would be to indicate the stable without the horse. What was the action?

Here is the avenue, here the circles, with dancing and singing traditions. To the instructed eye, overhead are domes and cubes and, above all, the pyramid of the five nightly planets; the sun circle without, the sun within, the moon calculated in the heavens, the moon as the Great Mother central. But the line of action is from the north-east—the ray from the fish-father, the Heol, through the entrances to the sun obelisk at the centre of all. And it goes on past the obelisk into the Great Gateway.

The Heol is the oldest stone and the true father, a kind of Adam. In it ritually was hidden the sword—there is a convenient crack into which it can fit.

The upright so-called 'altar' stone was an *obelisk*, which, as for Rā at Heliopolis in Egypt, caught the light upon its gold-and-silver-covered height. In Ireland we know that Crōm the old god was an upright stone covered with gold in the centre of a circle of 12 stones (one of the chronicles of St Patrick gives us this).

Here the sun comes first as a child, the Maban, the child form of Ạn the spirit (or the later Hu), as a soft dawn light reaches the tip of the column, then as he grows the light moves down, strengthens and in a few hours illumines the whole shining mass. He is Beli. As he rose in the sky the vertical ray seemed to penetrate earth. Thus the god-force comes to man in luminous stone, as in Egypt. Did he, as in Egypt, have all three names of his three stages, as did the moon inner forms?

I am Khepera (the sun-beetle) in my ascent:
I am Amûn in my strength:
I am Atoüm in my descending.

Shall we say:
The Maban or Mabin-Õg or Hu (Hé)—ascending.
Beli, the sundisk or Õg—the established noon.
Lugaidh, Lugh, the Mercury of Light, Life and Death—descending into shadows.

Accompanying this fivefold entry, to the sixth form came priests from the avenue, probably releasing birds as the sun came to the tip of the pillar. The flaming phoenix of Egypt and Persia could be a form of this. A great sound of harps and singing arose. A solemn dance ringed the sarsen circle.

The Sacred Death

The high priest of summer therefore comes from the north-east. Yet Stonehenge is not mainly facing this way. The triliths rise to the climax of the south-west, and this is the place of the death of midwinter.

The sinking orb of 21–2 December departed through the huge arch of the south-west, 21 ft 6 inches high, over a further stone alignment now destroyed. The final gleam shone upon the tip of the obelisk, the weak old sun shines on the *stupa*-like stone aloft. At last darkness seized its prey, Lugh was extinguished, the light-god was gone. There are only traces of this. It was pretty surely a time of sacrifices. It is that side of the circle which has been mainly destroyed. Again and again as in the names raying out from the Exmoor Dunkery to the north-west we can see the pattern of death repeat. Was that side linked, then, with horror? Did the sun not depart alone? Was there some great suttee?

There is not much sign of the winter rebirth at the south-east being celebrated, as it was at the Llandin, which is Parliament Hill Highgate, where it shows in a hill-line, or at Cashel Aenghus, which is New Grange, Ireland. Winter here was death, summer was power. That is, all seasons are oriented here—there are at least 16 orientations—but nothing special seems to mark the south-east; there are simply clear views to the north-east and south-east, that is all.

It was, however, made obvious here that death was the gateway to life, through the greatest of arches. We return into the mother-womb of spirit. The trilithon is the higher form of the dolmen, a great arch of rebirth-renewal. I abide in that land for a while, then after six months I am reborn in strength.[10] The great force shoots into earth; it fires the spirit and empowers it. Of course renewal could have been at the spring equinox or

---

[10] Six months according to the Roman calendar that we use today, a period of 2.5 seasons or 7.5 months or 180.5 days plus a few more, if the Stonehenge-Egyptian reckoning we suggest is sound.

on May Day, that day of immense *numen*. But the complement of one Solstice would probably be another.

There were two general spirit realms, that of the natural forms—sun, moon, stars, seasons, animals, crops (of which sun, moon, the general heavens and the Earth itself were symbolized in the great temple's structure)—and the realm of the spirits of the ancestors, which was cultivated rather more by the earlier long-barrow people, who revered and lived with them as it were, with the great burial-earth temple open. Death and rebirth, if there was, as we have suggested, the burning of the dead more recently, means less of an attachment to them personally, more a concern for releasing their spirits. The sun cult lifts heart and mind from earth and night-moon fertility out into the sky. This was first a pastoral folk, then an agricultural one, and both watched the skies. The then Mediterranean climate made the sun fairly dependable—it was a rebirth form of deity.

So there is a great death, but a great birth and power-growth. The sun-spirit mounts daily for 6 of our months—2.5 seasons of the 5—he declines for 2.5, and all comes again. Even as you have seen him go by that arch, so he comes again, self-begotten, upon his obelisk. As he goes and comes, so we go and come. Life is eternal.

Other meanings remain covered; they are within the Druidic *mystique* and may not be written in books. But nothing here given is inconsistent with them.

The Site and the Owners

We have little knowledge of the ownership of the Stonehenge site before the seventeenth century; the area appears to have been common land. To the work of the late John Soul of Amesbury (*Stonehenge and the Ancient Mysteries*) we are indebted for as complete a list of ownerships as seems possible at this late date:

1620 Mr Newduck
1639 Sir Lawrence Washington
(unknown date) Mr Daubeney
1643 Laurence Washington Esq
1655 Lord Ferrars
(gap in particulars)
1723 T. Hayward (possibly Thomas Hayward, author of *A Life of Merlin*)
1727 Rev. W. Hyward, styled on account of his ownership 'Archdruid of the Island'
1770 The third Duke of Queensbury.

The duke bought the Manor of West Amesbury including Stonehenge and Daniel Defoe says he was prepared to 'embellish' it with evergreen trees. Mercifully he did not, but he did do other public works round the area, such as making 'rides' over the downs from Amesbury to Stonehenge, and he built a westward bridge over the Avon.

With his successors Stonehenge seems always to have been kept quite free for access until Sir Edmund Antrobus, fourth Bt., (earlier dates unknown), put up some barbed wire, apparently to protect it. His father however, the third baronet, had, when approached by antiquaries, declined 'to interfere with the privilege of free access enjoyed by the British public from time immemorial.'

When Sir Edmund died in 1915 the large Amesbury Abbey estate was offered for sale, Lot 15 being Stonehenge with 30 acres of downland adjoining. A local gentleman, Mr Cecil Chubb, bought it for £6,600.

Already in 1901 officialdom had mounted a campaign against access in the name of protection. The monument was enclosed with wire and a charge made for admission; it was scheduled under the Ancient Monuments' Protection Act of 1882. An elaborate and lengthy lawsuit followed, with the Chief Druid, George Watson MacGregor-Reid and distinguished supporters including Sir Oliver Lodge backing Mr Chubb against the Office of Works, and the judge finally decided in favour of the owner and therefore of the right of the public to access.

In 1918 Mr Chubb presented the Stonehenge site to the nation and Sir Alfred Mond received the title-deeds for the Office of Works. Only after thus becoming Stonehenge's possessor did the Office of Works really examine the fabric and take other measures from 1920 onwards. Free passes to the monument were granted to local residents.

All the same, free access was granted on the Solstice night and morning, until behaviour by crowds led to their total exclusion by electrified wire, and the admission of some kinds of Druids only, from 1963. After experience of this, the main Order refused to function under circumstances whereby the people—unruly or not—were kept away from the publicly-owned oldest national shrine on the day of the year designed for its cult. The answer should of course have been a few more police, not barbed wire.

III. The Llandin: Parliament Hill, Highgate with the axis to the Bryn Gwyn (Tower of London) and the Tumulus of Boadicea, National Site of the Great Mother

The dominant hills of the London area make an intriguing study. Lud Hill is the hill of Lugh the god of Light; beneath St Paul's cathedral is a considerable Druidic stone circle, as related in the memoirs of Sir Christopher Wren's son. This circle was revealed in the foundations of Old St Paul's, in the course of the rebuilding. The Bryn Gwyn is the White Mound of the Tower of London, and held the head of Bran, the deity of the raven, which totally guarded Britain against invasion until Arthur removed it in the belief that he alone should be guardian of the land. The Pen Ton held a Druidic stone monument of some kind, possibly to the Mother Goddess. And north of the little Primrose Hill, where Druidry resumed its eighteenth-century manifestation, are two notable hills that have played great parts in English history: Highgate Hill and Parliament Hill.

In a military sense these and the Hampstead heights command London. Up here 'trained bands' manoeuvred in times of danger; the Lord Mayor would come out as far as here on national occasions.

In every high seat of a deity, as seen for example all over the Mediter-

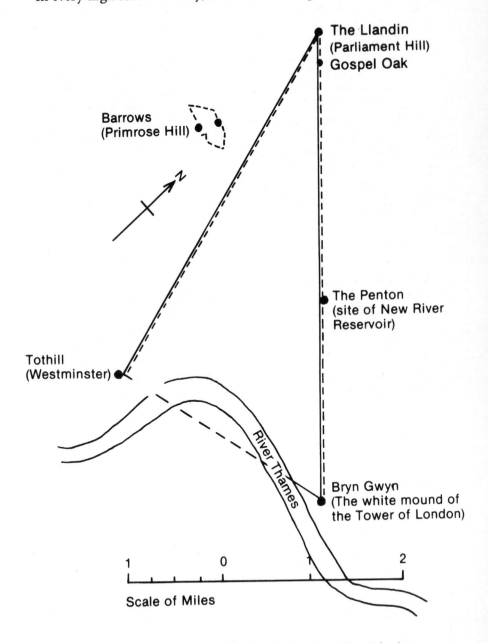

Triangulation of the Northern Heights for London (*Caer Llundain*).

ranean sites, the deity inhabits the real height and the temple a lower place or height. Delphi is the example that springs to mind. It seems highly probable that a mother goddess here presided over Highgate Hill, with its perpetual water on the summit and its traces of Druidic centres in names like 'The Grove'. But the hill below held the human earth-temple, a great Gorsedd place of three mound-and-ditch circles, a gathering-place of extensive tribes for cult and counsel.

What in particular determined the choice of this hill was what must to the neolithics have seemed a divinely-appointed sign: seeking for orientations as they were, here were three or four hills in a line pointing in a significant direction. The summit of the Llandin, the top of the Pen Ton, the spot called Gospel Oak and the Bryn Gwyn or White Hill of the Tower of London, are in a line directly towards the rising point of the midwinter sun. This cannot have seemed less to them than a miraculous finger pointing in the other direction to this site.

So we come to Geoffrey of Monmouth and the landing of the Trojans. Geoffrey's *History of the Kings of Britain*, accepted by subsequent generations and used by Shakespeare, is now generally regarded as wholesale lies. The story is as follows.

Brutus was the great-grandson of Aeneas who fled from the sack of Troy carrying his father Anchises on his back, and after the epic wanderings recounted in Virgil's *Aeneid*, founded Rome. His son Ascanius founded Alba Longa, and Ascanius' son Silvius had a son Brutus who made himself unpopular by unwittingly killing his father. Travelling to Greece, he found the descendants of Priam led by Helenus under bondage to a Greek, King Pendrasus. He established himself amongst them and eventually, since they had by then become 7,000 in number, they begged him to lead them off. Defeating Pendrasus and marrying his daughter Ignoge, Brutus sailed off to an island called Leogecia and in the proper manner with libation he asked the Goddess Diana whither they should sail to find a homeland. She appeared to him as he slept on a hind's skin and directed him to an island once inhabited by giants but deserted now, outside the Pillars of Herakles and under the sunset. 'There by thy sons shall Troy again be builded; there of thy blood shall kings be born . . .'

Accordingly, after a good harrying of Mauretania, they dodged the Sirens near the Pillars of Herakles (Straits of Gibraltar) and found more Trojans by the Tyrrhenian Sea, headed by Corineus. Via the Loire and Aquitaine and further fighting Brutus landed at Totnes, in Albion, where the Brutus Stone is still. Corineus took over the peninsular westwards and named it Cornwall from himself; Brutus also named Britain from himself. Corineus enjoyed wrestling native giants, especially one called Geomagot, twelve cubits tall. He flung him off the cliff at Plymouth, and his blood still stains a deal of the sea red in those parts.

Such jollities therefore surround the building of the third Troy or Caer Llud (the second Troy was Rome). Lud was the name of Casivelaunus' brother. It is difficult to tell whether it is all written of the area of Parliament

Hill or of the future London of the square city mile. It is noted as an indication of dates in a dateless narrative that Eli the priest was reigning in Judaea and the sons of Hector in Troy, whilst in Latium Sylvius Aeneas was third of the Latin kings.

In such manner was the Britain of Brutus born. The tale was so told to our ancestors as children but ours are not allowed to know it, in the interest of literal truth.

As so often, this apparently incredible tale contains truth disguised. First, Troy was the last considerable centre of the old mother-goddess cult in a world of buccaneering father-god Achaeans; hence, it is now realized, at least a great part of its fame and importance, for the fall of Troy meant the fall of a whole religious attitude and culture. Brutus therefore took a mother-goddess religion to a place marked out for it, one may say, in a strange land—this miraculous south-easterly orientation made by nature. Naturally dates have become completely confused and what might be as late as 900 BC has been given as the sixth century.

Secondly, a 'city' had and has a symbolical as well as a literal sense. No one has ever taken the heavenly Jerusalem for one of bricks and mortar, and because no trace whatever has been found of buildings hereabouts, this does not mean that there was not on the Llandin a religious and govern-mental assembly-place of great importance.

The huge enclosure of Parliament Hill has considerable traces of en-closing mounds and ditches, dug inwards–outwards in the manner that signifies a holy place and not military defence. The view over London is magnificent still and must have been much more so before building interfered. Here people could look down to the distant gleam of the Thames and over it at the white hill that marked the end of the ley, over which rose the infant sun of winter.

That this was a great centre for government of some kind as well as of cult seems likely from two facts: one is that up here is one of the half-dozen places that are by the old common law of England recognized as places of free speech which cannot be enclosed. A small pillar on the south-east slope of the hill is traditionally known as the Stone of Free Speech, and although the object itself is a rather vulgar Victorian replacement, doubt-less it preserves the name of the former stone. It did in fact mark a place where earlier meetings were freely held—and where now the Druids meet several times a year for ceremonies.

The other fact is that until the great Reform Act of 1832 voting for the local MP took place, not in the village, but on Parliament Hill. This very odd fact seems to speak of a long tradition of political importance.

We seem to have up here, then, a considerable centre for the tribes around, in later if not earlier neolithic times; a divinely-chosen spot where great leaders had been, a holy place to the water goddess living above, she who had created these hills to show men where to worship her and the direction of her epiphany. Quite probably it existed before the settlement of the marshy area of London and in fact named the city—to this day the

Welsh for London is *Caer Llundain*, the city of the pools.

The whole of Parliament Hill Fields with its natural woods and rolling grass is still one of the untouched spots of London. Here fairy forms and talking trees lingered for very long, and supernatural adventures are recounted by that very careful writer Arthur Machen.

In Roman times it seems to have been here that Boadicea (Boudicca) ranged her forces from the Iceni tribes and extensive lands further east and launched her ill-starred attack upon the well-disciplined forces of Suetonius Paulinus at Battle Bridge some five miles downhill. After her Druid, whose name has only come down to us as a name attached to a function, Swyedydd 'the one learned in the mysteries', had given her poison following disastrous defeat, it would have been customary for the body to be brought up to the last camping-ground for burning on the funerary pyre.

The Order of Bards, Ovates & Druids keeps alive the memory of this gallant queen's resistance to intolerable oppression by meeting each summer at her tumulus for midnight meditation before the Summer Solstice observance.[1] She is much more suitable as a Britannia figure than Nelson's mistress; over six feet tall, with copious red hair flowing past her waist, she possessed a stentorian voice. She stood against the regime of Nero, whose agents not only proposed to seize the whole, instead of a part, of her late husband's property, but totally refused to recognize the matri-linear succession common amongst the Celts; moreover they had raped her daughters—heirs to the throne in Celtic eyes.[2]

The Druids, it is evident, aided and abetted her. Manifestly their rising in Wales and defiance from Mona (Anglesey) was to draw off the Roman armies in that direction. It succeeded, and Boadicea swept down upon city after Roman city including Londinium. Terrified by the magical curses of the Druids, the soldiers had almost mutinied. They were being asked to cut down unarmed and unresistant reverend seniors who merely cursed them. But they did finally massacre that generation of political Druids. As they marched back they were met by the news that Boadicea, an avenging fury, had established herself and sacked Roman towns. Such was the punishment of heaven.

Paulinus was a longheaded general; he knew that in the open field his troops had little chance against the hordes of the enemy, whose fast scythe-wheeled chariots were a menace, and so with great skill he chose his ground near Islington, in the King's Cross area, where Battle Bridge keeps the memory. It was an enclosed site wherein the wheeling British chariots would have no space to manoeuvre. He awaited her attack.

Tacitus has the maddening habit of describing battles in some detail without giving a hint of where they occurred. Now Hampstead and

---

[1] This refers to the period of the author's chieftainship. [Ed.]
[2] For a fuller account of the origin of the struggle see p. 47.

Highgate forest areas were then continuous with Epping Forest, and in Essex was Boadicea's stronghold. A recent book on Boadicea places the great battle between Boadicea and Suetonius far away in the Midlands; but there really seems little ground for upsetting the earlier locations. According to this earlier version, she simply led her forces across, and their resting and rallying place was on Parliament Hill, in all probability. They descended thence upon this enclosed Roman terrain by chariot and waggon, a journey of some three miles, early in August in the year 61. The Celts were over-confident in their chariots and numbers. They even brought their families to witness the victory.

The Roman war machine, ably handled, won: the 'tortoise' of locked shields, the spears and daggers progressed pitilessly upon the Celts, now hampered by their discarded chariots and waggons and unable to escape. There was great slaughter. The defeat was final.

After the event it was normal for Celtic forces to withdraw to their camping-place; and Boadicea's suicide, to avoid the gross indignities put upon the defeated by Rome, whether it occurred on the battlefield or on Parliament Hill, would have meant a funeral pyre, for this people burnt their dead, thus releasing the spirit from the earthly shell as soon as possible. Reincarnation, or rather metempsychosis, was a distinctively Celtic faith: those who died bravely or in brave protest were received with honour in the land of the *sidhe* and returned soon to earth with noble parentage. Whether the tumulus on Parliament Hill ever contained these royal ashes is very doubtful, for there were no burial signs when it was excavated. Nevertheless, the fact that Boadicea's name is attached to it may perpetuate a memory of her dying or being burnt hereabouts.

The Llandin therefore gives us the Druidic site as a national centre. The later Druid Summer Solstice ceremony held here indicates the Chief Druid as the high priest interceding between heaven and earth, like the Chinese Emperor or the Inca of Peru, the Israelite high priest or, *mutatis mutandis*, the Archbishop of Canterbury. The same universal function attaches to the Winter Solstice originally conducted here: it is the mediation of the new birth of all things into light, the new sun-child of the Dark Goddess or moon of night.[2]

IV. Glastonbury

Ynys Vritin = Isle of Woad
Avalon = apple orchard (*avel* = apple, Gaelic)
The Tor; the Chalice Well; the Cavern; the Maze;
The Abbey of the Twelve Hides.

[2] For further information on ancient London including an essay by Ross Nichols see *The Aquarian Guide to Legendary London*, Eds. John Matthews and Chesca Potter, The Aquarian Press, 1990.

In the complex phenomena of Glastonbury's Tor and Chalice Hill, the Blood Well and the stalactite cave, not to speak of the deep awareness present in the ancient abbey zone, resides a mystic and psychic power which makes the area the true shrine of Britain's spiritual life. This is not too high a claim to make for this extraordinary place, where natural forces and man's devotion have combined under many forms.

Glastonbury is a sort of wide bowl with a hilly bottom, a great circle containing many things in its great sweep. The hills around; the plain stretching to the sea; the great fishlike hill which was a landing-place, Weary-all Hill; the conical Tor and its sisters, mainly its domed neighbour Chalice Hill, all have a depth of meaning which has to do with the great watery flats that stretch to the sea and were themselves an inland sea or lagoons. Drainage went on during the middle ages and Tudor times.

When the sea-mist rolls in and from a hill one overlooks a *nebelmer*, a sea of cloud, then as of old the hills stand out, there are the islands of Ynys Vritin, and one can see the shorescape almost as it was when the sea traders approached the two lake village ports, Meare, further out, and Godney, with their tin and lead trades. They were substantial marsh settlements, built on piles, Godney having 70 mounds to be excavated. Here was found the famous little bronze bowl, of local make (for they had many crafts), but seemingly old even in 300 BC or so. It is of fine workmanship, in two parts, rivetted, and with little decorative knobs. In Asia similar ones were used for ceremonial wine-drinking about 1000 BC. If, then, it is sacramental, the numbers may mean something: the knobs are in groups of 5 and 3, one an activity, the other a mystical creation number. The three groups of 3 make 9, a number of completion (and of witchcraft), the three groups of 5 make 15, and the number of knobs on the side of the bowl is therefore 24. If one adds the 3 on the bottom, it is 27, 9 × 3. Here then is one aboriginal 'chalice' for Glastonbury, linked with far-away religious practice.

The waterways, even if land was partly drained, must still have been more substantial than now when the later neolithic and bronze age traders came, for the villages were ports.

Whether Druidry can claim a substantial link here is debatable, for we can trace no Druidic settlement, although it is true that in the eighteenth century an avenue of ancient oaks went up to the top of the Tor on the north side, and that a little way up on the south side on the Pilgrim's way are old stones known as the Druids' Stones.[1] In keeping with the general saga of British mysticism, and the Arthurian traditions in which Druids share, the Order of Bards, Ovates & Druids in the Autumn of 1964 opened its relations with Glastonbury by an adventurous and somewhat hazardous general Gorsedd on the Tor, in accordance with the wishes of its late Chosen Chief.

The flood valley draining to the Severn estuary has, it seems, risen and

[1] See also p. 218 for a yew-tree link.

fallen several times above and below sea-level. It was in fact an inland sea much later than Roman times, and Meare was a tin-dealing port. The coming of Joseph of Arimathaea was to a berthing upon Weary-all Hill, where the miraculous staff whence came the Glastonbury Thorn was planted.

The Holy Thorn blossomed each spring and Christmas and still does; it is a Palestinian species. But it never does so if transplanted from Glastonbury—a strange fact. This was a Jewish-Gaelic enclave perhaps in the Romanized Brython world. There are drawings that show Joseph and his Eleven as a mystical Order, somewhat different from the conventional image of Joseph as foster-father of the divine Child. The sign of the fish was here, both zodiacal perhaps and Christian, and it was on the fish-shaped Wearyall Hill that they landed. On what altar did Joseph lay the Child? One remembers that Pisces was, and was known to be, the sign into which the world was entering, by the precession of the equinoxes.

Going back to the neolithic or an even earlier period however, early men cannot but have been struck with wonder at the twin hill island of the Tor and Chalice Hill. The taller hill was, from one side anyway, a symmetrical cone, from the other a ridge suggestive of a crouching beast. The other hill looked an almost perfect inverted bowl. Between them gushed out a supply of good red-stained water that never stopped—such was the benevolence of that local god amidst the brackish sea-wash. The supply comes from the other side of the Bristol Channel, from the Black Mountains, and in modern times has repeatedly saved the area from drought. This was holy water without doubt; however long you kept it, it never went stale or corrupted.

Another stream came from a cavern under the Tor into another pool nearby. The hills were male and female shapes in excelsis. Under the Tor, the mysterious limestone cavern showed stalagmite and stalactite formations of great beauty and produced blueish water. The impression of holiness grew.

Were the strange and suggestive shapes of hills and mounds and draining ditches really shaped into a vast Sumerian zodiacal scheme? It is tempting to assume it; the aerial survey shapes seem plausible. But if the drainage took place comparatively recently, then the design can hardly be the Sumerian one of 2300 BC or even 1300 BC unless the whole area has been raised much earlier by the falling sea-level. Still, the Bull, the Fish, the Boat Argo and the Dwarf-Giant do look very likely. Could some of this be correct, could some Sumerian motifs have come over later and been outlined in this way? The Graal quest path traced around the figures does seem to correspond to the High History account quite closely. A large slice of the mysticism of Glastonbury lies in this Glastonbury Zodiac work of Mrs K.E. Maltwood. However it is a vast and debatable subject difficult to treat in a short space.

The Maze on the Tor

Did early man shape the Tor with ridges into a maze shape? In some ways it looks remarkably like it, although the official verdict delivered by a group of experts on behalf of the Chalice Well Trust was negative. The famous Cretan maze pattern, known originally from a coin, has been found elsewhere, for instance in the floor of the nave of Milan cathedral by John Ruskin and engraved on rocks and laid out in turf as a kind of play pattern, a 'Troy', in at least two places in this country. It was therefore a fairly universal pattern.

The Cretan Maze.

As a mystical pattern in numerology its message is clear. Using the basis of the simple planetary numerology already indicated, the showing of the Cretan (or earlier?) pattern becomes an intelligible elementary teaching.

You enter upon the third ring in a scheme of 8 and weave outward, then enter the fourth. You then swing into the rhythm 7 — 5, and end with presumably 8 in the middle. This obviously forms a balanced scheme of numbers, each pair adding up to 8. It looks rather like an arch or hollow square, and perhaps other secret numbers are meant to be added in. The total number comes to 36, or 9 × 4 or, by magical addition, 9. Eight is the number of Mercury (Hermes), god of initiations.

The entrance, then, is into the third circle by way of energy in search, thence into second and first. We then go to fourth, then seventh, sixth and fifth; finally to the centre, presumably eighth.

In all systems of 7, 4 is the turning point between 3s. The outer 3 circles have first to be accomplished, the long and difficult ones, then is the turning

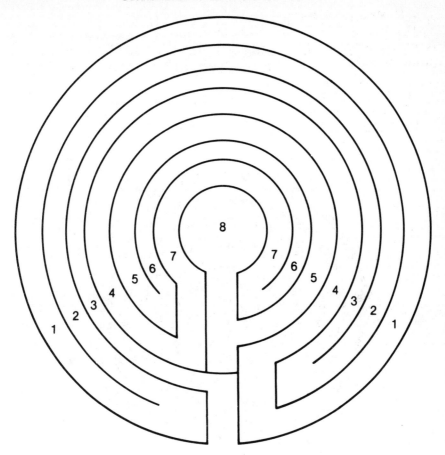

Note: Odd numbers run *deosil* — 3, 1, 7, 5 — and even numbers *tuathal* — 2, 4, 6.

The Cretan Maze Pattern.

point of the fourth circle, which, as a symbol basis, takes you at once to almost the highest, the seventh. Thence you firm up on the more outer sixth and fifth, and the fifth carries you into the centre, to the transcendental eighth.

So an energetic aim (3) should enable one to pick up balance (2) and accept authority (1) easily. Jupiter's balanced vitality (4) can then be absorbed and enables the vision in Venus of inner illumination (7) to lead you to the balance and intuition of the inner sun (6). It is the energy and aim of Mars (5) that finally releases the seeker into the presence of the transcendental and feminine Mercury-Mother (8, the centre).

It seems clear if this reading has any truth that, whatever the earlier age to which this work belongs, the Mother was then still the highest expression of deity. We know she was so in Crete. A lower sun then comes to mean vitality rather than its being the centre of the whole system. The number 8 was sacred very early and belongs to the Sumerian and Egyptian hierarchies of deities. It has also been held to be the number of the Eternal Return and of reincarnation.

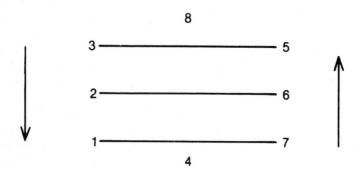

The Number Pattern.

Set out in the obvious way in pairs of circles, each pair totals 8; 4 is halfway, whilst 8 is the circle centre. Eight therefore is the dominant number, not merely a presumed centre. Of the circles the odd numbers run clockwise (deosil), the evens anticlockwise (tuathal).

Now, allowing for the pattern to be elongated in accordance with the shape of the Tor, and rather destroyed on one side, there seems to be a good fit. Such a pattern would be initiatory in a sort of first degree—it is a simple maze with a simple ethical message. But it culminates at the summit of the Tor. Can we believe it ended there?

Various disjointed pieces of evidence point to the former existence of a way down. In the nineteenth century there was a hole in the Tor down which things were dropped and heard very far below. There was a set of steps found in the nineteenth century, which was dug down a certain way but not pursued, only filled up again. Why? There are reports of covered ways and tunnels up to the Tor from the town below.

The limestone cavern is now firmly closed against all investigation by the local Water Board, who have it full of water and talk about water levels and safety.

The usual pattern in mystic initiations is a first simple testing (the Cretan maze) then a severe frightening experience under which people may fail— which could be a somewhat horrific descent precipitately into the hill— and finally a beatific revelation, i.e. the glory of illumined stalactites and stalagmites within. Revelatory teaching was given no doubt as well. This would parallel the cavern in Crete where Zeus was born.

This cave was open in the eighteenth century and its beauty was remarked upon. In this period Glastonbury enjoyed a boom as a 'spa'— the fashionable craze of the day, at maximum about the year 1751—and a queer vertical-sided bath existed to show where folk went into the water, as well as drinking it as a 'cure'. Apparently many improvements were effected. However the boom was only for a few years; Bath is not so far away and the water there is both hot and nastier—two great considerations.

The weird and disconcerting degree of power, whether of static electricity or something more psychic, that inhabits the Tor and the region near to it has to be experienced to be believed. As a youth the writer camped by the magnificent Tithe Barn in order to take part in the Rutland Boughton festival which promised at one time to launch Glastonbury as an English Bayreuth. Although he slept well, in the morning he was charged with an indescribable sensation perhaps akin to electrical vibrations. He knew nothing whatever of psychic phenomena at the time. Only years later was it known that an edict of the Glastonbury abbots laid it down that no one should sleep upon the soil of Glastonbury as it was inhabited by devils—another way of saying the same thing.

The devil was indeed a favourite character in medieval Christianity. So bad was his influence on the Tor that a church or tower had to be built on the summit to suppress him, and, one guesses, to block a way below to an initiation place; but he shook it down with an earthquake. Twice this happened, and the present St Michael's is a tower only. The devil seems to have tolerated it so far. Perhaps it is because the symbols on it are so doubtfully Christian. One side of the west-facing arch is the Holy Cow —a possible symbol for St Brighid certainly, but also for the Mother Goddess and—on the other side is the pair of scales which can be for St Michael, the angel of judgement, but also is the symbol of Thoth of Egypt. Michael of course is the usual surrogate for a chief heathen god, possibly Lugh or Beli.

Queer things happen in this tower: hippies sleep in it and cook meals, and recently a strange figure in white stood in it, immoveable, whilst the Order in its traditional manner laid hands upon the doorway as emblem of air.

Curious climatic phenomena are also observed about the Tor. Rainbows and apparent lassos of light are seen, and storms will divert from it. Some people cannot walk up the Tor at all but feel as though hurled from it. One vision was that it was shaped by men into a great lion whose voice uttered at times from the cavern within.

Until those likely to be in charge are of a greater spiritual awareness, it might one feels be a grave mistake to discover the Tor cavern, for if it has been what we surmise, centuries of neglect will have turned the power there sour. Someone used to such dealings has first to make peace with what may well by now be something malefic, before exploration is carried out. It is not therefore for the present sceptical and untrained authorities.

In contrast with the experience of a great neutral power, rather formidable on the Tor, sensations upon Chalice Hill are positively pleasant.

It is as though fruit is perpetually ripening there, but the apple trees which do grow on the hill are by no means sufficient to explain the feeling. One recalls that 'apple orchard' is one of this place's names.

A small watch-tower kind of settlement from the Arthurian period (fifth century AD) has been excavated on the Tor summit by Philip Rahtz with Mediterranean-type remains similar to those found at Camelot, not many miles distant. If that site was, as appears from the careful work done over several seasons from 1966 by workers directed by Leslie Alcock, the stronghold of a post-Roman chieftain, then the historic Arthur is quite likely to be here. It is a fine defensive position, with water supply and perhaps the remains of stables.

Before the excavations, the Order also seemed to trace at Camelot, with the help of an expert diviner, a processional way across it towards the south-east entry place, with stations at intervals, and an oval shape that was perhaps a games track. These would have been long pre-Arthur and only marked by soil pressures.

Glastonbury has, however, a far more substantial Arthurian link than this: it possesses Arthur's authentic burial place. The strange story of its re-finding twice has been given under Nine Arthurs (p. 132).

The archetypal pair Arthur (Aradr) and Guinevere (Gwynhwyvar) stand for part of a basic ritual to Druids. If there are human figures at all linked with Druidry these are they, rather than the over-distant Pythagoras or Abaris. Their mystic Merlin (Myrddin) stands for the high Druid of magical power.

Athur is a definite subhistoric figure, but he is also a mythical fertility shape and a watery one, quite understandable here. He is on the edge of the matriarchal—Gwynhwyvar has much more importance than is accounted for by a love-story. Arthur has something of the sacrificed king-god—he has a mortal hurt and lies in a state of life-in-death, although he is healed of his deadly wound. In this the myth varies from the simple sacrifice of the mainly Mediterranean examples of the Frazer thesis. The knights are a mixed bag, partly very ancient Welsh, partly much later French. The Graal Quest knights form the central hub: Gwalchmai and Gwalchaved balance each other, either Bedhwyvar or Peredur (Percival) starts the quest. The intruder from a later age is Lancelot; however this Gallicism may be a polite substitute for the old deity Lugh ('Lot'). Gawain (Gwalchmai the Hawk of May) is the Green Man, the healing one. Galahad (Gwalchaved the Hawk of Light) is the second generation (son of Lancelot) who achieves the quest; the first three had been too worldly. It is a kind of quadrated circle, points-of-the compass scheme.

The system and names are linked with the heresy and philosophical background of Pelagius,[2] a doctrine of numerations and spheres and a balance of good and evil, against which the sixth-century Gregory mission

---

[2] Pelagius, it is believed, may also have been a Druid, or at least influenced by Druidry. [Ed.]

was sent. It succeeded, but the semi-pagan system of thought may have carried on in Wales and been the background for the mystical sixth-century poems of Taliesin and Myrddin.

The Church in its wisdom has seen fit to completely conceal this first burial-place of our prototype of kings. Not even a plaque in the grass now marks where it was finally discovered.

Christianity in Glastonbury had mysterious origins and even more mysterious developments. The voyage of Joseph of Arimathaea to Britain carrying the Chalice of the Last Supper is one of those things that cannot be disproved or proved. A good deal of elaboration was added to it by later monkish wonder-seekers, hoping to increase the reputation of the abbey, just as holy relics from many questionable sources arrived and were set up in numberless shrines for the devotion—and contributions—of the gullible faithful. Still, there are established early accounts and facts.

If Joseph came here, perhaps dealing in tin, for he was a trader, he had already been to the mouth of the Rhône where Les Saintes Maries de la Mer is one of the oddest churches in Christendom. In aspect a grim fort, it holds a devotion to St Anne the Old Mother and to Black St Mary, an African associate or servant in the part which included the Blessed Virgin and Mary of Magdala. Later the infant Jesus was also added. It is the church of fishermen whose nets hang on the walls; it is centre to the annual gathering of the gipsies from a considerable part of Europe.

Voyaging hence Joseph's party continued to north Somerset and the haven of Wearyall in the inland sea. He planted his stave on the hill and it sprouted; its descendant is still there. On the other island (where the abbey now stands) he built a daub-and-wattle chapel—the first church in England, as was firmly believed by later centuries. This was carefully preserved within a later chapel. The sprouted stave was the Glastonbury Thorn from Palestine.

Some accounts make it two voyages: that Joseph came first with the Holy Child and his Mother, and after the Crucifixion with the Chalice and the Sacred Blood. The Chalice was buried in Chalice Hill, hence the redness of the perpetually-flowing water.

Some years ago a mystic traveller in Italy received a monition to attend a certain sale.[3] He found there, and bought, what appeared to be a Roman-Greek type of dipper, the kind which at feasts was dipped into the great *krater* or bowl of wine for easier drinking. It was made of glass and silver

---

[3] The traveller was Wellesley Tudor Pole, who lived in Glastonbury and founded the Lamplighter Movement. Apparently he hid the bowl in Chalice Well, where it was subsequently rediscovered by his niece, Kitty Tudor Pole, who received instructions in a dream to look beneath the rim of the well. The bowl was submitted to the most rigorous tests available at the time (c. 1930) and was investigated by Cardinal Gasquet. While in the Cardinal's library, the bowl apparently moved of its own volition, to be found standing on a medieval missal long-believed lost. In recent times, the 'Glastonbury Bowl' was kept in the Upper Room at Little St Michael's house, but has now been moved to a bank vault for safe-keeping. [Ed.]

in alternate layers in a remarkably skilful fashion belonging to the earliest Christian period. It then came to be lost or buried in Glastonbury; by a psychic directive message it was sought for and recovered much later. Whether it is or is not the dipper used at the Last Supper, it is of the period. Obviously, it was a valuable thing at that time and the usual idea is that the disciples were poor men. They did however have rich friends.

Stonehenge Measurements and the Greatest of Britain's Abbeys

From an unspecified time in the past dates the grant of the hides of land at Glastonbury to the early Church, maybe to Joseph himself, as fabled. Bligh Bond's measurements establish a strong link with the numerology of Stonehenge, as though the builders recognized such numbers as part of a universal and divine plan, something too mystical for the later church authorities to take, particularly an impenetrable Bishop of Bath and Wells; Bligh Bond was sacked for his pains as somehow heretical and an evil spiritualist 'dealing with devilish spirits'.

The abbey was a modest building in the twelfth century, erected around the mud-and-wattle church of Joseph of Arimathaea. In 1183 there occurred a great fire that destroyed most of it and a supreme age of building took over the construction by mystical plans of the main abbey between 1189 and 1303. The Chapel of St Mary, to enclose and protect Joseph's church, was designed by the famous Hugh of Avalon, later called St Hugh of Lincoln because later he was the main instigator of Lincoln cathedral. His was the delicate transitional period work of early English architecture, in the days of Henry II.

The length of the final abbey, including the King Ina and King Edgar chapels, was some 630 ft. It came to be reckoned as the greatest abbey in England and its abbot was the senior abbot in the House of Lords.

William of Malmesbury speaks of the mystical plan laid out in the mosaic of the pavement of the St Mary chapel, containing a 'sacred enigma' which included the zodiac. The original area was always given as 12 hides, gift of a mysterious King Arviragus. Now the abbey plan was in the proportions of the New Jerusalem (Rev. 21:16 etc.) that is 12 furlongs square or 1,440 acres, for the hide being 120 acres, the area is 144 × 10 acres, going by the 12 hides recorded in Domesday. Within them the king's writ did not run —it was, as it were, a sacred independent city and it paid no tax.

The Gnostics, whom the Celtic Church was accused of following, understood the New Jerusalem as an age of St John which was to succeed that of Peter. The last Glastonbury monk, Austin Ringwoode, foretold on his deathbed that the abbey would one day be repaired and renewed for 'the like worship which has now ceased' and that peace and plenty would then long abound. One Maelgwen or Melkin in the fifth century had prophesied the finding of St Joseph's tomb and in it of holy objects, two cruet vessels of silver and white, linked with the Holy Grail. Bligh Bond in *The Gate of Remembrance* (1918) gives the ground plan of the abbey, basing it upon a grid of 36 squares, each of 74 ft or 888 inches.[4] This rectangle shape,

9 squares by 4, is of 666 ft × 296 ft, or in square MY 26,640, i.e. 666 × 40. The area is 666,000 sq cubits. There are 36 squares and the sum of the numbers 1–36 is in fact 666. The cubits may be linked with the Egyptian cubit measurements of the stones of the Chalice Well-house (see p. 218). This number 666, the total of the magic square of the sun, links Glastonbury with Stonehenge, whose sun circles, as we have seen, are based upon 666, which appears repeatedly. In another way the abbey also measures up by numbers with the Holy Oblation in Ezekiel.

It thus appears that numerological links were deliberately built in between the revered heathen-philosophic temple and the church erected by the philosophic-minded generations of monks who followed the curiously mystic-minded St Bernard of Clairvaux, whose interest in the Qabalah and the scheme of the old Temple of Solomon in Jerusalem is now realized. They are reflected in the Qabalah mosaic and window at Chartres and quite possibly in the floor of St Joseph's chapel at Glastonbury too. A definite link has been shown between the measurements of the Chartres west window and the placing of the Sephiroth on the Qabalistic tree marked in the 'maze' on the floor.

Moreover, even if one ignores these numbers, the precision of the placing is most suggestive. The axis of St Benedict's church, the abbey, Dod Lane (a causewayed 'spirit path', coinciding with the Pilgrims' Way to the Tor), St Michael's, and Gare Hill (a former priory site) runs on exactly to the Stonehenge centre. The odds against this happening accidentally are considerable. The Christian Church was making a link with the temple of Druidry in what was to be the greatest abbey church of England and was already accepted as the most mystically holy. Little repulsion could, then, have existed towards Druids.

One thinks again of St Columcille's 'Christ is my Druid' and recalls that Columcille's master St Padraic was said to have been in Glastonbury for some time. There is a very old chapel there named after him, part of the abbey complex.

The Chalice Well Trust took over the administration of both Chalice Well and garden from the late Major Tudor Pole and has done good work. A beautiful garden has been created about the well; symbolic herbs and flowers abound.

For the cover of the present Chalice Well itself, Bligh Bond made a worthy design. Two bronze circles intersect, forming a *vesica piscis*; through them passes the spear, from hinge to fastening. So the two spheres of the spiritual and the material together form the womb of time which is incarnation. One divine purpose pierces them—the spear of truth. At Glastonbury the circles of the ancient past and of the future form the half-legendary present, but one powerful influence runs through all: the magic of the Tor.

---

[4] One recalls that 8 is the number both of Mercury and of Jesus, the number in fact of the spiritual teacher or way-shower.

The actual Chalice spring issues from the side of the Tor a little way up but accumulates in the dip between the two hills, thence seeping into the well. The well, if the stone at one side is taken as a sort of pointer, is 'oriented', north and south. Down the well the water level rises and falls; there is a large chamber at one side, a kind of man-sized niche.

Through the spring gush vast quantities of a chalybeate water from a stratum that stretches all the way from the Black Mountain area of Wales. Flinders Petrie gave it an Egyptian date, the stonework, he said, was in wedge formation, of the type used in the Pyramids, and tooled with stone implements only, like Stonehenge.

A researcher into types of measurement was living in 1962 at Little St Michael's House, near the well, and knew the difference between normal Egyptian and Egyptian royal cubits and between the foot of Edward I and the megalithic and the Celtic foot-unit. According to him, the queer-shaped, five-sided well-chamber was of Egyptian royal cubit measurement; nothing else was like it in England nor indeed in Europe, save for one building in the South of France.

Another appraisal, undertaken by the Chalice Well Trust, appears to link the earliest abbey construction with Egypt, for the stones from which the well and well-house were built, apparently now in the eighteenth century, had been taken from the ruined and abandoned abbey. This in turn meant that workmen trained in Egypt had been used in the ancient building, for it was the earliest part of the abbey that had been plundered for this. For the tooling certainly was of Egyptian traditional type—Flinders Petries had not been wrong—and the measurements were, as Eyre had said, by the Egyptian royal cubit, which would still have been in use in Egypt in the early centuries of Christianity.

Moreover research into soils by the Trust revealed a fact very pertinent to Druids. In the lower part of the well garden, where the eighteenth century had created a 'spa' bath, there had been a pool long before the well. A single yew-tree root was found and on analysis proved to have been alive in the Roman period. It was in line with extant yews and seems to show a ritual avenue up to the Tor. Such an ancient grove is the kind of thing seen at Great Yews near Salisbury on a larger scale. Now yews speak clearly of the Druidic mysticism. This makes it highly probable that Druids were here very early indeed and either planted or took over this ancient pattern of the dateless trees of death and eternity.

The picture develops further, for a few yards away is the entrance to the old crystalline cave now bricked around and barred up by the Water Board. There were therefore two pools: one of mysterious red water from unknown depths, never failing, and the other of a pure blueish limestone water from the depths of the crystalline cave whose stalagmites were no doubt an object of awe and quite possibly part of an initiatory sytem of wisdom-teaching.

The blue-white and the red pools, apparently from the male and the female hills, the pointed and lionlike Tor and the rounded apple-tree-covered Challis—the concept emerging, is one of the pre-Celtic Druids, the wiser ones, dominating over several grades of wisdom-teaching: the test for steadfastness, the maze; the test by horror, the descent into the Tor; the enlightenment in supernatural beauty into wisdom itself in the illumined depths of the stalactite cavern.

A personal memory may usefully close this section. When the writer first visited Glastonbury the Bligh Bond automatic-writing messages, alleged to be from monks of the past, had issued into definite statements and measurements of where King Edgar's lost chapel would be found, to the east of the high altar. The ground there was marked out with tapes. Not long afterwards digging discovered the bases of these walls exactly where indicated.

Part of our racial soul-roots are here at Glastonbury; others are at Stonehenge and Avebury. Did not the World Ash have three roots—an air root, a water root and a root in *hel*, the other world? Avebury, with its wide layout and hill above, is our air-root: Stonehenge, with its deep mystique is the other-world root and Glaeston is the root of holy and eternal water.

Star Channelling from Stone Down

To the north-east of the old place of the blood-red pool and of the Tor spring is the area called Stone Down. It is evident that from it was drawn part of the power channelled into the Tor—or the chamber within the Tor —and into the Chalice Well's predecessor.

The site of the present well, let it be repeated, is not where the chalybeate pool originally was. At first, when water levels were different, the water came into a pool at about where the eighteenth-century bath can now be seen—strangely changed, but recognizable—perhaps 100 yards westwards of the well.

Upon Stone Down were three menhirs in a north-south row. Parallel with the northernmost one is another stone to its west. Due north from it is a hillside spring. They are clearly shown on an old map. Unfortunately, only the well now remains to be seen. The orientations are intriguing. Directly north-east of the Tor tower (or the chamber beneath?) is the northernmost of the stones; and directly north-east of the former Chalice pool is this spring.

It is evident that the north-east was the channelling-down way, whether directly from the Summer Solstice sun or from other forces. The layout of so many monuments tells us this. So whatever star links may be discovered, it is evident that here is the path by which their influences were considered to have been passed into these two sacred features. This is not to say that pool and Tor had and have no autonomous powers of their own, merely that the neolithic wise men thought to boost them with this sort of influence.

Water from a rubeate pool was sister to white or blue water from a magical cave, the stalactite cavern beneath the Tor. Was there already the idea of the two healing or mystic snakes here, the twins of the Caduceus of Mercury? Wales had them as the red and the grey-green dragons or snakes, the *Ddrei Goch* and the *Ddrei Glas*.

So it must have gone on for centuries and there are likely to have been the mystic workers called Druids here, in the awesome Yew grove.

V. The Meini Hirion

The Penmaenmawr Circles: the High Working of Druidry and the Mysteries of Eryri Gwyn

Penmaenmawr is an outlying ridge from the Eryri Gwyn or Snowdon *massif*. It stands over the sea commanding in a great view Anglesey or Mona —the old centres of the kingdom of Gwynedd—and that sea which is central to the Celtic areas. Set in its midst is Man, isle of Manannan and Lir or Ler, the sea-gods. The site, nibbled by quarrying, rises some 1,200 ft above the sea and that little town called by the same name, the Head of the Great Stone, with its memories of the craggy face of Gladstone.

Meini Hirion, the circles set on this eminence, are remarkable. The larger circle had some 19 or 20 stones originally, 3–6 ft high; 8 of them now remaining upright, a few others are lying. Another small circle is some distance away to the north-east; the two link therefore as a large definite pointer to the precise Summer Solstice, the sun as power. The smaller set is of 5, probably originally 6, similar stones. If the greater circle had 19 stones, that would be a reminder of the faithfulness of its Great Mother the moon; if the lesser one was 6, it spoke of balance.

The greater circle has a slight ellipse, hardly noticeable, but which, according to Professor Thom, forms a practically perfect triangle in its structure; in other words, the main circle is of the finest possible workmanship.

These circles on the windswept moor, aligned to summer's high point, between them have two marker stones, one just outside the larger, another 113 ft from the centre of the smaller. The distance between the circles is no less than 829 ft.

The significance and status of a grove was based upon the type of circle it worked. Here we have one perfect in symmetry and commanding in height and vision. It is over the richest agricultural area, Mona the 'moonland' of the Great Mother, which, together with the Eryri Gwyn fastnesses of mountain, form the northern and main areas of national Wales, Land of the Cymru, the Brotherhood. This grove therefore had every right to be considered the major one of the large scene it overlooked from its Pisgah-height

Up here on Penmaenmawr fabulous history gives a series of a hundred towers; it was the great Druidic fastness, Braich y Ddinas (Ridge of the City), vividly described. Here is the account by Sir John Gwynn of Gwedur:

On the top of Penmaenmawr stands a high strong rocky hill, called Braich y Ddinas, whereupon is to be seen the ruinous walls of a strong and invincible fortification, compassed with a treble wall, and within every wall there are to be seen the foundation of at least a hundred towers, all round, and of equal bigness, in breadth some six yards every way within the walls; the walls of this same Dinas were in most places about three yards thick. This Castle when it stood was impregnable, and had no way to offer any assault unto it, the hill being high, rocky and perpendicular, and the walls very strong . . . By tradition we do receive it from our forefathers that this was the ultimum refugium, the strongest, surest, and safest refuge and place of defence that the ancient Britons had in all Snowdon to defend themselves from the incursions and inroads of their enemies, for the like place so strong, so impregnable, so defensive, is not to be found in all Snowdon; and besides, the greatness and largeness of the work showeth that it was a princely and royal fortification, strengthened both by nature and workmanship, seated on the top of one of the highest mountains in Snowdon, near the sea, and in the midst of the best and fertilest soil in all Carnarvonshire.

Actually Penmaenmawr had never been any such thing. There were simply a large number of strongly-built neolithic hut circles, and these bases gave rise to the legend. Most of them have now been quarried away. Penmaenmawr was, however, as with the Llandin, a great centre of mystic power. Men commonly conceive the spiritual in terms of the material, and the vivid metaphors characteristic of Welsh thought add to this tendency.

Up here was the Place of the Higher Powers, Ddinas Affareon. Up here the dragons drew the chariot of Ceridwen in her elevated forms. But here too was the Old Mother in her old sow form, who deposited on this height an eaglet and a wolf cub—the strong sight and the fierce spirit that characterize her.

Arthur (Aradr) has hereabout several cloudy and legendary forms linking him with the formidable picturesque crags of the great mountain. He is one of a pair of perpetually fighting giants, elementals of the heights, Aradr and Rhita Gawr, light and darkness perhaps, and along the summit ridge called *Lliwydd*, the Crest of the Breaking Wave, from its shape, is an ancient barrow-mound known as the *Carnedd Aradi*, Arthur's Grave (see also p. 142). After the last battle on the mountain slope his defeated knights appealed to the Powers for shelter. A great cavern in the mountain opened and they entered, the Lliwydd closed over them and there they lie, the *Lanci Aradr*, Arthur's Lads, awaiting the call when Aradr rises again at the day of the restoration of the Cymric lands when all things shall be well. They appear, clad in the light armour and leather of the period, to certain of the native dwellers thereabouts, usually in the Lleyn Peninsular in the west of Snowdonia, in the evening. They ask always, 'Is it yet time?' to which the reply still has to be 'No, it is not yet time . . . '

Below is the fastness of Dinas Emrys, an isolated hill—a good natural defence place — between Beddgelert and Capel Curig, from which Myrddin ruled as deputy for Ambrosius Aurelianus. From there as hierophant of the mysteries he had raised the phantasmagoria and quest of the Holy Graal, he had predicted and manoeuvred the last battles, he had designed the future kingships . . . just as he had caused the birth of Aradr, brought him forth and tested him for the kingship, so when the time came he removed him from the human scene over the waters of death in the dark barge.

According to the variant version in Nennius, King Vortigern, wishing to reestablish himself in Wales and to build a tower at Dinas Emrys, a most suitable and commanding site, found that everything he built was shaken down. It was the young Myrddin, the 'child without a father' whom Vortigern had been bidden to find, who pointed out that fighting dragons, red and white, were the cause. Their manoeuvres predicted further history to him, on the basis of which he advised Vortigern to flee. Vortigern bestowed Dinas Emrys upon Myrddin before being himself killed in battle.

When his active work in that place was done, there came about Myrddin the glass 'dome' or ship—symbol of another plane of being—and in it he was transported with the Thirteen Precious Things of the Island of Britain to Bardsey Island, at the end of the Lleyn Peninsular, Yns Enlli, an inaccessible place, later the refuge of thousands of monks, by tradition.

At what point in his career Myrddin has been seriously imprisoned by Viviane le Fée, daughter of the local lord of a castle at the Fontaine de Barentin in the ancient forest of Broceliande in mid–Brittany, is never clear; it seems as if we have two irreconcilable accounts, since he was tied up there for a number of years. We have also referred to another account linking him with southern Scotland. We may have in Myrddin a multiple figure standing for members of a dynastic family or grade of magicians—there is in fact a valley with a sort of Taliesin clan in North Wales—but it may simply be of those who had all reached a certain grade of skill in a college of Bards; the same sort of thing might well be in a Myrddin grade. It is Taliesin who seems rather to give the game away in the grading by his constant objections to other and lesser Bards whom he challenges to displays of erudite knowledge. It was at this evidently very medieval stage an affair of prestige and of noble or princely favour—a very 'courtly' atmosphere. *Myrddin* primarily means 'laughter', and *Taliesin* 'radiance' or 'glorious brow'. Thus the Myrddin quality expected could have been wit or magic, whilst the Taliesin quality was beauty, the 'radiance' of well-turned lines. Here are two pillars of song, two lines of inspiration.

It will be seen that the Welsh Arthur in this version is solely the nationalist hero, he is not the earlier mystic saviour; Glastonbury and the English traditions are out of the picture. He comes again solely to restore Wales. Myrddin is evidently a romanticized picture of a Chief Druid with functions as indicated by classical writers: he is the equal, nay the superior, of the ruler, of whom he is the trainer, religious mentor and general adviser.

Up somewhere near Penmaenmawr was a main grove of the Pheryllt; it was the grove which sometime before 1066 existed at Oxford and cannot really be separated from it. The apparatus for experimenting with metals (*ffer*) is not likely to have been actually on these heights, rather in valleys nearby; the circle was its temple no doubt. Certain tales sound rather like early experiments with steam power. Some sources use the expression *Calvyddydon Pherylltt*, which covers chemistry as well as metallurgy. But the dragons story from Dinas Emrys sounds like figures in alchemy; dragons are frequently pictured in alchemists' concurbits—those glass flasks in which workings were done.

It was near the top of Eryri Gwyn that the solution to one of the main plagues of Wales was found. The flood monster the Avanc, sometimes called the Giant Beaver, was finally cast into the beautiful tiny blue lake called Glaslyn, which goes down to the centre of the world. So is the flood of emotionalism, always difficult to manage in a temperamental people, stopped from flooding the whole area of man and is removed upon the heights of reason and sent down the vent-hole of beauty.

At the foot of a slope of the mountain is a centre of the Tylwdd Teg, the folk corresponding to the *sidhe* or elves in Eire. Not far away is a farm by a river where the watermeadows are a place of festivals and dances for the feys. They invite human lads and aim to induce them to take Tylwdd wives. It is a most chancy business marrying a fey however; if she is once touched with anything made of iron, you will find yourself in an elvish prison for quite a long time. It all sounds like the activities of an oppressed, perhaps a smaller, race.

The Meini Hirion stones themselves have about them strong psychic images. Even in wind and pouring rain (under which conditions the writer went to them) tall, dark-clad forms were perceived performing a serene rite; they were not unlike forms seen at Rollright but far more advanced in training.

Mysteries still remain in Snowdonia of which the modern Welsh know nothing. In the central part is a complete stone circle only to be seen under certain conditions. In one of the sub-mountains is a cache where remains of the Arthurian period, perhaps of the Arthurian band itself, can be found. But these things are like the Glastonbury Tor initiatory chamber; they are best left alone in this graceless generation, in the same way that the answer to the Lanci Aradi is: 'No, it is not yet time.'

The whole mountain is a place of visions and revelations. To the day and the night it holds up these giant symbols and is a haunt of eagles, birds of second sight. In a larger way the principle of the Twelve Knights as balanced order must always fight against anarchic giant force. They may for the time be defeated, but they live on and always come again.

VI. Callanish of the Seven Sites:
The Patriarchal Cult in the Outer Hebrides

Land of the Hyperboreans.
The Haebudes (Pliny).

'Ε Βουδαι (Ptolemy).
Ebudae (various geographers).
Innse-Gall = the isles of the strangers (Gaelic); these came from Lochlann
(Norway).

Norwegian dynasties were here until 1263, when Haco was defeated off
Largs, leaving an impoverished civilization. Norwegian blood is evident in
the tall, spare, sensitive and now rather delicate race, prone to tuberculosis,
fine in bone structure and with a great feeling for song.

Leverhulme did his best for Lewis and Harris which he bought, but his
factory was up against local bias and is now an educational centre. The
bitterness of the outer islands gives edge to memorable poetry: the
Canadian Boat Song is one example, another is the work of Adam Drinan:

> From the lone shieling and the misty island
> Mountains divide us and the waste of seas . . .
> No one foretold the children would be banished
> that a degenerate lord might boast his sheep . . .
> Come foreign rage, let discord burst in slaughter . . .

The Outer Hebrides range for some 100 miles with only two sea passages
breaking through, and those are very often impassable from the high seas
of the great Atlantic rollers. Tongues of the land project to the Atlantic, on
which knolls towards the western ends shelter the immediate tracts to their
east. The western side of the isles as a whole is good flat land with vast
beaches. The warm Atlantic drift means a mild climate like Devon's.

It is all immensely fertile; all manner of crops grow freely. Sheep develop
fine fleeces. When Britain was more or less Mediterranean in temperature,
this, with its additional warmth, may have been semi-tropical. Some
Mediterranean-type plants still grow, seals bask, South Uist had fine
forests until recently. A vast number of birds also rejoice in this long stretch
and even now it is one of the most Celtic of areas, where Scots Gaelic is
generally spoken. Its songs are famous, collected by Margaret Kennedy-
Fraser, and so until recently were its harping and piping.

The double island Harris-Lewis is a strong candidate for being the
Happy Land of song, dance and fruitfulness known as the Land of the
Hyperboreans. It was known to the Greeks; with the currents in summer
conditions travel out here presented no great problems. It was only when
the Phoenicians took over the Pillars of Herakles and allowed no other
ships than theirs to pass that Britain grew vague. Hence it is not really
surprising to find this is the area which, taking its circles and stones as a
group, has, Professor Thom considers, the most important set in all Britain.
A group of not fewer than seven are about the beautiful extensive loch,
Loch Roag, opening to the north-west. The most important set is that most
immediately met from the open sea, Tursachan Callernish. Briefly, this has
two circles and an ellipse, an avenue and five alignments, with a notable
menhir over a cist burial-place. The other six are mostly inter-viewable in

a way that provides declinations. There are four ellipses and several alignments. This area has not been accurately surveyed even yet.

The other monuments are: i) *Cnoc Ceann*, an ellipse whose circumference is 75 MY. It contains probably the tallest Scots stone, *Clach na Truiseil in Barvas*—19 ft × 6 ft × 4 ft. If it indicates the Steincleit ellipse 1.5 miles north then it possibly shows a declination for the star Altair. ii) *Cnoc Fillibhir Bheag*: concentric ellipses surrounded by a circle—a unique design. The figures are multiples of 2.5 or 2.5 MY. iii) *Ceann Thulabeg*, an ellipse, perimeter 422.6 MY. An orientation to a stone in another stone scheme and to two other sites, i.e. to 4 objects in all, is apparently a careful calendar observation. iv) *Airidh nam Bidearn*, a setting of stones for moon observation. Site v is of slabs positioned to observe 4 other sites. Site vi is a 10 MY stone ring between iii and iv.

There is little southwards in the rest of Harris-Lewis in the way of old stone sites until Taranshay. The Callanish group on Loch Roag, lonely and lovely, are sentinels over a long past. From several indications the general date is likely to be 1800 BC or more.

At the great Callernish, the *Tursachan*, the mourners or dancers, form an irregular sort of Celtic cross, with stones forming circles one inside the other, semi-centres round a great lith. Approaching from the landward side, the north, there appears an impressive avenue coming from about 10° east of north, eight stones each side, some 30 ft wide. The centre line of it passes the centre of the double cist burial, apparently that of a chieftain; it is small but divided seemingly into three chambers by 'groundfloor' stones. To this the avenue is an immensely stately approach, up this wide rising ground. Some ritual dance seems to be figured.

The centre axis extends into an accurate moon observation line southwards, whilst to the north it apparently marks the rising of the star Capella. This too indicates a date of 1800 BC.

The great circle (classified as 'type A' by Thom) has 13 stones, but in it pairs are twice arranged meaningfully. From the east one pair forms a gateway to this powerful tomb with its spirit chieftain obviously inhabiting the one great menhir west of centre; behind, another wider pair form a satisfying setting; beyond is a knoll and the sea. The menhir seems to look down upon the burial eastward.

Like transepts roughly east and west are lines of four stones each; they might well have been 6 each originally. They broaden and relate the scheme to the landscape; they interrogate the sky and sea. They guide up and down the sun to these portals at about the equinoxes.

By this time one may realize two further schemes, if alert to detail: there is a rather crowded arc of a circle of small stones to the north of the cist burial-place some 23 ft in diameter which was presumably once complete. Thom found its centre to be on the central axis of the wide avenue; moreover this axis meets the lines of the east and west stone rows at a significant point he called 'C', where the axis of yet another feature also converges, an ellipse with axis north–east, outlined by a bed of small

Tursachan, Callanish.

stones only viewable when the peat cover was at last lifted in the last
century. The ellipse is based on the 3–4–5 Pythagorean triangle, the axes
being actually 4 and 5 MY. The main axis shows the midsummer Solstice.

The alignment west shows the precise setting for the sun of either
equinox; the alignment east shows the rising of the star Altair 1800 BC.

To the direct south runs a line of 6 stones, their axis set upon the knoll
at the sea end, the Cnoc na Tursa. Again, those 6 stones might well once
have been 12.

The whole length of the temple's layout is some 400 ft. Up on the Cnoc
a wide sea view can be seen with the shores of Loch Roag some way south
and the succession of bays between headlands forming a fascinating view
eastward. Below, the 47 stones of Callernish can best be seen as a pattern
from here: the swerved cross of the greater monument, the lesser
Callernish shapes eastward.

The numerology of the stones, as now seen, clearly are of double origin.
The sun cult is shown by the north-east line and by the south-east, with
the numbers 6 and 12, recent in type. But the 13 stones of the main circle
have the moon stamped on them; so has the westward layout of the
cist-tomb.

These stones of the 13 mother-circle are finely and firmly set. They are
cleft but not further tooled. Contrast the Garyharmine circle—all beautifully finished. The great stone of the father-chieftain principle rises within
the moon-feminine circle, a kind of lingam-yoni suggestion recalling
Stonehenge's Heol-stone.

A small longheaded Mediterranean race came here first and put up this
intelligent tribute to the western Great Mother, building perhaps a birth-
chamber of initiation, not a cist at all. Then came a larger sea–going race
with long boats, sun circles and father stones. They adopted the little
people's ideas and adapted them; the marriage of cultures is probably, if
looked for, as clear here as at Stonehenge.

Father-stone and east and west sets of stones enriched Callernish. The
dour spirit of Protestant Scotland did not allow the stones to be dancers,
only false men—Na Fir Bhreige. The title of the main Callernish, is properly
a set of mourners. But earlier mourners did have dances at wakes, a
tradition that was kept up in old Catholic circles.

Was the Apollo cult here? Where was the 'round temple of wings'? Here
were plenty of wings and circles. Did the birds crowd round the circle?
Whence came here hecatombs of wild asses—rather a Persian touch?

The chieftain principle appears to reign here more unquestionably than
elsewhere, except maybe for Rollright with its Kingstone (also, one notes,
orientated to Capella). The absolute nature of the One stands out over the
complex initiation chamber or cist, over two circles and an ellipse, over
these stone rows with exact indications. Taking in the other six settings,
there are here the working tools of observances as complex as at
Stonehenge, with an approach avenue for all the singers, dancers and

players. Sea girdles the area, the sea whence these far-comers emerged, over which they freely moved, seas familiar to them.

Callernish is the clearest possible example of the surveying skills with which our ancestors were equipped when they came, directly or intermediately, from the culture's ripening place in Syria—not far off the time of the Israelite patriarchs. A legend has it that the princess daughter of the last reigning king of Judah married a chieftain-king of Scotland and so preserved the sacred dynastic line in the British direction. Maybe this is a chronicler's wishful thinking, but truly something of the prophetic and patriarchal dignities exist in the outer isles. One returns to that greatest stone, the Clach na Truiseil, contemplating the sea in solitary grandeur.

VII. Iona of the Dove: Union of Druid and Christian

I, Ia = land of the I, that is the island or *inis*. Also of the family called I.
Dûn I = the island's hill, or the island itself.
Icolmcill = isle of the dove (*colm*) of the church (*cill*), that is of St Colmcille.
Reilig Odhrain = the burial-place of clan I, names including Oran, and then of chiefs and first kings, some 48 Scots, four Irish and 7 Norwegian.
The Isle of Healing; the Isle of the Cunning Workmen; the Isle of the Druids.

> 'Where is Duncan's body?'—'Carried to Colme-Kill
> 'The sacred storehouse of his predecessors
> 'And guardian of their bones.'
> —*Macbeth*, II, 4.

There has always been a mystic-physical unity between Eire and part of the west coast of Scotland, especially Iona, joined by metamorphic rock well before life began. The tension is of a notable hardness. In Ireland again Iona's dazzling oyster-shell beaches are reflected at Glencolumcille. The same queer sense of the loss of time, yet knowledge of distant events, is in both areas. There is little need to bring newspapers to Iona; happenings are usually already known.

Dûn I is the apotheosis of the concept of the holy island, both in the isolation and the magical link. The fairy mound and the well of youth are there, and the cell—the tower of refuge. The circle bases of stone huts are as Druidic as they are Christian. Fused by the Gaelic spirit, two sets of values seem to be one.

Harmony was not to last on the theological side; a more official Christianity in the thirteenth century denounced all Druid customs in language of unmeasured violence and persecuted and even killed those steeped in ideas variant from those of Rome. Yet in Scotland this Greek-Celtic form of Christianity lasted longer perhaps than anywhere else; for about six centuries Rome did not establish what to her seemed order and dignity. Six centuries is a long time, long enough to build into the mind of a people a certain permanent stamp. And that stamp, as in Brittany, is

Druidic; intensely alive and sensitive, but serious, speculative and deeply ingrained.

Only two centres are possible for a restored Celtic unity: the Isle of Man, centre both of the Gaelic-Cymric sea and of the Scandinavian hegemony, and Iona, also central but bringing in the large area of Scotland more fully. Man was and could again be a convenient political centre, but there is really no question that the Dûn I of Columcille has the greater spiritual impulse, then and now. For centuries it was a beacon of civilization and learning. Not only did Shakespeare know of it, which means that it was of general repute at the time of James VI and I, but Dr Johnson was towed there in the wake of the industrious Boswell, showing off the glories of his native heaths. Its reputation in Scotland has been undiminished; always it has been a place to visit and linger.

There are certain parts of the Earth's surface where the spirit behind appearances seems to be closer, where a welling-up of power is felt, where the walls of the material are thinner—put it as you like, Iona is one of them. The psychic atmosphere can only be compared with Glastonbury's or that of the Jordan valley, and Iona's is on a higher plane. It is tempting to think that the events crystallized from this atmosphere into a locality, as seems to have happened around the Jordan. One considers again that pure hard crystalline stone binding Eire, Iona and the Caledonian lands.

The little isle had long been a mystical centre, filled with neolithic and Bronze Age relics, lying at one end of Mull with its several Druidic circles. Religion was nothing new here, nor was Columcille the first missionary hereabouts—Palladius came first and then, less fleetingly, St Ninian of Candida Casa (whitethorn) as early as the fourth century.

The Wolf, as Columcille was first called, was born in Donegal in 521. His father was grandson of the famous Niall of the Nine Hostages, High King 379–405, who had created a reign of terror round the coasts; his mother, Eithne, was royal also. She had a vision of her son's power when she saw a beautiful robe taken from her by an angel to cover a huge area of land including Alban, as Scotland was then called:

'Why do you thus quickly take away from me this lovely mantle?'
'For the reason that this mantle belongs to one of such grandeur and honourable station that you can keep it by you no longer.'

Columcille was trained under Finian at Moville, then in Celtic literature at Leinster and took vows near Dublin, in 545 founding a Derry monastery of which, in the manner of nobles, he became abbot. He preached, and founded some 300 churches, whilst his monastic foundations included Durrow and Kells. Yet Columcille was of much greater stature in history than any mere missionary, as he is often represented. With him we are at the time of the settlements of the Scoti in Scotland, the formation of a kingdom from two peoples round a centre and the creation of a civilized tradition that was Iona's.

The conquering race was Columcille's and he could have been a king of it, rather than creating kings. He had a violent overbearing nature to begin with—before he was Columcille, Dove of the Church, he was Crimthan the Wolf, and of status to be a High King of Tara, like his ancestor, had he not chosen the sphere of the Church. The Scottish Dalriada was an untamed Pictish area, now more or less Argyllshire, that his noble relatives had begun conquering from about the year 500 as an oversea extension of the Irish Dalriada (Antrim)—after all, it is only 12 miles from shore to shore. At first they had settled and had reduced the heathen Picts to virtual slavery fairly easily. But this redoubtable people, who had earlier been a main cause of the harrying of the Romans from large areas of northern Britain, gathered themselves under a warrior-king Brude and inflicted a resounding defeat in the year 560 on the Irish-Scots, whose own king, Columcille's relative, was killed. This was the challenge, it seemed, that brought Columcille into action as a settler-missionary to civilize this area and to unite the peoples—and, incidentally, to restore the suzerainty of his own race, the Christian Scoti.

Yet in the usual story this is not given as his motive. Columcille was a skilful copyist and illuminator of books—we still seem to have several of his manuscripts—and he copied the work of his father in God, St Finian of Moville, who was dead, but the owner of whose work demanded the copy, exercising what we should call copyright. But the law was not clear; Columcille claimed his copy as his own. When Diarmid, the High King of Tara, upheld the owners with the adage 'To every cow belongs her calf', Columcille incited his own clan, the Neills, to fight Diarmid. A great killing, 'The Battle of the Books', followed. So a synod excommunicated Columcille as the prime mover in the affair. He and his friends managed to have the sentence changed to banishment upon his undertaking expiation by winning souls for Christ outside Eire.

He set off therefore from Derry in the year 563 with 12 monks. The coast and area called Glencolumcille after him, though, also has claims to have been his departure place. Trying other areas first, his coracle was finally beached and buried on the brilliant horseshoe of sand now called the Bay of the Coracle, *Port a Churaich*. A party of high Druids appeared to welcome him, disguised in the account as two evil bishops, i.e. high Druids with fish-head crowns like mitres. They seemingly offered the use of a semi-circle of their huts, called the *Laraichean* or ruins, which were easily defensible, with 6 or 7 stone bases for wattle huts and also a well. Such an offer would have been very welcome.

There seems no doubt that Dûn I was a Druidic stronghold. Near the Bay of Youth on the other shore is the base of a stone circle which later Christians saw fit to knock down. Other places with the bases of buildings are the Garden of Young Hector, *Garadh Eachainn Oig*, at the top of the inlet, and *Port Goirtein Oimhair*, the Bay of Ivor's homestead, further eastward. Any of these could equally have been the settlement. The small island had on it no fewer than 360 menhirs, another mark of its religious status surely; of these nearly all have vanished.

Columcille was himself almost certainly of the Bardic Order, whilst at least one of his companions, Oran, was a fully-fledged Druid, so that the offer from the 'evil bishops' was quite natural. Not only there but also at the place of the later abbey Columcille took over Druid sites. His Christianity was of a distinct, Celtic, even individual, type. His community comprised a collection of round huts with a larger one, rather detached, for the abbot, a refectory with a great traditional stone and a fireplace, an oak-built church and a sacristy, a mill, a barn, a stable for horses (Columcille rode a white horse), a well and a surrounding mound-and-ditch. Later there were scattered sites with huts, more or less distant, known as 'deserts' which was where those desiring to be hermits, or to live so for periods, could do so.

There is an odd inconsistency about the record from the beginning. The area of the graves, at first on top of nearby knolls, but later moved down within walls, known as *Reilig Odhrain*, Oran's burial-place, was in fact that of the family of Hy, and names, including Oran's, were recorded for 15 years before any Christian settlement. This whole Oran element can very well be Druidic. The motives with which the extraordinary yarn about Oran was told defy analysis. Why should Columcille be told that his enterprise would not succeed without someone's being buried alive as a sacrifice? Is it credible that he would have done it? It is represented that Oran offered himself for this sacrifice and was buried standing upright in his monk's habit. Thinking to see how he was getting on, after three days Columcille ordered hm to be uncovered, whereupon Oran proceeded to discredit current Christian beliefs: 'Death is not a wonder and hell is not as it is described.' The Dove of the Church then cried, 'Earth on Oran's eyes lest he blab further!' The wolf Crimthan would seem to have arisen again in this tale. It does seem to show that the Druids were reputed to know further about the afterlife than the Christians, and if Oran had the normal Druidic assumption about metempsychosis from life to life, he could not be expected to accept the hell that, then as later, was a central fear-motive in the Christian love-religion. Fiona Macleod guesses that the whole legend is a symbolical survival, teaching some elemental mystery through sacrificial ritual.

That Columcille was an observer of precise shades in orientations, an essential part of Druidry, is evident if his cell, on the hill known as Tor Ab, the Tower of Refuge, immediately west of the present abbey church, is accepted as veridical. Three separate orientations speak here. The tradition is that the east itself is a place of balance, spiritual intelligence, judgement and control, at all seasons; the South-east is the place of rebirth belonging to the Mother who bears the new sun of midwinter; and the North-east is the place of highest inspiration and power, as the maximum sun-power of the year. Taking the centre of the cell to the centre of its entrance, where it would face, the angle is precisely east, to draw intelligence and judge-ment; the direction where the abbey's axis lies (probably the same now as then) is south-east, for a church is always a mother sheltering those reborn in baptism as her children; whilst the direction of the socket that held the tall crucifix is precisely north-east, to the place of highest inspiration.

This cross on the analogy of contemporary work would have linked the four-fold symbols of pre-Christian Egypt and the four Evangelists with a sun-circle or tail of a dragon in a Greek-style whole: Mark, a lion with wings in the hot south; John, eagle of rising light—or some other bird —to the east; the sheep, sometimes the fish, of Luke to the watery and brooding west; to the north, material side, belonged man, the over-earthy creature, with the head of Matthew the tax-collector. If the stone shown in the abbey was indeed the saint's pillow, his habits were even hardier than those of the Japanese or the discalced Carmelites with their wooden head-rests.

Iona was merely a base; all Pict-land was the objective. The essentially wandering nature of Celts is seen in the long venturesome journeys of these monks. Columcille, with Kenneth and Comgall as translators, set off for the court of their people's arch-enemy, Brude of the Picts. Druidry might be friendly with Columcille in Iona; it was not necessarily so elsewhere. Advised by the Chief Druid, Broichan, Brude refused them admittance. However, bolted gates flew open as they approached, so they entered. Shaken by this sign, Brude was won over and so, gradually, were his Picts.

Columcille always stood for political aims as well as a high culture: peace between tribes, a union under a monarch. To settle disputes the prince-abbot was always sent for, so that it was natural that when Brude died Columcille chose, and then at Iona consecrated, his successor Aidan, perhaps on the traditional coronation stone said to be one of the original Black Stones of Iona—black not because of colour but of the terrible things that befell anyone who broke an oath sworn on them.

Then the missionary statesman returned to Ireland to the council at Drumceat in 575: he achieved his main object, the independence of the Argyll-Dalriada kingship from Ireland; the Bards, his own Order, also were protected by certain rules and the tough women of Ireland debarred from actual military service. (One recalls that the redoubtable warrior-queen Maive had lived fighting hard to the age of 112 and was only then killed by an arrow.)

A map of the monks' travels would be a web that covers most of the Highlands and some of the Lowlands. Everywhere they seem to have found appalling squalor and ignorance plus oppression from the con-quering Irish. Yet, wider than this, the travels of Celtic monks took them to far places on the globe. Cormac went to Orkney and the Shetlands and probably to Iceland. Brendan spent most of his life at sea and probably, going by New World tradition, landed on American shores. The legend of his camping on a remote island and finding it was a whale's back is, however, a common explorer's yarn. Proverbially these monks were linked with the Druids by sailors: 'He who is wise will have two tillers to his rudder: the Art of the Druids for Luck of Wind and the Faith of Iona for stilling the waves.'

From the scattered hermitage 'deserts' and the various chapels it was arranged that orisons should constantly rise; always a monks was offering mass or praying, so that the rosary of communion with the divine should not cease. Upon a constant fountain of prayers the spiritual form of Columcille might be seen by a visionary like Blake.

In later years Columcille returned to his first loves, manuscript illumination and the writing of poetry: his two identified manuscripts are the *Cathach* (Psalter) and the *Book of Durrow* (Gospels). Half-a-dozen poems, both in Latin and in Gaelic, that appear to be his also still remain. He died just as the emissary from Rome, Augustine, landed in Kent, as agent of the disciplining and uncomprehending force that was destined eventually to wither up the fresh flower of the Celtic Church. Yet it held out in Scotland longer than anywhere else.

It is clear that Columcille identified the highest he knew as the Druidic, identifying it with Christ whilst repudiating superstitions:

> There is no *streod* that can tell our fate
> nor bird upon the bough
> nor trunk of gnarléd oak . . .
> I adore not the voices of birds
> nor Chance, nor the love of son or wife—
> my Druid is Christ, the Son of God.

The words are *mo drui, macDé*—'my Druid, son of God'—which does not sound as though he were contrasting the two but identifying them.

Columcille would use the Celtic mystique, whilst raising it to a more spiritual level. Thus he positively patronized fairy hills. *Sithean Mor*, Great Fairy Mound, is one of three; it lies towards the fertile tract called the Machair. The *sidhe* inhabited it and lit it up from within; musical sounds came from it. Monks are not supposed to witness the devotions of their abbot, but one once watched Columcille going up the hill and spreading out his hands:

> Holy Angels, citizens of the Heavenly Country, clad in white garments, came flying to him with wonderful swiftness and began to stand around the holy man as he prayed; and after some conversation that celestial band, as if perceiving that it was being spied upon, sped quickly back to the heights of the heavens.
>
> —Adamnan, *Life of St Columcille*

Sithean Mor had probably always been the centre of a horseback gathering circling the hill at Michaelmas, for Michael is, with Mary Mother and Columcille, the great protector, on shore and at sea. This observance went on until the eighteenth century at least.

There are many wells on Iona, but the preserved one is Columcille's alleged well by the abbey. A purely natural one is a little triangular tarn under a separate peak on Dûn I called *Tobar Na h-Aoise*, the Fountain or Spring of Youth. Pilgrims had to go there alone to receive the blessing and gift, and it must be at dawn, when the sun first strikes upon it. This would be a very old custom indeed.

Stone is naturally a great part of the island's mystique. A great dark square slab of stone still visible was the centre table of the refectory. The main stone of Iona's formation, as mentioned, is of incredible antiquity and hardness, fire-formed before the first life appeared, an Archaean serpentine marble. The link with Eire is not only mystic but is of the most substantial; it is a rock whose tension can transmit every vibration.

> The beginning of Iona is almost part of the beginning of earth itself . . . when the first oceans condensed in the hollows of its hot surface—then it was that the Archaean rocks of which Iona and the Outer Hebrides consist were formed on the sea-bottom. They contain no fossils . . . no living creature yet existed.
>
> —E.C. Trenholme, *The Story of Iona*

A little further west of Monks' Fort lay the Black Stones (according to the chronicler of 1695)—swearing stones of great holiness and power, with black effects upon anyone who broke oath. Upon one of them Columcille crowned Aidan King of Argyll, the first fully hallowed king in Britain. The stone used is supposed to be the present Coronation Stone. The Black Stones have all gone now, unless perhaps one is Columba's Pillow. Then there were lucky stones (you turned three white globes on a slab by St Oran's) until the Synod of Argyll ordered their removal. A certain number of holy Druidic stones were Christianized by having crosses cut on them. But the original number of 360 holy stones does recall both the beds of Diarmid and Grainne in Eire and the number of stones around the holy Kaaba at Mecca.

Thus the Druid ideas and the folk beliefs were not persecuted by the Celts of the Greek tradition at all; like the earlier Greek Christianity, it constantly sought to harmonize.

Columcille's spirit was ever with Nature. One of his poems describes the view from the mound overlooking the Port of the Coracle. He loved birds, holding a great festival for them, and horses, especially the white horse that worked on the farm. The bones of this beloved horse have been found carefully preserved.

He became of course more the legend of a power than a man, a name to bless with amongst other heavenly ones:

> May the herding of Columcille
> encompass you going and returning
> encompass you in strath and on ridge . . .

> The peace of Columcille be yours in the grazing
> The peace of Brighid be yours in the grazing

> The peace of Mary be yours in the grazing
> And may you return safeguarded.
>
> *Carmina Gaedelica*

His day of the week was Thursday:

> Thursday of Columcille benign
> Day to send sheep on prosperity
> Day to send cow on calf
> Day to put the web in the warp
>
> *Carmina Gaedelica*

He was a prophet, a more cheerful one than those of older times. One old Gaelic prophecy runs:

> Seven years before the Judgment
> The sea shall sweep over Erin at one tide
> And over blue-green Isla:
> But the Island of Columcille
> Shall swim above the flood

But his own prophecy is:

> In Iona of my heart, Iona of my love,
> Instead of monks' voices shall be lowing of cattle;
> But ere the world shall come to an end
> Iona shall be as it was.

Celtic Christians are often called Culdees and this is a correct usage for the time, but strictly the name should be kept for the order founded much later by St Maelruain about 787.

Iona and its Celtic Christianity became a national symbol for Scottish unity and national aspiration. Kenneth MacAlpine, the first king of a united Scotland, was buried there and there followed him some 48 kings of Scotland, 4 of Ireland and 7 of Norway, seen gathered in separate great tomb-areas in 1549: 'Tumulus Regum Scotiae' and 'Hiberniae' and 'Norwegiae'. The last of these kings was Shakespeare's Duncan. The effect even now is weirdly impressive.

Constant raids killed monks, ruined buildings and disorganized life, yet the creative essence of the place caused revivals. The greatest was the abbey's reappearance following a Benedictine foundation in 1200, together with an Augustinian nunnery; but this marked the end of the Celtic Church. From 1499 until 1578 the abbey church was a cathedral. In 1615 it was annexed to the Protestant Bishopric of the Isles. In modern times the Duke of Argyll presented it to the Presbyterian Church of Scotland, and in 1930 George McLeod founded the Iona Community there. In all these centuries in one or another form therefore the magic has worked: Iona has given a religious leadership.

Also the magic of the gigantic Staffa formation has worked, the place of the 'staves' or basalt pillars, the great sea-cave that was probably a place of Druidic initiations. It produced a poem from Keats as Iona did not, and great music from Mendelssohn. His sister asked him to tell her something of the Hebrides. 'It cannot be told, only played,' he said, and thereupon played the theme which was afterwards to become the Hebrides Overture.

Iona's worthiest literary tribute is that which comes from the great Dr Johnson in 1773. Well-known, it is still worth quoting fully:

> We were now treading that illustrious island which was once the luminary of the Caledonian regions, whence savage clans and roving barbarians derived the benefits of knowledge and the blessings of religion. To abstract the mind from all local emotion would be foolish if it were possible. Whatever withdraws us from the power of the senses, whatever makes the past, the distant or the future predominate over the present, advances us in the dignity of thinking beings. Far from me, and far from my friends, be such frigid philosophy as may conduct us indifferent and unmoved over any ground which has been dignified by wisdom, bravery, or virtue. That man is little to be envied whose patriotism would not gain force upon the plain of Marathon, or whose piety would not grow warmer among the ruins of Iona.
>
> *Journey through the Western Highlands*

The final impression should not be of the past, however powerful, but of the intense life of this typically Celtic land, and from the pen of Fiona Macleod:

> . . . here on the hill slope of Dûn I the sound of the furtive wave is as the sighing in a shell. I am alone between sea and sky—nothing but a single blue shadow that slowly sails the hillside. The bleating of lambs and ewes, the lowing of kine, these come up from Machair . . . these ascend as the very smoke of sound. All around the island there is a continuous breathing . . . The seals on Soa (Seal-Island) are even now putting their breasts against the running tide; I see a flashing of fins here and there in patches at the north end of the Sound and already from the ruddy granite shores of the Ross there is a congregation of seafowl, gannets and guillemots, skuas and herring-gulls, the longnecked northern diver, the tern, the cormorant. In the sunblaze the waters of the Sound dance their blue bodies and swirl their flashing white hair of foam . . . they seem to me like children of the wind and the sunshine, leaping and running in these flowing pastures . . .
>
> *Iona*

Each of these centres of neolithic Druidic activity we have tried to describe makes its own particular impression. On Iona the union of natural static electricity in stone, qualified first by Druidic use, with the high endeavours of dedicated men over many centuries, gives the psychic quality a peculiar stamp: a lightness and universality, as distinct for instance from the neutral heavy power experienced at Glastonbury or from the sensation of frenetic racing activity at the Merry Maidens. These phrases can be only indications, for the words do not exist that can convey adequately such distinctions.

VIII. The Temples of the Boyne to the Great Mother

New Grange: Grainne (pron. 'graun-ye'), the sun mother.
Bruagh na Boinne: the palace or settlement on the Boyne river.
Cashel Aenghus: the home of Aenghus mac-in-da-Ōg.
Dowth or Dubadh: Duma of the Mound of Bones.
Knowth: Duma of the Mound of Tresc; also Cnoc Bua, the Grave of Bue.
These have angulations with:
Tailtin or Teltown: grave-mound of Tailte.
Tara, Termuir or Teamhair: 'height'; Seat of the Bell-branch Kings of All Ireland. May also mean Bull-place, cp. Gaullish Taranus.

The Land of the Boyne

Bruagh-na-Boyne is the settlement or house on the Boyne, Boinne or, as goddess, Boanna. It is the eastern part of a large area. Further west is the *Sliabh-na-Caillighe*, the Hag's Mountain, the place of the trio Banba-Fohla-Eire, with all its myths. This Triple Goddess in her Eire form married Lugh at Tailteann (Tailtin) or Tailte. The feast of high summer in August's beginning, the former holiday of banks, Lughnasadh or Lammas, is their recurring wedding. She is his sister and bride; his sister as one of the band of Lordly Ones, virgin as the earth is ever-virgin, renewing her purity in the bath of winter; whilst as mystic bride of the light-god she causes the fertility of all things. Three are her forms: as bride, Eire; as mature mother, Fohla; as crone and sinister power, Banbha.

Three of the main hill-mountains of Eire illustrate these. The 'tricksy' form of the young goddess is Grainne, who leads Diarmid in such an apparently disastrous way, the crescendo of the tragedy being upon Ben Bulben; the mate, crafts patron and mother is Brighid, nurse of the infant Jesus and soul-mate of Padraic, at Mount Croaghpadraic. Finally the 'old hag' form is seen in Maive (Medbh), the fighting queen of Connaught in the War of the Bulls, who ruled until the age of 112 from Knocknarea.

Diarmid has had the seed of love implanted in him, he is the favoured one of the great god Aenghus Ōg of the greatest sanctuary, Bruagh-na-Boyne, the castle or sanctuary on the holy river. He can draw to him any woman, it seems. Hence it has to be his fate to be drawn against his will to elope with a divine woman—deity comes to him in that shape. His love has been set upon human loves therefore he has to have a divine love forced upon him—and it seems to him almost as a punishment. He will not go all the way with the divine, he protests and refuses. The chase becomes one over the years, over all the days . . .

The nights are nights of the old incubations for initiation, in the dolmens probably erected by each male for his own rebirth temple in the hills and mountains to the west, the Boyne's catchment area. No one has ever explained this profusion of dolmens here and elsewhere. It would be the easiest thing for legend to change the places of incubation for vision and transformation into 'beds' in the mating sense. But this expression may hold a deeper meaning: a 'bed of Diarmid and Grainne' might bear the meaning of the couch where the blessed vision of the teaching goddess appeared nightly to the pilgrimaging Diarmid. It was she who had led him out into the wilderness as it were.

What he—or she—was departing from was the conventional warrior type of gross feasting and marriage, the materialism of the elderly Finn. He was correctly mated and over-righteous; then conventionally jealous and vengeful, he thought that revenge would really be sweet. But it wasn't because it never is. He had to learn another principle, that death may teach life. It is true that Grainne, apparently unabashed, carried on again as Finn's wife, having taught him a lesson. She is ageless as Helen of Troy, who after at least 10 years cheerfully returns to Menelaus none the worse for wear —it has been guessed that she may really have been a valued cult statue. Grainne is jeered at by the Fenians as worthless; we are not told her reactions. Perhaps as a sun goddess she had natural periods of eclipse.

With this legend we are at the end of the long saga of the Fenians, their wars and aggressions, the wars caused by cattle raids. The Brown Bull, the Black Bull, and some special cows, are supposed to have been the causes of these epic wars between the peoples of Connacht and Ulster, old Queen Maive on one side and Cúchulainn leading the men of Ulster smitten with strange impotence on the other.

Eire as Earth Mother

The basic Earth Mother has an island in Bantry Bay and a hill behind the Twelve Bens. She leapt on the Lochcrew Hills and dropped stones from her apron and they became monoliths and circles, just as the Devil dropped the stones at Stonehenge. Or she turns people into stones, often 'dancing' ones. Upon the Hag's Mountain is Cailliagh Durra's House, a megalith; and the 'Hag's Bed' is near Monasterboice.

The Earth Goddess was changed mainly into Beara, one of the denigrations that set in with Christianity. The less pleasant form of the first trio became the Three Hags, Babh, Aine and Beara. Babh, the war specialist, divided into a still more unpleasant trio—Neman, Macha and the bloody Morrigan, who feasts on corpses and weaves entrails. So, if each of the original three bred another three, and each of these does so again, we should have $3 \times 3 = 9: \times 3 = 27$ goddess forms; but the 9 we have seems enough.

In each of the trios one is youth, one motherhood or maturity, and one age. And as the three are one, it is to be expected that Beara renews her youth and again the old moon becomes the new and then again becomes the full. Seven times, i.e. a magical or infinite number of times, she becomes young again, and then she is be-christianed, takes the veil and dies, like the swan-children of Lir. She is tribal, for her children are tribes and races. She is of the sea, with a hint of Aphrodite; her voice is heard in rushing water, or visions are seen in pools. She is of the crop and hides in the last sheaf, decked out as a 'maiden' or 'granny'.

If this Great Mother is thus prevalent, what of her mate? Ignoring for the moment her human lover Diarmid, we take him as Lugaidh or Lugh. He indeed spreads over much of Europe. He is Lud of Ludgate Hill, Lug of the Latin *Lugdunum*, which is the Roman name of several towns; he is Lugaidh and seems to be the same as that 'Dispater', god of the dead, whom the Romans rendered as Mercury. He is the power of light but also of darkness; and as he is identified with the guide of souls, Mercury, the deity of the underworld, these partial definitions seem to point to a deity of reincarnation. For Caesar and the rest tell us definitely that the Celts believed quite practically in metempsychosis. What, then, can be the god of the dead amongst such a people but the god of rebirth also? This would be quite naturally typified as deity of both darkness and light.

He is, however, usually taken simply as light;[1] he inhabits the great hills, he dominates both Paris (Montmartre, Hill of Mercury) and London (Ludgate). Here by the Boyne is the 'grave' of Lugh, which probably merely means his temple, a dolmen with a stone circle on Kileen Hill, Louth, having incised carvings, it is said, like New Grange. Further south are the Wicklow Mountains, and there is the 'bed' of Lugh, the mountain called Lughnaquilla.

These then are the centre figures, the Juno and Jupiter, of the Tuatha dé Danann race of gods with the divine son the love-god Aenghus, whose 'house' or *cashel* is the great temple.

At the Bruagh area itself we find a great triangle of megalithic mounds with chambers, and also a significant line of orientation, in an area strewn with other considerable remains. Not far to the south-west is Tara of the famous hall and crowning place, also now found to be neolithic to start with. Not far west is Tailte, where Lugh weds Eire and where also, going by the *Book of Ballymote*, were the funeral games for Lugh's wife or nurse. It is exactly on the line of latitude with New Grange and here is a straight orientation to the north-east from Tara to Knowth and the round tower near Monasterboice. New Grange, Knowth and Dowth form a triangle also pointing north-east.

Cashel Aenghus, The House of the Love-God, New Grange

New Grange is a very superficial way of labelling a group of ancient shrines, and in fact it is almost surely Grainne, feminine sun-shape, not Grange. *Cashel Aenghus*, the House of Aenghus Ōg, the ever-young son of the Dagda, who is Angus-mac-in-de-Oc in the Manx version is a better

---

[1] One place, however, where he is the setting sun and death is Exmoor, where the names of stones and stone groups from Dunkery Beacon seem quite decisive.

name for the sacred place where Aenghus' cult was and where he conjured back the spirit into the corpse of Diarmid O'Dyna, Grainne's mate, after he had been slain by the mystic boar. 'I will send a soul into him, so that he may talk to me each day,' says Aenghus in the *Pursuit of Diarmid and Grainne*. A poet brought four *ranns* (riddling stanzas) to Finn Mac Cumhal, putting him under *geisa*[2] to comprehend it:

> I saw a house in the country
> out of which no hostages are given to a king.
> Fire burns it not, harrying spoils it not.
> Good the prosperity with which it was conceived the kingly house.

Finn says, 'I understand that verse . . . it cannot be burned or harried so long as Aenghus still lives.'

The answer seems to be the burial-place of the Dagda, of his sons Lugaidh and Ogma, of Etan (Etain), indeed of most of the cycle of the Tuatha de Danann. Later tradition insists that it was also the burial-place of the High Kings of Tara.

Going back to the archaeological layout, one surveys it thus: Cashel Aenghus, unlike the other tumuli, has around it not merely a ring of retaining stones for the earth, but a ceremonial circle well away from it. This has or had 38 big stones. The cairn was about 260–280 ft in diameter at the base, but irregular, sloping up to a top perhaps 205 ft across, going by earlier reports, and thus steeply sloped. Much 'slip' has come down. Lhwyd reports a single great stone on top. The height was perhaps 40–50 ft.

Of the ceremonial circle, two stones were big entrance stones and an extra great stone, the incised blocking-stone of the entrance, so we can make it 39 (13 × 3) if we wish. This entrance is precisely south-east. Besides this incised entrance-stone only two other external stones are carved.

New careful reconstruction gives us a second rectangular space or second entrance above the normal one. The magical dawn ray was guided through this square upper entrance. The parallel structure in Greece is triangular. Is there any significance in this? Eire, one remembers is the island of the four castles and the four districts or kingdoms—Ulster, Leinster, Munster and Connacht.

The ray, then, ascends for about 28 ft under a roof angled at that rise with overlapping stones. There is then the central chamber with its dome of more overlapped stones, like the Treasury of Atreus in Greece. It appears that these ascend in spiral. The spiral is the symbol of growth in nature. The top of this little 'dome' is a flat stone. They have not yet uncovered the top of this, so we do not know if any symbols are the other side, but the underside is plain. Piles of stones and earth were heaved up—there was

---

[2] *Geisa*: a magical command, which made it one's duty to do or not do a certain thing.

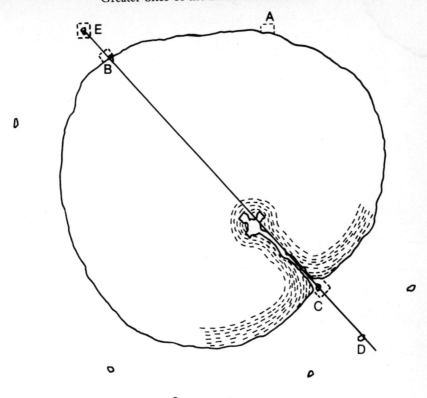

Construction:-

DC = 56.304, CB = 256.496, BE = 27.2, DE = 340 FT.

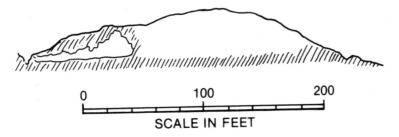

0   100   200

SCALE IN FEET

From *New Grange* by Sean P. O'Ríordan and Glyn Daniel.

Cashel Aenghus, New Grange.

a flat platform calculated as having been up there.

What do you do with holy light, having obtained it? At Stonehenge it seems probable that the upright stone altar was clad in metal that shone—the Egyptian obelisks were, and in Ireland there is record of a great circle with a gold-covered stone in the midst, dealt with by Padraic. Here we have a space with the remains of three great bowls or dishes and one shallow one intact.

This place we know was despoiled and raided several times; it was said to have possessed great treasures. Possibly a suspended crystal caught and flashed down the ray, but we have no evidence. We do have the bowls, and these suggest water or a holy potion. The intact dish has two shallow cupholes, perhaps for eye bathing to cure or to induce vision.

At the Bryn Celli Ddu burial-chamber in Anglesey a pottery bowl was placed on the midsummer axis, from which the magic number of the sun was angled out to 12 stones. Over the bowl was found a stone with the strange symbol taken for the Mother Goddess.

In Cashel Aenghus there are three recesses, the most important to the north-east, or, if the entrance is included, there are four. We have four dishes. One suggests tentatively that the ray so carefully brought in was caught in something—stone or suspended bowl of water—and its power quartered into either three or four dishes of water. There are three large bases of oblong chargers perhaps 30″ × 18″, and the one smaller shallow complete dish with hollows, say 24″ × 15″, the hollows being of 2.5″ diameter.

This is as far as we can go. We can speculate and point out that the idea of holy water in which inheres a sun-power is very old, that in this century the Bach remedies consist of just this, the surfaces of bowls of water being covered by various petals and then exposed to sunlight; and that water was repeatedly poured out in sun sacrifices in Egypt. Presumably it was Boyne water that was used—the whole Bruagh area is the floodplain of the river. In a time of Mediterranean climate it might have been a dusty area. We have three temples at least there, and numerous burial-chambers. This area has some parallels with the Nile in fact—a holy burial area with great structures like pyramids, a meandering river that supplied needed water and gave fertility.

The axis of the long chamber lies north-west–south-east, but of the cross-chambers, that on the right is the larger and evidently the main one and faces north-east. In this north-eastern chamber were found two of the stone basins. This may emphasize the primacy of this direction. If the centre has this remarkable dome of Mycenaean build, aspiring upwards, and, as now shown, a carefully-built spiral, the eastern part is in its way as remarkable for the wealth of various incised shapes sculptured upon it. In particular there are lozenges and 8 circles.

As this is the most decorated and apparently holy part of the temple, it is worth noting that 8 in the middle ages and perhaps earlier had always been a sacred number: the square of matter intersected by the two triangles of spirit, going up and down:

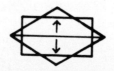

True, this is of the philosophy of Plotinus, but the shape might well represent some earlier concept. Eight 'compass-points' were known to early man.

Are circles, seemingly representing suns, to be taken as days, after the fashion of the North American Indians?

Of the two carved stones in the circle outside, the one corresponding to this north-eastern aspect has two large connected spirals on it with lozenges. Do they link with the spirals within? The pair look rather like the kind of glyphs one takes in France for mother-goddess emblems, and they might be just that, but degenerated into a meaningless formula by a later culture. One must never forget that the French main pre-historic culture is so much earlier. It might seem something that the external stone marking the north-west axis has a similar mark, if the stones are taken to represent both the midsummer sunrise and sunset.

If, opposite to this direction of the rising midsummer sun, we find in the direction of the setting midwinter sun a ship and several circular mazes, can they be taken as of significance? The ship could be a ship of death; it looks like an Egyptian one, with a sun of the underworld over its mast. At the edge projecting into the central chamber a fern-leaf has been incised. Now ferns have always been extremely magical and emblematical of the *sidhe*. This too could be meaningful.

Cashel Aenghus was not particularly packed with bones when found; there were a few incinerated remains only. It can well be taken to have been an initiation or incubation temple. Here are the basins and a very wide shallow sort of 'bath', and even now a great hollow stone is still called the Womb of Mary. The external roof seems to have been studded with quartz pebbles that would give a glitter—the possible origin of these queer phrases about 'glass domes' that occur in the Welsh. These pebbles are now being restored.

Of the three great tumuli, only that of Aenghus is called by old writers a *cashel*; the rest are *dumas*. Yet, in spite of the ship of death and the spirals, the impression grows that the Cashel Aenghus, if of better workmanship than Dowth, is yet less meaningful. Dowth, being earlier, is by virtue of this fact much nearer to the more meaningful symbolism used in France. Knowth is even earlier and has amazing incised stones.

So we pass to the other two great mounds that complete the triangle to the north, the duma of the Mound of Tresc (Knowth) and the duma of the Mound of the Bones (Dowth, also called Dubadh).

Knowth

Tresc, now in the hands of the excavator, seemed on a visit to be the most evocative of the three. Something was there, and it seemed it had been used by 'fairy' forces—it felt quite different. It is roughly oriented in the usual significant direction, north-east. It might signify that it is also known as the Grave of Bué, *Cnoc Bua*.

No excavation of the main central mound of Knowth has been carried out, only of the kerb-stones, of which 34 have been exposed between an earlier dig (Macalister) and the recent one. The main mound is 100 yds in diameter and 36 ft high.

The hill on which the temple stands is some 200 ft high and the monument's date is now reckoned as 3000–2500 BC, extremely early, the time of the Brittany remains. Around it are 11 small tombs now excavated; their entrances all face that of the main structure.

The main tumulus is built in completed layers and around are decorated kerb-stones. Marking the main tomb's entrance is one with seven concentric rectangles and across them a great perpendicular furrow, rather as at New Grange; there is also a transverse scratch across four of them. Elsewhere there are decorative circles and wavy motifs—perhaps the snake motif. Outside it all is a kind of dance-space of long arcs of stones some 23 yards long and a small circular enclosure paved with quartz.

The monument's entrance faces west. The tomb was once 126 ft or 127 ft long but 13 ft has been destroyed. There are 81 orthostats and 33 capstones. The chamber is about 7 ft high, square in shape. There is rich decoration; 25 orthostats altogether are carved. There is only one stone basin.

The subhistory and traditions here are even more important than elsewhere. It seems so far as names go to have been the main castle of the main dynasty of kings, that of North Brega, a large area including Tara. These monarchs therefore were hosts to the regular gatherings at Tara. In the annals and chronicles, Knowth is 'Cnodba' ('nova'), and it would appear that the North Brega kings used it as their title-castle from perhaps the eighth century AD down to the Normans, who took it over as a stronghold of their own.

So far six ancillary grave-temples and passages in varying states of completeness, two souterrains with low domed structures anticipating New Grange, and five hearths have been unearthed. The apparatus for an advanced civilization has been shown, town-dwelling, with industries and a fairly large population already at this date of 3000–2500 BC.

An orthostat forms the south-east side of the chamber. One end, that is, to the north-east, the other south-west, whilst the outer side faces south-east and the inner face is to the north-west. Thus the outer face is to the rising sun of midwinter, and one corner is at the north-east.

In the apparent welter of circles, cuphollows, curly lines, triangles and 'fir-trees', one series eventually stands out. Nearly at the bottom are A, two concentric circles with a central dot. Above is B, a much larger triple concentric circle pattern. Higher again is C, a still larger four-fold concentricity. On the right of B is a spiral of about the same size. Spread partly below and to the right and partly between B and C are six curled lines, sometimes with heads, which seem to be snakes, if one goes by the usual interpretation in Brittany.

Snakes may be part of the sun's magic or they may be his (or her) enemies. On the whole early man thought of snakes as wise mysterious creatures, an ambivalent attitude crystallized sharply in Egypt where snake monsters impede the underworld water journey of Rā, but where also the divine cobra is one of the highest emblems of the wisdom of the Pharaoh.

The series would seem to record the increasing size of the sun either as it rises or as it becomes larger and larger for longer and longer, as the season goes on from 21 December. Elsewhere we have a series of three sun-shapes, as externally on a kerb-stone at Dowth; and at Knowth in fact there is also a trace that seems part of an even smaller circle-and-dot below A making a fourth; this might well mean four special days reckoned about that time of year.

Besides the rebirth of the small winter sun, on this stone would seem to be shown its midsummer greatness. For just on the north-eastern tip is a remarkable figure of eight rays coming from a dot, and above are four semicircular rows of dots. Four again, and 4 × 2 rays. Eights and fours are continuously linked with the sun in this culture. The carving of this is far finer than any of the rest. If this interpretation is fair, then perhaps at the other corner we should find symbols of darkness, midwinter sunset at the south-west? We do in fact find there solid downward-pointing triangles, and we have speculatively reckoned lozenges and triangles as contrary symbols to circles and *deosil* (anti-clockwise) spirals. On this south-west tip is a *tuathal* (clockwise) spiral and the 'fir-tree' or 'herring-bone' design, which, if it is a tree, might indicate shadow.

All this is on the richly decorated outer side, but the inner is almost equally full of symbols. This inner face is to the north-west, the place which in part is where the sun never comes, the north, which is therefore the place of darkness and foreboding, and in part of the west where the sun sets in summer.

If the south-east was marked by the young sun appearing below, this side is marked by watery rather than snake symbols on the lower part. Water, one recalls, has always been the opposite of fire. The official report of the Royal Irish Association sees here a man represented upside down— is this the falling sun, darkness, even 'the hanged man' of the later Tarot tradition? Prominent on this side is an elaborate set of concentric circles like a maze, and across and out of it seems to be a passage running downwards. There is no other treatment of a circles design like this one. Could it in fact be a maze, and this passage a relief way out? At this place of darkness, in this maze of a soul-trap, the way out is only downwards . . . for this is the place of death. Also on this face are lozenges, possible emblem of the more material aspect of things, if the circle-spiral is that of the more spiritual.

Taking both sides and all the ornamentation therefore of this remarkable stone, it seems to confirm the scheme of interpretation built up from others of these Bruagh temples.

It appears that in later times Bronze Age men were there and this lasted into the Roman period; afterwards it was in regular squatters' use, but something more is likely, for there is a floor and domestic activity is shown. There are several burials with some beads and other things. In 1175 the place was fortified by Normans; and by then it was all reckoned part of the Grange of Mellifont Abbey.

A twelfth-century bard treats Knowth as one of the great entrances to the underworld: 'There are Three Dark Mysteries of Ireland: the Cave of Knowth, the Cave of Slanga (Slieve Donnard) and the Cave of Fern'

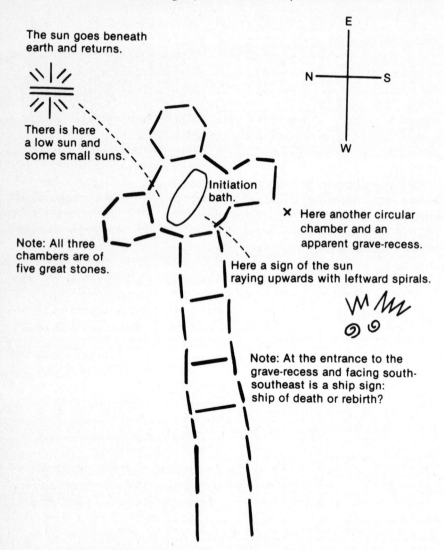

The sun goes beneath earth and returns.

There is here a low sun and some small suns.

Note: All three chambers are of five great stones.

Initiation bath.

✗ Here another circular chamber and an apparent grave-recess.

Here a sign of the sun raying upwards with leftward spirals.

Note: At the entrance to the grave-recess and facing south-southeast is a ship sign: ship of death or rebirth?

Outside the mound at the east are four inscribed suns as at the Barclodiod y Gyres:

Dowth or Dubadh.

(probably the Cave of Dunmore, and not Wexford).

Lastly, it is suggestive that from one period comes the report that Knowth was the dwelling place of the King of the Cats. Cats are closely associated with magical power . . . in Egypt there is the powerful Bast.

Dowth

Dubadh or Dowth, the Bone Mound, has a candle-lit approach. Narrow were the entrance and the long chamber, and one has to dip down; moreover, both walls and candles drip. The whole affair is smaller and rougher than is Cashel Aenghus, but is that much nearer to the earlier tradition.

Here was a main and obvious type of initiation or even 'baptizing' bath, hollowed from a noble piece of stone: a 'womb of Mary' indeed. It had been found smashed and is reconstructed, so that its positioning is not authentic. Another initiating bath, smaller, was off it at an angle in another chamber.

The long chamber is 'correctly' oriented, that is to the north-east. The clues sought were found. The inner stone at the south-west octagonal side, that is the stone turned towards the point where the sun's course reaches apogee in summer at north-east, has on it a sign unseen elsewhere, an upward-pointing series of pillars which might well be a more special way of representing rays. There is also a close-woven maze-pattern just there. There are spirals which perhaps confirm the identification. A stone similarly oriented in the left-hand chamber has quadrated circles.

Opposite, to the south-west side, at the inner side facing the midwinter death of the sun and his rebirth, is a strange but I think understandable symbol:

One hardly needs to compare the Amerindian symbols ⟁ and ⟰ being sun-up and sun-down respectively, to realize that this is a double emblem of the departing and rising of the sun. Precisely in fact what the midwinter sun does. A left-hand path spiral is traced around it, appropriately to the 'evil' time of the year. The whole is carved, again appropriately, low down on the stone. Other small suns or quadrated circles accompany the symbol.

Outside, the only external stone of the retaining wall to be carved, one to the direct east, has on it four suns, very similar to those on the passage grave of Barclodiod y Gyres on Anglesey. Two were ringed, two not. The sun passes twice over the east in his yearly course, and there are two types of sun . . .

A larger round chamber, without any of the indications that appear to make temples of these chambers, has a recess of it facing a sort of south-east that might well be a resting place for corpses. It has at the entrance a more formalized but recognizable ship sign, again the ship of death.

So what of it all? The Tuatha took over in these three noble structures the prehistoric initiatory function, that may also have included death ceremonies, and it became to them a place of magic, where one raised the spirits of the dead, and a holy place where the hero-gods of the cycle slept.

And what did death or sleep or 'house' mean? It is the greatest house, the one with the stone circle, that is the 'house' or 'cashel' connected with the God of Youth ruling the land of the young, Tir-na-n'Ŏg. In another version probably of a more ancient people, he is the son of the god, the Dagda, who 'feels' an extremely old concept and not at all Celtic. He has a cauldron of plenty on a gargantuan scale, a boiling up of primitive mating —in the great spoon a man and woman could lie together. The cauldron was a vast hole in the earth. But Aenghus is more refined, an advance, the next generation, a deity of beauty and of Celtdom, beautiful of hue. No lying in earthy spoons for him; with his mate, the swan-maiden Caer, he flew off over the lake, two great white birds.

The heroes were here because, shall we say, those seeking the light slept here. It was a place for incubation with the spirits, where the holy dream came to the aspirants. You also burnt the bodies and placed here the bones of some revered or holy relatives, to be in the sacred atmosphere. Above them went the holy spiral chimney up to heaven, for memories of the culture of those who lived in the hills—who indeed built sham hills to live in, which had ways in and out at the top—left an idea about ways up that were human-made. One thinks of Babylon's ziggurats. Was the original Jacob's ladder a 'chimney'? 'They climbed the steep ascent to heaven' is not an exclusively Christian sentiment. Was it a spiral staircase to heaven?

And those four great spirals and some other designs, perhaps originally up over the entrance, and the five big stones out in front there: what are they? Guardian spirits in the stones perhaps, as we subconsciously feel them even now (and see them with faces in Corsica), whilst a flavour that comes from the phallic period makes us think also of ancestors. What of the spirals? Only general indications of mysteries perhaps, for they had seemingly lost the more precise meanings of the symbols. Circular types of engravings on monuments may mean several things: eyes, symbolic of the 'eye-goddess' of the eastern Mediterranean; the sun, the equivalent of days; or circular mazes if spiral, with overtones of luck, movements perhaps of ways in and out of birth and death and initiation. Some of these meanings they might earlier have had, but here they may only have kept a generalized sense and were perhaps mainly decorative.

What of the numbers 4 and 5? Four spirals repeat the motif of four suns facing the east: perhaps there was something about four special days at the high centre or centres of the year. Four is a basic number of foundation, suitable to a feeling of assertion of something fundamental at a ceremonial entrance, and the spiral itself might still have had this earlier 'mysteries' feeling hanging about. The five stones, again, are a number connected with the senses and the Mother.

The lozenges seen everywhere might be a meaningful up-and-down, sun-up and sun-down symbol, signifying life and death, and above all, midsummer and midwinter: the general principle of opposites. It could also represent the serpent-power formalized.

One would like to know what sensitives have felt, if any have slept within this shrine. What shades from sleep, from what beautiful land of Aenghus Ōg, could slip into the relaxed mind? W.B. Yeats spent some time in it. Knowth is distinctly fairy and untouched, and one feels something different there. The others by comparison are more turbulent. Knowth certainly belongs to a much older people, who knew at least something of its own traditional symbols and placed them meaningfully, while Dowth is intermediate with New Grange.

Teltown and Tara

From Cashel Aenghus two great sites are on significant leys and form a pointing shape. The essences of each therefore may be considered as having relevance to the temple of the old Mother and the love god.

In Greece any considerable site has several developed expressions: there is the theatre, the gymnasium and places for athletic contests of all kinds, the place for meetings, political and philosophic debate—the agora—and the temple which links with and qualifies all, for all activity is guided by one or another deity. So it was with these Danaans of a very similar culture: games, politics, debate, the worship of the gods, the dance, formed a linked whole, not so distinctly articulated as with the more conscious Greeks, but with similar elements, although we have fewer traces of the drama. Tara has five-yearly sports competitions and the assembly of the Bell Branch Kings, Tailtin the large-scale races presided over by Lugh's fostermother.

At Tailtin or Teltown is the rath of the games of the Lughnasadh season —a wide stretch where games boundaries can be traced around and under agriculture. At one end presides the long mound called that of Lugh's 'nurse' or foster-mother, in the ancient Celtic tradition of fostering and of sending young boys to be reared in larger households. Funeral games held here were like those held for Hector as told by Homer, presumably held also at the great cursus with the long barrow near Stonehenge. It is all at the Festival of High Summer, the Festival of Lugh or Light, 1 August by the present calendar: time of sacrifice, of first harvests, of the destructive force of the Mother Goddess. But also it is the time of the wedding of Earth, Eire, by Lugh the Light-God, a season of marriages all over the land. The complexities of the festival are many and have been the subject of a large and thorough book.[3]

[3] MacNeill, Maire, *The Festival of Lughnasa*, Oxford University Press, 1962.

The unopened mound appears to run east-northeast–west-southwest, plus or minus a few degrees, at the sunrise of early August. It should be a sort of shrine. Games and cycle contests have been linked with Tara in quite recent years; the magic still works.

The High Hill of Tara

Although known as Termuir and Teamhair (pron. 'tyow-ar'), meaning 'height', in fact this bastion of Irish history is not very high at all (512 ft) but it certainly commands a wide view over Tara's Plain. Perhaps it used to be higher—hills often were. This wide rise of land had a mound and ditch, with early wooden fortifications on them, constructed pretty well all round its summit. Within this sacred acropolis were sacred things of all stages of antiquity . . .

To take those things likely to have been basic first, we have the Mother Goddess, the homunculus and the monster. The homunculus masquerading as 'Adamnan', who looks like the horned god Cernunnos and the Celtic archetypal child, the Maban, mixed, may be seen on a stone on the local graveyard and was maybe at the entrance to a rock-cut maze starting thereabouts. Excavation has not yet confirmed this, but such bits of dig as have taken place have shown rock-cut trenches that might well be this, that link with the findings in Crete. Who knows but that the bull of Eire may prove to be a minotaur?

The rock cuttings were abruptly revealed by the Arkites, of all people, whilst bashing the valuable site mercilessly about with the full consent of its besotted owner (in spite of the negatives of the Irish authorities) to find the Covenant Ark, throwing aside magnificent torques, bones *in situ*, megaliths and all as piffle before the wind. The Covenant Ark would bring in the golden age to confirm the British as the Chosen Race of Israel. Where did the Irish come in? As continuations of Canaanites perhaps—one could even find a 'proof', for the next letter to 'C' is 'D', and in the centuries they have of course shifted the initial letter one on: who cannot recognize Danaan in Canaan? Simple.

The Mother Goddess is there in a huge circular earthwork 220 ft across, dedicated to the goddess Grainne, and in a well a little down the hill. Indeed this hill is surrounded with wells halfway down its sides, at the right water-level; and the fertility goddess turns up again with a 'house' and is there called a 'She-Husbandman' with the improbable name of Mairisius—one notes the 'Maire' stem masculinized.

Here she has a well, Nemnach, and one thinks of the grove Nemedh. Another well is called Caprach, and one thinks of the stem 'Capr' and the fertile goat-god. This well is also called the Physician, the White Cow and the Dark Eye: that is curative water, fertility-making springs and the beauty of dark liquidity in water and eye alike.

We have now accumulated a number of known mother-goddess emblems: the circle (plan of both fort and 'house'), the wells themselves, the hints of sacred groves and of fertility goats (masculine complements to the Goddess), and sustaining cows (perhaps actual breasts as hillocks). And this eye, now called dark, maybe was originally light, i.e. the sun: or, as complement to that, the Dark Eye might be the moon. One wonders if excavation will reveal any incised stones with intensive spirals, often held to be the eye emblems of the Goddess, as at the Hal Taxian temple, Malta. Certain pairs of spirals certainly do seem to be eyes; the only question is whether they all were or whether the alternative mystical explanation of the larger spirals at any rate, given by Rachel Levy in *The Gate of Horn*, that they represent the maze of death and birth, in and out, is not equally likely.

The Mata of Tara has not been interpreted as a monster attached to a stone, but as a warrior. Much of this Tara investigation turns on rethinking and using comparison and commonsense. A monster with plenty of arms takes us back to other monstrous creatures, to the great boar of Wales that rushed all over the land and swam out to sea; to the Giant Beaver, the Avanc, that bunged up Lake Bala and caused a world flood; or even the great cow called the Green Stripper of Eire. A simpler thought would be an octopus.

Mother, magic child and monster, then, give us a start. One can proceed to the Grave of Maine, probably an early sanctuary with a sacred stone. Near it were three Druidic stones which seem to have borne names attached hereditarily to Druids, perhaps corresponding to three offices whose bearers were successive Druids. They may have been foundational and initiatory stones. No trace of them remains; all we know of them is from a later literary source.

The other main structures are the Fort of the Kings and the mound it encloses, the assembly hall and the Fort of the Synods. The Fort of the Kings is a huge double ramparted area whose longest internal measurement is 775 ft. It was created by the great King Cormac—he was the main builder of this whole complex, and dates about AD 250—and he carefully deformed it in order that it might be blessed by the intrusive mound of the foundress or goddess now going under the name of 'Tea', i.e. 'dea', which seems to mean nothing beyond 'goddess'. Within the enclosure side by side are the circle called the 'seat' that seems to represent the former kings' dwelling (about 30 ft across): perhaps a hall with a throne: and the central and larger circle of Cormac's own 'house', if house it was, whose area is 88 ft × 80 ft.

On its mound now sits the Fail Stone of Destiny, as alleged by Petrie, but defaced with a modern memorial inscription; it was probably brought from the Mound of the Hostages, Niall's lot, a little way away. Other people say this is not the Lia Fail at all but that it went to Scone and is now the Westminster Abbey throne and crowning stone.[4] Something basic still

[4] The earlier Gaelic account gives us the Stone of Tara as coming from Palestine with Jeremiah and a princess. In the fourth century BC the prophet Jeremiah, figuring as the Ollamh (ollave or high poet) Fodla, after the death of the last reigning prince of Judah, came with his daughter, the heiress, to Eire, bearing with him the crowning stone of the Judaean princes and also accompanied by a scribe. The records indicate that she married

responds in each of us to the idea of a holy stone; see how deeply the Stone Ages have sunk into us. Mayors and royalty lay foundation stones; every Christian altar must either be of stone or have a stone let into it, and this is what is consecrated. Hardly anyone is unmoved by the actually not very large Stonehenge.

This Fal or Fail stone guaranteed that a scion of the house of Milesius should always reign; it objected if anyone else attempted to be crowned. So it belongs to the Milesian invasion race, before the People of the Gods, the *Tuatha de Danann*.

In the Fort of the Kings, perhaps at his 'house', King Cormac had a visitation by one of the beautiful fairy people bearing the musical bell-branch which gave him the vision of the world of the *sidhe*. It demanded his nearest and dearest as a test, but later gave them back. Cormac entered the *sidhe* world awhile, where all is brilliant, musical and lovely; but he returned to complete his work upon Earth. Others did not. There was a more or less open door then to this country which was under the sea, or in the hills, or simply transcended the workaday world. Many were rapt into it, usually in periods of nine something—days, weeks or years—that is, a magical or dream period. Marvels were told on their return. As in England, the Other World may have been that of previous inhabitants, Little or Littler People, with mound-dwelling habits and skills in herbs or with animals. On the whole, though, that formula does not fit Eire very well, since the *sidhe* are often represented as of full or even giant size, clad in brilliant clothes and masters of music: to hear their music was the first step to entrancement. The Wild Hunt, with the miming of the Goddess and her mate in brilliant clothes and plenty of witchy calls and bells, perhaps some form of music we should now think of as eastern, calculated to hypnotize somewhat, that is perhaps more like it . . . a marvellous excuse to vanish for a while for any maiden or youth, turning up again at the ritual period, with tales of marvels such as the Irish well know how to pitch, received with awe. A worn or aged appearance was confirmation, for after a *sidhe* period you were returned bedraggled. These are doubtless unworthy speculations.

Cormac probably erected the House of Mead-Circling, the assembly hall, again replacing something earlier. Here we have literary evidence to play with. Two ancient works, the *Yellow Book of Lecan* and the *Book of Leinster*, purport to give us the exact plan of this great 700 ft-long structure. Knights, minstrels, Druids, servitors and so on are elaborately arranged in longways rows, which correspond to the layout found in the mounds more or less as they slope up the hill. The king sits not at one end but at one side, near the middle, this corresponding to a high stretch of ground whence he could have commanded the hall.

Eochaid, the then High King of Tara, and that thenceforward the stone became Eire's crowning stone. The block is of a blue sandstone veined with red, 22 × 13 × 11″ dimensions.

To this high period of great heathenism we may attribute with some confidence the sacrifice of animals by burning, the existence of a regular sacred fire and also of a vernal equinox celebration and Samhain fires. All these are shown by the remains. It is quite maddening that we have no more of them.

Of the considerable kings in the post-Cormac period, the one who waged skilful and directed war abroad was Niall of the Nine Hostages. Hitherto Irish kings had pretty well kept to Eire; the securing of their own loose domains and their own enjoyable little brotherly wars between chieftains were sufficient. Niall, however, with great persistence harried Roman Britain and the Continent. His dates are given as 379–405. Niall has merited a remarkable stone in a Donegal church, the Catholic church at Glencolumcille, which the writer has seen. The figures have stiff pointed caps and stiff coats. No one seemed to know anything about it, and it must have been thought of later date. Niall's 'hostages' were the slaves and noble youths he brought back. For such extensive operations, nine hostages would seem a mere pittance; but perhaps they were very notable ones. Amongst them certainly was one Succet from Gaul, who was noble or even royal.

The next-but-one king was Laoghaire (Leary) MacNiall, to whom is here attributed a 40 ft square fort, with doors to the four quarters. In his reign Succet landed as the missionary Padraic, and Laoghaire would neither listen to nor receive him. His father, he said, had taught him to hate enemies, and he was not going to learn to love them. This Laoghaire swore faith to the men of Leinster by the sun and moon and three other pairs of elements, and when he broke faith and attacked to enslave the Leinstermen, the elements avenged it—he was struck by lightning. So the elements were deities all right.

The Fort of the Synods—three were held here, at long intervals, Padraic's being only the first—has been so cut up by the search for the Ark that little can be gleaned from it, save to indicate it as 100 ft in diameter. Patrick's activities were mainly the checking over of the extant laws, striking out those which were hopelessly heathen but keeping what he could. As a Celtic noble, he would not be too hard on the laws of his race and caste. Then the Bards put the new substitute parts into poetry, to be memorizable like the rest. All laws had to be poetic.

Padraic, of course, had a grand time. The official story that he was trained in Italy is obvious nonsense—Gaul is the furthest he could have gone in order *not* to have had knocked out of him his Irish chieftain's characteristics. He assembled a host of followers, just like a chieftain's, and did things in a big way, burning idols and driving out snakes (did Eire ever have any?) whilst with a little tact the colleges of Druids, communities already organized, came over to his teachings. All he had to do was to link up existing symbolism; (they already had a figure Esus from Gaul), add the Maban as the child Christ and adapt the old goddess Maire as Mary and her more vigorous form Brighid as the infant's nurse, and there you were.

If anyone can believe that one missionary, however energetic, could even in a reasonably long period start the hundreds of monastic and conventual foundations attributed to Padraic, let him look at the later and more factual records of the centuries; the great Benedict did not, at the height of his fabulous influence, achieve any such marvels. If Padraic gave some new ideas to existing bodies, however, it is quite credible. He may even have really taken round a small army of workers and remodelled them a good deal.

So it all passes into the Christian period and decays, and by AD 400 or so the great wooden hall where the mead circulated was pretty well gone and the other structures, all wooden, were disappearing. The great vision of Cormac's heathendom, with its brilliant colours, its warriors and riders, the more open way to the *sidhe*, the spells and the runes disappeared in reality to reappear vividly in the world of literature. Druids became Culdees and a new seriousness doubtless descended.

Summary of the Trio

At New Grange, as we have seen, the ancient ideas recorded themselves on stones, indications are of burials and worship, and the way up is a corbelled roof like the Atreus 'Treasury' at Mycenae, which shone in the new winter sun. At Tara there were few, if any, early incised stones, although the Mound of the Captives, opened up, seems to have afforded a few later incised figures; mostly the structures and perhaps the cult figures had been of wood. Tara was primarily civil; its kings attempted political power. New Grange was a great temple. Tailtin was the sacred games place. It is the Greek cultural trinity.

The same difference is noticeable in England between Avebury and Stonehenge: one is for a large more mundane dance assembly, probably gathered for some great spectacle; the other is the shrine of father-sun and cattle-horns-mother deities, whose priests told men the seasons to sow and reap. The games element is represented by the cursus nearby.

These comparisons can only be suggestive, for if one statement is truer than any other, it is that every megalithic structure is in fact different from every other, however many features are in common. A few definite idols would help; but the fact seems to have been that anyway in these islands this religion was singularly non-idolatrous, the neolithic mind being symbolical in texture. In Eire we hear of idols; Padraic burnt some, so presumably they were wooden. No idols appear in the Dublin Museum, however. Passionate Christians may of course have utterly destroyed them in righteous fury, but it seems unlikely that none would have remained at all. So far as a limited knowledge goes, what we do have is the fertility figure Sheila Na Gig over church doorways, a degenerated fertility and good luck figure, only abolished by a scandalized Church about the middle of the last century or later, yet surviving here and there.

By idols it is possible that chroniclers usually mean menhirs, which are sometimes carved with faces as in Corsica. These could well be overthrown; the surprising thing is how menhirs managed to stay up, even though no Irish one perhaps reached the size of the 67 ft Men er Hroeck in Brittany, the great male emblem beside that clearest marked shrine of the Mother Goddess, the Table des Marchands.

There will now be given a more speculative attempt to interpret the motives of these remote ancestors of ours.

Cashel Aenghus: a Freer Interpretation

By the holy river was the land of the gods, where a good sort of stone made it easy to entomb the bodies or ashes of ancestors, those who prophesied through the priests. But time had gone on, and it was understood that here were also great powers of light from above, as well as holy unions with growth-powers linked with earth and ancestors. Those who knew had converted the chiefs to the need for a proper House by the Boyne, a *Bruagh na Boinne*, for these great ones, something worthy of them, and an abstract art had developed which was able to represent the different sides of these natures.

The dark world of mazes into which part of you went at death was surely illumined by some version of the sun that seemed to cause all life here. So a spiral united both ideas: it was round and like an eye, as the sun, yet devious as the old spirit ideas with their mazes. And then, going away, that was what happened to the sun in the evening. And at one time of the year he seemed to threaten to go away permanently to the south and it grew darker and darker. It was desirable to design the temple in order to bring him back and appreciate and praise his gift when he halted for a day or so and then returned. The south-west was where he vanished, the south-east was where he reappeared.

Up north was the sunless earth part. Perhaps it belonged to the dead who had no sun on their plane—certainly it belonged to roots and seeds which grew in dark places, and to water which was usually down below. The right sign would seem to be a triangle of earth or water, going up or down, or both.

As the sun grew bigger and stayed longer, so his daily and seasonal death seemed worse. At the north-east was his greatest power, which was in the summer, a very high light indeed, when the greatest things happened. You would point towards it to receive the power. His death then became the worst, and of the dark north the north-west was the most deathly part of the boding area.

Why not build a place where the new ray could come in and give, as it was believed, tremendous power to young people through its conversion of water into a spirit gift? It could also come down symbolically into the mazes of earth . . . The great power of summer should be used, amongst other things, for the great initiation of a man into the tribe when he was about 25–30. It should and could also be stored up in the stones facing the right way and properly dedicated by sun designs, power later to be drawn off as needed.

For these purposes the House was built in the land of the gods. It had a great stone across the entrance, proclaiming it the temple of an infinite number of suns and mazes, showing also the sun-ray coming vertically down at midday and percolating into the whorls of the spirits. The entrance itself had an ordinary tall oblong entry for the elders and others, but another higher up for the spirit of light. Along this upper way of the gods it went, right up into the corbelled roof of the great chamber, then was directed to a prepared bowl that deflected part of the power down for use. Light was really a child newly arrived, and a picture on the wall facing his entry showed the kind of high-powered boat wherein he was rowed on his arrival.

Directed down, the power rayed into a special bowl of water, a bath of illumination, with two shallow cups in it for the water blessed in this way. Here the priests bathed their eyes and were given the second sight; and others were given healing for their eyes or for other troubles.

This took place in the central chamber at the turning point of mid-winter, when it was still cold and dark. But in the bath in that chapel facing leftwards into the dark of winter sunset, where there was shown the boat and also symbols of the bigger sun, little boys of seven years were given their first initiations. There was nothing very powerful facing that way inside, but some triangles joined into lozenges showed reflections of the idea of the dove with earth and sky or water shown below, ideas which belong in that direction.

The great death of midsummer was different. Outside at that point was a model cyst-coffin plan. Round it were broken circles and knots, as life was broken and the spirit tied up. Three cup-eyes were filled with the death rays. Inside, a triple maze showed three ways opening out of one another in which the soul could wander.

However, the greatest concern of midsummer was the coming of the highest power of energizing, of *mana*. Magically it was drawn in, first outside by that huge standing stone precisely at the north-east, then watched outside by two great eye-spirals for the two days it stayed much the same, together with the two diamonds filled with water showing that it was all balanced between the summer sun-eyes and the winter-darkness. Inside, all the great whorls of suns faced that way and welcomed the power into the north-eastern chapel. There were three suns radiating from the opposite chapel, half-a-dozen on the big jamb of the entrance to the centre chamber, and decorations of suns and many other things on the stone roofing overhead. What a couple of days those were! All the high power was being drawn in with chants and gestures by the priests, whilst the highest initiations of the men who were ready took place at the north-east in the biggest bath. They were now fully taken into the senior bands of their tribes, took honorific oaths and were given armlets and headbands.

There were three of these initiating baths altogether as well as the curative one in the middle. The third—or the second in life-order—was in the north-west chapel at the very end as you came in, and watched by great circle eyes and the great fernleaf of the fairy ones, where the worst of the mock-death tests were given to the boys being initiated into manhood at 14. They were cut about, starved and made to catch game with their bare hands for weeks before being brought in half-dead to the temple, given the fairy healing and acceptance by the eyes of the goddess.

The light god or goddess who had entered at midwinter and was in full power at midsummer had only partly descended to help men in all this. This divinity dwelt in the upper passages and above all in the dome. Deity really belonged to the sky, to either of the great lights. As the light became less on Earth, deity went up to the heavens again, up the spiral steps that had been prepared in the corbelling, through the spirit door at the top and past the shining quartz pebbles of the roof that showed their glory. The temple was now cleared and lit ready for the midwinter rebirth. The part of deity that belonged to the fertility passages and wandering ghost-track below sank into the earth and prepared an earth-ship, with seeds and little lights. At last the young Maban of the Ōg appeared again, launched in it.

Who were the deities? Had they names? The Dagda is the later earth-god without doubt; he has a pit in the ground which is the great cauldron of plenty. Yet is he not also the sun, in another aspect? For he has the one eye of the sun-god. The Dagda may be bisexual, for there is the great spoon in which man and woman can lie together, and Eire has a sun goddess in Grainne. The Dagda's harp calls to and regulates creation by sounds. Certainly his son is a higher spirit: *Aenghus*, son of the Dagda, *Mac-in-da-Ōg* son of youth, with his mate, are capable of changing into great white swans —the Dagda would have been more likely to change into a great ogre. Aenghus is the love-god who marks his followers with charms that attract. But he is no longer purely neolithic, he is Bronze-Age and Celtic and a Danaan. The primitive Dagda is more like the earlier deity of the Bruagh-na-Boinne House.

IX. *The Rollright Darkness*

The Rollright complex is on the borders of Oxfordshire, three miles north of Chipping Norton, on a ride above the villages of Great and Little Rollright, Little Rollright being perhaps half a mile and directly on the ridge trackway. There was a narrow sunken lane approach since built up and this kept it lonely until recently and an attraction for misuse—not only have organized Druids and regular witch covens used it, but very different folk and for less reputable purposes.

Earlier it was called 'Rowldrich', which speculatively may have come from Rholdrwg, wheel of the Druids. This is Stukeley's perhaps bogus suggestion. Domesday has Rollandri = rollandright, the Right of Roland, the well-known Christian champion—which would imply some strong pagan opponent. But there are big Roland figures which were set up in Germany and represent an earlier pagan god, connected with a wheel—

possibly Wedel, a figure grasping a wheel.

The crowded nature of the site, the stones cheek by jowl and half-buried sometimes, is opposed in type to most of the work of the neolithic Druids who are on the whole workers with carefully measured and spaced-out stones, and, if it is a real circle, it betokens a completely different culture. The stones traditionally cannot be counted, like the Castlerigg Circle stones, and the circle actually called the Countless Stones, 500 yds south of Kit's Coty House; and this is so, for it depends upon how you reckon buried, fallen and overlapping stones, and no two people reckon alike. One may hear visitors counting and reckoning from 70 to over 90. Approximately 60, however, one may say is the number. There are other crowded circles, like Lounhead, but they do not give this impression of 'busy-ness' and deliberate crowding.

The circle is about 100 ft across; the stones are mostly low but taller ones are here and there: at the due north point is one standing 7 ft 4 inches high. Some 84 yds distant to the north-northeast (29°), over into Warwickshire, is the isolated, tortured-looking lith called the King Stone. Practically at right angles with it, 220 yards to the west-northwest, was the lith called Gough's Stone on a barrow, now untraceable. More or less due east (94°9′) at about 390 yards is the group of the four uprights of a burial chamber with a fallen capstone; these are the Four Whispering Knights, on horseback. Probably they have been pushed in further together, for agricultural space. The 60-odd stones of the main circle are known as the army of the King's Men.

Perhaps the surroundings as well as the site say something. Between the villages of Great and Little Rollright the ridge is 700 ft above sea-level, overlooking the river Stour one way, the river Swere the other, and Long Compton to the north-east.

Geographically the extended monument splits not only between Oxfordshire and Warwickshire but also between two owners, and by a very ancient trackway running west-southwest and east-northeast, marked by a traceable line of menhirs, forming a sort of sacred way to an old ridge-top burial ground. These burials are of late Bronze Age date and are cremations.

The indications are that this was primarily a Cymric settlement area; the word Cotswold derives from the Celtic *coed* = a wold. Anciently, all this was part of Wychwood Forest and part of the Wold (wild). This was in fact very much of a border district. Within Wychwood stood formerly a number of well-known stones now disappeared—Frethurstone, the Hoar Stone, and the Hawk Stone. On the Oxford side stood a circle as large as Avebury, 900 yds across, part of which remains as the Devil's Quoits. The whole area was thus famous for standing stones, and the actual name of Stanton Village not far away is *stan tren*, the stone enclosure.

Camden knew Rollright well; he considered it Danish and called it the second wonder of the land—Stonehenge was the first. Stukeley, who found the whole area heathland, considered the King Stone a relic of an

Archdruid's barrow. In this he was clearly wrong for it is an isolated stone.

The oddly crowded stones, the erosions of the oolitic limestone and their peculiar relationship have given rise to legends. The story is one of baffled ambition and guardian witchcraft. An ambitious local king (unnamed) is assured of ruling all England if from the Rollright site he can see Long Compton. Coming along with his men to fulfil this simple requirement, he found that Mother Shipton (surrogate for a witch of any kind) had caused the ground to rise in the manner it now does and so prevented the view. So when he happily chanted:

> If Long Compton I can see
> King of England I shall be

she cried:

> Rise up stick and stand still stone
> King of England shalt thou be none.
> Thou and thy men hoar stones shall be
> And I myself an Elder Tree

and there he is, the King Stone, with fairies dancing round him, and his men are in that magic circle.

But the raising up of an earth ridge by magic is a feat little if at all known in legends; could there not be another explanation? If Professor Thom is right, from the top of the mounded-up circle quite probably one could originally have seen Long Compton. Then as the mound wore down one had to strain to see it, then one could not see it at all. So someone must have raised something . . . the folk-mind could have worked that way.

Returning to the king, some of his knights had meanwhile been conspiring against him a little way off; they were concealed in stone too, as those four knights that whisper together. Alternatively, they may have whispered dark prophecies.

Mother Shipton is indeed an elder tree; there are a number of elder bushes near. In Saxony she is better treated—personified as the much respected and feared Dame Elder. She is, however, considered completely unholy in Ireland. At Midsummer Eve the elder is traditionally cut, whereupon the king moves his hand. Also the fairies dance round him.

Until 1882 the stones were unprotected; visitors could chip off bits without restraint and did so. Now they are in the careful charge of an owner who values them.

To Professor Thom, the strange nature of Rollright suggests that probably the circle is the ring of support for a large earthern mound, which has vanished as they usually do. But what of the invariable central cist stones within, usually too large for people to trouble to shift? Professor Thom suggests that they were used for roadbuilding; but it would be a determined roadbuilder who would prefer to use the fairly massive cist stones when there are smaller ones. There is no sign of their having been drawn out, so he would have had to split them on the spot. Also, is there any other example of such a large round barrow?

Yet allowing for its being the supporting stones of such a barrow, Rollright is in effect a true circle, having the orientations that the mound had before the earth vanished. Going by the outlier stone, it is oriented to Capella.

It may be accidental, but the arcs of the circle looking to the Whispering Knights or to Gough's Stone have closer and more upright stones than the rest of the periphery. The above legend shows the likelihood of a matriarchal kind of cult—the witch protects her own stones.

Summing up orientations and other indications, we have the one definite marker stone in the circle to the north; a main marker-stone, the King Stone, points north-northeast to Capella, which is at 'square' (90°) to Gough's Stone west-northwest. Practically due east is the chief's tomb or the Whispering Knights. Does this mean an oracle? Whispering or murmuring is often found to indicate such a use. The general menhir-marked trackway is running east-northeast–west-northwest. Professor Thom says guardedly that these entrance-marked orientations of Rollright may be entrances or simply markers. There could have been a processional way between the circle representing some ceremonial sanctification and the chieftain's tomb to the east. The King Stone may equally have been an object of reverence as well as of time-observation to Capella. Some dozen surveyed sites use the star Capella as time-marker. In 2000 BC Capella was more prominent than now; it was useful from late autumn until rather before midsummer. Rollright shares with Woodhenge the observation of Capella; the other sites to do so are mostly in Scotland. Thus it is possible that the people who erected both circles had come down from more northerly latitudes where Capella is a few days more useful as a calendar and time-marker. Between these two orientations ran a sacred way for the dead, up to the hills not far away.

These observations make it clear that the main construction of Rollright must have been some 2000–1800 years BC, and although from other remains it may seem that the culture of the Belgae, 300–200 BC, was there, this race clearly inherited something already structured. Possibly it may already have been in the denuded state in which it is found now.

Rollright also had a magic connected with water—the ford of the river Swere or tributaries below. At night, about midnight, the stones move down the hill to drink at the stream, near the burial chamber. Both king and knights move down to the Spinney Spring, just as the Carnac stones go down to the sea on Christmas Eve. In so far as this monument has a sun-link, it could be down here to the south-east or winter rebirth place of the infant sun from the Great Mother.

The drinking shows that the stones were inhabited by human spirits. If one thing is clearer than another it is the thirst of the dead. Holes are left in pottery coffins for drink of some kind to be poured in, beer is poured on to and into the places of the dead in Britain, before the gibbering ghosts can speak to Aeneas in Virgil they must quaff blood poured into a trench. Not all menhirs by any means are humanized, but the continual mention of dancing linked with names of stones implies it, whilst here they are an 'army' and 'knights'.

The combination of a barrow surround used as a circle, a mysteriously-vanished cist-grave, a rare orientation (more circles are directed to the sun) and mistaken use by a later race, gives the confused background against which cult use is seen.

At the writer's third visit there was a vision as of a quite dark-skinned people coming from the eastern direction carrying large leafy boughs for ritual purposes. They seemed a folk here for a short period only, but the intensity of their life was such as to impregnate the whole area inescapably. They might be relatives or those seen at Meini Hirion, but a duller branch of those dignified and intellectual beings.

By indications of these various kinds one deduces that the location in later times belongs to the magic-working, crowding, Nature-regarding culture that might be expected from a people drawing power from the earth current of the north. Burgeoning Nature is the work of the force known as Pan, expansive, ruthless, regarding only the natural forms and its own devotees. Pan dances down the valleys in old Arcadia, maddening the he-goats and rams, with a following of young folk and of middle-aged matrons. Sensible men shunned Pan, finding his effect on their wives very strange indeed. True, this Belgic race (if Belgic it was) has not gone so far as the wild nocturnal festivals on mountains that the Greeks knew, when kids and lambs were torn apart by the revellers, mostly women, quite unconscious of what they were doing; but in their rapt branch-waving they are moving in that direction in their duller way.

This is the only site known to the writer that can be said to have been witchy in use in the conventional sense. All fertility cults—and this certainly was that—have something dark in them, for man does not live by fertility alone but normally moves by a higher purpose that informs and contains it. Pan is not a respectful or respect-inducing form but reckless, gay and savage. As a release from tensions he is useful; as anything more, mischievous. Pan always needs mastering, whereby he becomes a powerful servant; the insouciance of the unconscious is only good up to a certain point.

It is little wonder that for many Rollright becomes the typical setting for witch observances, often peculiar rather than authentic. It is at the opposite pole from the Cornish Merry Maidens, a planned ritual circle, little interfered with, having much force still to be used—at the right vibrations.

X. *The* Dawns Myin
or Nineteen Merry Maidens of Cernow (Cornwall)

About the extreme western areas, whether of the Hielands in the Hebrides, Wales in the Lleyn Peninsular, or Eire in the mysterious stone and pillar at the furthest west point of these islands, hangs mystery that can almost be touched. Cornwall is an intensification of this general experience. Whilst Land's End itself is perhaps less impressive than the horrifying Breton Pointe du Raz, the area west of Merazion constitutes a land thick with mystery. It is thick with ancient monuments, most of whose angulations to each other are significant, and in spite of the work by John Michell, *The Stones of Land's End* (1974), much more work needs doing here.

Darkness in a psychic sense hangs about many of these valleys, as though generations of wreckers had left unraised elements of themselves. Yet they also hold oases of light. One of these is perhaps the best-known circle of Cornwall. Fortunately it has not been spoiled, for the Cornish seem to have inherited a reverence for stones and not to have let themselves be carried away by fanaticism such as that which destroyed a large part of Avebury and of the circles of Wales.

Bolerium is a granite plateau only attached to the rest of Britain by a bridge four miles wide from Hale to Marazion. Its length, south-west–north-east is 10 miles. This is the Land of the Giants who still raise great granite blocks. Over 100 menhirs, stone circles and other gigantesque works are or were in these 14 parishes known as Western Penrith. The craggier tors and cairns are attributed to the giants who were only dealt with finally by Brutus' Trojans. Following them came Druids and the Greeks and later the Celtic, usually half-Druid, saints, of whom there is an extraordinary profusion, largely linked with Brittany also. Phoenicians arrived for the metal and white clay trade, and the Greeks followed. This was one of the fusing grounds for Greek philosophy with Druidic ideas; perhaps these were the final judgement of the Hermetic traditions themselves, as distinct from revivals. Sacred areas, *llans*, kept independent privilege and administration, like St Buryan's parish which contains the Merry Maidens, one of the richest areas in all these monuments.

Boscawen-Un's 19 stones plus a central stone is maybe the most interesting circle, central to a great scheme of alignments: a flattened circle based on the *vesica piscis*. The longer diameter is about 30 MY and the great perimeter is three times that, which is a frequent ideal with the circle builders. The leaning central stone points eastward. Welsh triads know the Boscawen-Un as one of the three mighty Gorsedd places. According to William Borlase's *Antiquities of the County of Cornwall* (1766 and 1769) the inclining stone in the Boscawen-Un centre was for the election of a prince or to pass a decree.

However, now the Merry Maidens (*Dawns Myin*) is the better known site, surrounded by varied stone shapes. A round barrow and further away two tall stones (15 ft and 13.5 ft) all line up to the north. There are holed stones (sighting stones?) to the north-east and west-northwest. The circle's eight alignments include stones towards Capella, Antares and Arcturus. As a calendar, it marks the May-year sighted two different ways on a barrow, on a fougou[1] and on St Buryan's church. Capella marks February and Antares May, whilst Arcturus is August.

The Merry Maidens is a very complete set of 19 squared granite blocks, some 4 ft tall. It overlooks the sea not far from Lamorna, some two miles south-east of St Buryan, near the hamlet of Boleit. It is on a slight hill and is 77.8 ft across, by Thom's reckoning, has an entrance to the east, pointer stones to the west, and two stones of 12 ft and 16 ft called the Pipers are linked with it. Although in the 1890s it was reported as having 15 stones only and some fallen, the re-erections appear to have been quite correct and do not really cloud the impression that we have here the least interfered with of all the circles in Britain. Borlase rather curiously does not mention it—maybe it was temporarily concealed by bush growth, as was the Long Man. Professor Thom lists it as a true circle ranking with Meini Hirion, and with no sign of an ellipse, however slight.

Its builders may have lived due north of it, for around Carn Kininack tumulus there seems to be a dwelling-place of Pictish type. Certainly other megalithic work is very near; only a mile north of St Buryan is an ellipse of another 19 stones, averaging 4 ft 7 inches tall, with an eccentric menhir within it. One recalls once again that 19 is the sacred number of the moon's cycle. One-and-a-half miles north-west of Upton Cross is an ambitious structure of three circles in a row, known as the Hurlers, lacking many stones, the line running north-northwest; the northerly circle is 100 ft across, the centre one 135 ft and the southerly one is 105 ft, whilst 200 yards west are two large stones also called Pipers.

Earlier names are unpromising; the name 'Boleit' is said to mean 'a place of slaughter' and the Merry Maidens circle itself was formerly 'the Giants' Grave'. The repeated Piper's Stones, however, remind one that people do not dance around stones without making rhythmic sounds and that the herdsmen's pipe must be one of the earliest instruments known.

This peaceful and always unified place gives evidence of one characteristic that true circles always had: the ability to store power. T.C. Lethbridge felt a current more powerful than any he had experienced at other sites:

> As soon as the pendulum started to swing . . . the hand resting on the stone received a tingling sensation like a mild electric shock and the pendulum itself shot out until it was circling nearly horizontal to the ground. The stone itself . . . felt as if it was rocking and almost dancing about.
> —*Legend of the Sons of God*, p. 15

Lethbridge was a scientific worker who was also an honest psychic; his reports can be trusted. Others besides him have had similar experiences at

---

[1] Fougou: ancient stone-lined pits discovered in Cornwall, usage unknown. [Ed.]

this circle, where the Cornish Bards have several times held Gorseddau.

It is interesting to note that Lethbridge, divining for age by pendulum, found that the movements seemed to record the circle as of 2540 BC, and the Pipers as 2610 BC. The usual guess has been much later.

How did the stones receive their electro-magnetic vibrations in the first place? Lethbridge regards them as deposits of bio-electricity:

> If you have a large number of excited people dancing wildly round in a ring, you obviously generate a great deal of this bio-electricity. If you carry out this performance in rings formed of stones with gaps between them, you have a form of dynamo . . . Electromagnetic fields of stones, trees and water will absorb bioelectricity from outside . . .

Power so stored can be drawn off and used by those who 'tune in'. People who understand the witch cult will understand this. The concept of bio-electricity now appears to be scientifically respectable.

We have therefore in the Merry Maidens a circle as near as possible untouched, retaining to our own day such power as the neolithic circle-builders—and those working later in the same tradition no doubt—built into it. The granite retained it as stone can and as trees can only do more temporarily. That here it was a beneficent power is a matter of psychic sense rather than evidence, but it does give that feeling. To those who are sensitive, the Merry Maidens is an unforgettable experience of peaceful and creative energy that no other circle quite gives.

DRUIDIC WISDOM

Preliminary Note:

Druid teachings are drawn from many sources. In reality, a good deal of this wisdom exists at an archetypal level, and can be accessed with proper training. That wisdom which is written down can be found in the Order's course, much of the writings of the authors mentioned in the Foreword, and in the early Welsh and Irish texts, although these are often difficult to obtain or obscure to interpret.

The author has gathered here a number of excerpts from these different sources to enable the reader to gain a glimpse into the depth and richness of Druidic wisdom. [Ed.]

The Early Welsh Heavens: Regulation of the World

The following is based upon the learned articles of Alun Llewellyn published in the *Aryan Path*, interpreting the difficult old Welsh of the ancient books of Wales, largely the *Black Book of Caermarthen*.

'Many things about the nature of things, the stars and the immortal Gods,' says Caesar of the Druidic wisdom. Certainly the ancient books of Wales give us these, and one dominant scheme of the heavens, perhaps rather altered but based clearly upon the late-classical Erigena, or John Scotus, John the Scot (he was Irish), whose work dates from c. AD 860. His *De Divisione Naturae* pictured man's evolution inwardly through the three spheres: [1]

The first was both land and water, *Tellus*—later known misleadingly as *terra*, with which later generations failed to link the seas also.

The second was of all that moves under the dominion of time; it comprises sun, moon and planets and is called *Mundus*.

[1] A confusion still exists between John Scotus Erigena (810–77) and Johannes Duns Scotus (1265–1308). The two were mixed by William of Malmesbury in the twelfth century. The earlier Scotus is meant here. [Ed.]

These touch the sphere above themselves in the night sky—the highest sphere of creation, the *summa rerum*.

In exposition, John Scotus Erigena indicates the third (above) as first:

I   God, or that which is not created:

II   Then come ideas expressed in constellations, which in turn create within time the world of the planets.

III   Third comes the local division of space and time contained in sun and earth. The union of the One with the Many was the essence of the divinity, the Logos or Reason of the world.

Three old books—*The Book of Aneurin, The Book of Taliesin* and the *Black Book of Caermarthen* mainly have a precise vocabulary derived from seamanly observation of the stars for practical voyaging purposes, and show minds trained in thought, with an already-formed system to which they applied the scheme of Erigena. Each planet and sphere had its defined place and precise name. The poems, some of them dating from well before AD 800, make their own this kindred philosophy, which was lost and gone by AD 950.

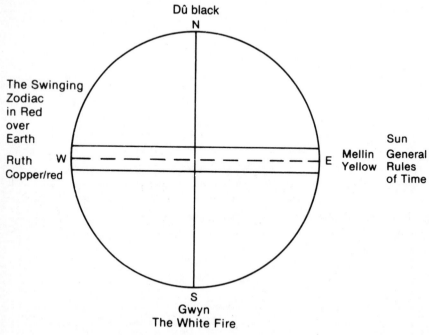

The Cymric Quarters of the Heavens and their Work.

Before 781 Clement the Monk and some followers had settled in Gaul at the future emperor Charlemagne's invitation. Clement's teaching is represented by part of *The Book of Taliesin* (fol. 79). He writes in terms of the seafarers who need the heaven's workings and steered by the pole star and the meridian.

The day was in three parts: the morning hours 4 a.m. to noon, called Asia and Dawn; from noon to 8 p.m., called Africa—the land to the south, of the high sun; and from 8 p.m. to 4 a.m., the time when the sun never was, called Europe.

The *south* is *gwyn*, which is white; the *north* is *dû*, black. The copper-red of *ruth* is the *west* and yellow, *mellin*, is *east*. Between them is the Spindle of Necessity, the line pole to the meridian; the planets are weaving around it in time's three divisions—classically called Clotho, Lachesis and Atropos.

The night of the stars shaped Earth through the pole's circling. The inner star that orders the seas is Vega. The horizon is marked by Sirius. Now at the last hour of the year, 21 December, Sirius is south, Vega is north and between them exactly is the pole star. So stands the balance on the verges of the year.

There are now five spheres of the creation: the *primum mobile* or first

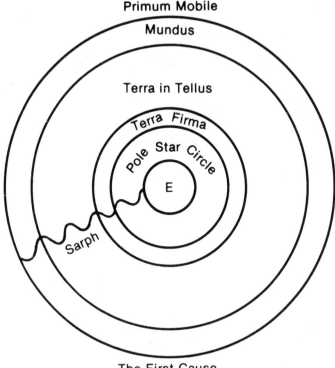

Primum Mobile

Mundus

Terra in Tellus

Terra Firma

Pole Star Circle

E

Sarph

The First Cause

The Spheres of Creation.

cause; the outer sphere, the pole star's circle of Earth at centre; *Mundus* or the planetary all-motion scheme; then two spheres of earth—*terra-in-tellus* and *terra firma*, the first comprising land and water, the second land only, where man dwelt.

The five planets have their functions quite definitely allotted: Mars stood for movement and energy, Venus for light, Mercury governed the seas, Jupiter was for circular movements and origin, Saturn for limitation. Each planet had its note in the octave of the great scale:

> Like a song sung, like a harp strung,
> like pipe to lip, like viol to bow,
> Star and sea and shore and sky
> number their notes in arpeggio
> through the scheme of scales in the key of light . . .
> —Alun Llewellyn

The circle over the seas below the constellations, drawn by Mercury, is yellow. The circle near the firmament—the heavens of earth, the stars of ocean—is of Venus, and is black. The circle which is the margin or order under the firmament, the highest circuit, this is the red Saturn. And these three circles form the *Zone of Planets*.

The *Zone of Sun* is the sphere of time starting from the east, over the inner station which is Earth. The inner sphere of fire that caused the Earth and the limit of ocean and the definition of time, this is the *moon's* meridian, and it is white. The Earth's seasons within the stars, that close off this world

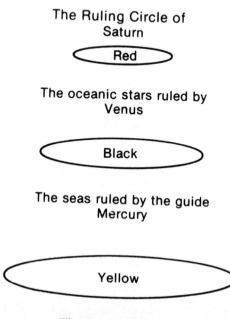

The Ruling Circle of
Saturn

Red

The oceanic stars ruled by
Venus

Black

The seas ruled by the guide
Mercury

Yellow

The Zone of Planets.

form the *zodiac*, swung between Cancer and Capricorn, and this is red. Earth itself and the arc over it, east to west, is the path of the daily *sun* of yellow.

Each luminary and planet is a division, *diu*:

Y-eu:	Jupiter, or origin.
Sad–URN:	Saturn, 'seated amongst stars'.
Maurth:	Mars, inner point of an emergent heaven.
March-YR:	Mercury, border of the rim of ocean.
GUENER:	Venus, star of the sea, vital spirit of ocean, and leader of the sun.
SUL:	The sun, the focus of meridian upon the pole.
LLUN:	The moon, measure of the stars.

Inwards from the origin of all things, the *primum mobile*, the coiled Sarph the star-serpent, shown in the Milky Way, is coming from night through the spheres, reaching at last into man and his head, lodging in man's intelligence.

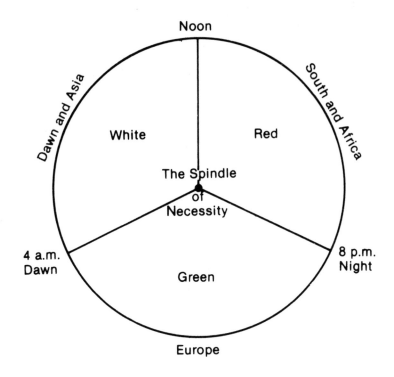

The Coloured Dial of Time.

The *Triple Dial of the Sun*, which is the microcosm of the Earth's system, is as follows:

> The *light order* rising in the shape of dawn, the margin set for the circuit is the left quarter-circle, 4 a.m. to noon, and is white.

> The *boundary* against the world's structure, the limit of light—the lower sector of the dial untouched by the sun—is 8 p.m. to 4 a.m. and is green.

> The *confine* at the season's edge, the end of sun's travel over the earth, is the right sector, noon to 8 p.m. and is red.

But this Third is not from the *Black Book*, it is supplied from the *Red Book of Hergest*. A hint may be given from the story of Llew Lau Gyffes in *The Mabinogion*. He is the ruler doomed to death who yet returns a second time as the Lion of the Long Hand, that is, the sunset's rays.

In these skies Arthur's was the polar circle, sovereign of the world, around which all revolved and which never sank below the horizon—

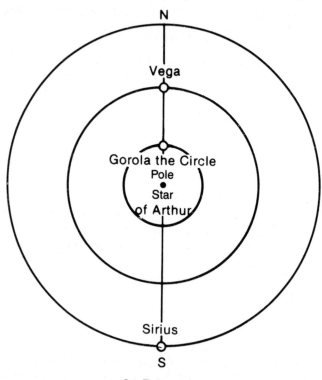

on 21 December

The Axis of the Heavens.

Gorolad, the unsinking star circle. Venus, the least predictable planet, in its more circular course, became Arthur's three wives, all called Gwenhwyvar, who vanish when captured by Mordred and come again. The name is an elaborate build-up: *Uen-er*, horizon of the sea, whose limits are *Vyfar*: combining they become *Uen-vyfar*, defined limits of the sea's horizon, and so *Gwynhwyvar*. The other goddess form means the inner circuit over the ocean, thus *Kyrrid*, the circle, over ocean, *uen*, becomes *Kyrriduen* or *Ceridwen*. Thus Gwenhwyvar is the horizon and Ceridwen the nearer circle of waters.

The Book of Taliesin implies that each division of the Druids had its proper astronomical study: the Druids themselves the fixed stars, the Bards the planets, and the Ovates the spiritual intelligence of the night.

In Wales after the Romans we see that a culture remained, continuous with the classical learning on the one side and with the old Druidic traditions on the other. Druidry may have gone underground, but it was obviously there in most areas of Britain and more particularly in Ireland, Wales and Scotland, which were never conquered by Rome. If anywhere, we are justified in looking for Druidic wisdom in these areas. And much of this learning about planet-deities and astronomy and the highly poetic material inspired by them may well be the kind the older Druids composed and memorized in their forest academies and groves of learning:

> The rim of Ocean is for Earth
> the inner horizon of the sphere of Sun
> that woke to make a sky for the air of the world.
> The unfixed stars from which the Ocean came
> the concept of the circling planets from which the Sun was born—
> This is the structure of Time set around men
> by the courses of the world.
> —Gododdin Gomynnaf, folios 23 and 20

When we find therefore, in one of the most significant places of Ireland, at the furthest west point of the European land mass, Dunmore Head, an Ogham inscription that is thought to be of AD 400–500 cut in a sharp-edged monolith some 8 ft tall, written across the westward-aiming edge running:

Erc makima ki, Ercias modof inias

which may be translated:

> Ocean, the inner shore of the working of this world—
> Ocean, whose further shore is set against the movement of Time in Night

we recognize the kind of philosophy it comes from.

Another version might be:

The starry heaven by night meets the
futher shore of ocean: her nearer shore
encircles the workings of our world.

Vertically below the Ogham stone is set upright on the rock beach the large
white oval stone known as the *Liour*, like an egg of a giant bird, or the
Omphalos stone of a lost civilization. For what lost world of knowledge
is it a testimony, a birth-stone?

II. *Wisdom from the* Barddas

Controversy has raged over the *Barddas* of Iolo Morganwg.[1] Briefly, he

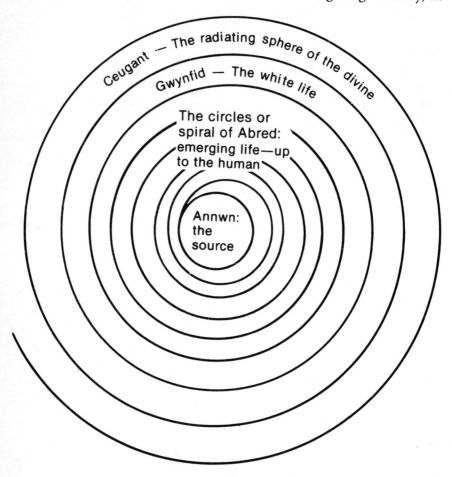

The Circles of Creation.

[1] Published by D.J. Roderic (Llandovery), Longman & Co (London) in 1862.

convinced his generation of the soundness of his learning and was instrumental in reviving Druidic forms and ceremonies in Wales and England,
especially the now invariable use of a circle of stones at Gorseddau. A later
generation found no sources and considered him an imaginative fraud. A
still later one has found a great deal of earlier work, possibly improved and
edited, incorporated by him in his vast *oeuvre*, but has not yet really worked
out which is what. The following passages give what appears to be some
of the earlier wisdom.

To set the scene, the following diagrams illustrate the general scheme of
the Circles of Creation, a system linked with late classical philosophical
schemes.

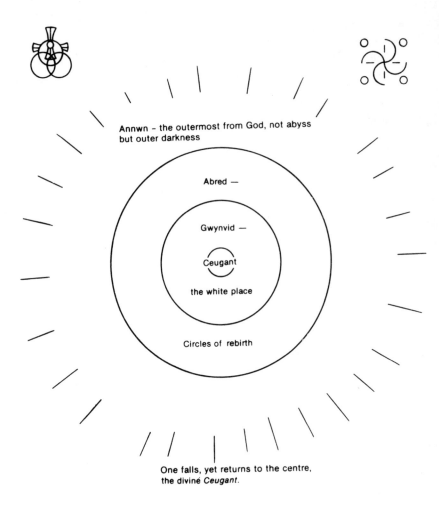

Annwn – the outermost from God, not abyss
but outer darkness

Abred —

Gwynvid —

Ceugant

the white place

Circles of rebirth

One falls, yet returns to the centre,
the divine *Ceugant*.

The Celtic Church Version of the Circles of Creation.

Origins

When God pronounced His name, with the word sprang the light and the life, for previously there was no life except God Himself. And the mode in which it was spoken was of God's direction. His name was pronounced, and with the utterance was the springing of light and vitality, and man, and every other living thing, that is to say, each and all sprang together. And Menw the Aged, son of Menwyd, beheld the springing of the light, and its form and appearance, not otherwise than thus, /|\ , in three columns; and in the rays of light the vocalization—for one were the hearing and seeing, one unitedly the form and sound, and one unitedly with the form and sound was life, and one unitedly with these three was power, which power was God the Father. And since each of these was one unitedly, he understood that every voice, and hearing, and living, and being, and sight, and seeing, were one unitedly with God.

It was from the understanding thus obtained in respect of his voice, that he was able to assimilate mutually every other voice as to kind, quality, and reason, and could make a letter suitable to the utterance of every sound and voice. Thus were obtained the Cymraeg, and every other language. And it was from the three primary letters that were constructed every other letter—which is the principle secret of the Bards of the Isle of Britain; and from this secret comes every knowledge of letters that is possible.

Thus are they made: the first of the signs is a small cutting or line inclining with the sun at eventide, thus   / ; the second is another cutting, in the form of a perpendicular, upright post, thus | ; and the third is a cutting of the same amount of inclination as the first, but in an opposite direction, that is, against the sun, thus   \   ; and the three placed together, thus /|\ . But instead of, and as substitutes for these, are placed the three letters 'O''I''W'. And it was in this manner that the Bard inserted this name in his stanza, thus,

> The Eternal, Origin, Self-existent, Distributor—holy be the lips
> that canonically pronounce them;
> Another name, in full word,
> is O.I. and W—OIW the word—Ieuan Rudd sang it. [2]

The three mystic letters signify the three attributes of God, namely, love, knowledge, and truth; and it is out of these three that justice springs, and without one of the three there can be no justice. Which one so ever of the three stands up, the other two will incline towards it; and every two of them whatsoever will yield precedency and pre-eminence to the third, which-ever of the three it may be. It was according to this order and principle that three degrees were conferred upon the Bards of the Isle of Britain.

Pray, who was the first that made a vocal song in Cymraeg? Huè the Mighty, the man who first brought the Cymru into the Isle of Britain; and he made

---

[2] 'W' is always the thin Welsh *oo* or *eu* as in French.

the song to be a memorial of what happened to the nation of the Cymru from the age of ages. And he inserted in it the praise of God for what the Cymru had received at His hand, by way of protection and deliverance, also the sciences and regulations of the nation of the Cymru.

The three elements of letters are /I\ ; that is to say, from a combination of one or other of the three are letters made. They are three rays of light. And of these are made the sixteen gogyrvens, that is, the sixteen letters. According to a different arrangement there are seven gogyrvens, the seven and seven score words in the Alphabet of the Cymraeg being no other than a sign of worthiness; and it is from them that ever other word proceeds. Others say seven score and seven hundred words.

Einigan the Giant beheld three pillars of light, having in them all demonstrable sciences that ever were, or ever will be. And he took three rods of the quicken tree, and placed on them the forms and signs of all sciences, so as to be remembered; and exhibited them.

A Catechism
Q: Who was the first that obtained understanding respecting letters?
A: Adam first obtained it from God in Paradise, and his son, Abel the Innocent, learned it from his father. Cain the Murderer, Abel's brother, would have fame from the good things of the world, but Abel would not, except from sciences that were pleasing to God, and from understanding and learning relative to what God did or desired. Wherefore Cain envied his brother Abel, and slew him feloniously and treacherously. Then the sciences, which Abel caused to be understood, were lost. After that, Adam had another son, whose name was Seth; and he taught him the knowledge of letters, and all other divine sciences. And to Seth was a son, whose name was Enos, who was educated by his father as a man of letters and praiseworthy sciences in respect of books and learning. It was Enos who was the first that made a book of record, for the purpose of preserving the memory of every thing beautiful, commendable, and good.
Q: What were the first books that were first known to the nation of the Cymry, and what were their materials?
A: Wood, that is, trees, and that mode was called Coelbren, from which comes the Coelbren of the Bards, as it is still on record by the nation of the Cymry. There was no other mode of dealing with letters known to our nation before Christ came in the flesh.

The Bardic Secret
'O''I''W' are the three letters, and in very old books 'O''I''U', because 'U' was used instead of 'W', in the olden times. It is the secret work of the primitive Bards, which it is not lawful to speak or utter audibly to any man in the world, except to a Bard who is under the vow of an oath. The letters may be shown to any one in the world we like, without uttering the vocalization, which, under the protection of secrecy, is due to them, though

he be not under an oath; but should he utter them in speech audibly, he violates his protection, and he cannot be a Bard, nor will it be lawful to show him any more of the secret, either in this world that perishes, or in the other world that will not perish for ever and ever.

The Sacred Symbol

/ I \ This symbol is called the three columns, and the three columns of truth, because there can be no knowledge of the truth, but from the light thrown upon it; and the three columns of sciences, because there can be no sciences, but from the light and truth.

Gogyrvens

The three primary gogyrvens are / I \ .

There were sixteen gogyrvens before the faith in Christ; after that eighteen, then twenty.

Talhaiarn[3] appointed twenty gogyrvens.

The Three First Words of the Cymraeg Symbol

These are the three first words of the Cymraeg: the Name of God, that is 'O"I"U'; the name of the sun, perception, and sensation, that is SULW; and Bo (others say 'Byw').

The Name of God is a substantive verb; the sun is a substantive noun; and *sulw* is a substantive adjective—which was clear before the perfect Cymraeg was lost.

There are three series of symbols of literary sciences: the symbols of Coelbren, the symbols of music and the symbols of numbers.

The three pillars of memory and history are: vocal song; letter; and symbol. A symbol is a form that is understood, and, being understood, shews at sight that which really exists which would require many letters, or much vocal song, or speech and oration, before it could be properly understood.

The Birds of Rhiannon

The Birds of Rhiannon sang until the Angels of Heaven came to listen to them, and it was from their songs that were first obtained vocal song and instrumental music; vocal song being that which is sung by the lips to melody and harp.

Here is the *system of symbols*. There have been three symbols remembered and preserved from the beginning by the Bards and Sages of the nation of the Cymru, namely:

1. The symbol of the word and speech, that is, letter. It is from the symbols that a visible word is formed, and from the words a visible language, and visible vocality.

[3] Not to be confused with Taliesin. [Ed.]

2. The symbol of harmony and tone, that is, the signs of the sound and utterance of vocal song, and instrumental song.

3. The symbol of number and weight.

The symbols of number are exhibited under the signs of the ten vocal characters of word and speech, that is, the ten characters of the primitive letters, which are kept secret by the Bards of the nation of the Cymru under the obligation of a vow, and may not be divulged other than to a Bard under the sworn vow of life and death. Nevertheless, for the purpose of instructing the common people, the sworn ten characters are not the means, but the trite signs of number, such as are in the memory and knowledge of a civilized country and nation.

The Coelbren of the Bards

Thus says Llywelyn Sion:

After the intestine war of Owain Glyndwr,[4] the king[5] forbade paper and *plagawd* to be brought into Cymru, or to be manufactured there, in order that it might prevent epistolary correspondence between a Cymro and a Cymro, and between the Cymru and the people of a bordering country and of foreign lands; and this to revenge the siding with Owain, which was observed everywhere on the part of every man in Cymru. He also forbade the Bards and Poets to go their circuits and to visit the different families officially. Then was remembered, and brought into use, the ancient custom of the Bards of the Isle of Britain; namely, the cutting of letters, which they called the symbols of language and utterance, upon wood or rods prepared for the purpose, called Coelbren of the Bards—and thus was it done. They gathered rods of hazel or mountain ash in the winter, about a cubit in length, and split each into four parts, that is, the wood was made into four splinters, and kept them, until by the working of time they became quite dry. Then they planed them square, in respect of breadth and thickness, and afterwards trimmed down the angles to the tenth part of an inch, which was done that the cuttings of the letters, that is, the symbols, which were cut with the knife on one of the four square surfaces, should not visibly encroach upon the next face; and thus on every one of the four faces. Then they cut the symbols, according to their character, whether they were those of language of speech, or of numbers, or other signs of art, such as the symbols of music, of voices, and string.

And at both ends of two *pillwydd*, they made necks, as places for strings to tie them firmly together at each end of the symbolized sticks. And when the whole are thus bound tight together, the book that is constructed in this

---

[4] Owain Glyndwr was born AD 1349. He began to wage war against the English king about AD 1400, which was continued for about 15 years, when Owain died, i.e. AD 1415.
[5] The Cymric chieftain fought against two kings successively, against Henry IV, and against Henry V, the latter of whom succeeded to the throne AD 1413, two years before the death of Owain.

manner is called PEITHYNEN, because it is framed; the *pillwydd* at each end keeping all together, and the *ebillion*, or lettered staves, turning freely in the *pillwydd*, and thus being easy to read.

There are forty sides to the *ebillion* in every *Peithynen*; after that, another *Peithynen* is formed, until the conclusion of the poem or narrative.

Ten symbolic characters of utterance, in respect of language and speech, have been in possession of the nation of the Cymru from the age of ages before they came into the island of Britain, which were a secret under vow and oath among the Gwyddoniaid, these persons being Poets and men of vocal song and sciences of wisdom before there were regular Bards. It was in the time of Prydain, son of Aedd the Great, about one thousand five hundred years before Christ was born in the flesh of the pure and blessed Mary, and in the time of Aedd the Great, that regular Bards were instituted, and authorized office and licence assigned to them. After that, the Coelbren of the Gwyddoniaid was improved, as occasion required for its being understood and read, until there were sixteen symbols in the Alphabet.

And it was in the time of Dyvnwal Moelmud, about six hundred years, by record and computation, before Christ was born in the flesh, that the sixteen symbols, and their order for the preservation of language and speech and every memorial of country and nation, were divulged, because no other method could be found to be so good for maintaining the memorials and sciences of wisdom, and the privileges and usages of the nation of the Cymru, and its appurtenances. And the ten symbolic characters are kept to this day as a secret by vow and oath; and no man except those who have taken the oath, knows them. When the sixteen became generally open to all the nation, the Coelbren was further improved and extended, till it consisted of eighteen in the time of Beli the Great, son of Manogan; and after that of twenty; and, in the time of the Blue Bard, of twenty-one, or, as another record says, of twenty-two; and so many are there of primitive letters in the Cymraeg, such as are beyond this number, as far as thirty-eight, being called secondaries.

Memorials of Wisdom by Triads

Before the knowledge of letters was obtained, there was no other memorial than vocal song, authorized by three Chairs, and the voice of an efficient Gorsedd. There were three efficient Gorseddau that preserved memorials, namely, the Gorsedd of Bards, the Gorsedd of the court of lord and law, and a conventional Gorsedd of country and nation. And every memorial was efficient that received the countenance of three Gorseddau, of one or other of the three Gorseddau of country and nation; that is, the countenance of the same Gorsedd three times under the proclamation and notice of a year and a day.

The three characteristics of God: complete life; complete knowledge; and complete power.

The three states of existence of living beings: the state of Abred in

Annwn; the state of liberty in humanity; and the state of love, that is, Gwynvyd in heaven.

The three necessities of all animated existences: a beginning in Annwn; progression in Abred; and plenitude in heaven, that is, the circle of Gwynvyd; without these three things nothing can exist but God.

There are three things that constantly increase: fire, or light; understanding, or truth; and the soul, or life. These three will prevail over every thing, and then Abred will end.

There are three Unities, and they cannot have any secondary to them: one God; one truth; and one point of liberty; and in these three all goodness is rooted in respect of power, goodness, and knowledge.

The three witnesses of God in respect of His works: His infinite power; infinite knowledge; and infinite love; for there is nothing that these attributes cannot accomplish, cannot seek and cannot wish.

The three places of the being and existence of all that lives: with Cythraul in Annwn; with light in the state of man; and with God in Gwynvyd.

There are three expressions on the circle of Ceugant: pride, perjury and cruelty; because of free will, and endeavour, and pre-arrangement, they force existence upon things that ought not to be, and that cannot accord with the indispensables of the circle of Gwynvyd. And by making this assault, man falls in Abred even to Annwn. The chief and most grievous is pride, because it is from this that the other two oppressions are derived; and it was from pride that the first fall in Abred occurred, after the original profession to the species and state of humanity in Gwynvyd.

There are three circles of existence: the circle of Ceugant, where there is neither animate nor inanimate save God, and God only can traverse it; the circle of Abred, where the dead is stronger than the living, and where every principal existence is derived from the dead, and man has traversed it; and the circle of Gwynvyd, where the living is stronger than the dead, and where every principal existence is derived from the living and life, that is, from God, and man shall traverse it; nor will man attain to perfect knowledge, until he shall have fully traversed the circle of Gwynvyd, for no absolute knowledge can be obtained but by the experience of the senses, from having borne and suffered every condition and incident.

The three principal states of created animation: Annwn, in which was their beginning; Abred, which they traverse for the sake of collecting sciences; and Gwynvyd, where they will end in plenteousness to the utmost extent of power, knowledge, and goodness, so much that more cannot possibly be had.

The three principal co-existences of the circle of Gwynvyd: love as far as its necessity requires; order until it cannot be improved; and knowledge as far as it can be conceived and comprehended.

What is not conceivable is the greatest of all, and the immeasurable of what is not in place:

God is the greatest of all, and the immeasurable of intelligence;
And there can be no existence to any thing but from intelligence;
And the non-existence of all things comes from what is not in place.

The Name of God

Some have called God the Father HEN DDIHENYDD because it is from His nature that all things are derived, and from Him is the beginning of every thing, and in Him is no beginning, for He can not but exist, and nothing can have a beginning without a beginner. And God the Son is called LAU, that is, God under a finite form and corporeity, for a finite being cannot otherwise know and perceive God. And when He became man in this world, He was called Jesus Christ, for He was not from everlasting under a finite form and body. And the man who believes in Him, and performs the seven works of mercy, shall be delivered from the pain of Abred, and blessed for ever be he who does so. Jesus Christ is also called GOD THE DOVYDD;[6] and he has also other names, such as PERYDD,[7] and GOD THE NER,[8] and GOD THE NAV.[9]

This extract is from a list of *Damhehion Beirdd Ynys Prydain*.

Iau: a Dialogue

Disciple and his Master.

Disciple: Why is *Iau* (yoke)[10] given as a name for God?

Master: Because the yoke is the measuring rod of country and nation in virtue of the authority of law, and is in the possession of every head of family under the mark of the lord of the territory, and whoever violates it is liable to a penalty. Now, God is the measuring rod of all truth, all justice, and all goodness, therefore He is a yoke on all, and all are under it, and woe to him who shall violate it.

Disciple: Who then is Hu the Mighty?

---

[6] *Dovydd* = *domitor* = the Tamer.
[7] *Perydd* = the Causer; the First Cause, the Creator.
[8] *Ner* = Energy, the Powerful.
[9] *Nav* = the Former Ones, the Creator. Sion Cent has a poem, 'The Names of God' into which he has introduced all these, with the exception of *Hen Ddihenydd*, and *Perydd*, thus:

Duw, Dafydd mawr, Ionawr, Iau.
Ener, Muner, Ner, Naf ydyw.

(See Iolo MSS p.285)

They are also, with many others of undoubtedly Druidic origin, still used by the Cymru as epithets for the Deity.

[10] It would appear that the *iau*, or 'yoke', being the badge of power on the part of him who imposed it, was so designated from a combination of bardic symbols, which indicates preservation, creation, and destruction, and which was one of the earliest forms of the Divine Name. Iolo Morganwg interprets *iau* as meaning 'the recent, or last manifestation of the Deity—Mithras, Mithra'; from the adjective which literally signifies 'younger'.

Master: Hu the Mighty is Jesus the Son of God—the least in respect of His worldly greatness whilst in the flesh, and the greatest in heaven of all visible majesties.

The Circles

These are the Circles: the Circle of Abred, in which are all corporal and dead existences, the Circle of Gwynvyd, in which are all animated and immortal beings, the Circle of Ceugant, where there is only God. The wise men describe them thus, in three Circles.[11]

And God caused that every living and animate being should pass through every form and species of existence endued with life, so that in the end every living and animate being might have perfect knowledge, life and Gwynvydd; and all this from the perfect love of God, which in virtue of his divine nature He could not but exhibit towards man and every living being.

All living beings below the Circle of Gwynvydd have fallen in to Abred, and are now on their return to Gwynvydd. The migration of most of them will be long, owing to the frequent times they have fallen, from having attached themselves to evil and ungodliness; and the reason why they fell was, that they desired to traverse the Circle of Ceugant, which God alone could endure and traverse. Hence, they fell even unto Annwn, and it was from pride, which would ally itself with God, that they fell, and there is no necessary fall as far as Annwn, except from pride.

Disciple: Did all who reached the Circle of Gwynvydd after the primary progression of necessity from Annwn, fall in Abred from pride?

Master: No, some sought after wisdom, and hence saw what pride would do, and they resolved to conduct themselves according to what was taught them by God, and thereby became divinities, or holy angels, and they acquired learning from what they beheld in others, and it was thus that they saw the nature of Ceugant and eternity, and that God alone could endure and traverse it.

Disciple: Does not the danger of falling in Abred, from the Circle of Gwynvydd, exist still as it did formerly?

Master: No, because all pride and every other sin, will be overcome before one can a second time reach the Circle of Gwynvydd, and then by recollecting and knowing the former evil, every one will necessarily abhor what caused him to fall before, and the necessity of hatred and love will last and continue for ever in the Circle of Gwynvydd, where the three stabilities, namely, hatred, love, and knowledge, will never end.

---

[11] The Three Circles of Existence are probably represented in the old enclosure such as Avebury, and in the wheels on ancient British coins.

Disciple: Will those, who shall return to the Circle of Gwynvydd after the fall in Abred, be of the same kind as those who fell not?

Master: Yes, and of the same privilege, because the love of God cannot be less towards one than towards another, nor towards one form of existence than another, since He is God and Father to them all, and they will all be equal and co-privileged in the Circle of Gwynvydd, that is, they will be divinities and holy angels for ever.

Disciple: Will every form and species of living existence continue for ever as they are now? If so, tell me why?

Master: Yes, in virtue of liberty and choice, and the blessed will go from one to another as they please, in order to repose from the fatigue and tediousness of Ceugant, which God only can endure, and in order to experience every knowledge and every Gwynvydd that are capable of species and form; and each one of them will hate evil of necessary obligation, and know it thoroughly, and consequently of necessity renounce it, since he will perfectly know its nature and mischievousness—God being a help, and God being chief, supporting and preserving them for ever.

Disciple: How are these things to be known?

Master: The Gwyddoniaid, from the age of ages, from the time of Seth son of Adam, son of God, obtained Awen from God, and thence knew the mystery of godliness and the Gwyddoniaid were of the nation of the Cymru from the age of ages. After that the Gwyddoniaid were regulated according to privilege and usage, in order that unfailing memory might be kept of this knowledge.

After that, the Gwyddoniaid were called Bards according to the privilege and usage of the Bards of the Isle of Britain, because it was after the arrival of the Cymru in the island of Britain, that this regulation was made; and it is through the memorials of Bardism and Awen from God that this knowledge has been acquired, and no falsehood can accrue from Awen from God.

In the nation of Israel were found the holy prophets, who through Awen from God knew all these things as described in the Holy Scriptures. And after Christ, the Son of God, had come in the flesh from Gwynvyd, further knowledge of God and His will was obtained, as is seen in St Paul's Sermon. And when we, the Cymru, were converted to the faith in Christ, our Bards obtained a more clear Awen from God, and knowledge about all things divine beyond what had been seen before, and they prophesied, improving Awen and knowledge. Hence is all knowledge concerning things divine and what appertains to God.

According to the three principal qualities of man shall be his migration in Abred: from indolence and mental blindness he shall fall to Annwn; from dissolute wantonness he shall traverse the Circle of Abred, according to his necessity; and from his love for goodness he shall ascend to the Circle of Gwynvyd.

Disciple: In what place is Annwn?

Master: Where there is the least possible of animation and life, and the greatest of death, without other condition.

Disciple: In what does the nature of death and mortality consist?

Master: In its characteristics, where one is the cause of another, as heaviness is the cause of darkness, and both the cause of corruption, and corruption the cause of both.

Disciple: Of what, in respect of materials, were formed living and dead beings, which are cognizable to the human sight, hearing, feeling, understanding, perception, and the creation of the imagination?

Master: They were made of the *manred*, that is, of the elements in the extremities of their particles and smallest atoms, every particle being alive, because God was in every particle, a complete Unity, so as not to be exceeded, even in all the multiform space of Ceugant, or the infinite expanse. God was in each of the particles of the *manred*, and in the same manner in them collectively in their conjoined aggregation; wherefore, the voice of God is the voice of every particle of *manred*, as far as their numbers or qualities may be counted or comprehended, and the voice of every particle is the voice of God—God being in the particle as its life, and every particle or atom being in God as His life. On account of this view of the subject, God is figuratively represented as being born of the *manred*, without beginning, without end.

The First Men

Disciple: Who was the first man?

Master: Menyw the Aged, son of the Three Shouts, who was so called because God gave and placed the word in his mouth, namely, the vocalization of the three letters, which make the unutterable Name of God, that is, by means of the good sense of the Name and Word. And, co-instantaneously with the pronunciation of God's Name, Menyw saw three rays of light, and inscribed on them figure and form, and it was from those forms and their different collocations that Manyw made ten letters, and it was from them, variously placed, that he invested the Cymraeg with figure and form, and it is from understanding the combination of the ten letters that one is able to read.

Disciple: Who was the first that instituted the worship and adoration of God?

Master: Seth, the son of Adam, that is, he first made a retreat for worship in the woods of the Vale of Hebron, having first searched and investigated the trees, until he found a large oak, being the king of trees, branching, wide-spreading, thick-topped, and shady, under which he formed a choir and a place of worship. This was called Gorsedd, and hence originated the name Gorsedd, which was given to every place of worship; and it was in that choir that Enos, the son of Seth, composed vocal song to God.

Disciple: Who was the first that made a vocal song?

Master: Enos, the son of Seth, the son of Adam, was the first that made a vocal song, and praised God first in just poetry, and it was in his father's Gorsedd that he first obtained Awen, which was Awen from God; hence has arisen the usage of holding the Gorsedd of Vocal Song in the resort and Gorsedd for worship.

Disciple: What was the name that the wise men first had, whose employment was vocal song and laudable sciences?

Master: One was called Gwyddon, and many Gwyddoniaid; and they were so called because they followed their art in woods, and under trees, in retired and inaccessible places, for the sake of quietness, and the meditation of Awenic learning and sciences from God, and for the sake of quietness to teach the sciences to such as sought them, and desired wisdom by means of reason and Awen from God.

The Instruction for Mankind

God made all living beings in the Circle of Gwynvyd at one breath; but they would be gods, and attempted to traverse the Ceugant. This, however, they could not do, wherefore they fell down to Annwn, which unites with death and the earth, where is the beginning of all living owners of terrestrial bodies.

There are three kinds of light, namely, that of the sun, and hence fire; that which is obtained in the sciences of teachers; and that which is possessed in the understanding of the head and heart, that is, in the soul. On that account, every vow is made in the face of the three lights, that is, in the light of the sun is seen the light of a teacher or demonstration; and from both of these is the light of the intellect, or that of the soul.

God is one, and there is only Himself who is God. Love thy God with all thy soul, with all thy heart, with all thy strength, with all thy endeavour, with all thy understanding, and with all thy affections. For it is He, and no other being, living or existing, that made thee, and doth maintain thee, with all His might, and with all His mercy.

Do not love or seek an image instead of God, whether of wood or stone, of gold or silver, or of any other material, and whether it be represented in colour or in effigy; for thou has never seen God; and who has seen Him? Do not take this world, or any other world, however glorious it may appear to thee, in the place of God; because they are not God, but the work of God, for thy great good, and for that of others, millions of times beyond the extreme limits of thy understanding and comprehension. Do not take riches or possession of any kind, or the regard and greatness of the proud and sinful world, in the place of God. Take not either relation or friend, male or female, for a God. Do not place thy aim, thy heart, thy intention, thy affections, or thy confidence upon one or other of these things, or upon anything that will cause thee to trust less to God, because of the claim and possession thou has in them.

If thou doest so, God will turn His face from thee, and will leave thee to stand on thy own footing, and on the rotten foundation of the things which thou worshippest.

Kill not, and do no murder upon any account whatsoever. Do not take away life of either man or beast, except to prevent thyself from being killed, as when thou killest the enemy that would kill thee, when thou canst not escape, and leave him his life; or when thou killest an animal to obviate hunger, when thou canst not have food otherwise that will keep thee from dying. He that slays shall be slain; and though the body may not be slain, the soul shall be slain. If he escape in this world, he shall suffer grievously in the next world. Blood must be rendered for blood; God hath sworn it.

Take not from any living being his property, by treachery, or cunning, or extortion, or oppression. Take not, in any of these ways, his goods, or understanding, or time, or opportunity, or memory, or art, or anything that belongs to one or other of these particulars.

Though it may be against thy father or mother, against thy brother or sister, against thy son or daughter, against the wife of thy bosom, against thy own life, yet tell the truth. For the falsehood, of whatever kind it may be, will be against thy own soul—it will be told, exhibited, and performed against God and His truth.

The Transcendent Threes

The three principal employments of God: to enlighten the darkness; to invest nonentity with a body; and to animate the dead.

The three agents of God in making the worlds: will; wisdom; and love; and from these three comes omnipotence.

Three things beyond all the research of man's sciences: the extreme limits of space; the beginning and end of time; and the works of God.

Three things in man that will include every other goodness: bravery; peace; and godliness.

There are three things in man, that are the most odious of all to God: craftiness; avarice; and becoming hardened against praiseworthy sciences.

The three primary materials of everything: fire, that is, light; water; and earth. That is to say, the first of every material was fire, and the particles of light; the second was water, whereby things were discriminated; the third was earth, by which all things were corporalized—all things else were mixed—and these were called the three primary elements. Others say there are three primary elements: water, which was the beginning; after that, earth; and it ended with fire; and hence ensued imperishableness.

The three burstings of Lyn Llion: the first, when the world and all living beings were drowned, except Dwyvan and Dwyvach, their children, and grandchildren, from whom the world was again peopled—and it was from that bursting that seas were formed; the second was, when the sea went amidst the lands, without either wind or tide; the third was, when the earth burst asunder by means of the powerful agitation, so that the water spouted forth even to the vault of the sky, and all of the nation of the Cymru were drowned, except seventy persons, and the Isle of Britain was parted from Ireland, and from the land of Gaul and Armorica.

The three administrations of knowledge, which the nation of the Cymry obtained: the first was the instruction of Hu the Mighty, before they came into the island of Britain, who first taught the cultivation of the earth, and the art of metallurgy; the second was the system of Bards and Bardism, being instruction by means of the memorials and voice of the Gorsedd; and the third was the faith in Christ, which was the best of all, and blessed be it for ever.

The Universal Druid Prayer

Grant, O God, Thy protection;
And in protection, strength;
And in strength, understanding;
And in understanding, knowledge;
And in knowledge, the knowledge of justice;
And in the knowledge of justice, the love of it;
And in that love, the love of all existences;
And in the love of all existences, the love of God.
God and all goodness.[12]

Elements

There are five elements: earth, which is *calas*; fluidity, which is water and freshness; air, and hence all breathing, every voice and speech; fire, and hence all heat and light; and *nwyvre*,[13] whence proceed all life, intelligence, knowledge, and power from will and desire.

The Parts of the Human Body in which are the Faculties

1. In the forehead are the sense and intellect;

[12] Also from the *Carmina Gaedelica* by A. Carmichael, Scottish Academic Press, 1972.
[13] Equivalent of *aither*.

2. In the nape is the memory;
3. In the upper head are discretion and reason;
4. In the breast is lust;
5. In the heart is love;
6. In the bile are anger and wrath;
7. In the lungs is the breath;
8. In the spleen is joyousness;
9. In the body is the blood;
10. In the liver is the heat;
11. In the spirit is the mind;
12. In the soul is faith.

Thirty-Seven Remarkable Sights
1. The Circle of Arianrod;[14]
2. The White Throne;
3. Arthur's Harp;[15]
4. The Circle of Gwydion;[16]
5. The Great Plough-tail;[17]
6. The Small Plough-tail;
7. The Great Ship;
8. The Bald Ship;
9. The Yard;[18]
10. Theodosius's Group;[19]
11. The Triangle;
12. The Palace of Dôn.[20]
13. The Grove of Blodeuwedd;
14. The Chair of Teyrnon;[21]
15. The Circle of Eiddionydd;
16. The Circle of Sidi;[22]
17. The Conjunction of a Hundred Circles;
18. The Camp of Elmur;[23]
19. The Soldier's Bow;
20. The Hill of Dinan;
21. The Hen Eagle's Nest;
22. Bleiddyd's Lever;[24]
23. The Wind's Wing;
24. The Trefoil;
25. The Cauldron of Ceridwen;[25]
26. Teivi's Bend;
27. The Great Limb;
28. The Small Limb;
29. The Large-horned Oxen;[26]
30. The Great Plain;
31. The White Fork;
32. The Woodland Boar;
33. The Muscle;

[14] The daughter of Dôn, and styled in the *Triads* (Myv.Arch.ii.73) one of 'the three beautiful ladies of the Isle of Britain'. This constellation is the same as the Corona Borealis. Mentioned in *Hanes Taliesin*, Ap.Myv.Arch.i.19.
[15] The Lyre.
[16] The son of Dôn, one of 'the three sublime astronomers of the Isle of Britain', Tr.89 third series: The Galaxy.
[17] The Great Boar.
[18] Orion.
[19] The Pleiades. Mentioned in *Hanes Taliesin*, Ap.Myv.Arch.i.19.
[20] Cassiopeia.
[21] The title of one of Taliesin's poems. Myv.Arch.i.65.
[22] The zodiac, or ecliptic. Mentioned in *Hanes Taliesin*.
[23] Styled in the Triads as one of 'the three monarch bulls', Tr.73 third series.
[24] There was a king of Britain of this name, who flourished from 859 to 839 BC. He founded Bath.
[25] Mentioned in *Hanes Taliesin*.
[26] The Twins.

34. The Hawk;   36. Elffin's Chair; [28]
35. The Horse of Llyr; [27]   37. Olwen's Hall. [29]

Nine Achievements Amongst the Cymru

Tudain Tad Awen's achievement was the securing of memory by eloquent verse.

Rhy Vawn's achievement was the establishing of the principles of justice in the law of the land, for record, verse and secure memorial.

Hu Gadarn's achievement was the forming of social order for the Cymru for their removal from Taprobane (Ceylon) to the Island of Britain.

Prudain son of Aedd Mawr's achievement was pacifying the co-inhabitants of the land by justice, under a chief confederate ruler Dyvnwel.

Moelmud's achievement was the establishing of laws and ordinances against disorder.

Severus' achievement was a fair work athwart the Isle of Britain against assaulting hosts—the Wall of Tyne.

Manawydan the Wise's achievement was against the deceit of treachery in the deep prison of Oeth and Aiweth (Anoith).

The achievement of Llew was the appointing of the skin of the sheep as the depository of learning, a reward of song.

The achievement of Arthur the Emperor over the laying of weakness on the coat of the fleeing Saxon; before the army he was the best commander.

Thirteen Precious Things of the Island of Britain
(from the Bosanquet Collection)

There are various versions of this list.

1. The sword Dyrnwyn of Rhydderch Hael, which if any man drew except himself, burst into flame.
2. The Basket of Gwyddno Garenhir, which multiplied food placed in it a hundredfold.
3. The Horn of Bran Galed: whatever liquor was desired was found in it.
4. The Chariot of Morgan Mwynvawr: one who sat in it was immediately wherever he wished.
5. The Halter of Clydno Eiddyn, stapled to the foot of his bed: in it would he find whatever horse he wished.
6. The Knife of Llawfrodded Farchawg, which served 24 men at meat all at once.
7. The Cauldron of Tyrnog which boiled no meat for a coward but cooked at once for the brave. [30]
8. The Whetstone of Tudwal Tudclud which sharpened the sword of a

---

[27] The son of Bleiddyd—Shakespeare's Lear.
[28] Elffin (Elphin) is said to have first discovered Taliesin, in a leathern bag fastened to one of the poles of a weir. He is frequently mentioned by the Bard.
[29] A distinguished character in Welsh Romance.
[30] See p. 145, poem.

brave man for sure killing, but for a coward its sharpness was unavailing.

9. The Garment of Padarn Beisrudd which suited well a man of gentle birth, but did not fit a churl.

10. and 11. The Pan and the Platter of Rhegynydd Ysgolhaig, wherein was found whatever food was required.

12. The Golden Chessboard of Gwenddolen, whose chessmen made of silver played a game for themselves when placed upon it.

13. The Mantle of Arthur; whoever was placed under it could see everything and be seen of none.

III. The Celtic Tree Alphabet

This, being printed in an eighteenth-century work,[1] was despised by scholars. It bears every mark of being quite early, from the Beth-Luis-Nuin (Nion) alphabet period. It was part of the kind of wisdom taught in the Druidic forest academies. Robert Graves did good work on it, and this, with modifications, is from his *White Goddess*. It is old Irish Gaelic in language, but some links are with Welsh.

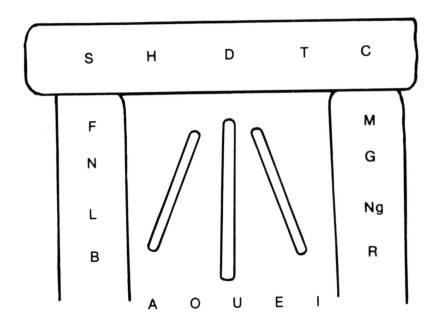

The Unhewn Dolmen of the Letters.

[1] Roderick O'Flaherty, *Ogygia*, Mackenzie, Dublin, 1793.

The Song of Amergin I (as arranged by Robert Graves)[1]

Year of thirteen-month dates	The voice of God is speaking:	Tree Alphabet Consonants
Dec 24–Jan 21	I am a stag of seven tines	Beith the Birch
Jan 22–Feb 18	I am a wide flood on a plain	Luis the Rowan
Feb 19–Mar 18	I am a wind on the deep waters	Nuinn the Ash
Mar 19–Apr 15	I am a shining tear of the sun	Fearn the Alder
Apr 16–May 13	I am a hawk on a cliff	Saille the Willow
May 14–June 10	I am a fair amongst flowers	Huath the Hawthorn
June 11–July 8	I am a god who sets the head afire with smoke	Duir the Oak
July 9–Aug 5	I am a battle-waging spear	Teinn the Holly
Aug 6–Sept 2	I am a salmon in a pool	Coll the Hazel
Sept 3–Sept 30	I am a hill of poetry	Muinn the Vine
Oct 1–Oct 28	I am a ruthless boar	Gort the Ivy
Oct 29–Nov 25	I am a threatening noise from the sea	Ngetal the Reed
Nov 26–Dec 22	I am a wave of the sea	Ruis the Elder tree
Dec 23	Who but I knows the secret of the unhewn dolmen?	

Song of Amergin II

Who but myself knows the assemblies of the dolmen-houses upon Slieve Mis?	A row of dolmen-houses is on this Kerry Mountain.
Who but I knows truly when the sun shall set? and what is the length of the sun's month?	Enoch: full material in the Book of Enoch.
Who is it foretells the ages of the moon?	The astronomer—or calculator from the Aubrey Holes at Stonehenge.
Who brings forth the cattle from the house of Tethra and places them in due order?	Tethra's Cattle are the stars wandering over heaven, i.e. the five planets, known by the calendar.
For whom will the fish of the laughing ocean make a welcome?	For him who knows the tides.
Who orders the year from hill to hill in its progress?	From point to point in the year's progress the days of the Blessed Saints lead on.

Invoke then, People of the Sea, invoke the Poet
that he may compose a spell for you:
For I, the Druid who sets out the letters in Ogham—
I, who part the contestants in battle—
I will approach the Rath of the Sidhe
seeking a cunning poet, so that together
we may concoct good incantations;
For I am a wind of the sea.

[1] *The White Goddess*, Faber & Faber, 1961.

The last line may be taken as: 'I am an incarnate spirit from the mysterious deep.' Ogham is the alleged Bardic Alphabet, cut in strokes at angles on the corners of wood or stone. A rath (pron. 'rah') is an earth fortress, usually circular. The *sidhe* are the fairies, who, as mentioned previously, are larger than the English kind, inhabit hills and probably represent an earlier race.

The vowels (buried under the threshold) are:

The Sweet Cauldron of the Five Trees

A Ailm the silver fir	I am the womb of every holt	Birth is everywhere

O Ohn
   the furze—
   and the egg
   (the young-sun of
   the equinox)
	I am the blaze on every hill	Initiation upon hills, in dolmens

U Ur
   the heather
   (passion—the bees—
   centre of the year)
	I am the queen of every hive	The love-goddess

E Eadha
   the white poplar
   (autumn equinox—
   age and the spirits)
	I am the shield to every head	The repose of the warrior

I Iodha (Iar)
   the yew
   (winter solstice,
   the wheel of destiny)
	I am the tomb of every hope	Death—and hope's gateway

IV. Irish-Gaelic Poetic Wisdom

Spirit

I am the Wind that blows over the sea,
I am the Wave of the Ocean;
I am the Murmur of the billows;
I am the Ox of the Seven Combats;
I am the vulture upon the rock;
I am a Ray of the Sun;
I am the fairest of Plants;
I am a Wild Boar in valour;
I am a Salmon in the Water;
I am a Lake in the plain;
I am the Craft of the artificer;
I am a Word of Science;
I am the Spear-point that gives battle;
I am the god that creates in the head of man the fire of thought.

Who is it that enlightens the assembly upon the mountain, if not I?
Who telleth the ages of the moon, if not I?
Who showeth the place where the sun goes to rest if not I?
—Uttered by Amergin, as he visited Eire.

Finn and The Salmon of Wisdom

Murna, after the defeat and death of Cumhal, took refuge in the forests of
Slieve Bloom, and there she bore a man-child whom she named Demna. For
fear that the Clan Morna would find him out and slay him, she gave him to
be nurtured in the wildwood by two aged women, and she herself became
wife to the King of Kerry. But Demna, when he grew up to be a lad, was
called Fionn, 'Finn' or the Fair One, on account of the whiteness of his skin
and his golden hair, and by this name he was always known thereafter.

His first deed was to slay Lia, who had the Treasure Bag of the Fianna tribe,
his relatives, which he took from him. He then sought out his uncle
Crimmal, who, with a few other old men, survivors of the chiefs of Clan
Bascna, had escaped the sword at Castleknock, and were living in much
penury and affliction in the recesses of the forests of Connacht. These he
furnished with a retinue and guard from among a body of youths who
followed his fortunes, and gave them the Treasure Bag.

He himself went to learn the accomplishments of poetry and science from
an ancient sage and Druid named Finegas, who dwelt on the river Boyne.

Here, in a pool of this river, under boughs of hazel from which dropped
the Nuts of Knowledge on the stream, lived Fintan the Salmon of Knowledge, and whoso ate of him would enjoy all the wisdom of the ages. Finegas
had sought many a time to catch this salmon, but failed until Finn had come
to be his pupil. Then one day he caught it, and gave it to Finn to cook, bidding
him eat none of it himself, but to tell him when it was ready.

When the lad brought the salmon, Finegas saw that his countenance was
changed. 'Has thou eaten of the salmon?' he asked. 'Nay' said Finn, 'but
when I turned it on the spit my thumb was burnt, and I put it to my mouth.'
'Take the Salmon of Knowledge and eat it,' then said Finegas, 'for in thee the
prophesy is come true. And now go hence, for I can teach thee no more.'

—From the Ossianic Cycle: The Coming of Finn MacCumhal,
T.W. Rolleston's version, *The High Deeds of Finn*, Harrap & Co, 1910.

The Hazel (Coll)

A cabin on the moutain-side hid in a grassy nook,
With door and window open wide, where friendly stars may look;
The rabbit shy may patter in, the winds may enter free
Who roam around the mountain throne in living ecstasy.

And when the sun sets dimmed in eve, and purple fills the air,
I think the sacred hazel-tree is dropping berries there,
From starry fruitage, waved aloft where Connia's Well o'erflows;
For sure, the immortal waters run through every wind that blows.

I think when Night towers up aloft and shakes the trembling dew,
How every high and lonely thought that thrills my spirit through
Is but a shining berry dropped down through the purple air,
And from the magic tree of life the fruit falls everywhere.
                    —'A.E.' (George William Russell)

Five Trees

Burn not the sweet apple-tree of drooping branches, of the white
blossoms, to whose gracious head each man puts forth his hand.

Burn not the noble willow, the unfailing ornament of poems;
bees drink from its blossoms, all delight in the graceful tent.

The delicate, airy tree of the Druids, the rowan with its berries,
this burn; but avoid the weak tree, burn not the slender hazel.

The ash-tree of the black buds burn not—timber that speeds
the wheel, that yields the rider his switch; the ashen spear is the
                    scale-beam of battle.
                    —Juban's advice to the fire-ghillie of Fergus MacLeda.

The Myth of the Cattle Raid of Cuailgne
(Tain bo Culgny)

Against the thundering Brown Bull of Cuailgne
who roars, who lets forth the rains
as the cows hasten forth, off to the pastures—
Against the Cuailgne Bull the hosting of Connacht
wide as the onset of night, from the west came.

Champion of the Bull of the East is the shapeshifting
Cuchulainn of Murthemney
son of the sun, brilliant his hues in battle:
yet for a time the hosts of Connacht can overcome him.
Red was the bull the Fennbenach, Finnbenach the champion
of the whole Fianna Fail, and Fennbenach the Red
was the sun of the east.
Of the west and its cloudy night
was then the brown of Cuailgne, the great bull taken captive
for the glory of Maev. And broad was his back,
the play-space upon him was the playground for fifty young children.

And these bulls were the rebirths of the honourable keepers
they who kept safe the white swine of the Sidhe:
in Tir-fa-Tonn in Tir-na-nOg
the folk are sustained by the flesh of these swine only.

And Fergus Mac Roy fought for the glorious Maev
and for Finn MacCumhal the shapeshifting beauty of Cuchulainn
the fountain of fire in the battle
the Tain Bo Cuailgne, the raiding of the cattle.
For Maeve were her seven sons the Maines
sons of Maga, and Ferdia his company
the Firbolg boisterous in battle, full of war and strong ale:
the skilful men of Leinster; and Cormac son of Conor
the exile from Ulster . . .

Against them was seen to be one, and he but a stripling
yet in battle a dragon, and the whole host was crimson
because of him, and see from his head
came fountains of colour as he cast the strange weapon.
But despondency lay upon the son of Sualtan.

As he lay at evening by the grave-mound of Lerga in gloom and dejection, watching the camp-fires of the vast army encamped over against him, and the glitter of their innumerable spears, he saw coming through the host a tall and comely warrior who strode forward, and none of the companies through which he passed turned his head to look at him or seemed to see him. He wore a tunic of silk embroidered with gold, and a green mantle fastened with a silver brooch; in one hand was a black shield bordered with silver and two spears in the other. The stranger came to Cuchulain and spoke gently and sweetly to him of his long toil and waking, and his sore wounds, and finally said: 'Sleep now, Cuchulain, by the grave in Lerga; sleep and slumber deeply for three days, and for that time I will take thy place and defend the Ford against the host of Maev.'

Then Cuchulain sank into a profound slumber and trance, and the stranger laid healing balms of magical power to his wounds so that he awoke whole and refreshed, and for the time that Cuchulain slept the stranger held the Ford against the host. And Cuchulain knew that this was Lugh his father, who had come from among the People of Dana to help his son through the hour of gloom and despair.

So Lugh of Lugh n'Aquilla the high point
came after the Morrigan came, who perched as a crow perches
ready to feed upon blood, and they speaking together
Cuchulainn rejected her, and she as a great eel in the ford
lay and entwined his feet . . .

When the Brown Bull of Cuailgne, sent back into Connacht,
met the Bull of Ailell the white-horned and white-breasted,
the brown bull of Night slew that beast of the white horns.
For seven years a peace was made, the peace of the Ridge of the Bulls,
between Maeve and Ailell of the west, and of the east all the
Fenians of Ulster.

                    —Rhythmed version by R.N. from T.W. Rolleston

Children into Swans

Cruel to us was Aoife
Who played her magic upon us
And drove us out on the water—
Four wonderful snow-white swans.

Our bath is the frothing brine
In bays by red rocks guarded;
For mead at our father's table
We drink of the salt blue sea.

Three sons and a single daughter
In clefts of the cold rocks dwelling—
the hard rocks, cruel to mortals—
We are full of keening tonight.
—Transformation of the Children
of Lir, Fionuala's song.

Tir-fa-Tonn

Delightful is the land beyond all dreams,
Fairer than aught thine eyes have ever seen.
There all the year the fruit is on the tree,
And all the year the bloom is on the flower.

There with wild honey drip the forest trees;
The stores of wine and mead shall never fail,
Nor pain nor sickness knows the dweller there,
Death and decay come near him never more.

The feast shall cloy not, nor the chase shall tire,
Nor music cease for ever through the hall;
The gold and jewels of the Land of Youth
Outshine all splendours ever dreamed by man.

Thou shalt have horses of the fairy breed,
Thou shalt have hounds that can outrun the wind;
A hundred chiefs shall follow thee in war,
A hundred maidens sing thee to thy sleep.

A crown of sovranty thy brow shall wear,
And by thy side a magic blade shall hang,
And thou shalt be lord of all the Land of Youth,
and lord of Niam of the Head of Gold.
—*The Fenian Cycle*, Niam of the Golden Hair
describing Tir-fa-Tonn to Oisin.

Conditions to a King

Thou shalt not go right-handwise round Tara, nor left-handwise round
Bregia.[1]
Thou shalt not hunt the evil beasts of Cerna.
Thou shalt not go out every ninth night beyond Tara.
Thou shalt not sleep in a house from which firelight shows after sunset, or in
which light can be seen from without.
No Three Rods shall go before thee to the house of Red.
No rapine shall be wrought in thy reign.
After sunset, no one woman alone or man alone shall enter the house in which
thou art.
Thou shalt not interfere in a quarrel between two of thy thralls.
—*Geise* given to Conary as King of Erin,
declared to him by Nemglan.

[1] Bregia is the plain east of Tara.

THE EIGHT-FOLD
YEAR-PLAN

Preliminary Note:
Just as Christmas or New Year's Day act as markers and orientations for us through our year, Druids—both ancient and modern—use a cycle of eight such traditional observances, to both honour and connect with the sun, moon and Earth and to provide a cyclical rather than linear framework around which to orient their lives.

The ceremonies have developed through the Order's history, some parts being recent additions, some parts being of unknown antiquity, some coming from chiefs in Britain, some from chiefs in Brittany. But the most important aspect of each observance is an attunement and recognition and celebration of the quality of the particular time and place. The Mysteries of Eleusis, the rite of Alban Elued and the Christian Harvest Festival, for example, are all recognizing and connecting with essentially the same thing: the time of ripeness, of reaping, of gathering in.

Sometimes Druid ceremonies are formal gatherings, particularly when held in public places such as on Glastonbury Tor. But at other times, they are more informal, and are held in forest glades or in private gardens. The wording of the ceremonies reflects these varying degrees of formality. The most formal take place using the traditional wordings, while the most informal will use no prepared wordings, but will be guided by the chief of the rite and the participants responding to the spirit and inspiration of the place and moment.

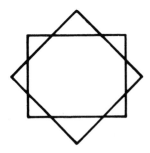

A complete description of each of the eight ceremonies is given in the Order's postal course, but we give here notes on the significance and associations of the eight-fold cycle, together with the complete text of the Order's Bealteinne ceremony as performed at Glastonbury.

[Ed.]

The Eight-fold Year-Plan

Let us begin by setting out briefly the eight-fold scheme of the year in symbols and astrology:

Candlemas: ≈ *air* *2 February*	Imbolc or Brighid, the mother as crafts patron and nurse. A time of natural beginnings. Symbols: lights and water. The Scots year used to begin now. It is the festa of the Armenian firegod Mihr (Frazer). Ploughing the first sod now takes place in Ireland.
Alban Eiler: or *Spring Equinox* ♈ *fire* *21 March*	Festa of the earth-realm, the fertile ground at our feet. Main symbol: the trefoil, the first footprints of Niwalen and Olwen. Other symbols: buds, blossom, seeds, the white-green cloak.
Beltane: ♉ *earth* *1 May*	Bealteinne, the good fire—fire of growth well-rooted and shown in blossom. This is the first of summer, the English summer maiden Niwalen and her father Celi (Cole), his smoke and sap.
Alban Heruin: or *Summer Solstice* ♋ *water* *21 June*	The eternally moving circle of water around earth's shores, boundary of earth and sea, and of two halves of the year. Main symbol: vervain (verbena), the plant of sight. Other symbols: flowers, leaves, mead. The hospitable feast—the giving back of that which is freely given. Mercy, truth and love come from the highest sun: the golden cloak.
Lughnasadh: or *Lammas* ♌ *fire* *1 August*	The marriage of Lugh or Lugaidh (light) with Eire (earth); autumn begins and the harvest. A time of sacrifice: the games are held for the funeral of Lugh's foster-mother. Baking of the first loaf (lammas).
Alban Elued: or *Autumnal*	The eyes lift to the distance, the circle of the sea's horizon. The time of the main harvest. The main symbol is the wheatsheaf—the ripened achieve-

Equinox	ment shown in the circle, the freedom symbolized by the
♎ *air*	ocean. Other symbols: wine, fruit, the red-bronze cloak.
23 September	

Hallowe'en:	Samhuinn, the union of two worlds.
♏ *water*	The cauldron and the herbs, the yew-bough of death and
31 October	the eternal, the summons and invitation to the spirits to partake of four foods of the dead, which are burnt. Symbols: protective angelica and garlic.

Alban Arthuan:	Eyes lift to heaven, the pole star and the Bear.
or	Main symbol: the mistle.
Winter Solstice	The death and birth of the sun, turning-point of the year.
♑ *earth*	Extinguishing of lights, making of the new fire, re-
21 December	illumining of the star, the great light and the lesser lights. The black cloak.

The Pairing of the Opposites

The nature of the ceremonial year is best realized by the circle of designed opposites which are complementary.

Alban Arthuan, the Winter Solstice, is the rebirth of the tiring sun from the Great Mother as Mabinog and is clearly a mother-goddess ceremony. Opposite it, Alban Heruin, the Summer Solstice, is the most powerful of the magics: it is the high point of the father–sun's achievement in this hemisphere, light in excelsis.

Alban Eiler and Alban Elued, spring and autumn equinoxes, have very similar ceremonies; each has a lady bearing significant symbols of gifts from earth: the storage of wine and the seeds for sowing in spring, in autumn the achieved ripened crop of wheat. As the wine is symbol for old stored wisdom, so the wheatsheaf is valued experience from life. Either ceremony can be given seasonal attributions, but the produce of the earth is emphasized.

The Gaelic-Cymric observances have not the same universality. Imbolc clears away rubbish, washes the face of the earth and implants the first seed. It is clearly a motherhood symbol. Six months later, on 1 August, is Lughnasadh, the triumph, the mating, and the death: the height of foliage and the formation of seeds, the mating of Lugh with Eire, the death of John Barleycorn by Frazer followers, the sacrifice of the year, the killing of one mate by the Mother Goddess and the taking of another. Both ceremonies therefore are essentially of the Mother Goddess.

Bealteinne and Samhuinn have in common the contrasted magics of seasons. Bealteinne on 1 May has the supreme magic of blossom, the heavy magic of earth, the spells of the *sidhe* people, with the pentagram. Samhuinn has the more awesome magic of the death of time, the coming back to Earth of those who have passed its boundaries, a look into the depths of time-lessness and the open doors between worlds.

Essential Elements of Each Ceremony-Season and Some Linked Deities

Alban Arthuan—Death and birth; the *mistletoe* of renewal and healing, Ceridwen and Hu-Hesus.

Imbolc—Cleansing and planting; primal woman as Earth; Brighid.

Alban Eiler—Seeds and wine; stimulus, blossom, magic; the young male lover, Aenghus Ōg; the spring maiden in several shapes.

Bealteinne—The good fire and mystic pentagram with the Mayflower; the flower maiden, Niwalen or Olwen.

Alban Heruin—The High Point of Light, the clearing of sight, the male sun-festa; Ōg or Teutates, father or grown son.

Lughnasadh—The mating of Earth and Heaven: the goddess Earth at height, with the ripening of Light; Lugh.

Alban Elued—The garnering of the wisdom of life: the wise old man, the Dagda; or Ceridwen as Nurse of Seeds.

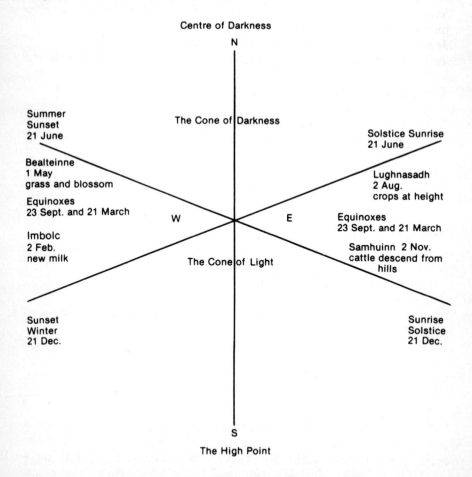

Man's Natural Compass and Calendar of Light.

Samhuinn—The timeless ones; the yew, tree of eternity; the crone-grandmother; Ceridwen as Sibyl.

It will be noted that only three of these rituals are distinctly masculine; the others show aspects of the Mother Goddess and the extent to which the moon directed Druidic ideas.

The majestic swing of the seasons is early man's cross of matter and creation. It gave him also the arc of light and the orb and maybe the cattle-horns of fertility.

The Bealteinne Ceremony

Introduction at the foot of Glastonbury Tor
Herald: O Companions, what is your manner of pilgrimage here?
Pendragon: We have come to this place of the ancient years, where the spirit was made known to man, to contact that spirit anew.
Herald: Seek then in the ancient way, between the two pillars.
Scribe: In the Holy Vale of Avalon the pillars are manifested as the Tor and the Well.
Herald: Let us dedicate our purpose by them.
(*All proceed to the Tower on the Tor.*)
Chief: (*proceeding to Tower and laying hand on it*)
In this Tor and Tower we honour the symbol of supernal fatherhood. (*All follow and touch.*)
(*Water-bearers bring round water bowl filled with Chalice Well water.*)
Chief: In the water from this eternal well of health we taste the sweetness of motherhood. (*All drink.*)

Opening of the Gorsedd of Bealteinne in the Isle of Avalon
(*Herald, blower of the horn, addresses at the centre with a trump each of the four quarters.*)
Herald: Hear the call of the Gorsedd.
All say loudly: Hear.
Chief: Let us begin by giving peace to the quarters, for without peace can no work be.

Peace to the North
Peace to the South
Peace to the West
Peace to the East.

All: May there be peace throughout the whole world.
Chief: Since it is known that there is peace, we may begin our work, trusting in the clear vision that comes from inner harmony and in the God/dess of Truth. The rich land of Wessex reflects truth from many mirrors.

Herald: (*Approaches May Queen and Earth Mother, both at West as Patronesses of the ceremony.*) Has the Queen of the May any message for the Chiefs of the Order?

Queen or Earth Mother: The Queen of May, the Lady Elen of the Blossoms, daughter of Celi the fire of growth, is here with her Queen-Mother Ana of the Earth; they send their greetings and welcome to the Chiefs of the Bardic and Druid Order and invite them to approach their presence.

(*Herald repeats message to Chiefs at the East.*)

Pendragon: We receive with duty the message of the May Queen and the Earth-Mother and wish to be guided to them. (*Herald leads Chiefs to the West.*)

May Queen: O Chiefs, receive from us these gifts of the season of May: our own blossom, the flowered Whitethorn that guards the sacred Oak, and the young flowers that glorify the Earth. May they lift the hearts of all.

Bardic Chief: O Lady Elen, May Queen of the Tor of Glastonbury, and Lady Ana, Great Mother of the Earth, we thank you for your gracious gifts. Duir the sacred Oak is indeed guarded either side by the Whitethorn Huath and the Holly Teith. May the Oak, emblem of eternal life, the May-blossom, emblem of magical power, and the Whitethorn, emblem of purity and defence, be with us during all of this, your season of budding flowers. (*Chief returns to the East.*)

Scribe: Let us offer the words that have been the bond between all Druids:

> Grant, O God/dess, thy Protection
> And in protection, <u>Strength</u> (*words underlined spoken by all*)
> And in strength, <u>Understanding</u>
> And in understanding, <u>Knowledge</u>
> And in knowledge, <u>the Knowledge of Justice</u>
> And in the knowledge of justice, <u>the Love of it</u>
> And in the love of it, <u>the Love of all Existences</u>
> And in the love of all existences, <u>the Love of God/dess and all Goodness.</u>

Pendragon: Will you, O Herald, bid now the Gathering?

Herald: By command of the honoured Pendragon I announce that the Gorsedd in Avalon is now open.

The Eisteddfod follows with talks, poetry, music and sometimes dancing.

The Closing

Bardic Chief: Arthur after his battles for unity went to the land of the *sidhe*. He comes again when there is need. He sleeps and does not die. He is dark to us when the light of this mortal world blinds us.

Sword-bearer: Behold this sword (*unsheathing and uplifting it*) Excalibur, which rose from the lake of still meditation and was returned to it again. The sword of spirit, of light and truth, is always sharp and always with us, if our lake be stilled. (*Takes the sword to Chief.*)

Scribe: Here are not only the Tor and the Well. There is the third wherein they become one.
Herald: What mean you by this?
Scribe: The Cave contains all, both the dragon and the treasure. The two pillars are the entrance thereto.
Herald: When Arthur descended to Annwn few there were that returned with him.
Sword-bearer: Excalibur is the symbol of the way of the few. (*He holds the sword before the Chief.*)
Chief: Whilst this sword is unsheathed, promise you all that the Earth our home and mother shall be protected and illumined by the swords of our spirits and wills. (*Sword is placed horizontally in front of the Triad who then place their hands on the sword.*)
All: We swear it.
(*Sword is sheathed and Sword-bearer returns to his place.*)
Chief: We ask the help of the four archangels and saints of our islands who are regents of the four gates, that we may keep this promise worthily:

To the East, Raphael in his golden cloak, overshadowing George of England.
To the South, Michael of the red flame and the sword, overshadowing
Davydd of Wales.
To the West, Gabriel of the blue water, overshadowing Padraic and Dana
of Eire.
To the North, Uriel of the fruitful dark earth, overshadowing Columcille of
Iona. (*Faces centre at East.*)
May the harmony of our earth-forces be complete.

(*Office-holders move to the four quarters and make the Cry of Peace:*)

May there be Peace in the North,
May there be Peace in the South,
May there be Peace in the West,
May there be Peace in the East.

All: May there be Peace throughout the whole world.
Scribe: Let us remember those who have passed from us to another plane of life, especially those linked with this work. (*Scribe reads from Order Scroll.*)
All: (*All hold hands in ring.*)

We swear by peace and love to stand
Heart to heart and hand in hand
Mark, O Spirit, and hear us now
Confirming this our Sacred Vow.

Chief: This Gorsedd ends in peace, as in peace it began. Let us withdraw in peace, and may there be peace outward and inward until we meet again.
All: So be it. (*Exit sunwise, Chief last.*)

An Explanatory Note to the Beltane Ceremony

The festivals of Beltane and Lughnasadh form a magical pair: at Bealteinne comes the magical five-fold blossom of the May, whitethorn and black-thorn, with that of other trees also, in late spring; and the end of summer comes with Lughnasadh, when crops are brought in—the end-period of heat, the calendar-beginning of autumn at the beginning of August: the wheel of the year has reached its apogee and is rolled down as the sun begins visibly to lower his height in the skies.

In the ceremony of Beltane, it was found very early that the features used as symbolical formed themselves at Glastonbury into a pattern that could hardly be mistaken. Any tall stone at the east has always represented air; one naturally therefore backed the ceremony to the Michael Tower. Water is used for cleansing the circle: it was naturally brought from the Chalice Well of curative water just below. The cave in the Tor below was then the natural place to assume for the other elements, the fire-dragon and the earth-treasure. The ritual's words came to adapt to this *mise-en-scène*, and

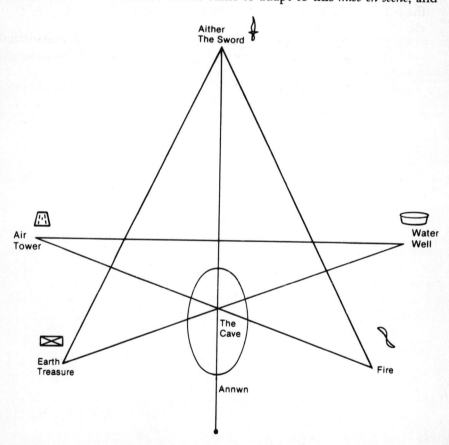

The Glastonbury Pentagram Scheme.

the elevation of Excalibur therefore automatically became the top member of the pentagram, *aither* or spirit.

Four paths unite in the cave, the lower centre, and three in the sword, the upper union of centres.

The four paths into the cave are air and water, the two pillars, and earth and fire, the treasure and the dragon. The pillars guard the entry; that is, intuitive knowledge (air) and the trained emotions (water). Realism with thought (earth) and enthusiasm (fire) form the permanent bases.

In the sword unite three elements: it is made from earth (carbon) as iron ore, from water (hydrogen) in the hardening of steel and from fire (oxygen) in annealing. It is drawn in symbol from the *stone* at the proving of Arthur, from the *lake* when given by Nimuë, and from the *dragon* after its killing by the hero as Arthur the sun-god. The sword itself is *aither*, creative spirit, a higher form of fire, and is elevated in the fourth element, air, the intelligence.

The scheme is therefore one of four-fold bases united in the cave, and of the essences of three elements uniting in the symbol of the high sword, elevated in a fourth.

The lower four angles form an elemental scheme of four, a quadrangle enclosing a vesica or cave. Intelligence (air) and emotion (water) form with spirit (sword) an upper trio. The lower two bases, earth and fire, are the essential and practical, 'having one's feet on the ground' and possessing enthusiastic energy. The cave is the alembic or alchemic cucurbit where all fuse.

EPITOME

Druidry emerges from this examination into origins and history as a very real and vital mystery teaching, not fully revealed here but the essentials conveyed.

The concept of spirit is clear and central: it is in the syllable for air = spirit = Hé, Heu'c, Hu or 'E in various forms. This seed, point, or grain of mustard seed, grows to a giant; it is Hu Gadarn, the Herakles of humans, the Esus-spirit of the grown racial figure in the Cymru tree, the Taranus of the four divisions as bull in animal form, whose voice in thunder is the Creator's.

The circle is the working form of this spirit: the centre is the seed-point or basic sound, the circumference the limit of its radiations or if regarded as sound, a chord coming from its basic note. The turning and raising of the circle is spirit's movement in developing power; the cone is its projection, the isosceles triangle the glyph. The *gorolad* of the heavens is the polar circle of Arthur; the other heavenly circles all have their special qualities. All so-called deities are figures for the savage or uninstructed mind, the most Druidic being the Hu-Aesus axis illumined for Wales in the Gwion-Taliesin progressions through the four stages or forms. As are the quarters, so are the wisdoms and their transformation: the fast hare is still of earth, the emotional fish water, the intelligent wren air—but the fire, the vital transformation, is in the seed (Hu again) which the Great Mother causes to grow into Taliesin, the Radiant Brow.

The circles of creation spiral up from the deep of Annwn through the multiform creation—between the various forms of which are no real barriers, only brotherhood in the circle—finally moving into the White Life, as far as man's spirit may go, for beyond is the radiance of Ceugant only.

The four qualities and necessary developments of man ray into him from, and are expressed by, the quarters and their figurings as the knights, the saints, the types of creatures, the four elements, the contrasting colours. Circle and quadratures form a permanent chart for many applications.

The other four, the half-quarters or 'cross of Andrew', are important in a lesser way: they are taken to correspond with more local (but equally deep) observances.

The physical dance-circle contains the wild ecstatic shrieks and leapings, akin to the Dervishes, of earlier days, and later the more stately but perhaps more effective circulations. The circle originates, intensifies and expresses the power so raised, and if of wood or stone also, it stores and transmits power even to centuries ahead.

Looking at the evidence of angulations and orientations, longer and shorter, these imply an immense sense of purpose and grasp of direction not at all to be expected in earlier man on the older suppositions, but more to be expected if the snake from the stars is really inspiring him. His mind appears to move on abstract and wide-ranging levels. Ley lines and orientations have to be set out and grasped more fully before evaluation is possible; but calculations such as those from the Great Menhir to England, and triangles such as the twin ones based on the Glastonbury-Iona axis, with upper points falling one way upon Lindisfarne, the other upon the area just off Western Ireland where the visionary Hy Brazil/Tir-na-n'Ōg/Atlantis was repeatedly reported—and mapped—give some conception of the viewpoint involved, almost as from a different dimension.

Over all manifestation are the triple powers expressed in infinity: light, universal air and pure water unlimited. These are the truly supernal elements in which men's souls chiefly express themselves. Well after these comes the limitation of the solids of earth. Thus the watery spring, the tree and the stone are the holy things. Together with air-fire the water spring is the principle of purity in matter and the tree is the embodiment of the earth qualified by this purity, hence the cult of a great group of holy trees. The tall stone aspires into air and is linked with it, the infinitely soft and invisible with the infinitely hard forming between them a rod or heap upon which spirit plays. Fire is the holy transformer perpetually at work upon material things, an intensive form of holy air, a specialized form of holy light, the agent of the deific force that strikes from heaven. It is the essence of life itself.

Sound at the circle and creative centre perhaps begins as 'Hé-hay', the sound of breath. Awen—'ah-oo-en'—or the mystic Hebrew 'E-háy-yeh' ('I am that I am') is the triple sound that evolves creation, that causes the Three Worlds or Orders of Being: Light, Air and Water. Earth is 'tellus', the height 'ah', the depth 'oo' and manifestation or the surface between 'en'. Light or fire is the life spirit playing through these positions.

Which came first, the Word or Light? Perhaps they are the same thing . . . beyond our grasp. They are merely how it appears to us.

Sun and moon, which are fire and water in higher forms, are the twin pillars or horns, the two great servants of spirit: this power moves between them. They are the alchemic trio. Such a sign as this is typically Druidic:

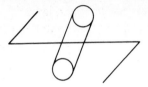

I am in the place between sun and moon, where the lightning-flash (or thunder-bolt) of the Creator strikes.

After evolution through all phases of life, from vegetable, fish and animal to lower man and finally to the safety of Gwynfid, whence is no back-sliding, the human spirits pass to the clouds, to the moon for rest, to the sun for purification then out of this system to develop in different worlds. It is a noble vision, surely, quite comparable with the Hindu philosophic vision that is somewhat limited by attempts at numbers and datings.

Druidry proves to be wholly philosophic, that is, a scheme of universal application, not resolved into any one humanized shape, as with most religions. It does use a local, highly flexible pantheon to illumine aspects of deity to those who can only think with the aid of such shapes. Hu-Esus illustrates very well the halfway between a principle and a figure and is in fact Druidry's chief one: the point, the principle of growth, the hero, the Breath Hu or Hé. Upon the oak-tree Esus' name naturally suggested Jesus upon the Cross and an initial unity between Druidry and this religious system seemed pre-ordained.

BIBLIOGRAPHY

Druidry

Carr-Gomm, Philip, *The Elements of the Druid Tradition*, Element Books, 1991.

Elder, Isobel, *Celt, Druid & Culdee*, Covenant Publishing Co., 1962.

Kendrick, T.D., *The Druids*, Cass, 1927.

Owen, A.L., *The Famous Druids*, Greenwood Press, 1962.

Piggott, Stuart, *The Druids*, Thames & Hudson, 1985.

Rutherford, Ward, *The Druids*, The Aquarian Press, 1983.

Spence, Lewis, *The History & Origins of Druidism*, The Aquarian Press, 1971.

Festivals

Bord, Janet and Colin, *Earth Rites*, Paladin, 1982.

Farrar, Janet and Stewart, *Eight Sabbats for Witches*, Hale, 1981.

Kightly, Charles, *The Customs and Ceremonies of Britain*, Thames & Hudson, 1986.

MacNeill, Marie, *The Festival of Lughnasa*, Oxford University Press, 1962.

Touslon, Shirley, *The Winter Solstice*, Jill Norman & Hobhouse, 1981.

The Grail Quest and Arthurian Studies

Ashe, Geoffrey, *Avalonian Quest*, Methuen, 1982.

Jung, Emma, and Franz, Marie-Louise von, *The Grail Legend*, Hodder & Stoughton, 1971.

Knight, Gareth, *The Secret Tradition in Arthurian Legend*, The Aquarian Press, 1983.

Matthews, John, *The Grail: Quest for Eternal Life*, Thames & Hudson, 1981.

——, *The Elements of the Arthurian Tradition*, Element Books, 1989.

——, and Green, Marian, *The Grail-Seeker's Companion*, The Aquarian Press, 1986.

Stewart, R.J., *The Mystic Life of Merlin*, Arkana, 1987.

Tolstoy, N., *The Quest for Merlin*, 1987.
Weston, J.L., *From Ritual to Romance*, Doubleday/Anchor, 1957.

Paganism, The Western Tradition, Celtic Matters

Adler, Margaret, *Drawing Down the Moon*, Beacon Press, 1979.
Bancroft, Ann, *Origins of the Sacred*, Arkana, 1987.
Carmichael, A. (ed), *Carmina Gadelica*, Scottish Academic Press, 1972.
Collis, J.S., *Triumph of the Tree*, Cape, 1950.
Graves, Robert, *The White Goddess*, Faber & Faber, 1961.
Gray, L.H., *Mythology of All Races*, 1918.
Hartley, Christine, *The Western Mystery Tradition*, The Aquarian Press, 1968.
Hazlitt, W.C., *Dictionary of Faiths and Folklore*, 1905.
Markale, Jean, *Women of the Celts*, Inner Traditions, 1986.
Matthews, Caitlín, *Mabon and the Mysteries of Britain*, Arkana, 1987.
——, *Arthur and the Sovereignty of Britain: King and Goddess in The Mabinogion*, Arkana, 1989.
——, *The Elements of the Celtic Tradition*, Element Books, 1989.
——, and John, *The Western Way*, Arkana, 1985.
——, and Jones, Prudence (eds), *Voices from the Circle*, The Aquarian Press, 1989.
Merry, Eleanor C., *The Flaming Door: The Mission of the Celtic Folk-Soul*, Floris Books, 1983.
Murray, Liz and Colin, *The Celtic Tree Oracle*, Rider, 1988.
Porteous, A., *Forces and Folklore*, 1918.
Powell, T.G.E., *The Celts*, Thames & Hudson, 1983.
Ramsay, Jay (ed), *Prophet, Priest and King: A Selection of Ross Nichols' Poetry*, Element Books, 1991.
Rees, Alwyn and Brinley, *Celtic Heritage*, Thames & Hudson, 1989.
Ross, Anne, *Pagan Celtic Britain*, Routledge & Kegan Paul, 1967.
——, and Robins, Don, *The Life and Death of a Druid Prince*, Rider, 1989.
Rutherford, Ward, *Celtic Mythology*, The Aquarian Press, 1987.
Toulson, Shirley, *The Celtic Alternative: A reminder of the Christianity we lost*, Century, 1987.

Sites

Atkins, G.S., *Stonehenge Decoded*, Souvenir Press, 1966.
Atkinson, R.J.C., *Stonehenge*, Hamish Hamilton, 1956.
Bord, Janet and Colin, *Mysterious Britain*, Paladin, 1974.
——, *The Secret Country*, Paladin, 1978.
Borlase, W.C., *Antiquities of the County of Cornwall*, 1756 and 1769.
——, *The Dolmens of Ireland*.
Brennan, Martin, *The Stars and The Stones*, Thames & Hudson, 1982.
Burl, Aubrey, *Megalithic Brittany*, Thames & Hudson, 1985.

Critchlow, Keith, *Time Stands Still*, Gordon Fraser, 1979.

Dames, Michael, *The Silbury Treasure*, Thames & Hudson, 1976.

——, *Avebury and Silbury*, Thames & Hudson, 1988.

Devereux, Paul, and Thomson, Ian, *The Ley Hunter's Companion*, Thames & Hudson, 1979.

Evans, Sir Arthur, paper to the Folklore Society, 1895.

Graves, Tom, *Needles of Stone Revisited*, Gothic Image, 1986.

Hickey, Elizabeth, *The Legend of Tara*, Dundalgan Press, Dundalk.

Holiday, F.W., *The Dragon and the Disc*, Sidgwick & Jackson, 1973.

Lethbridge, T.C., *The Legend of the Sons of God*, Routledge & Kegan Paul, 1972.

Levy, Rachel, *The Gate of Horn*, Faber & Faber, 1948.

Lockyer, Norman, *Stonehenge*, London, 1906.

Malone, Caroline, *Avebury*, B.T. Batsford, 1989.

Matthews, John, and Potter, Chesca, *The Aquarian Guide to Legendary London*, The Aquarian Press, 1990.

Michell, John, *The Stones of Land's End*, Thames & Hudson, 1974.

——, *The Earth Spirit, its Ways, Shrines and Mysteries*, Thames & Hudson, 1975.

——, *The New View of Atlantis*, Thames & Hudson, 1983.

——, *A Little History of Astro-Archaeology*, Thames & Hudson, 1989.

O'Kelley, Claire, *Bruagh-na-Boyne and its Monuments*.

O'Riordan, Sean, *Tara*.

Pennick, Nigel, and Devereux, Paul, *Lines on the Landscape*, Hale, 1989.

Renfrew, Colin (ed), *The Megalithic Monuments of Western Europe*, Thames & Hudson, 1983.

Revenshill, T.H., *The Rollright Stones and the Men who Erected Them*.

Roberts, Anthony, *Glastonbury: Ancient Avalon, New Jerusalem*, Rider, 1978.

Russell, Vivien, *West Penwith Survey*.

Screeton, Paul, *Quicksilver Heritage*, Thorsons, 1974.

Stewart, R.J., *The Waters of the Gap*, Ashgrove/Arcania, 1989.

——, and Matthews, John, *Legendary Britain: An Illustrated Journey*, Blandford Press, 1989.

Thom, A., *Megalithic Sites in Britain*, Oxford University Press, 1967.

Watkins, Alfred, *The Ley Hunter's Manual*, The Aquarian Press, 1989.

INDEX